AMERICA'S RIGHT

AMERICA'S RIGHT

ANTI-ESTABLISHMENT CONSERVATISM FROM GOLDWATER TO THE TEA PARTY

ROBERT B. HORWITZ

polity

First published in 2013 by Polity Press

Polity Press
65 Bridge Street
Cambridge CB2 1UR, UK

Polity Press
350 Main Street
Malden, MA 02148, USA

ISBN-13: 978-0-7456-6429-3

A catalogue record for this book is available from the British Library.

Typeset in 10.5 on 12 pt Sabon
by Toppan Best-set Premedia Limited
Printed and bound in the United States of America

The publisher has used its best endeavours to ensure that the URLs for external websites referred to in this book are correct and active at the time of going to press. However, the publisher has no responsibility for the websites and can make no guarantee that a site will remain live or that the content is or will remain appropriate.

Every effort has been made to trace all copyright holders, but if any have been inadvertently overlooked the publisher will be pleased to include any necessary credits in any subsequent reprint or edition.

For further information on Polity, visit our website: www.politybooks.com

CONTENTS

Preface   vi

Acknowledgments   viii

1 Introduction   1

2 Anti-statist Statism: A Brief History of a Peculiarly American Conservatism   23

3 Religion and Politics: The Rise of the New Christian Right   63

4 Two Generations of Neoconservatism: From the Law of Unintended Consequences to the Cleansing Fire of Violence   112

5 Richard Hofstadter's "Paranoid Style" Revisited: The Tea Party, Past as Prologue   157

6 Dogmatism, Utopianism, and Politics   202

Notes   211

Index   266

PREFACE

Conservatism has been the most important political doctrine in the United States for nearly four decades. It has dominated the intellectual debate and largely set the national policy agenda, even during years of Democratic electoral control. But twenty-first-century conservatism has moved far beyond even the "Reagan Revolution" of small government, lower taxes, and a respect for tradition. Contemporary American conservatism practices a politics that is disciplined, uncompromising, utopian, and enraged, seeking to "take back our country." An unlikely alliance of libertarians, neoconservatives, and the Christian right has launched anxious and angry attacks on the purported homosexual agenda, the "hoax" of climate change, the rule by experts and elites, and the banishment of religion from the public realm. In the foreign policy arena it has tried to remake the world through the cleansing fire of violence.

This is *anti-establishment conservatism*, whose origin can be traced back to the right wing that battled both the reigning post-World War II liberal consensus and the moderate, establishment Republican Party (also known as the Grand Old Party or GOP). This book examines the nature of anti-establishment conservatism, traces its development from the 1950s to the Tea Party, and explains its political ascendance.

Books on conservatism litter the journalistic and academic landscapes. Indeed, the treatment of conservatism has become somewhat of a scholarly cottage industry. What is different about *this* effort is its attention to both domestic and foreign policy, and the weaving of these two facets of anti-establishment conservative thought and action into one coherent narrative of change over time. *America's Right* also revisits and reassesses some of the older, dismissed theoretical assessments of the conservative movement, most notably that of the mid-twentieth-century historian Richard Hofstadter. This revisit allows students of conservatism to circle back to the 1950s to see how public intellectuals and scholars like Hofstadter interpreted a moment of political ferment not unlike our own. *America's Right* then applies and adjusts some of those interpretations to help make sense of the current conservative moment.

The book begins in the 1950s, when conservatism shifted from its pre-World War II isolationism to embrace a double "rollback": of the New Deal and of international communism. Anti-establishment conservatism's fusion of libertarian and traditionalist principles found its political expression in the candidacy of Barry Goldwater, GOP standard-bearer in the 1964 presidential election. Goldwater's crushing defeat did not subdue anti-establishment conservatism; its political entrepreneurs built the institutions that served to channel the ongoing discontent with liberalism. *America's Right* analyzes these institutions and how they helped facilitate the reemergence of anti-establishment conservatism in the late 1970s. It examines the two movements most responsible for this rejuvenation: the new Christian right and neoconservatism. The millenarian underpinnings of anti-establishment conservatism came to the fore after the 9/11 attacks, and informed the rationale for the George W. Bush administration's invasion of Iraq in 2003. Finally, the book explores the most recent manifestation of anti-establishment conservatism: the Tea Party.

While *America's Right* is broadly sourced, it is written for the general serious reader. I have tried hard not to use academic jargon or assume great familiarity with social and political theory. Where I employ big concepts – such as secularism, pre- or post-millennialism, American exceptionalism, and the like – I endeavor to define them simply and clearly. Where I explore a theory – such as Hofstadter's "paranoid style" – I try to explain it straightforwardly and with rich context. The vast majority of the notes are bibliographic citations, although I do employ the occasional textual note where it aids in explaining an issue in the main body of the text. Readers who wish to see a comprehensive bibliography can go to my webpage on the University of California, San Diego Department of Communication website: *http://communication.ucsd.edu/people/faculty/robert-horwitz.html*.

Because of the topic and the writing pitch and style, I hope the book will have some general audience readership. As a synthetic overview of history and political sociology that spans the politics of the post-war period and ends with the Tea Party movement, this volume is, I think, of contemporary topical interest and will have a decent shelf life for students interested in a longer perspective on American politics.

ACKNOWLEDGMENTS

Many people generously contributed to the formulation, writing, and final production of this book. I was fortunate to present two of the draft chapters to the University of California-San Diego (UCSD) Conservative Movements workshop, and received much advice and useful criticism. I taught pieces of the research in undergraduate and graduate courses as the research was unfolding, and thank those students for allowing me to explore. I especially thank three graduate students in the Department of Communication: Muni Citrin, Stephanie (Sam) Martin, and Reece Peck.

Several friends and colleagues read large parts or the entire manuscript in one of its draft forms, including Patricia Aufderheide, Amy Binder, Amy Bridges, Peter Dimock, John Evans, Michael Evans, Lew Friedland, Jeffrey Minson, and Michael Schudson.

Introduced to me by my mother-in-law, former professor of theology Jack Rogers generously and patiently gave me much-needed help in my sections on religion. Charles Drekmeier, my undergraduate mentor forty years ago and as sharp as ever, provided a critical reading of the early chapters.

Eliott Kanter of UCSD's Geisel Library helped me track down many obscure references. Larry Gross got me in touch with John Thompson, editor extraordinaire of Polity Press. Justin Dyer provided inspired copy-editing. I thank you all.

I could not have written the book without the help of my dear friend and colleague Val Hartouni. She read the entire manuscript more times than I'm sure she cared to, offering engaged discussion, keen insight, comradely criticism, and encouragement. She is a treasure.

The final editing push and manuscript preparation could not have been done without the expert writing and editorial flourish of my wife, former bookkeeper, auto mechanic, newspaper journalist, and elementary school teacher Libby Brydolf.

INTRODUCTION

North Iowa Tea Party billboard, Mason City, Iowa, 2010.

The ACLU [American Civil Liberties Union] has got to take a lot of blame for this [the terrorist attacks of September 11, 2001]. And I know I'll hear from them for this, but throwing God . . . successfully with the help of the federal court system . . . throwing God out of the public square, out of the schools, the abortionists have got to bear some burden for this because God will not be mocked and when we destroy 40 million little innocent babies, we make God mad. . . . I really believe that the pagans and the abortionists and the feminists and the gays and the lesbians who are actively trying to make that an alternative lifestyle, the ACLU, People for the American Way, all of them who try to secularize America . . . I point the thing in their face and say you helped this happen.

> The Reverend Jerry Falwell, on the Christian Broadcast Network's *700 Club* television program (September 13, 2001)

Man-made climate change is "patently absurd . . . junk science . . . a beautifully concocted scheme . . . by the left . . . just an excuse for more government control of your life.

> Former U.S. Senator and 2012 Republican presidential hopeful Rick Santorum, on the Rush Limbaugh radio show (June 8, 2011)

I, _____, pledge to the taxpayers of the (_____ district of the) state of _____ and to the American people that I will: ONE, oppose any and all effort to increase the marginal income tax rate for individuals and business; and TWO, oppose any net reduction or elimination of deductions and credits unless matched dollar for dollar by further reducing tax rates.

> Taxpayer Protection Pledge signed by 234 of 240 Republican members of the U.S. House of Representatives, and 40 of 47 Republican members of the U.S. Senate in 2011. Authored by Americans for Tax Reform, a lobbying group headed by Grover Norquist

What we might call the "anti-establishment" right wing now defines American conservatism. It has by and large taken over the Republican Party. A movement long in the making, with roots in the Goldwater presidential campaign of 1964, anti-establishment conservatism achieved major success with the election of Ronald Reagan in 1980. It subsequently orchestrated the congressional opposition to the Clinton presidency in the mid-1990s, including shutting down the government and impeaching the president. Effectively securing the executive branch in the George W. Bush era, it helped drive the country to war in Iraq in 2003. During the years of the Obama presidency, anti-establishment conservatism has become the foremost face of the Republican Party, manifest in the populist rage of the Tea Party and the stunning obduracy of Republicans in Congress.

Instances of the anti-establishment right's forthright positions are now legion. In debates involving matters of science, for example, anti-establishment conservatives, such as Rick Santorum in the epigraph above, consistently ignore the overwhelming consensus among climatologists that human activity and industry are largely responsible for the perilous warming of the planet. Many conservatives of this tendency still hold out against Darwin's theory of evolution in favor of "creation science," and make every effort to stop "God being thrown out of the schools" (to paraphrase the Reverend Jerry Falwell in our opening epigraph) by getting at least equal billing for creationism or intelligent design in high school biology classes. In foreign policy, anti-establishment conservatives pressed relentlessly for the invasion of Iraq without proper regard to the actual evidence of the existence of Saddam Hussein's alleged weapons of mass destruction. The George W. Bush administration, epitomizing anti-establishment conservatism in the aftermath of the terrorist attacks of September 11, 2001, insisted on the direct link between Saddam Hussein and al-Qaeda long after the claim had been thoroughly refuted. By many credible accounts, the administration cooked highly equivocal intelligence to appear substantive and conclusive. It engaged in tortured legal logic to find that torture was not torture. And it fixed facts to support preconceived policy determinations in areas of particular interest to business and religious constituencies. Indeed, the administration effectively turned over certain government agencies or departments to select religious groups.

In our current moment, congressional Republicans engage in an unbending, mantra-like advocacy of tax cuts and deficit reduction in the face of any and all economic conditions – showing that they do not have a real economic policy, but rather a canonical system of political beliefs. As became evident in the fraught congressional brawl over raising the federal debt ceiling in the summer of 2011, the Republican agenda revealed itself as a weird cross between duplicity and self-delusion, with demands for severe deficit reduction and balanced budgets notwithstanding the enormous, and unopposed, deficits run up by recent Republican presidents. Republicans failed to defeat President Obama in the 2012 election in a campaign replete with intemperate flights of fancy on the right. The GOP also failed to retake the Senate. Some Tea Party movement supporters insisted that President Barack Obama was not an American citizen and was secretly a member of the Muslim faith. In their view the president was intent on ruining America through his "socialist" policies – with the North Iowa Tea Party even equating Obama's "Democrat Socialism" with Hitler's "National Socialism" and Lenin's "Marxist Socialism" in the notorious billboard pictured at the opening of this chapter. One Tea Party-identified candidate for the Senate in 2012 declared that a woman could not become pregnant from "legitimate" or forcible rape because under such circumstances "the female body has ways to try to shut that whole thing down." During the debate over President Obama's healthcare bill, Tea Party supporters exclaimed with urgent fury, "Keep the government out of my Medicare!" – apparently not comprehending that Medicare is a social insurance program administered by the U.S. government.[1] At the same time, of all the political actors on the stage during the 2008 financial crisis, it was the Tea Party that possessed the political vocabulary capable of expressing the disgust of the class bias and unfairness of the government bailouts of the banks, insurance, and mortgage companies responsible for the financial collapse.

What is going on here? What is anti-establishment conservatism and where did it come from? Why is it so dogmatic and sometimes even at odds with empirical reality? And how has it triumphed – at least in terms of capturing the Republican Party, if not the political climate as a whole? The latter assertion may seem overstated in the wake of Obama's reelection, but it is the case that the right has pretty much set the political agenda in the United States for almost four decades. The answers are rooted in conservatism itself, especially its American version.

Conservatism embodies a venerable, coherent, if sometimes conflicted set of values rooted in an appreciation of the importance of tradition and the social world we inherit, a theory of individual freedom and property, and a deep suspicion of the power of the state. European conservatism has typically been oriented toward the concern with tradition and cultural inheritance. In contrast, American conservatism, born of classical liberalism's focus on the individual, has usually gravitated toward theories of freedom and property. In this outlook, liberty and property are inescapably linked. Property makes it possible for a human being to develop in mind and spirit, that is, for an individual to be free. Property in effect underlies personhood: it provides an individual with perspective, privacy, responsibility, and a concrete place in society. A person has the natural right to the possession and use of his or her property; indeed, private property is among the most fundamental of natural rights. Without property, a person has no concrete free existence. He or she is inevitably dependent on others, especially government, and hence essentially unfree. Property, thus, is a sacred moral value, the key to individual freedom and the prerequisite of a free society. Against the modern liberal notion of equality, conservative thought declares human beings as essentially unequal in their natural gifts and abilities. Freedom can thus only consist in the ability of each person to develop without hindrance according to the law of his or her own personality. Hence of fundamental concern to conservatism is the power of the centralized state and its threat to liberty and property.[2]

While conservatism reaches back centuries, how its principles manifest concretely has varied considerably. Like most belief systems, there are many versions that fall under the label of conservatism: some have to do with the view of human nature; others focus on the lessons drawn from history (originally the lessons drawn from the shock of the French Revolution). The distinct form of conservatism that is dominant in any given historical period depends on the conditions of that period and the other political philosophies with which conservatism does battle, including battles internal to the conservative creed itself. Our current dominant form of conservatism in the United States, which I have called anti-establishment conservatism, has a complex but readily traced historical pedigree. That lineage enables us to understand its profile and disposition.

American conservatism has always differed from its European counterparts in its virtually unalloyed embrace of individualism and capitalism, and its selective hatred of the state. Late nineteenth- and early twentieth-century American conservatism (then known as classical liberalism) was defined by its stout, repressive, and successful defense of laissez-faire capitalism and property rights, often legitimated by the ideology of Social Darwinism (the "survival of the fittest" applied to human society).[3] Interference with the invisible hand of supply and demand, even if well intentioned, was understood to disrupt the natural negotiations that make the market function so well. If this meant suffering for those who lost in the competitive struggle, it was the unfortunate price of both liberty and productivity. The operative maxim was: the government that governs best is that which governs least.

But the Great Depression weakened faith in American business and its sundry ideological supports. The policies initiated under the Democratic presidency of Franklin Roosevelt – known as the New Deal – ushered in various forms of state intervention, some of which, pushed by a newly empowered labor movement, had a social democratic cast of mitigating inequality and of promoting basic public controls over markets. In the 1930s and 1940s, what we might call the "old right," rooted in business and straddling the Democratic and Republican parties, set itself against the Roosevelt administration. The old right decried the New Deal as fostering economic collectivism and redistribution. For the conservatives of the 1930s and 1940s, like their predecessors in the "Gilded Age" from the late 1860s to the mid-1890s, the market was the democratic sphere of liberty. It was government that threatened freedom. Indeed, for conservatives the experience of the twentieth century was that in the name of equality and with the professed aim of improving life for the masses, the state alarmingly accrued power and weakened property rights. In so doing, the state undermined the fundamental condition of liberty that emanates from property, undercutting freedom writ large. The old right thus called for the "rollback" of the New Deal. Its critique of the state in many respects extended to foreign policy. In the period between the two world wars, American conservatives tended toward isolationism. They counseled avoidance of entangling political commitments – especially in European affairs, which, after the experience of World War I, conservatives saw as intractable. And because spending on armies and armaments required higher taxes and thus inevitably produced inflation, the old right was convinced that a militarized foreign policy would lead inevitably to the dreaded concentration of governmental power.

Voters, however, did not agree. New Deal Democrats were consistently returned to office. (To be sure, the New Deal coalition had its own conservatives – on racial matters and labor unions, concentrated in the Democratic South.) By the early 1950s, the old right – still anti-New Deal and isolationist – split more or less into two key factions. The dominant bloc essentially made its peace with the New Deal and with America's post-war internationalist, interventionist foreign policy of the containment of communism. This dominant bloc was "establishment conservatism" or moderate Republicanism, centered (actually or metaphorically) in the Northeast, tied to Wall Street and large corporations, led initially by GOP 1944 and 1948 presidential nominee Thomas Dewey, and then Dwight Eisenhower. In essence, establishment conservatism made its accommodation with liberals and with theory and doctrine in the overweening pragmatic effort to protect private enterprise and foster its advance. By and large, establishment conservatism accepted what historians label the post-war "liberal consensus": that is, the basic New Deal order of modest welfare state, Keynesian economics (i.e., a fiscal and monetary policy of government spending to increase aggregate demand) and the application of disinterested social science in pursuit of the national interest, and interventionist foreign policy of containment of communism – but a milder, less state interventionist, less expensive, less labor-dominated, more business-friendly version.

Anti-establishment conservatism, the other faction that emerged from the dissolution of the pre-war old right, developed as a movement in opposition not just to the liberal consensus of the post-war period, but to establishment conservatism as well. Located principally in small business and its political affiliates, geographically rooted in the Midwest and West, but also scattered amongst a welter of anti-communist and political fringe groups (some of which identified as Christian religious organizations standing up for God and western civilization), anti-establishment conservatism continued the call for the rollback of the New Deal – and for the ousting of the Republican establishment. Barry Goldwater, the Arizona Senator who emerged as one of anti-establishment conservatism's leaders, denounced establishment conservatism as "me-too Republicanism." "Me too" conveyed sharp criticism of the established Republican Party's collaboration with Democrats in the post-war liberal consensus. In contrast, anti-establishment conservatism advocated the rollback of the centralized New Deal state in favor of a principled individual liberty. The rollback metaphor also applied to foreign policy. This signaled a major ideological shift. By the early 1950s, virtually all segments of the old right turned away from isolationist foreign policy. But whereas establishment conservatism largely accepted the policy of containment, anti-establishment conservatism called for the military defeat of international communism. Anti-establishment conservatism denounced containment in favor of aggressive, muscular, and – if necessary – nuclear action against the Soviet Union and its satellites. Roll communism back.

Anti-establishment conservatism thus carried on the pre-war old right's loathing of the New Deal but turned away from its foreign policy isolationism. It combined or "fused" two strains of thought: an economic libertarianism with a socially conservative Christian traditionalism. These strains resided in some tension. The libertarian form, derived from eighteenth- and nineteenth-century European liberalism (and particularly the English philosopher John Locke), was founded on principles of the freedom of the individual, limited government, a capitalist economy, and the social contract to protect private property.[4] The market was a mechanism of virtue because of its efficiency and its promotion of individual freedom. The traditionalist strain, rooted in a religious, essentially Christian sensibility, understood society as a community woven into a web of values and obligations that binds individuals to one another, united by belief in a transcendent being and an objective moral order. A particular reading of Edmund Burke, the eighteenth-century British parliamentarian and political philosopher, formed the basis of traditionalism. Burke emphasized order and social harmony, the necessity to balance freedom with self-restraint and duty. We have obligations toward those from whom we inherited our world, Burke maintained. Likewise, we have obligations toward those who will inherit the world from us.[5]

What bridged the differences between the two strains of conservatism was a shared loathing of the New Deal and of communism. In the fusion of traditionalism and libertarianism, the moral force of property was understood to guarantee individual freedom, the traditional family, and communal virtue. The Bible and the U.S. Constitution were understood as textual guides. Known at the time as "fusionism," anti-establishment conservatism presented an ideologically charged version of customary conservative beliefs in laissez-faire capitalism and private property rights, limited government and low taxes, the defense of the traditional family, the original meaning of the Constitution, anti-communism, and stout national defense. Best articulated by William F. Buckley, Jr.'s *National Review* magazine, fusionism adopted a peculiarly anti-statist statism, allowing the movement to support interventionist anti-communist foreign policy and the massive military-industrial complex that served it, while in the same breath condemning the growth of the federal government as a threat to individual liberty, personal responsibility, and self-reliance.[6] Anti-establishment conservatism's grassroots, located largely in the West and later in the South, were nurtured on this ideology while sustained materially by massive government spending on defense.

A right-wing populist revolt against the post-war liberal consensus, including the consensus's Republican establishment supporters, fueled the Goldwater movement in the early 1960s. Establishment conservatism's vigilance against communism, which included the New Deal itself as a form of proto-communism, was judged by the revolt to be woefully deficient. Winning only 38.5 percent of the popular vote, Goldwater lost big in the 1964 presidential election, but the forces set in motion by his defeat laid the ideological and institutional groundwork for anti-establishment conservatism's subsequent ascendance. Diminished by the Goldwater defeat, the movement didn't disappear; rather it went into rebuilding mode. It re-grouped, built institutions and recruited leaders, attracted money from right-wing businessmen, mobilized conservative Christians politically, and, sixteen years later, helped bring Ronald Reagan to the presidency. Since that 1980 victory, anti-establishment conservatism has manifested in an effective, if somewhat discordant alliance of reenergized anti-New Deal business, the Christian or evangelical right (embodying social conservatism), neoconservatism (disillusioned liberal intellectuals who moved to the right in the 1970s), and the libertarian conservative tradition now embodied by the Tea Party movement. Anti-establishment conservatism has effectively become the new establishment. Conservatism today is of the anti-establishment variety. This book traces that development.

What are the features of contemporary anti-establishment conservatism? Principled to the point of being dogmatic, fundamentalist in style and inclination, apocalyptic in rhetoric, anti-establishment conservatism brooks no compromise. Indeed, it derides the old maxim that politics is the art of the possible and deems those who live by that adage as weaklings, sellouts, even traitors. The old "me-too Republican" insult has been replaced by the RINO acronym – "Republican in Name Only." Politics for anti-establishment conservatives is, for all intents and purposes, Manichean, a life or death struggle between good and evil. My use of religious metaphors is, plainly, by design, for a convinced, intransigent, faith-based style of politics has become characteristic of contemporary American conservatism, one that seems to attack the very notion of a public good. The old hard-line libertarian saw, "taxation is theft," increasingly animates conservative politics. In this view, taxation beyond some very restricted level of collective security is illegitimate, which makes the entire thrust of twentieth-century progressive politics essentially criminal. While this may be an extreme view, going far beyond the older, states' rights-based conservative criticism of *federal* taxes as opposed to *local* ones, the extreme seems now to pervade all contemporary conservative politics. The Taxpayer Protection Pledge referred to in the opening epigraphs to this chapter conveys this outlook. For anti-establishment conservatives, taxes and government spending have become as much a moral matter as a political or economic one. Government, in this moral calculus, squanders hard-earned taxpayer dollars on programs that reward bad behavior. But when politics become ensconced within a deeply moralistic framework, negotiation and compromise become next to impossible. One's opponents do not just differ on policy matters; their very opposition is confirmation of their bad intent, perhaps, even, their evil nature. Contemporary conservatives are apt to vilify their adversaries in a way that recalls historical religious battles. Their deeply held values tend to over-whelm inconvenient facts and evidence in a way that recalls religious fundamentalists explaining away the contradictions found in Scrip-ture. Faith over facts.

Indeed, current-day conservatism puts the lie to the wry dictum attributed to the late Democratic Senator Daniel Patrick Moynihan: "You're entitled to your own opinions; you are not entitled to your own facts." Virtually everything to anti-establishment conservatives – facts, science, expertise – is politics: that is, unsettled, untrue, and open to contestation. An aide to President George W. Bush, widely reputed to be Bush's closest adviser, Karl Rove, conveyed this perspec-tive in a noted 2004 interview with the journalist Ron Suskind. In Suskind's retelling:

> The aide said that guys like me were "in what we call the reality-based community," which he defined as people who "believe that solutions emerge from your judicious study of discernible reality." I nodded and murmured something about enlightenment principles and empiricism. He cut me off. "That's not the way the world really works anymore," he continued. "We're an empire now, and when we act, we create our own reality. And while you're studying that reality – judiciously, as you will – we'll act again, creating other new realities, which you can study too, and that's how things will sort out. We're history's actors . . . and you, all of you, will be left to just study what we do."[7]

Although in recent decades the right has attacked liberals and liberal-ism for their supposed relativism and lack of a clear moral center, the aide's comments in fact betray the right's affinity with a world-view – these days laid at the door of postmodernism – that reality and truth are not fixed. Rather, politics is the power to define reality, to make truth. This articulation of what amounts to Leninist van-guardism, which at the same time casts some doubt as to the objective nature of reality, is rather stunning for a perspective that presumably cleaves to traditional notions of self-evident facts, timeless truths, and foundational texts.

The anti-establishment right thus reveals itself to be a complicated mix of conservative principle, fundamentalism, and truth-creating exercise of will, engaged in a radical effort to overturn settled law, norms, and institutions. How has conservatism evolved into such a state that it seems at odds with its moderate and intellectually prin-cipled origins in the likes of Edmund Burke, the French political thinker and historian Alexis de Tocqueville, the British statesman Benjamin Disraeli, and even, in comparison to what we see today, William F. Buckley, Jr.? If conservatism is in historical and theoretical terms a political philosophy and practice tied to notions of continuity, prudence, and incrementalism, of securing restraints on human passions and creating social institutions that foster, in Burke's phrase, "public affections," how is it that current American conservatism has become so fervent, so furious, so revolutionary? How are we to understand the tension in anti-establishment conservative ideology between the ostensibly fixed knowledge provided by an inerrant Bible and Constitution with the suggestion, by, it would appear, Karl Rove and others, that reality and truth are infinitely malleable? What explains the rage of the Tea Party movement and the elected representatives affiliated with it? And why has this brand of conservatism become so successful? These are the central questions this book tries to answer.

One noted explanation for the dogmatic turn of conservatism is that of the "paranoid style in American politics," formulated in 1963 by the historian Richard Hofstadter in his effort to comprehend the popular movements around Joseph McCarthy and Barry Goldwater. In Hofstadter's view there was legitimate debate to be had about American foreign policy and the danger of the Soviet Union, Keynesian economics and government spending, the influence of labor unions, and the like. What concerned Hofstadter was the *style* of popular conservatism. What he found so significant and disturbing about McCarthyism was the *way* the senator and his followers engaged in political argument (conspiracy mongering), expressed their political subjectivities (as rage), and understood themselves (as patriotic victims, in McCarthy's old phrase, of "a conspiracy so immense"). And, in the end, it wasn't a matter of simply style. The paranoid outlook affected substantive political content, transforming otherwise legitimate political disputes into fevered charges of betrayal and treason, the violation of natural law or God's will, and resulted in a poisoned political climate and the widespread abuse of people's rights. Hofstadter understood right-wing movements as manifestations of a periodic, punctuated upwelling from a permanent reservoir of anti-intellectualism, even mass irrationalism, in American life. Those drawn to the paranoid politics of McCarthyism and Goldwaterism were, in Hofstadter's analysis, deeply distressed by the pace and direction of post-World War II social change, and judged their group position in American society to be under grave threat. They were convinced that "America has been largely taken away from them and their kind, though they are determined to try to repossess it and to prevent the final destructive act of subversion."[8] Behind these convictions, Hofstadter submitted, was the powerful phenomenon of "status anxiety," the psychological sense of loss of rank and place, of an intense feeling of victimhood, and the need to find and punish those responsible for this. The result was a curiously crude and almost superstitious form of anti-communism which discovered in elites (even Republican presidents!) individuals of wholly evil intent who conspired against the public good, and found in the modest American welfare state alarming economic policies that posed an existential danger to the fabric of free society.[9]

Jump forward forty-plus years. The rage and conspiracy mongering following the election of Barack Obama – and the generally dogmatic tenor of conservative politics in the George W. Bush years – have prompted a Hofstadter revival of sorts among political commentators and social scientists. Again, the antipathy to taxes and government spending, the anxiety about what conservatives perceive as the increasing control by the federal government over American life are, of course, familiar themes, legitimate subjects of even passionate political disagreement. What startled, again, was the *style* of conservative politics, particularly that embodied by the Tea Party movement but hardly confined to it: the rage and invective that accompanied the critique of government spending and the so-called nanny state; the racist rhetoric and fantastical fixation on President Obama's birth certificate, citizenship status, religious affiliation, and reputed association with terrorists; the outraged claims, backed by no evidence whatever, that the Democratic health care reform bill of 2009–10 called for "death panels"; accusations that the scientific consensus on climate change was a politicized hoax perpetrated by leftist elites. It's hard not to summon up Hofstadter's concept of the paranoid style after encountering the ubiquitous Tea Party slogan, "We want our country back!" Back from whom? Back to what? To a simpler, happier time when nice white Christian people ran an America that itself confidently ran the world? Indeed, Hofstadter's description of the paranoid style of the early 1960s is so apt for our current moment it feels slightly uncanny.

In the paranoid style, as I conceive it, the feeling of persecution is central, and it is indeed systematized in grandiose theories of conspiracy. But there is a vital difference between the paranoid spokesman in politics and the clinical paranoiac: although they both tend to be overheated, oversuspicious, overaggressive, grandiose, and apocalyptic in expression, the clinical paranoid sees the hostile and conspiratorial world in which he feels himself to be living as directed specifically *against him*; whereas the spokesman of the paranoid style finds it directed against a nation, a culture, a way of life whose fate affects not himself alone but millions of others. Insofar as he does not usually see himself singled out as the individual victim of a personal conspiracy, he is somewhat more rational and much more disinterested. His sense that his political passions are unselfish and patriotic, in fact, goes far to intensify his feeling of righteousness and his moral indignation.[10]

But incisive description is not adequate explanation. As many of Hofstadter's critics were quick to point out, the problem with the theory of the paranoid style is that its social psychological approach makes it easy to label as atavistic and irrational those political actors and behaviors with which the researcher happens to disagree. At the end of the day, Hofstadter's analysis is a description of a political style, tied to a grand social psychological theory. Hofstadter posed a macro argument (certain social structural conditions produce status anxiety) and a micro argument (people anxious of their place in the world exhibit a paranoid, conspiracy-mongering political style) – with nothing in between. A central flaw is the absence of a middle level of analysis to connect the two. This book focuses on this middle level of analysis. It traces the concrete institutions responsible for mobilizing and channeling anger, anxiety, and ideas in particular conservative directions, and that produce particular kinds of conservative political subjectivities and a distinct conservative political culture. In this approach, institutions and ideas are co-constitutive. To understand the ascendance of anti-establishment conservatism, we must trace the development of ideas in the rough and tumble of politics in historical context, and understand the networks of money, media, and organizations that the anti-establishment conservative movement has built to channel those ideas over the last four-plus decades.

Of particular interest to this study are the Christian right and the neoconservatives, inasmuch as these particular groups developed the ideas and networks that reenergized anti-establishment conservatism beginning in the 1970s. Politics are often defined by what (and who) one hates. Arriving separately on the American political scene, the Christian right and neoconservatism each articulated deep loathing toward the worldview and politics of the cultural upheaval of the 1960s. This abhorrence grew into an expansive critique of the modern liberal state, which Christian fundamentalists and evangelicals believed (with some justification) had turned against them, their institutions, and their values. The logic of the equal protection and due process protections of the Fourteenth Amendment to the U.S. Constitution – the so-called rights revolution – expanded in the 1960s from the legal protection of racial minorities against discrimination to a defense of pluralistic values in the public sphere. Pluralism, particularly in the form of the ban on school prayer, and the striking down of laws against contraception, abortion, and sexual expression, upended the fixed moral truths that essentially had been embedded in American society by virtue of its Protestant-based civil religion. The rights revolution, and the "counterculture" that accompanied and fueled it, had the effect of challenging the relatively insular, protected world of conservative Christians generally, and particularly through tax, education, and labor policies. Fearful for their institutions (especially their private schools and their lucrative radio and television networks), fundamentalists and conservative evangelicals denounced liberal government and the value system they believed lay behind it, labeling that value system "secular humanism." They were especially scornful of a federal judiciary that had begun to apply the Fourteenth Amendment in cases involving Christian institutions. As this book will show, while fundamentalists supposedly withdrew from the secular world to concentrate on salvation, in fact they were very much part of the politics of anti-communism and anti-civil rights. Nonetheless, it *is* the case that by the late 1970s, conservative Christians, newly mobilized politically and brought into the Republican fold with the help of former Goldwater political entrepreneurs, became a key constituency in the Reagan electoral coalition. Since 1980, the Christian right has been acknowledged as the "base" of the Republican Party.

Neoconservatism was neither an electoral constituency nor a grassroots movement. Rather it was an influential intellectual inclination that began with a trenchant critique of government overreach and the unintended consequences of liberal public policies. Although in general supportive of the New Deal, neoconservatives turned to the right because they believed the federal government by the late 1960s was guilty of engaging in social engineering. At the root of government overreach, epitomized in their view by the anti-poverty Great Society programs of Lyndon Johnson's administration, was a "New Class" of unproductive liberal public sector professional elites whose ill-advised and costly endeavors to re-make social behavior served to fortify their own position and power. The New Class's will to power came largely at the expense of virtuous "producers": that is, at the expense of those honorable laboring members of society, including businessmen, who actually produced economic value and added to the real wealth of the nation. By implication, the New Class did not add value; indeed, its members were parasitic on those who did. Neoconservative New Class analysis represented a right turn in the anti-elitist politics historically identified with American populism.

Distinct movements, the Christian right and neoconservatism by the mid-1970s discovered they shared intellectual affinities and moral convictions. The neoconservative critique of the New Class in many respects mirrored the Christian right's critique of secular humanism. Both groups blamed big government for creating the nation's ills and imperiling private enterprise, which, naturally, also served to align them with certain business interests. The Christian right and neoconservatism both also held that the United States was faltering in its leadership of the free world. They shared an unabashed belief in American exceptionalism: that is, in the conviction as to the beneficent, universal nature of the American values that necessarily accompany U.S. military ventures abroad; that war was the preferred means to defeat America's external enemies and, in the case of the neoconservatives, the way to spread democracy to blighted parts of the globe. And they shared an appreciation of religion as providing the moral and cultural foundations for a wobbly, even endangered, liberal democracy. As leaders of the two groups began to interact, they increasingly came to share material networks and resources as well as ideas. They implored business to help spread the ideas, and business responded generously. The same foundations, corporations, millionaires, and CEOs began funding neoconservative and religious initiatives, think tanks, advocacy organizations, symposia, and publications; Christian right and neoconservative leaders began attending the same conferences; their writings appeared in each other's newsletters and journals.

The corporate underwriting of right-wing Christian and neoconservative ventures highlighted a third element in a reconstituted anti-establishment conservative alliance: big business. Having for the most part signed on to the post-war liberal consensus, big business ditched it in the 1970s in a revolt against regulation and tax policy and accommodation with organized labor. Although the business mobilization against government was swift and consequential, business was in many ways a follower, not a leader, of the anti-establishment conservative zeitgeist formulated by the intellectuals associated with the

Christian right and especially the neoconservative movement. Here the role played by the neoconservative essayist and organizer Irving Kristol was crucial.

Kristol et al.'s ideas were powerful in this moment when the New Deal political coalition had begun to break down and the old liberal consensus policy tools had become less effective. The national Democratic Party's commitment to civil rights led to the defection of the white South from the party. Organized labor had already been transformed, beginning with the 1947 Taft–Hartley Act, from a crusading social movement to just another interest group – and a diminishing one – of the Democratic coalition. The Vietnam War split the party. The 1970s marked the beginning of the decline in American hegemony: the Vietnam War sapped American global political leadership and economic globalization had begun to lessen America's post-war economic supremacy. Keynesian economic tools seemed unable to cope with the combined high inflation and unemployment of the 1970s. Together, the New Class and secular humanism critiques called into question a core principle of the modernist liberal consensus – that disinterested social science and policy expertise could be marshaled in the service of the national interest. Instead, neoconservatives and Christian evangelicals challenged – in their minds, exposed – expertise as politics and power. The essence of the New Class critique was that expertise was simply a masquerade for a particular kind of group self-interest. Liberal professionals in the government and non-profit sectors used their educational credentials and the language of expertise to gain power. This, too, had a deeper, historically pregnant religious dimension. The idea of a disinterested social science-based policy elite was in many respects the secular embodiment of the liberal Protestant Social Gospel. In that tradition, science, including social science, was a prime tool in achieving the kingdom of God on earth. At the time of the formulation of the Social Gospel around the beginning of the twentieth century, building the kingdom of God meant civic action to rectify social problems – which entailed Christian engagement in the world largely for the betterment of the working class and the poor. By the New Deal, the goal had become secularized and generalized as the common or national interest. Elite values of nonpartisan, disinterested social science were to be mobilized in the service of the people.[11] But fundamentalist Christians had been at war with the Social Gospel from the outset. The Social Gospel's assumption that humans, rather than God, could and should affect social outcomes was nothing short of blasphemy to conservative Christians.

When in the 1970s the new Christian right, echoed in a more secular way by neoconservatives, criticized government actions as anti-religious or as social engineering, they were channeling central elements of the old battle with the Social Gospel into the new fight with liberals over the nature of liberalism and, concretely, the expansion of the Fourteenth Amendment-based rights revolution. To the Christian right and neoconservatives there was no such thing as disinterested social science; that was simply a mask for partisan liberal policy. This battle allied these newer constituents of the anti-establishment right to the old Goldwater libertarians, and fueled what would become the conservative class war on expertise in general. The attack on expertise as a form of liberalism became a key element in what came to be called the "culture wars."

The political figure who embodied the anti-establishment conservative outlook was Ronald Reagan. It was around Reagan's 1980 candidacy that coalesced the interlocking sets of conservative issue groups, the mobilization of material resources, and the articulation of a powerful political ideology of victimhood. Government was the problem; the citizenry was its victim. Reagan's candidacy especially galvanized the Christian right. He famously declared his allegiance to the anti-establishment conservative alliance, saying to the August 1980 National Affairs Briefing of 15,000 religious leaders, "Now I know this is a nonpartisan gathering and so I know you can't endorse me, but I only brought that up because I want you to know that I endorse you and what you are doing."[12] Reagan was and remains conservatism's idol. But Reagan is also in some ways an ambiguous figure. Whereas he benefited from the populism of the newly mobilized Christian right to gain the presidency and satisfied that constituency with occasional policies, more often he offered mere rhetorical flourishes, and in the end Reagan's presidency was not much beholden to it. The actual Reagan revolution was for the most part a capitalist revolution, a re-conquest that reconfigured the relationship between the state and the economy in the partial dismantling of the welfare state, the deregulation of many industries (and consequent decline of labor union power), the privatization of a number of public functions and services, and the partial transfer of risk from corporations and government to individuals – what has come to be labeled neoliberalism.[13] Reagan was a more complicated politician than was once thought, as several new scholarly studies suggest. Denouncing taxes, Reagan raised them several times in the course of his presidency. Condemning government spending, his administration nearly tripled the federal budget deficit. Having supported on the campaign trail a constitutional amendment that would have prohibited all abortions except when necessary to save the life of the mother, in office Reagan did comparatively little about abortion. And ranting against the Soviet Union as the "Evil Empire," Reagan engaged Soviet leader Mikhail Gorbachev in serious negotiations over massive reductions in nuclear arsenals and the possible sharing of missile defense technology.[14] This is not to say Reagan was no conservative. Hardly. It was Reagan who realigned the state toward the interests of business. But notwithstanding his top billing in the conservative pantheon and contrary to his own rhetoric, Reagan engaged in old-style give-and-take politics. Beyond well-timed rhetoric, Reagan did not much serve the interests of strict conservative ideologues or the Christian right or the neoconservatives. Still, the fact that Reagan is revered for anti-establishment right-wing policies he often didn't carry out is telling, for conservative politics since Reagan, endlessly invoking his legacy, has been largely of the anti-establishment variety.

It wasn't until 9/11 that anti-establishment conservatism saw its broadest hopes and policies put in place under George W. Bush. The terrorist attacks of September 11, 2001 set the stage; the debacle of the Iraq War was the result. As neoconservatism evolved into its foreign policy-focused second generation, the intellectual movement came to share with the Christian right not just a harsh critique of liberalism, but the deep structure of millenarian utopianism. Neoconservative influence from the 1970s, first in hawkish foreign policy lobbying organizations and later in dominance of defense policy institutions, put the movement in a strong position when the fear and sense of risk became amplified by the attacks of September 11. The second generation of neoconservatives ignored its forebears' watchword of the dangers of social engineering and unintended consequences of public policy in favor of utopianism and the cleansing fire of violence in foreign affairs. This meant strong support for a confrontational policy legitimated by the belief in American exceptionalism. The idea that the United States is the embodiment of God's gift of freedom and constitutes the greatest earthly force for good the world has known has always fused elements of nationalism and religion. Muscular versions of American exceptionalism distinguished the thinking of the Christian right and neoconservatism, and figured heavily in the Bush administration's militaristic Middle East policy. Christian right support for the U.S. wars in the Middle East proceeded in some significant measure from the pre-millennialist belief in the Rapture and the "end-time," in which the world's destruction enables Christ's return and a new, perfect world to emerge. During the Persian Gulf War of 1991, for example, the veteran prophecy writer Charles Taylor advised his followers that the war was preliminary to the Rapture.[15] If not the Antichrist himself, suggested conservative evangelical organizations and preachers, Saddam Hussein could well be a forerunner of the Evil One. In many evangelical readings of the New Testament's book of Revelation, the return of Jesus requires first that Jews return to the biblical boundaries of ancient Israel. War on Iraq would hasten this process. Thus many evangelicals regarded the invasion of Iraq as not simply an instance of a just war, but the realization of the prophesies of Revelation. Second-generation neoconservatism's utopianism lay in an analogous apocalyptic belief in the United States' ability to hasten universal democracy and a global free market through the creative application of violence.

Christian right and neoconservative brands of conservatism, influential since the late 1970s, became fully joined and embraced by the Bush administration in the wake of the fear and heightened perception of risk following September 11. President Bush himself said that he sensed a "Third [Great] Awakening" of religious devotion in the United States that coincided with the nation's struggle with international terrorists, a war he depicted as "a confrontation between good and evil."[16] Fusing Christian right and neoconservative worldviews, Bush disclosed in a 2007 interview, "It's more of a theological perspective. I do believe there is an Almighty, and I believe a gift of that Almighty to all is freedom. And I will tell you that is a principle that no one can convince me that doesn't exist."[17] The parallel millennial beliefs of the Christian right, neoconservatism, and the Bush administration coincided in the disaster of Iraq.

I have referred to the Iraq War as a debacle a few times now. I am hardly alone in this judgment. Many prominent diplomats and scholars, including retired Army general William Odom, the preeminent conservative newspaper columnist George F. Will, and former Secretary of State Madeleine Albright, called Iraq the worst foreign policy disaster in U.S. history.[18] The lineaments of this assessment are now well understood. The direct American combat role in the Iraq War proceeded for almost nine years, with nearly 4,500 American military and at least 100,000 Iraqi civilian casualties at an unknown cost (officially $750 billion but estimated at far higher – well beyond $3 trillion when long-term medical costs and replacement costs of troop and equipment are factored in), and the internal displacement of 2.7 million Iraqis and exile of another 2 million.[19] The war siphoned off money, manpower, and attention from the military engagement in Afghanistan. The American military effort did remove the vile dictator Saddam Hussein from power. But as of this writing the viability of the Iraqi government remains in doubt, neighborhoods in major cities have been ethnically cleansed, infrastructure remains shattered, and basic services such as electricity are marginal at best. Indeed, the very "state-ness" of the country remains a question, given the strong tendencies of Shiite, Sunni, and Kurdish communities toward separation and perhaps partition. Contrary to the self-assured pronouncements of Bush administration policy-makers, there were no Iraqi weapons of mass destruction. And contrary to the hoary expectations of the backers of the war, a would-be democratic Iraq did not become a model for other Arab states. A severely weakened Iraq is no longer a regional counterweight to Iran; indeed, many analysts point to Iran's heavy, if below-the-radar, influence on Iraq's ruling parties. U.S. intelligence agencies concluded that the Iraq conflict was a prime source of recruitment for the global jihadist movement.[20] In short, the Iraq War proved to be an utter fiasco, a dreadful monument to the law of unintended consequences abroad and at home.

Domestically, the Iraq War was perhaps the most far-reaching political event of recent years, for two interrelated reasons. First, when combined with the large tax cuts the Bush administration enacted in 2001 – which lowered tax rates across the board on income, dividends, and capital gains, and effectively eliminated the estate tax (and hence mostly reduced the taxes of America's wealthy) – the huge expenditures on the Iraq War caused the federal budget deficit to balloon. Bush increased the budget deficit by $6.1 trillion, far more than any other administration in history. Thus when the housing collapse and financial crash ensued in 2008, the increased indebtedness meant that the U.S. government had far less room to maneuver than it otherwise would have had. The high deficit/debt made Keynesian remedies under the incoming Obama administration much more difficult to sell politically. Worries about the (war-inflated) debt and deficit constrained the size and effectiveness of Obama's economic stimulus.[21] And, of course, the effectiveness of a domestic stimulus package in an increasingly globalized economy already made its effectiveness less likely. The second far-reaching consequence was that the crisis intervention spending remedies that were put in place to deal with the near economic collapse mobilized a ferocious conservative populist political reaction in the form of the Tea Party movement, reanimating the anti-establishment conservative politics that had been temporarily discredited by the multiple failures of the Bush administration.

As stated previously, it was the Tea Party that proved most capable of expressing the disgust of the class bias and unfairness of the government bailouts of the banks, insurance, and mortgage companies responsible for the financial collapse. The government was seen as aiding the elites. This view superficially is true inasmuch as the structural bias of the state causes it to engage in crisis management in ways that safeguard the financial infrastructure of a capitalist economy. But it is also the case that the game *is* rigged on behalf of elites. Paradoxically, it is in part the very success of anti-establishment conservatism – the force that animates the Tea Party – that has made this so. After thirty-five years of hard ideological work, anti-establishment conservatism has succeeded in getting large sections of the American people to view government as the problem. This has consequences. When government is the problem, the public institutions historically built to check the power of structurally powerful entities, business corporations first among them, become eroded, hollowed out, and corrupted – and subject then to legitimate contempt and calls for their elimination. And in point of fact, since the 1970s and economic globalization, the old Keynesian solutions have proved less effectual and the old New Deal social democratic ideal has seemed more financially problematic. The conservative triumph does not come in a political vacuum, after all. But when the very idea of disinterested social science policy in the national interest is in doubt, there is no reason for the actual policy elite to pursue its activity in the pursuit of a non-existent ideal. The governmental elites then become the personification of what is held in contempt. If government is by nature ineffective and oppressive, even perhaps evil, why not try to "drown" the beast?[22]

The scope of the book by chapter

If this, chapter 1, sets the stage, chapter 2 addresses the birth and development of modern American conservatism. It surveys the post-World War II political landscape, in which the old right found itself having to adapt to the liberal consensus of the New Deal and the interventionist, but bounded, foreign policy of containment of communism. The chapter traces the emergence of anti-establishment conservatism and its characteristic anti-statist statism, and its embodiment in the 1964 Goldwater campaign. The forces set in motion by Goldwater's defeat, in conjunction with the erosion of the New Deal coalition owing to civil rights and the Vietnam War, laid the ideological and institutional groundwork for the victory of Ronald Reagan sixteen years later.

Chapter 3 traces one key element of that ideological and institutional groundwork, the rise of the new Christian right. In so doing, the chapter reconstructs a condensed history of evangelical Protestantism in America, the split between church modernists and fundamentalists, the supposed withdrawal of the latter from the world, and their reemergence to the realm of politics in the 1970s when they found their institutions under threat from the consequences of the expansion of the Fourteenth Amendment.

Chapter 4 discusses the evolution of neoconservatism from its roots in skeptical social science of domestic policy to its embrace of war as the preferred form of foreign policy. The chapter traces the intellectual affinities and institutional connections between neoconservatism and the Christian right and how, together, in a common critique of the New Class and secular humanism pursued through networks of foundations, think tanks, and media, they reinvigorated anti-establishment conservatism in the 1970s.

The neoconservative critique of the New Class underlies the sense of victimhood that propels the populist rage of the Tea Party movement, the latest manifestation of anti-establishment conservatism and the central focus of chapter 5. The Tea Party is a continuation of the revolt against elites, in which regard Richard Hofstadter's "paranoid style" is a powerful analytical device. The Tea Party pursues the long-term political goal of anti-establishment conservatism: to shrink support for and dismantle government.

Chapter 6 concludes the book with an exploration as to how utopianism has shifted from the political left to the political right. Anti-establishment conservatism is utopian and now rules the Republican Party. Its utopianism is largely responsible for the GOP's current dogmatic politics.

— 2 —

ANTI-STATIST STATISM
A Brief History of a Peculiarly American Conservatism

At the end of World War II and into the 1950s, American conservatism faced a difficult set of challenges. It had grown out of step with the broad changes wrought by the New Deal and the war and with what appeared to be the political consensus that had emerged in their wake. Cold War liberalism, or the "liberal consensus," effectively defined the post-war dominant political bloc. Domestically, the liberal consensus affirmed the positive role of the state in the economy. This meant the essential acceptance of Keynesian economic principles, heavy government investment in infrastructure and defense industries, and the preservation of the most important New Deal programs and institutions. Pushed by the social democratic commitments of a powerful labor movement, the Roosevelt administration brought some degree of public control over markets. Still, state intervention under the New Deal was designed to ameliorate market failures and mitigate the most unequal income distributional patterns but by no means was to displace private enterprise. Capitalist economic growth was seen as the key to prosperity and the diminution of social conflict. While at the outset there was contemplation of extensive state supervision through initiatives such as the National Recovery Administration, after the first few years of the Roosevelt administration, government intervention largely aimed to perform crisis management and foster economic growth through spending, to regulate but not plan economic activity or radically redistribute income. The so-called second New Deal of 1935–6 placed less emphasis on government planning and more upon restoring competition among smaller economic units. This formulation is too neat, of course. Most scholars suggest that the Roosevelt administration put forward any number of economic policies with mutually contradictory rationales, hoping that some would work.[1] The New Deal order was built on a unionized workforce with good wages and benefits in mass-production industries subject to various kinds and levels of government regulation. Safety-net institutions minimally provided for those unable to work. Industries undermined by various economic forces, including excess competition, were stabilized by subsidies, price supports, and entry controls.[2] Politically, the New Deal consisted of a coalition of liberals, big-city political machines, labor unions, ethnic, racial, and religious minorities (especially urban Catholics, Jews, and, as time went on, African-Americans), some farm groups, and, crucially, the South.[3]

In foreign affairs the liberal consensus affirmed another version of the positive role of the state. But first, a quick primer on the key schools of thought. Scholars speak of four basic conceptual approaches or schools to international relations. *Realists* see rivalry and conflict among nation-states as unavoidable and thus they approach the international system in terms of states exercising power, whether military, economic, or diplomatic. They orient policies and actions according to what they see as in the best national interests of the United States. Realists have little concern for the internal nature of other regimes or human rights issues; what matters is the external behavior of states. *Paleo-conservatives* (sometimes called Jacksonian nationalists) tend to take a narrow, security-related view of American national interests. They strongly distrust multilateralism and international institutions such as the United Nations, and at the far end of the continuum tend toward anti-foreign and anti-immigrant sentiments (otherwise known as nativism) and isolationism. They take as a watchword John Quincy Adams's 1821 declaration that "[America] goes not abroad in search of monsters to destroy."[4] *Liberal internationalists* aspire to transcend the amoral nature of power politics. While they don't forswear the use of military force in international conflicts, they place trust in multilateral institutions, international law, and diplomacy. The United States must pursue its national interests in foreign affairs, but liberal internationalists view those interests far more broadly than do realists or paleo-conservatives. Human rights and the internal nature of other regimes are very important in their worldview; diplomacy is much preferred to military force. Like liberal internationalists, *neoconservatives* tend to be internationalist in basic orientation, concerned with democracy, human rights, and the internal politics of states. They believe that U.S. power, including, notably, military power, can – and must – be used for moral purposes. But unlike liberal internationalists, neoconservatives exhibit deep skepticism about the ability of international law and institutions to solve serious security problems and they tend toward unilateral American actions.[5] At the risk of simplification, we can say that realists and paleo-conservatives are oriented toward interests, whereas liberal internationalists and neoconservatives are oriented toward values. All of these schools believe, with varying degrees of intensity, in American exceptionalism, that the United States is a special nation whose democratic values are universal and whose policies are designed to bring the blessings of liberty to other peoples of the world. Although these categories are useful markers, one needs to be careful not to hypostasize them. People and groups do not always fall cleanly into any particular school, and on any given foreign policy issue – especially in the context of a national security crisis – there may be marginal coherence between a school's principles and the policy adopted.

The post-World War II liberal consensus in foreign policy consisted of the acceptance of a permanent role for the United States in international affairs, manifesting in large military outlays to limit communist expansion and support for new international institutions such as the United Nations, the World Bank, and the International Monetary Fund. The policy order of the day – to become known as the Truman Doctrine, after the Democratic president – reflected a balance of power realism: the containment of communism through a combination of diplomacy, permanent American military presence abroad (particularly in Europe, through the North Atlantic Treaty Organization, or NATO), and military and economic assistance to nations deemed vulnerable to the blandishments or depredations of the communist movement. The Marshall Plan for European Recovery to rebuild a war-devastated Europe embodied the approach toward foreign aid: make American capital available to governments that chose an open economy and the development of capitalist markets. Scholarship has revealed that much if not most foreign aid outside of Europe was actually military; U.S. military assistance included covert operations, assassinations, and secret financial infusions to political organizations and parties deemed favorable to "western," that is to say, liberal capitalist, interests. Even within Europe, the Marshall Plan's economic assistance was complemented by covert political actions and subterfuge.[6] The Truman Doctrine's realism consisted of an overt commitment to international institutions and a covert one to subversive actions.

The Korean War set the pattern of engaging the communist enemy with U.S. conventional military forces or by proxy armies in conflicts in the colonial or semi-colonial "periphery" or "Third World." This included the support of dictators if they were perceived as forestalling communism and safeguarding western interests. As the historian Odd Arne Westad puts it in startlingly neutral terms, the Cold War marked an elemental ideological clash between the United States and the Soviet Union over the concept of modernity – in ideal typical form, market-based liberal capitalist vs. state-centered, "social justice" collectivism – whose clash largely played out in the countries emerging from colonial domination.[7] In President Truman's view, broadly shared by Americans, the Cold War also represented a fundamental spiritual conflict pitting those who believed in God and morality and the dignity of the individual against atheism and materialism and the apotheosis of the state. Containment policy thus had a distinct theological dimension.[8] And while the clash over the model of modernity frequently devastated the Third World countries that played host to superpower hostilities, for example the wars in Korea, Vietnam, Angola, and a host of others, the superpowers observed a generally successful effort to keep any given conflict bounded. U.S. containment policy entailed a practice not to engage the Soviet Union directly or in its post-war geographic sphere of influence much beyond a war of words and spies. The Truman Doctrine committed the United States to building a large nuclear arsenal but not to using nuclear weapons offensively. Ideally, the atomic bomb would never be used again; it was to act as a deterrent to Soviet aggression and as a key asset in the complicated game of international power politics. Containment, in other words, was not the "rollback" of communism. Containment policy was designed to restrain Soviet expansionism in the short run without risking the expansion of hostilities into direct, out-and-out, and especially nuclear, war. The grand theorists of containment hoped that the Soviet system would change or collapse in the long run.[9]

This summary is, admittedly, absurdly condensed. Although the Truman Doctrine recognized that a nuclear war was generally not winnable, much post-war military policy was concerned with how to use the nuclear option. Nuclear weapons arsenals were built to stupendous levels.[10] Moreover, the existence of the Bomb underlay the evolution of the national security state and consolidated power in the Office of the President, contributing mightily to the "imperial presidency" characteristic of post-war American politics.[11] Still, containment meant putting limits on U.S. military actions, including threats to use nuclear weapons. And I do not mean to suggest that the post-war liberal foreign policy consensus simply emerged casually, without

debate or conflict. President Truman had to vanquish Commerce
Secretary Henry Wallace's much more dovish "Popular Front" liberalism in the 1948 presidential election. Wallace, considered the heir
to Franklin Delano Roosevelt (or FDR), campaigned on his Progressive Party platform of turning American nuclear weapons over to the
United Nations and of funding a large reconstruction program for
America's war-ravaged ally, the Soviet Union. Truman fired Wallace
as Secretary of Commerce in 1946 after the latter publicly opposed
containment. On the other side of the political ledger, Truman had
to contend with the right's nascent preventive war position and its
embodiment in a very popular General Douglas MacArthur.[12]

The old right, the New Deal, and containment

The original sin of the New Deal, in the eyes of the pre-war old right,
was its fostering of the growth of federal power. As discussed in the
introductory chapter, the fundamental political concern of American
conservatism is the threat to liberty and property from centralized
state power. In conservative political theory, property makes liberty
possible. Indeed, in the sociologist Karl Mannheim's analysis, the
concept of property in the conservative worldview retains the scent
of the set of pre-modern inarticulate privileges of personhood and
honor conveyed in the relationship of an owner and his property.
"Property in its old 'genuine' sense carried with it certain privileges
for its owner – for instance, it gave him a voice in affairs of state,
the right to hunt, to become a member of a jury. Thus it was closely
bound up with his personal honour and so in a sense *inalienable*."[13]
Mannheim's articulation may yet be too European with its focus on
honor. Still, in the American context, the notion that property conferred the liberty and independence necessary to be a citizen of the
republic was a central theme of Jeffersonian democracy and largely
echoes Mannheim's observations.

   By intervening in the market and limiting what an owner could do
with his property, the state thus was seen to imperil liberty. Accordingly, the old right demonized the New Deal, seeing it as the American
variant of collectivism and the enhancement of state power characteristic of fascism and communism. Franklin Roosevelt had betrayed
the true meaning of American liberalism: laissez-faire. The American
Liberty League, organized in 1934 by some prominent conservative
Democrats (including the 1924 and 1928 party nominees for president, John W. Davis and Al Smith, respectively) and funded by several

big industrialists (especially the du Pont family), opposed the New Deal along these lines, as did leading Republicans such as 1936 presidential candidate Alf Landon and the prominent GOP senator from Ohio, Robert A. Taft. The Liberty League denounced the New Deal as an unconstitutional centralization of power. It characterized FDR's Agricultural Adjustment Administration, for example, as "a trend toward Fascist control of agriculture."[14] The old right was galvanized by businessmen reacting to the practical weakening of their prerogatives. The National Association of Manufacturers (NAM), the trade association of small and medium business, worked hard against the New Deal. NAM mobilized businessmen to oppose labor unions and advocated for the rights of management, both practically and ideologically. Opposition to the New Deal found intellectual cogency in the critique of economic planning by the Austrian-born economists Ludwig von Mises and Friedrich Hayek (with the occasional reach back to the ideas of Edmund Burke and Alexis de Tocqueville).[15] Some businessmen engaged in efforts to institutionalize conservative ideas, among other things subsidizing academic appointments for Mises and Hayek through the William Volker Fund, and bankrolling the post-war Mont Pelerin Society, the elite international society of intellectuals and businessmen devoted to defending the free market against economic planning and socialism. Business supported other groups devoted to conservative causes and ideas, such as the libertarian Foundation for Economic Education, publisher of the monthly magazine *The Freeman*.[16]

Congressional conservatives, Democrat and Republican alike, opposed the spread of federal power and bureaucracy, defended states' rights, and rebuked deficit spending and welfare. Some of the conservative congressional opposition was principled, some personal, and some based on the usual assortment of sectional interests, including, prominently, southern Democratic legislators' efforts to preserve white supremacy. Most southern congressional Democrats were happy to support FDR on economic matters – especially since much New Deal spending essentially created projects in the South paid for by taxes from northerners – but fought his administration on civil rights. Southern congressmen also evinced hostility toward labor unions and opposed any government policy thought either to assist organized labor or potentially deprive southern farmers of cheap black labor. The Roosevelt administration's need for southern Democratic support, as well as the fact that southern legislators dominated the congressional committee system, dampened whatever initiatives might have been proposed to alleviate the condition of

African-Americans. New Deal liberals failed even to go after the infamous poll tax. As the historian George Mowry observes, until the Truman administration, the Democratic Party operated with a subtle understanding: the South would support the national party in its leftward ideological evolution in exchange for the party leaving the South alone with regard to white supremacy and labor relations.[17]

To the more fiery congressional conservatives, the expansion of the federal government under the New Deal was an odious transgression of the American way. In the words of one, it was akin to "Hitlerism." Democratic Senator Carter Glass of Virginia, for example, described the New Deal as "an utterly dangerous effort of the federal government to transplant Hitlerism to every corner of the nation."[18] Congressional conservatives formulated a bipartisan "Conservative Manifesto" in 1937 calling for tax cuts and a balanced budget (just as present-day Republicans do).[19] Unlike elite sources of opposition to the New Deal, populist opponents, organized around charismatic public figures such as the "radio priest" Charles Coughlin, tended to be hostile to capitalism (or at least evinced anticorporate and anti-Wall Street rhetoric) but shared the anxiety about the concentration of governmental power, especially governmental power in the hands of a secular elite (and that was often identified as Jewish).[20]

Yet incensed laissez-faire industrialists and congressional conservatives, not to mention the furious right-wing groups on the populist fringes of opposition to the New Deal, had to swim against the tide. New Deal Keynesian economics and the establishment of the rudiments of a welfare state were widely perceived as having succeeded, their results popular with voters. Franklin Roosevelt was reelected in 1936 with 60.8 percent of the popular vote, winning all states but Maine and Vermont. When FDR's policies didn't work, especially the cutback in federal spending largely responsible for the recession of 1937, Republicans gained at the polls. The GOP picked up eighty-one House and six Senate seats in the 1938 midterm election. But conservative opposition to the New Deal on utilitarian grounds – that welfare economics destroyed individual initiative and hazarded general prosperity – appeared counterfactual, even nonsensical. Indeed, between 1933 and 1940, U.S. gross domestic product increased from $68.3 billion to $113 billion (in 1929 dollars), one of the strongest eight years in U.S. economic history, exceeded only by the World War II period.[21] The continuation of prosperity in the post-war period defied widespread expectations of an economic slowdown. As Richard Hofstadter put it in the context of the 1964 Goldwater campaign,

> As they [the ultra-right spokesmen] see it, we have been committed for many years, for decades, to economic policies which are wrong morally and wrong as expedients, destructive of enterprise, and dangerous to the fabric of free society. At the same time, every informed person recognizes that we have become much richer doing all these supposedly wrong and unsound things than we were when we had hardly begun to do them.[22]

On the foreign policy front, the pre-war old right tended toward non-interventionism and unilateralism, if not outright isolationism. In today's foreign policy terms it would be labeled paleo-conservative. The opposition to internationalism had several sources but at bottom was rooted – naturally – in the old right's wariness of the state. Old right intellectuals such as Felix Morley, one of the founders of the weekly newsletter *Human Events,* and Frank Chodorov, who edited the previously mentioned conservative journal *The Freeman* (and who, with William F. Buckley, Jr., founded the Intercollegiate Society of Individualists in 1953), noted that modern war, and an interventionist foreign policy more generally, centralized power in the state and promoted socialism – and thus threatened freedom. The military draft, moreover, commandeered and regimented citizens for war, further aggrandizing state power and weakening individual freedom.[23] The old right generally supported war in the aftermath of Pearl Harbor (although the more conspiratorially inclined always claimed that the Roosevelt administration had had advance knowledge of the Japanese attack and allowed it to transpire in order to rally a properly reluctant United States to war). But true to isolationist form, the old right counseled the retreat from foreign commitments at the end of World War II. Yet with Europe laid waste and vulnerable, and with the Soviet Union widely perceived to be pursuing an aggressive, expansionist program, broad opinion – stoked by dire pronouncements from the Truman administration – held that the United States was the only world power capable of checking Soviet expansion. The Truman administration, convinced of the danger of Soviet totalitarianism, met the post-war challenge by centralizing foreign policy and military affairs in the executive branch under the National Security Act of 1947. Among other things, the National Security Act created the National Security Council, the Central Intelligence Agency, and the Air Force – which had been a branch of the Army, and now was given primary responsibility for the U.S. nuclear arsenal. Actual responsibility for the atomic bomb was vested in the president.[24]

Pre-war old right positions carried over into the immediate post-World War II period. Their ablest articulator was Ohio GOP Senator Robert A. Taft. On the domestic front, Taft engineered – over President Truman's veto – a reduction of union power with congressional passage of the Taft–Hartley Act in 1947.[25] By imposing limits on labor's ability to strike, restricting union shops, and requiring labor leaders to affirm non-communist credentials, Taft–Hartley helped demobilize the labor movement and hence diminished its power in terms of broader social movement politics. This helped halt any further expansion of the New Deal. In the foreign policy arena, too, Taft reflected old right proclivities. He had opposed U.S. entry into World War II prior to Pearl Harbor because he did not see Nazi Germany as a serious threat to the liberty of the United States. A militant anti-communist, Taft laid the blame for the post-war Soviet threat at the feet of liberals and Democratic leaders who "preferred wishful thinking to facts, and convinced themselves that Stalin would co-operate with them to create a free world of permanent peace," as he wrote in his slim, accessible 1951 treatise, *A Foreign Policy for Americans*. He denounced the postwar settlement: "So at the negotiating summits at Teheran, Yalta, and Postdam they handed Stalin the freedom of eastern Europe and Manchuria, and prepared our present peril."[26] Likewise, Taft saw the State Department as having lost China to the communists.

Although he condemned liberals and Democrats, Taft did not accuse them of treason, as did many on the right. That charge underlay Senator Joseph McCarthy's attacks on the presence of communists in the federal government, and was echoed by others who, for example, accused the State Department of selling out the Nationalist Chinese to the Chinese communists, and General George Marshall of conspiracy at the Yalta Conference.[27] Taft hewed to traditional conservative non-interventionism, arguing that the post-war international role of the United States should be limited. He especially opposed committing U.S. armed forces for the protection of Europe. "War should never be undertaken or seriously risked except to protect American liberty," Taft declared, and the military assistance of post-war Europe surely did not meet that criterion.[28] Despite its evil, Soviet communism posed no immediate threat to the United States, Taft asserted. Rather, the Truman administration imperiled the liberty of Americans by concentrating state power through its secret centralization of national security policy. To meet the communist menace,

Taft advocated mild forms of strategic action: publicity, spying and infiltration, support for forces in friendly or neutral countries – and the purge of communists and fellow travelers from the U.S. government.[29]

Taft's positions reflected the key themes of pre- and early post-war old right thinking on foreign policy. But the non-interventionist position was in many respects internally contradictory. If the USSR was understood as just a state with interests adversarial to the United States, normal international relations or even a hands-off approach could be pursued as American foreign policy. But if Soviet communism was, instead, as many, including conservatives, believed, anathema to human liberty and by its very nature bent on enslaving the world, then the mild strategies put forward by Taft and fellow non-interventionists to meet the communist challenge did not really seem up to the task. After Pearl Harbor and World War II, America might well have to go "abroad in search of monsters to destroy" to maintain its own liberty and security. As President Truman told Congress in the 1947 address that established the doctrine that bears his name (a request of $400 million in military and economic assistance for post-war Greece and Turkey), "This is no more than a frank recognition that totalitarian regimes imposed upon free peoples, by direct or indirect aggression, undermine the foundation of international peace and hence the security of the United States."[30]

Truman's view that a threat to freedom anywhere was now a threat to the freedom of the United States carried the day, so much so that by the early 1950s the old right's non-interventionist anti-communism became a political liability. Taft lost the 1952 Republican presidential primary to the ideologically moderate former Army general Dwight Eisenhower. Notwithstanding the tough language of the 1952 Republican Party platform, Eisenhower stuck with the Truman Doctrine upon assuming the presidency. Eisenhower was a convinced internationalist. This prompted a debate among conservative intellectuals about the correct policy toward world communism. The debate also played out in Congress in the fight over the Bricker Amendment. Reintroduced in the Senate by old right isolationists in early 1953, the Bricker Amendment was the name for a series of proposed amendments to the Constitution designed to restrict presidential authority in foreign policy and to serve as a weapon in the right's fight against the United Nations. Unhappy with the assertion of foreign policy preeminence in the presidency, conservatives also feared that various U.N. conventions would bring American citizens under the jurisdiction of foreign courts without the protections of the

U.S. Bill of Rights (not unlike arguments against the International Criminal Court decades later). Although the defeat of the Bricker Amendment was only a narrow one, it signaled the end of any serious policy of isolationism.[31] By the mid-1950s, the debate within conservatism was won by the rising interventionist wing, marked by the founding of what would become the key conservative journal of opinion, *National Review*, under the leadership of William F. Buckley, Jr. In a sign of how far conservative opinion on foreign affairs had shifted, *Human Events*, the isolationist old right journal founded in 1944 with historic links to the America First Committee, had also become an advocate of interventionism in foreign affairs. In short, the unique danger of post-war international communism and the perceived domestic political price of an isolationist foreign policy under these new conditions induced the old right to shed its traditional anti-interventionism.

The triumph of the post-war liberal consensus fused aggressive anti-communism with the power of the presidency and signaled the acceptance of the supremacy of the executive branch in foreign policy. From then on, the vast majority of conservatives joined the post-war foreign policy consensus, but with their own piercing spin. They continued to direct their ire at liberal duplicity not only because, in their judgment, it was the liberals' appeasement of Soviet expansion that had created the post-war communist problem in the first place – always the cry of the sellout at Yalta – but also on account of liberal weakness and half-heartedness in facing the communist menace.

Anti-establishment conservatism: Interventionism and fusionism

The switch from foreign policy isolationism marked the emergence of anti-establishment conservatism. Now interventionist, the new wing of conservatism called for total mobilization against communism and for unilateral preventive military action against the Soviet Union and China. Rejecting the logic of mere containment, anti-establishment conservative intellectuals, some of whom were former communists who had turned on their past creed, committed themselves to the military paradigm of all-out war, quick victory, and limited losses – even in a nuclear age.[32] Barry Goldwater's *Why Not Victory?*, published just a decade after Taft's *A Foreign Policy for Americans*, placed a capstone on the shift in anti-establishment conservative foreign policy thinking. In Goldwater's view, the Truman

Doctrine was flawed because it implied the possibility of peaceful coexistence. Instead, the United States should engage in an aggressive policy of rolling back communism, of liberating subject populations from their communist overlords.[33]

Anti-establishment conservatives now saw the New Deal and international communism in roughly similar terms. Both were threats to liberty; both had to be rolled back. President Truman was wrong to commit American troops to Korea without congressional approval, they complained, but now that the United States was involved militarily in the Korean peninsula, it should go all-out and take the war to the Chinese puppet masters directly. The new conservative interventionists thus backed General Douglas MacArthur's aggressive designs to strike bases inside China during the Korean War, and denounced Truman's cashier of the decorated general. MacArthur stood in favor of preventive military attack, with nuclear weapons no less. Anti-establishment conservatives also applauded Senator Joseph McCarthy's efforts to purge the federal government of alleged communists (although some conservative intellectuals were wary of McCarthy himself).[34] If the Cold War represented a practical and spiritual struggle between freedom and despotism, between religion and atheism, in the view of anti-establishment conservatives it was a struggle that liberals (and many establishment Republicans) were manifestly unfit to lead.[35] Yet lead the liberals did, often, in the eyes of the anti-establishment right, treacherously and viciously. That America was beset by internal subversion was a strong theme in the early post-war period. McCarthyism writ large had resonance in popular and conservative congressional circles because of the conflict between the elevated sense of U.S. power and the country's apparent impotence in making international affairs conform to its designs. Such impotence, McCarthy and his followers argued, could only be explained by internal betrayal.[36] Notwithstanding that the loyalty oaths had been set in motion by the Truman administration as part of the post-war national security state, in the eyes of the right it was the liberals who embodied domestic treachery.[37] The New Deal and containment represented, in McCarthy's famous soundbite, "twenty years of treason" by the elite, by "the bright young men who are born with silver spoons in their mouth."[38] Part of McCarthy's success was in his weaving of class resentment with anti-communism. Whereas McCarthy was a figure of fear and revulsion to liberal America, the senator became a martyr of the anti-establishment right. The lesson drawn by conservatives from his fall was not that his anti-communist crusade had violated the democratic process, rather that the liberal establishment would use its great power to crush its critics.[39] The strident defense of McCarthy against the treacherous liberal establishment continues to this day.[40]

Linked by anti-communism and revulsion toward the New Deal, early 1950s anti-establishment conservatives fell into two main theoretical tendencies: libertarianism and traditionalism.[41] Property, as we have seen, was considered the foundation of liberty, especially in the libertarian analysis. The market, too, was understood a virtuous institution because of its economic efficiency and its promotion of individual freedom. The libertarian Austrian economists Ludwig von Mises and Friedrich Hayek (and from them through the Mont Pelerin Society to Milton Friedman and the Chicago school of economics) brought a political-economic dimension to the notion of the virtuous market. They argued that the nature of knowledge in a modern economy was local and concrete; the myriad decentralized preferences and decisions of buyers and sellers made the market system succeed. Centralized planning could never work because planners could never know enough to manage an economy. The knowledge possessed by economic planners was arid and abstract, whereas the dispersed knowledge that guided ordinary participants in economic life was concrete and rational, imbued with everyday, personal significance. Indeed, the elite's presumption of the rationality of planning was dangerous hubris. Any attempt at economic planning not only skewed the economy and undercut the rights of the individual but also led inexorably to the creation of a powerful, centralized state and hence ultimately to totalitarianism. The state thus posed an existential threat to individual liberty. The formula was simple and bold: state interventionism in the economy led to centralized planning led to totalitarianism. In its opposition to the state, the libertarian strain of anti-establishment conservatism drifted toward a kind of market fundamentalism. The market was a wise and moral institution whose genius must not be second-guessed. In the heat of their opposition to planning and socialism, cemented by fear of totalitarianism, libertarians seemed to elevate the market to an almost sacred status.[42] Libertarianism's most famous spokespersons in the immediate post-war period were the economist Hayek and novelist Ayn Rand. There were key differences within libertarianism, of course. For Hayek, the "road to serfdom" began with economic planning; for Rand, following in the Social Darwinist footsteps of Herbert Spencer and William Graham Sumner, that road was paved by misplaced altruism.[43] Capitalism was a naturally moral system that allowed heroic risk-takers to rise to the top. Their risk-taking added to the overall value of society. (In today's political rhetoric, capitalists are the vaunted "job creators.") Any fuzzy-headed disruption of this system traduced individual liberty and undermined the lessons of personal responsibility and self-reliance. For Rand, selfishness was a virtue; altruism leads to collectivism leads to dependence and moral degradation.[44]

Anti-establishment conservatism's other strain, traditionalism, had a more communal understanding of society. It recognized the mutual obligations that bind individuals to one another, united by belief in an objective moral order guaranteed by God. Edmund Burke was traditionalism's key influence. Burke's horror at the excesses of the French Revolution led him to propose a social contract theory based not on reason (which ultimately led to regicide and terror), but on a partnership across the living, the dead, and the not yet born, the visible and the invisible world – secured by a transcendental power that confines human liberties and curbs passions. Without the restraint of human passions, individuals do not learn personal responsibility. Untrammeled selfhood leads to the disintegration of civil society, argued Burke. The restraining power is government. Within a bounded liberty, other social institutions and practices that foster "public affections," including the attachment to the family and "the little platoon we belong to," manners, and particularly religion and property, facilitate the perpetuation of society itself.[45] "We begin our public affections in our families. . . . We pass on to our neighbourhoods, and our habitual provincial connections."[46] Each generation is indebted to the cumulative achievement of generations past. Notwithstanding the importance of tradition and habit, there is a flexibility in Burke, an unwillingness to participate in the spouting of political abstractions. Even as he maintained that government must limit liberties and restrain human passions, he declared, "But as the liberties and the restrictions vary with times and circumstances, and admit of infinite modifications, they cannot be settled upon any abstract rule; and nothing is so foolish as to discuss them upon that principle."[47] Burke's conservatism was an orthodoxy built on notions of tradition and incrementalism. Unlike libertarianism, Burkean traditionalism did not display a strict adherence to a pre-set ideology. That is to say, it was not fundamentalist.

Drawing on the lessons of Burke, the traditionalist strain of conservatism held that civilization is fragile and easily disrupted. Modern western societies in particular are weak and unstable, a consequence of liberalism's abandonment of belief in an objective moral order and the transcendental values that emanate from that order. Indeed, for many traditionalists, the abandonment of the idea of an objective moral order underlay the affinities between liberalism and communism. Like communists, liberals were said to believe in human perfectibility through the use of reason and sought to achieve the elimination of social defects and individual differences through the exercise of state power. Roman Catholic theology constituted another philosophical tradition that fed this strain of anti-establishment conservatism. Catholicism linked liberalism and communism through materialism. Materialism denies the existence of both deities and souls, and makes humans and their natural inclinations the measure of all things. In the eyes of traditionalists, human beings are inherently flawed, hence individuals must be subordinated to an objective, religious order. New Deal liberalism had broken with this conception. Instead, the New Deal represented an advanced stage in the long process of secularization and the rupture with classical teachings. At bottom suspicious of democracy and equality, traditionalist conservatives believed that the survival of the republic presupposed the virtue of citizens and required a highly educated elite as guardians of civilization.[48] William F. Buckley, Jr. served as both a great interlocutor and disseminator of these ideas, and a practical organizer of those of like mind. Buckley's grand aim was to create an intelligent, respectable Burkean conservative movement. In addition to *National Review*, Buckley's column, "On the Right," was syndicated in 1962 to more than 300 newspapers. An occasional panelist on *Answers for Americans*, an early 1950s televised conservative public affairs program, Buckley hosted *Firing Line* on network television from 1966 until 1999.[49]

Although libertarianism and traditionalism each expressed belief in the inviolability of private property and condemned "collectivism," some traditionalists worried about the rampant individualism that could accompany raw capitalism. In their own way, traditionalists understood the rationalizing, destabilizing juggernaut of the capitalist mode of production. The elemental insight of Karl Marx was that capitalism's dynamism tended to unsettle every aspect of human existence, transforming social life into an impersonal, abstract, and calculating form of experience. As capitalism advances in a society, Marx wrote, "[a]ll that is solid melts into air."[50] Traditionalists clearly did not draw on Marx, but they understood that capitalism could weaken the habits of the past they so valued. Government, in their view, thus had a responsibility to deal somehow with the consequences of capitalism. (Even Hayek believed this, much to the disgust of Rand.) But the traditionalists submerged this responsibility within a broader requirement that government regulate morality because, unguided, the masses could turn to cultural and political evil. Government had an obligation to foster virtue – not so much in regulating the market as in enforcing public, that is, Christian, morality.

Seeking to strengthen the intellectual basis of conservatism, a new generation of intellectuals under the leadership of James Burnham, Richard Weaver, Russell Kirk, Frank Meyer, and William F. Buckley, Jr. (all of whom were heavily involved with *National Review*, by all accounts the hearth of post-war American intellectual conservatism) inaugurated the fusion of libertarianism and traditionalism. "Fusionism" and anti-establishment conservatism are one and the same. In the United States – and perhaps only in the United States, because of its standing as the unique nation, beacon of liberty, democracy, and equality of opportunity to the rest of the world – the libertarian concern with individual freedom and the traditional concern with moral order and virtue coincided. What made the fusion of libertarianism and traditionalism fraught is that the order it wished to maintain rested not on traditions emanating from the mists of time and scores of generations à la Burke, but on founding documents – the Declaration of Independence and the Constitution – and revolutionary doctrine forged, in the words of Peter Berkowitz, "by men in the heat of the political moment and constructed with numerous painful compromises."[51] In contrast, European conservatism derived from its reaction to the French Revolution. This is the basis upon which the celebrated political scientist Louis Hartz could claim that liberalism – in the classical sense of individual freedom and natural rights – is the foundational American political ideology from which all American political ideologies, including conservatism, cleave. Americans are by nature Lockean liberals, in Hartz's view, because America lacked a feudal tradition that had to be destroyed. The state's purview was generally seen as limited to protecting property relations among equal producers.[52] And as American conservatism developed, a faith in the abstract, ultra-rational market became one of its distinguishing features.

In comparison with European conservatism, the American variant is more optimistic, more materialistic, and more individualistic.[53] God could be said to stand behind capitalism. Among religiously inclined anti-establishment conservatives of the 1950s, the market, especially because of its contrast to communist planning and collectivism, acquired a kind of biblical sanctity.[54] The market is where individual freedom is exercised and realized. This permitted anti-establishment conservatives to criticize the welfare state not on the basis of a utilitarian argument (that state intervention in the economy didn't work – we already noted that post-war prosperity clearly contradicted that contention), but on the basis of a *moral* claim: the welfare state undercuts the fundamental conservative principle that effort should lead to reward. It thus destroys human dignity, individual autonomy, and personal responsibility. And ramping up this lesson, the welfare state therefore places freedom, democracy, and virtue in jeopardy. The perceived decline of freedom and capitalism went hand in hand with the decay in the belief in God and absolute truths.[55] As Barry Goldwater stated on the campaign stump in 1964, "Something basic and dangerous is eating away at the morality, dignity, and respect of our citizens – old as well as young, high as well as low."[56] Hence another link to anti-communism: the unbridled growth of the welfare state destroys the society's morals, making society submissive and weak in the arduous fight against communism. Goldwater intoned, there "could be no peaceful coexistence with Communist power as long as they do not believe in God."[57] And, squaring the political circle, he declared, "You will search in vain for *any* reference to God or religion in the Democratic platform."[58]

Fusionism established the key features of mid-twentieth-century American anti-establishment conservatism that carry on to the present day: militant anti-communism, libertarian defense of freedom, individualism, and the market; and traditional concern with the moral order and community. This is not to say that fusionist doctrine magically smoothed over the conflicts between its libertarian and traditionalist strands. Those strands stood in serious intellectual tension, and lively debates appeared in *National Review* throughout the 1950s and 1960s. Libertarians today still clash with traditionalists. At the most obvious level, the libertarian championing of capitalism is based on a view of human freedom that prizes reason, change, growth, social mobility, and, in the idiom of the 1950s, "rugged" individualism. In contrast, traditionalism values authority, continuity, stability, local attachment, virtue, and the existence of social hierarchy. For that reason, some traditionalists, such as Russell Kirk and Richard Weaver, admired agrarian societies and harbored nostalgia for the antebellum South. Libertarians, rooted in the Enlightenment, speak of freedom and natural rights. Traditionalists, ultimately tied to religious philosophy, speak of virtue.[59] What united the tendencies in the 1950s were their common loathing of New Deal liberalism, especially its creation of a large federal bureaucracy and a commanding presidency, and their fear and hatred of communism.[60] Perhaps not surprisingly, Protestants drifted toward the libertarian strain of fusionism, while those with Catholic roots tended toward traditionalism. It is worth noting that, in the context of the history of American conservatism, fusionism signaled the arrival of Catholics and the Catholic philosophical tradition.[61]

But for both libertarian and traditionalist intellectual strains of anti-establishment conservatism, the new embrace of interventionist anti-communism in foreign policy meant the "dejected" acceptance, in William F. Buckley's phrase, of the growth and centralization of the otherwise evil state in the realm of military affairs.[62] The exemption of national security from anti-establishment conservatism's high-minded anti-statist critique is of considerable significance. It meant that in the post-war transformation of conservative ideology, notwithstanding the anguish about the size, power, and intrusiveness of government – particularly the federal government – conservatives of every stripe tended, over time, to support the foreign policy purview of the president in ways that undercut Congress's role and that justified the concentration of power in the executive branch. In this respect they joined the liberals who, since Woodrow Wilson's academic days, had advocated the centralization of power under an agenda-setting president. This shift was rather breathtaking, even if it was desultory and evolved over several decades. Senator Robert Taft had denounced President Truman's unilateral dispatch of American troops to South Korea, charging that Truman had "simply usurped authority, in violation of the laws and the Constitution."[63] The struggle over the Bricker Amendment in 1953 reflected a serious effort on the part of congressional conservatives to pare back the power of the president in the arena of foreign policy, aiming to limit his ability to make executive agreements. But by the Nixon presidency, anti-establishment conservatives such as Barry Goldwater, who had argued against presidential power as a principled position in the 1960s, reversed themselves. Now, strikingly, it was the conservatives who defended the imperial presidency. And in the aftermath of the attacks of September 11, 2001 and the advent of an unlimited war on terrorism, a prominent strain of conservatism went even further. It put forward a theory of extraordinary presidential power not only to conduct foreign policy unilaterally, but also to ignore congressional legislation and to surveil, detain, interrogate, torture, and assassinate based on the president's commander-in-chief constitutional authority, known as the theory of the "unitary executive."[64]

But let's not get ahead of ourselves, as the reversal of conservatives on the issue of presidential power evolved over two decades. What was always a little strange about American conservatism, in the historian and political scientist Clinton Rossiter's summary evaluation, was its worship of free enterprise, because unchecked capitalism creates some degree of social devastation. Accompanying the esteem of the market was an audacious anti-statism – except, as we have seen, with regard to national security, where this was trumped by anti-communism.[65] As Arthur Schlesinger, Jr. noted early on, American conservatism's embrace of the market and its demonization of the state tended to come into conflict with its avowed allegiance to Edmund Burke's notion of established traditions and institutions. This was true even of the traditionalists. Writing of Russell Kirk and his traditionalist compatriots, Schlesinger observed that once "they leave the stately field of rhetoric and get down to actual issues of social policy, they tend quietly to forget about Burke and Disraeli and to adopt the views of the American business community." Kirk, for one, denounced federally sponsored school lunch programs as a "vehicle for totalitarianism" and Social Security as bearing the marks of "remorseless collectivism." Schlesinger concluded acidly, "But for all his talk about mutual responsibility and the organic character of society, Professor Kirk, when he gets down to cases, tends to become a roaring Manchester liberal of the Herbert Hoover school."[66] In other words, the conservative traditionalists tended to defer to the libertarian champions of laissez-faire capitalism.

From the grassroots

Thus far this account has focused largely on the emergence of the movement of *intellectual* conservatism that emerged in the mid-twentieth century. It is important also to understand the practical political and the populist conservatism that lay in the grassroots, and how these strands met up, informed, and invigorated one another. As Karl Mannheim argued long ago, we can never really understand changes in a style of thought unless we study the social groups that are the carriers of these changes.[67] This, of course, raises the question of the complex relationships between elite factions and the grassroots base on which they often depend. It points to the importance of the institutions that mediated between elite and base – the journals like *The Freeman* and *National Review*, the conservative intellectual talkshops like the Mont Pelerin Society and Foundation for Economic Education, the early think tanks like the American Enterprise Association (to become the American Enterprise Institute), whose views and positions trickled down into more popular conservative vehicles – and the businessmen who funded these efforts and also brought the ideas into their boardrooms, factories, and labor contract negotiations.[68] One striking example of the interpenetration of elite and grassroots anti-establishment conservatism was the unusual popularity of Hayek's *The Road to Serfdom*, which stemmed in part from the fact that the book was condensed, popularized, and distributed by the editors of *Reader's Digest* in April 1945. Mass media, of course, are of signal importance in circulating ideas and mediating between intellectual elites and the grassroots. It may be a grossly self-serving claim by Hayek's followers that the condensed version was read by millions of Americans. Still, *Reader's Digest* had a circulation at the time of more than five million, and the condensed version of *The Road to Serfdom* was provided to subscribers, as well as each American serviceman, at home and abroad. An additional 600,000 copies of the condensed version were later printed and distributed through the Book of the Month Club and by non-profit civic groups. In February 1945, a picture-book version was published in the mass-circulation *Look* magazine, later made into a pamphlet and distributed by General Motors.[69]

And then there is the matter of the grassroots itself. Underneath the post-war liberal consensus, challenging and refuting it, lay a powerful undercurrent of still largely inchoate – or at least largely unorganized – disagreements, anxieties, animosities, fears, and resentments. A central point of Rick Perlstein's study of the making of the 1964 Goldwater presidential campaign is how the post-war consensus was something of a myth, a liberal piety. The academic literature was celebrating an American consensus even as it was breaking apart.[70] In many respects Perlstein's claim should not be all that surprising. After all, the supposedly placid 1950s were punctuated by a sharp, sometimes virulent anti-communist nationalism whose most visible manifestations were the crusades by Senator Joseph McCarthy and the House Un-American Activities Committee (HUAC). The trade unions purged communists from their leadership in the early post-war years. Loyalty oaths and blacklists pervaded the 1950s.[71] HUAC distributed hundreds of thousands of copies of FBI Director J. Edgar Hoover's report, *Communist Target: Youth*, and commissioned the film *Operation Abolition*, both of which documented how communists duped American young people into opposing HUAC's efforts.[72] In short, a fervent anti-communist popular culture permeated the country in those years. Numerous far-right organizations abounded in the late 1950s, such as the radio ministries of

Christian fundamentalists Carl McIntire and Billy James Hargis. The Christian Anti-Communism Crusade, led by Dr. Fred Schwarz and backed by several large corporations and hosted by notable popular culture celebrities, put on mass rallies asserting that, among other things, Soviet Premier Khrushchev's disciplined apparatus operated in American cities and could start a riot or a strike at any time.[73]

Among the most prominent of these groups was the John Birch Society (JBS), which helped spur local conservative mobilization by providing organizing strategies and resources. The Society's frenzied anti-communism exercised considerable early influence on grassroots conservatism.[74] It played a prominent role in the movement that thrust forward Barry Goldwater as the conservative standard-bearer of the Republican Party in the early 1960s. Built by Robert Welch from the anti-New Deal National Association of Manufacturers and the libertarian Foundation for Economic Education, the JBS proclaimed the progressive income tax, the Federal Reserve, and increased business regulations to be part of the Soviet takeover of the United States. President Eisenhower, especially vilified for his support of a nuclear test ban, was said by the Birchers to be under the control of the Communist Party, as, they claimed, was 40 to 60 percent of the federal government.[75] Other JBS positions resonated with those of many right-wing groups of the period: support of states' rights, repeal of the income tax, impeachment of Supreme Court Chief Justice Earl Warren, withdrawal from NATO, elimination of foreign aid. The JBS, incidentally, was a principal distributor of the FBI's *Operation Abolition* at the community level. Welch warned apocalyptically of an October 1952 attack on America by Stalin.[76] Conversely, the JBS sometimes dismissed the actual threat from the Soviet Union as fiction, a ploy by internal communists to increase the power of government and hence move the United States toward the hated creed. The boundary between "legitimate" anti-establishment conservatism and the radical right was often murky in the 1950s, a fact that led *National Review* to break with the John Birch Society – first, in a polite 1962 critique of Welch, and later, in a denunciation of the JBS generally – in order to separate right-wing conspiracy theorists from respectable, if anti-establishment, conservatism.[77] The aim of *National Review* was a stridently anti-communist conservatism that would champion a Goldwater against the "me-too" eastern Republican establishment, but a conservatism that struck a distance from utopian and conspiracy theories.

The conviction that a liberal consensus prevailed in the 1950s and 1960s required an account and dismissal of the importance of groups such as the John Birch Society. Indeed, it was the assessment of the right wing as "extremist" and in decline that allowed mainstream commentators to visualize the maintenance of a post-war liberal consensus.[78] The standard critique of the right wing in this period depicted its adherents as uneducated and dispossessed, part of a declining class suffering from status anxiety and exhibiting a paranoid style of politics owing to a futile revolt against modernity. The members and supporters of right-wing groups were understood as motivated by fear of displacement. Daniel Bell put the thesis most succinctly in a widely noted 1955 volume he edited called *The New American Right* (updated and expanded as *The Radical Right* in 1963):

> What the right wing is fighting, in the shadow of Communism, is essentially "modernity" – that complex of attitudes that might be defined most simply as the belief in rational assessment, rather than established custom, for the evaluation of social change – and what it seeks to defend is its fading dominance, exercised once through the institutions of small-town America, over the control of social change. But it is precisely these established ways that a modernist America has been forced to call into question.[79]

The radical right needed to be taken seriously. But the danger it posed would pass. As modern, rational, science-guided administration solves social problems and helps elevate people to a new middle class, Bell argued, these atavistic malcontents would be integrated into the fabric of progressive American life.[80]

Whereas the authors of *The Radical Right* believed the populist right wing of the mid-century was a reactionary, declining small town anti-modern rump, subsequent empirical scholarship showed that this right wing consisted rather of educated, white-collar, even professional men and women who saw their own lives and communities as tributes to individual entrepreneurial success and moral steadfastness.[81] This was particularly true in what has become known as the Sunbelt, where the long post-war economic boom, fueled initially by federal public works projects such as dams and then by federal defense spending, created new sources of wealth and new communities. An estimated 82 percent of all manufacturing jobs created between 1950 and 1962 could be traced to aerospace expenditures in the Los Angeles, San Diego, Orange, and Santa Clara counties of California and accounted for 62 percent of the net influx of new residents.[82] A similar dynamic, if smaller in overall numbers, affected other western states. By 1962 about one-third of Utah's personal income was dependent on defense.[83] In the South, defense and other federal spending was instrumental in moving rural populations into more urban settings, creating employment and raising their standards of living considerably.[84] Nourished by federal outlays that subsidized suburbanization, southern and especially western conservative populists weren't anti-modern throwbacks; on the contrary, they thrived in the new scientific industries connected to defense industry research and development and the precision engineering of the aerospace plants.

Lisa McGirr's study of Orange County, California provides a compelling snapshot of mid-century grassroots conservatism, which celebrated the free market and entrepreneurial endeavor while fiercely defending traditional values and denouncing liberal collectivism. Even though the fulcrum of post-war economic life in Orange County and other burgeoning cities of the Sunbelt rested on the enormous sustained federal government outlays for defense and the indirect government subsidization of suburbanization, these communities tended to demonize government, its regulations, and the institutions of the welfare state. In defense of their status as homeowners, taxpayers, and parents of schoolchildren, they articulated an anti-statist libertarian outlook, yet steadfastly exempted the military-industrial complex from the perceived evils of government growth and spending. In this respect, grassroots anti-establishment conservatism largely mirrored the intellectual version of the fusionist *National Review*. Indeed, McGirr shows how ideas proffered by the John Birch Society and journals such as *National Review* were disseminated at the local level, providing the core ideas around which the local movement could be built.[85] The influence of Ayn Rand's novels was also felt in grassroots conservatism.[86]

For both the national anti-establishment conservative intellectuals and the Sunbelt grassroots, vocal hatred of centralized state power grew profoundly mute in the face of the defense outlays deemed necessary to challenge communism abroad. In a parallel exercise of ideological work, economic success was understood as the result of individual risk-taking, self-reliance, and hard work – not the result of opportunities directly made possible by extensive state intervention through defense spending. Woven within this libertarianism were normative concerns over the decline in religiosity, morality, individual responsibility, and family authority – the perceived decay of which, in anti-establishment conservatives' perspective, went hand in hand with the growth of centralized federal power. McGirr's most intriguing argument is that conservative individualism was embedded in the built environment. Orange County's privatized, sprawling suburban model of development resulted in a form of built environment that served to reinforce individual property rights, home ownership, and isolation at the expense of public space and town centers that might have created a different sense of public and community responsibility and belonging. And when liberal political culture was perceived to have begun creeping into Orange County – at first through a 1960 Anaheim ACLU meeting to abolish the House Un-American Activities Committee, later through progressive educational policies (the theory of evolution, new reading materials, the United Nations as a subject of study) in the public schools – conservative political activism became an important avenue of sociability, largely through the actions of women.[87] In a new region where change seemed unremitting, the right offered a reassuring message of solidity, of moral certitude, of strong moorings to the Dust Bowl Protestants who had streamed into southern California a generation earlier. Delighted to find employment opportunities in the West, they were resistant to challenges to their traditional religious worldview and institutions.[88] Orange County became known as a fervently conservative Republican haven, a region where a rising class diagnosed social problems as the result of liberal tampering with an otherwise harmonious, self-regulating social system.[89] In short, the exemption of defense spending from right-wing anti-statist ideology allowed grassroots conservatives to project an individualist, self-reliant political subjectivity.

The web of identifications, concerns, and resentments emanating from the grassroots conservative undercurrent of the early post-war decades was much more widespread than the limited membership roles of the John Birch Society would indicate. Indeed, one can more adequately account for the extent and depth of the phenomenon by appreciating the exhilaration that accompanied the presidential candidacy of Barry Goldwater, around whose persona the grassroots and the intellectuals converged. Elected to the Senate from Arizona in 1952, Goldwater made his political mark in the chamber as champion of state "right to work" laws and taking the fight to "union bosses" whom he considered both corrupt and dangerous in their socialism. These stances and his denunciation of the Eisenhower administration's 1958 Keynesian-inspired federal budget brought Goldwater to the attention of the industrialist rump that had maintained its staunch opposition to the New Deal and organized labor, and found itself intensely disaffected with moderate "me-too"

46

Republicans. The latter were increasingly identified as the eastern establishment, the perceived highest representative of which was New York Governor Nelson Rockefeller.[90]

As the historian Michael Kazin notes, the longstanding American class and sectional antagonism of the South and West toward the Northeast was articulated early in the nineteenth century with the rise of Andrew Jackson. Jacksonian Democrats championed honest frontier producers against the consumers of the Northeast – the rich, the proud, the privileged corrupted by European atheism and decadence.[91] By the mid-twentieth century the impulse described by Kazin played an important part in internal Republican Party politics. Born of contempt for New Deal liberalism, the nascent anti-establishment conservative movement also displayed a profound feeling of homelessness within the Republican Party. The "Committee of One Hundred," led by Clarence Manion, a lecturer, weekly radio commentator, and former dean of the University of Notre Dame Law School, was a group of conservative industrialists unhappy with moderate Republicanism. Together with *National Review*, young collegiate conservatives, and anti-communist groups such as the John Birch Society, the committee initiated a subterranean grassroots campaign to draft Goldwater for president in 1960.[92] Of course, the buzz around Goldwater had to be stoked, channeled, and funded. F. Clifton White, the draft Goldwater movement's young captain, claimed that his efforts simply "gave direction and focus to a great grassroots movement."[93] There is some truth to White's claim of modesty. Clearly, as this account suggests, there was a broad and deep conservative populist undercurrent in American society. But most scholars also point to White and company's brilliant under-the-radar strategy that engineered the early 1960s takeover by anti-establishment conservatives of GOP county and state organizations as key to Goldwater's nomination in 1964.[94] It is safe to say that a mutually constitutive relationship evolved among an embryonic grassroots conservative populism, an invigorated anti-establishment conservative intellectual movement, and a talented, funded, cadre of right-wing political activists and entrepreneurs in the early 1960s.

Particular organizations and outlets of the new anti-establishment conservatism were of signal importance in Goldwater's rise. The recently established organizations such as the Intercollegiate Society of Individualists (founded 1953) and Young Americans for Freedom (founded 1960), nurtured by the new generation of intellectuals and sustained by the journals *The Freeman*, *Human Events*, *Modern Age*, and *National Review*, tapped into and helped shape the populist undercurrent into a political movement by giving it a name, a philosophy, a brand, and, with Barry Goldwater, a leader. William Rusher, the political professional who published *National Review* and served as senior editor of the journal, was, with Clarence Manion, another political entrepreneur important to the draft Goldwater movement. Manion conceived the idea for a book to give life to the emerging anti-establishment conservative doctrine. He enlisted L. Brent Bozell, one of the founders of Young Americans for Freedom, and friend, eventual brother-in-law, and co-author with William F. Buckley, Jr. of a 1954 defense of Senator Joseph McCarthy,[95] to ghostwrite such a book under Goldwater's imprimatur. The book was envisioned not only to burnish Goldwater's national presence, but also to convey in popular form the principles of the new fusionist, anti-establishment conservative creed. William Rusher provided financial backing.

Goldwater's resulting 1960 manifesto, *The Conscience of a Conservative*, marked the ideological shift from Taft non-interventionist conservatism to the pro-interventionist anti-establishment conservatism of the fusionists. The book extolled liberty, property, and individualism, leaning toward the libertarian side of the fusion. "Every man, for his individual good and for the good of his society, is responsible for his *own* development. The choices that govern his life are choices that *he* must make: they cannot be made by any other human being, or by a collectivity of human beings."[96] Government, necessary only for the maintenance of the social order, historically has proved to be the chief instrument for thwarting individual liberty. *Conscience* declared the United States a "republic, not a democracy" – for only a republic, characterized by limited government subject to checks and balances, can halt the tendency toward statist collectivism. The Constitution was at its core a means to restrain government power, particularly centralized power. Thus Goldwater championed states' rights – not, he claimed, because he opposed the civil rights of Negroes, but because constitutionally the federal government must not impose its will upon the states.[97] He denounced the "socialistic" programs of the Democrats and government intervention in agriculture because, echoing Hayek's *Road to Serfdom*, "[f]arm production, like any other production is best controlled by the natural operation of the free market."[98] Indeed, much of *Conscience* was an unacknowledged ode to Hayek. The overweening power of labor union leaders posed a grave threat to economic stability and political processes. The graduated income tax was a confiscatory scheme whose purpose was the redistribution of wealth. Welfarism was the form that collectivism now took in the effort to subordinate the individual to the state: it created dependence and gave government the ultimate in political power. In sum, the danger to America lay in those who champion the state: the liberals.

Turning to foreign policy in the second half of the book, Goldwater declared the Soviet Union a dire threat. Yet, he charged, American leaders were searching desperately for a means to appease the Soviet Union as the price of national survival. But survival was less important than freedom. The United States had been a patsy to communist determination; Soviet expansionism had been made possible by American weakness and the fantasy of coexistence. The Soviet Union was incapable of change, and had declared its intention to bury the West. Thus our strategy, Goldwater declared, must be offensive in nature. We must win the struggle. To do this the United States must achieve military superiority, withdraw diplomatic recognition of communist nations, use foreign aid sparingly and strategically, encourage captive peoples to revolt against their communist masters, and embrace the development and use of tactical nuclear weapons. "We must . . . make . . . the cornerstone of our foreign policy . . . that we would rather die than lose our freedom."[99] *The Conscience of a Conservative* was in William F. Buckley's view the key text of the era, consulted by conservative politicians and studied by newly initiated young Republicans.[100] To the extent that the extensively distributed *Conscience* reformulated in a more accessible way the tenets of Mises and Hayek, the book continued the percolation of elite conservative ideas to a grassroots distressed at the reigning liberal consensus and desperate to have its unease acknowledged and suitably articulated in the political arena. In *Conscience* Goldwater gave voice to the three passionate resentments of mid-century anti-establishment conservatives: loathing for the ever-growing power of the federal government and the liberals who made that growth possible, hatred of the impotence of American foreign policy vis-à-vis Soviet belligerence, and despair over me-too moderate, establishment Republicanism.

Goldwater, always professing diffidence at the effort to draft him in 1960, threw his support to Richard Nixon at the Republican convention. But the conservative juggernaut with Goldwater as its poster-child was only in its beginning phase. During the Kennedy years of the early 1960s the undercurrent of unhappiness with liberalism and moderate eastern establishment Republicanism grew, and into the legions of the draft Goldwater movement came many skilled activists who would later serve as political entrepreneurs in forging the new right in the 1970s. Among these was Phyllis Schlafly, president of the Illinois Federation of Republican Women. Schlafly authored a scathing denunciation of hidden eastern establishment "kingmakers" who had engineered a policy of aiding and abetting Soviet communism, and had continually sabotaged strong, authentic conservative presidential candidates. If *The Conscience of a Conservative* marked the effort to concretize the intellectual basis of anti-establishment conservatism in a slim, accessible primer, Schlafly's *A Choice Not an Echo* was a campaign book that captured and reflected the conspiratorial view of politics characteristic of grassroots conservatism of the time. Labeling Democratic foreign policy an "America Last" policy, Schlafly accused the secret kingmakers of setting American foreign policy as a way to protect their personal investments in Britain and Western Europe. The Marshall Plan and foreign aid were a huge boon for them. And who were these kingmakers who moved with ease in and out of both political parties? A power elite of financiers, publishers, government officials, and some foreigners revolving around the Morgan and Harriman banking interests, eastern establishment Republican figures Nelson Rockefeller, Henry Cabot Lodge, and C. Douglas Dillon, with the *New York Times* acting as the chief cheerleader and propaganda arm. *A Choice Not an Echo* crystallized the popular suspicion that the United States was beset by domestic subversives – including senior established Republicans – who lorded over the machinery of power. And while intensely pro-capitalist, the book reflected reigning conspiracy theories toward big-business internationalists.[101]

Schlafly's remarkably successful little book championed Goldwater. Unlike the eastern establishment Republicans, Goldwater represented a choice, not a me-too echo (although Schlafly's vilification did not include President Eisenhower, just the people around him). To Schlafly, Goldwater was guardian of the beauty and necessity of simple solutions – in stark contrast, for example, to the "egghead complexities" of the State Department. (The State Department was always a particular bugaboo for the right.) The book was a kind of conservative populist inversion of the left-wing sociologist C. Wright Mills's famous 1956 book *The Power Elite*. Whereas Mills discerned the emergence of a post-war elite in politics, business, and the military that acted to instantiate the military-industrial complex and a cruel corporate capitalism, in Schlafly's reading of that same historical period a largely secret group of internationalists had sabotaged the Republican Party's conservative candidates and undermined capitalism and democracy. *A Choice Not an Echo* seemed to distill (and shape) many of the core beliefs of the period's conservative populists. Hundreds of thousands of copies of Schlafly's book proliferated on the campaign trail in 1964. By election day, it had reputedly sold 3.5 million copies.[102]

Out of the ashes: The Goldwater defeat, new mediating institutions, and the remobilization of resources

Lyndon Johnson trounced Barry Goldwater in the 1964 election (61.1 to 38.5 percent of the popular vote), but that did not much diminish the conservative undercurrent. What the electoral drubbing did do was facilitate the reassertion of moderate Republicans over the party machinery.[103] The able activists who were so dynamic in the Goldwater campaign, now purged from high GOP posts by the Republican establishment, regrouped, learned from their mistakes, and continued to create organizations and institutions that took the best models from the liberal enemy. Thus, institutionally, anti-establishment conservatism used the Goldwater defeat as a lesson and a springboard to fight the liberal establishment (which, of course, included not just liberal Democrats but also the moderate wing of the GOP). As William Rusher and others argue, the Goldwater defeat laid the foundations for the eventual conservative victory in 1980 and beyond.[104] While Rusher's conclusion is self-serving, there is no reason to doubt the basic trajectory of his claim. Just as William F. Buckley, Jr. established *National Review* because he felt that *The Nation* and the *New Republic* had provided the key debating forums and intellectual firepower for the New Deal, so the anti-establishment conservatives laid a parallel set of institutions and networks in the 1960s that largely aped those of the left. The Intercollegiate Society of Individualists (ISI) and Young Americans for Freedom (YAF) had been organized to counter the liberal National Student Association (NSA); Americans for Constitutional Action (ACA) and the American Conservative Union (ACU) were organized both to counter the liberal Americans for Democratic Action and to take on the Republican Party establishment; the American Enterprise Institute and the Hoover Institution were intended as conservative think tanks to counter the Brookings Institution. The John Olin Foundation was to serve as the conservative version of the Ford Foundation. The *Wall Street Journal* positioned itself as the conservative counterpoint to the *New York Times*.

These organizations were consciously created to set up a conservative "counter-establishment."[105] The ISI and YAF offered a kind of conservative apprenticeship service, which, it was hoped, would in time expand into a national young conservative training ground – an idea that would be adopted by the Heritage Foundation and other conservative think tanks in the 1980s. John A. Andrew, III, a former YAFer, shows the YAF lineage of many important conservative politicians and political entrepreneurs, including Richard Viguerie, Howard Phillips, Patrick Buchanan, Lee Edwards, M. Stanton Evans, Richard V. Allen, and John Terry Dolan, among others.[106] These and other able operatives, a great many of whom were veterans of the Goldwater campaign, not only built organizations, they became consummate political entrepreneurs in later periods, skilled at brokering contacts, cementing intellectual affinities, raising seed money, and bringing together previously separate organizations on the anti-establishment right. The growth and proliferation of conservative think tanks in particular marked a new phase in the mobilization of resources – money, ideas, expertise, media access, personal and institutional networks – on behalf of conservative causes. As Sidney Blumenthal suggests, this was the rise of a conservative counterestablishment in which the anti-establishment conservative movement largely displaced the institutions of the Republican Party both as a wellspring of political ideas and in the exercise of power. William Rusher's hope for a principled conservatism that would flourish within the GOP and perhaps take it over was largely realized in the late 1970s. The interlocking networks of think tanks, journals, and foundations were key institutions in that takeover.

The American Enterprise Institute (AEI, née Association) began in 1943 as a business counterweight to the New Deal brain trust inside the Roosevelt administration. In its early years the AEI examined then-current public policy or laws as judged within the context of free-market ideology, and published hundreds of pamphlets under a series called National Economic Problems. William Baroody, Sr., who, as an impresario of conservative intellectuals, built the AEI with the contributions of many leading corporations, served as the policy and speech-writing adviser in the Goldwater campaign. He envisioned the think tank as an alternative "intellectual reservoir," outside the left-controlled university system.[107] But the AEI was a minor player until it received a big boost in the early to mid-1970s, attracting financial support from conservative organizations such as the Lilly Endowment and the Scaife, Earhart, and Kresge foundations, and from corporate donors including General Motors, U.S. Steel, Republic Steel, Mobil Oil, and Standard Oil. The AEI began not just to evaluate proposed public policies but also to advocate policies, especially the deregulation of the economy. Echoing time-honored anti-establishment conservative themes, AEI reports declared that regulation not just was costly and inefficient, but also undercut freedom. William Baroody, Jr., who took over the AEI, continued his father's intellectual entrepreneurialism, drawing into the institute's orbit many neoconservatives, those former liberals who had moved to the right (the focus of chapter 4). Some of the AEI's prominent associates joined the Nixon administration. By 1977, the AEI was spending $1.6 million on its public outreach programs. The institute's corporate donor base grew considerably, and in the 1980s additional gifts from the Bradley Foundation and Olin Foundation permitted further expansion.[108]

A central figure in envisioning this conservative counter-establishment was Wall Street mogul and Nixon Treasury Secretary William E. Simon. It was Simon who, with (perhaps more accurately, under the guidance of) Irving Kristol, putative father of neoconservatism, advocated the establishment of foundations to seed conservative think tanks that in turn might halt anti-corporate sentiment and policies. Simon served as president of the Olin Foundation and as a trustee of the Templeton Foundation, and on the boards of the Heritage Foundation and Hoover Institution.[109] Together with Kristol, Simon formed the Institute for Educational Affairs (IEA) in 1978 to funnel money to conservative causes. A primary aim of the IEA was to cultivate young people by providing fellowships to promising conservative students and funding nearly two-score conservative student publications on various college campuses. This was but a small step in an effort to recapture the universities, mass media, and liberal foundations from the "elitist . . . political intellectuals" who had fostered the "egalitarian-authoritarian" programs responsible for the destruction of the country.[110] Kristol and Simon were hardly alone in advocating a pro-capitalist mobilization. Lewis F. Powell, Jr., before he was appointed to the Supreme Court, pointedly warned the U.S. Chamber of Commerce in 1971 that "the American economic system is under broad attack," and that corporate philanthropy was supporting the very institutions – the college campuses, the liberal pulpit, the media, the intellectual and literary journals – that were attacking business. Effectively aligning himself with the cause urged by Kristol and Simon, Powell argued it was high time that business defended itself by entering into the realm of public ideas to "enlighten public thinking."[111] In short, business needed to cultivate a cadre of intellectuals able to participate in the routines and conventions of policy expertise and savvy enough to elicit media attention. Hayek, in fact, had been advocating this since 1949.[112] Businessmen finally heeded the advice. From the early 1970s, they increased corporate donations to conservative think tanks and greatly enlarged business's lobbying presence in Washington. Through such associations as the Business Roundtable and a reinvigorated Chamber of Commerce, backed by reports from the conservative think tanks they helped fund, business lobbied hard and successfully against legislation that was seen to increase the purview of regulatory agencies or augment the power of unions and consumers. In the 1970s, employers began to abandon good-faith labor bargaining, exploiting loopholes in the National Labor Relations Act to delay the National Labor Relations Board's administrative proceedings, sometimes for years. Business lobbying aided in the defeat in the House of Representatives in 1977 of the effort to create a Consumer Protection Agency; likewise, business pressure led to the scuttling in 1978 of proposed legislation that would have made it easier for unions to organize workers. The perceived inability of Keynesianism to deal with the simultaneous phenomena of high inflation, unemployment, and economic stagnation ("stagflation") provided the discursive space for new business-friendly intellectuals to insert ideas about "capital formation" and supply-side economics into policy discussions. Indeed, supply-side economics, the theory that cutting taxes (particularly the taxes of those with high incomes, including capital gains) and reducing regulation would expand the economy, reduce inflation, and raise government revenues, was peddled by Irving Kristol and the economist Jude Wanniski as a political strategy under the guise of an economic theory.[113]

The Heritage Foundation, further to the right than the AEI and more actively involved in conservative political advocacy especially on Capitol Hill, commenced in 1973 under the leadership of Edwin Feulner and Paul Weyrich, with initial financial support from beer magnate Joseph Coors and later big money from Richard Mellon Scaife. More interested in influencing policy than simply analyzing it, Heritage aggressively targeted policy-makers and the opinion-making elite, closely tracking bills and legislation, providing experts for key legislators and their staffs, and peddling opinion pieces in elite media outlets. Upon assuming the presidency of the foundation in 1977, Feulner created a "Resource Bank" which, in the words of the foundation, was designed "to take on the liberal establishment and forge a national network of conservative policy groups and experts." Over the years, according to Heritage's self-report, the Resource Bank grew to encompass more than 2,200 policy experts and 475 policy groups in the United States and other countries.[114] A favorite of the Reagan administration, Heritage issued a "Mandate for Leadership: Policy

Management in a Conservative Administration," which was said to be the policy blueprint of the newly elected administration in 1981. By the late 1970s and early 1980s, the AEI and Heritage were complemented by a large number of additional conservative think tanks or centers at universities to concentrate on particular policy issues. The Cato Institute, perhaps the most important of the later wave of think tanks, began in 1977 with the expressed purpose of defining a libertarian policy agenda. Other entrants included older organizations that were invigorated with new funding, such as one of the longest established of the libertarian organizations in the United States, the Foundation for Economic Education, founded in 1946 through the Los Angeles Chamber of Commerce and publisher of the influential monthly magazine *The Freeman*. Newer organizations and think tanks include the Center for the Study of Public Choice (1957), the Hudson Institute (1961), the Center for Strategic and International Studies (1962), the Institute for Contemporary Studies (1974), the Ethics and Public Policy Center (1976), the Manhattan Institute (1978), and many more. Various big businessmen, the energy and chemical billionaires David and Charles Koch first among them, bankroll right-wing foundations and lobbying groups to the tune of hundreds of millions of dollars.[115]

The importance of ideas

Institutions are crucial to the understanding of social change, but the simple existence of institutions does not explain change. How the ideas they disseminate come to claim allegiance and help create political identities is vital. Ideas take root under specific historical conditions. The historical circumstance of key relevance here is the dialectical success and ultimate fragility of the New Deal coalition – of the concrete development of modern liberalism itself. Recall that the New Deal coalition rested in part on a balance between Keynesian state intervention in the economy and a playing down of civil rights. As the national Democratic Party began moving toward the support of civil rights, what with President Truman's decision to racially integrate the armed forces in 1948, the inclusion of civil rights legislation as part of his Fair Deal agenda, and especially Lyndon Johnson's strong support of the Civil Rights and Voting Rights Acts in 1964 and 1965, the political proclivities of anti-establishment conservatives and previously New Deal-supporting southern white supremacists began to coalesce. Barry Goldwater's position on states' rights created an ideological opening for the anti-establishment wing of the Republican Party with white Democrats in the South, especially in the wake of the 1954 *Brown v. Board of Education* decision outlawing the segregation of public schools and the vortex of politics surrounding race and civil rights.[116] A pragmatic coalition between racial and economic conservatives in Congress had already been in evidence in political maneuvering during much of the 1940s and 1950s, where conservative Republicans agreed to vote with the South against civil rights legislation in exchange for southern Democrats voting with conservative Republicans against some of Truman's economic legislation. Indeed, the anti-labor Taft–Hartley Act was the result of this inter-party conservative alliance.[117] The ideological alignment between racial and economic conservatism also was in evidence in the doings of Charles Wallace Collins, founder of the States' Rights Democratic ("Dixiecrat") Party in 1948. Collins had discerned and denounced the link between civil rights and increased federal power, warning in his *Whither Solid South? A Study in Politics and Race Relations* of the dual dangers of "Negro equality and State capitalism."[118] This was an astute political observation, for any piece of legislation that extended the planning capacity of the federal government could in principle become a direct challenge to the local, white supremacist arrangements of the South. The Dixiecrats thus initiated the linkage between racial stratification and property rights and states' rights, creating the ideological basis for an alliance with conservative Republicans outside the South.[119] The intellectual discussion for this would-be alliance was facilitated by the inclusion in *National Review* of a consistent flow of essays on states' rights, local autonomy, and southern anti-liberal politics.

One indicator of the fruits of this nascent alliance – and of the foundering of the New Deal order over the issue of race – was the presidential electoral map. Whereas southern whites maintained their Democratic political identities and party affiliations, as the national Democratic Party began pushing a civil rights agenda they typically crossed over to support Republican (and white supremacist) presidential candidates. Four-fifths of southern whites voted for Roosevelt in 1944, but only half voted for Truman in 1948.[120] The white supremacist States' Rights Democratic Party, running Strom Thurmond as its candidate, took Louisiana, Mississippi, Alabama, and South Carolina in the 1948 presidential election. In 1964, Barry Goldwater took those previously "solid Democratic South" states plus Georgia. And George Wallace, the Democratic Governor of Alabama, who inherited this alliance and broadened it in his quasi-racist American Independent Party bid for the presidency in 1968, took the same states as did Goldwater, with Arkansas substituting for South Carolina. Again, southern whites clearly still considered themselves Democrats, and the combination of that strong traditional political identification, incumbency, and safe seats maintained the Democratic Party's lock in the South in local and regional political contests through the 1980s. White southerners only began considering themselves Republicans with Ronald Reagan, and then really only after 1984.[121] But the post-Goldwater stances of anti-establishment conservatism on matters of race and, increasingly for the growing ranks of middle-class southern whites, economics, eventually built ideological links with southern white voters generally. Collins, Thurmond, Goldwater, and Wallace initiated a shift in political identity that eventually undermined the New Deal political coalition, particularly, though not exclusively, in the South.

This alliance between anti-statist economic conservatism and the maintenance of white privilege was hardly inevitable; as discussed earlier, southern white supremacist Democrats historically were among the strongest supporters of New Deal economic interventionism. Working-class northern white ethnic voters also backed the New Deal. But a series of divisive social issues in the 1960s and 1970s created conditions for polarization and the realignment of political identities. Much of this revolved around race and the federal government's various actions to realize the constitutional rights of African-Americans. Lyndon Johnson's Great Society programs were designed, among other things, to give substantive significance to the *Brown v. Board* decision and the Civil Rights and Voting Rights Acts, to pull African-Americans into the economic and political mainstream. The federal courts, following the logic of the expansive reading of the due process and equal protection clauses of the Fourteenth Amendment, pursued a parallel path with regard to affirmative action, school busing, welfare rights, and so on. These efforts led to resentment and backlash, especially among economically vulnerable whites.

George Wallace's appeal to the working-class or lower-middle class male, who was depicted as pushed around by an invasive federal government, threatened by crime and social disorder, discriminated against by affirmative action, and surrounded by increasing moral degradation, joined a barely coded racism to a populist anti-statism. Wallace's anti-statism extended mostly to issues surrounding race. Pro-labor (or, at least, pro-worker), Wallace never embraced laissez-faire economics. In that regard, he maintained the old southern link to the New Deal. It was race, the civil rights struggle, and the role of the federal government in that struggle, which lay at the center of the white anxiety Wallace tapped into, in the South and among working-class Democratic constituencies outside the South as well.[122] Wallace gave clearest shape to the new us vs. them metric of political identity, a political identity very different from that rooted in the New Deal. Wallace championed the little guy, the (white, moral) working middle class against an unholy alliance of liberal bureaucrats, permissive judges, the very rich, anti-war protesters, rioters, criminals, and welfare recipients. Wallace channeled resentments, giving voice to the presumably unrepresented (white) producer against government bureaucrats who spent public money on the undeserving (black) poor. As Wallace explained his support in a 1976 memoir:

> What kind of people backed me? Concerned parents who wanted to preserve the neighborhood schools, homeowners wanting to protect their investment, union members wanting to protect their jobs and seniority, small businessmen who wanted to preserve the free-enterprise system, attorneys who believed in the Constitution, police officers who battled organized demonstrators in the streets, and all the little people who feared big government in the hands of phony intellectuals and social engineers with unworkable theories.[123]

This was an early formulation of the "New Class" theory promulgated by neoconservative intellectuals. New Class theory mirrored Wallace's racial populism – the embattled honest little guy against the intrusive government eggheads – but without the racism. Like Wallace's rhetoric, the theory pitted virtuous producers consisting of business and the working class who were victimized by an adversarial, anti-capitalist elite of public sector professionals, lawyers, teachers and academics, union officials, mass media, and liberal foundations.[124]

Wallace ran in the 1964 Democratic presidential primaries and did surprisingly well in some northern states. But by the time the discourse had electoral salience – in the 1968 election of Richard Nixon – Wallace's *overt* racism was outmoded. It was Nixon who was able to capitalize on the racial unrest of the mid-1960s and the increasing white resentment of the efforts to tinker with wealth and power posed by the Johnson administration's Great Society programs. Nixon's so-called southern strategy in the 1968 presidential election conceded the overt racist vote to Wallace, replacing it with a softer, seemingly color-blind appeal to white metropolitan and suburban voters that aimed at tapping into their desire to protect their prosperous and (largely racially segregated) communities and treating this desire as innocent of racial animus. Nixon defended residential segregation as the class-based outcome of meritocratic individualism rather than the product of structural racism.[125]

Matthew Lassiter discerned in the "New South" a political identity and a new complicated dynamic of race and class roughly similar to that found by fellow historian Lisa McGirr in southern California, sociologist Jonathan Rieder in the white ethnic middle-class boroughs of New York City, and journalist and author J. Anthony Lukas in Boston.[126] The newly arrived white middle class had got where they were through hard work and initiative by the pluck of their boot-straps and their devotion to family and neighborhood. They saw themselves in the classic populist mold as producers – the people who worked hard and paid the taxes, increasingly squeezed by the welfare parasites below and the power-wielding, tax-avoiding upper-income liberals above.[127] The proto-libertarians whom McGirr found in Orange County differed profoundly in their support of laissez-faire capitalism from the longstanding New Deal orientation of the Jews and Italians of Rieder's Canarsie section of Brooklyn or the white working class whom Jefferson Cowie writes about in his history of the 1970s, *Stayin' Alive*.[128] But they were joined in their experience of feeling besieged by the external political forces they saw in liberalism. That by the late 1960s the federal government was expanding the reach of the Fourteenth Amendment, pushing the busing of children to integrate public schools, placing housing for the poor in middle-income neighborhoods, enforcing affirmative action for African-Americans in workplaces and universities, expanding welfare rights, was anathema to the self-conception of these working-class and middle-class whites, their understanding of legitimate politics, and their interests. They rejected race-conscious or equal protection liberalism as an illegitimate exercise in social engineering and a violation of the principle of merit. They were, and felt themselves, unwilling martyrs, aggrieved victims of the social experimentation of the liberal state, and vulnerable to the perceived lawlessness and immorality that encroached upon their communities by virtue of that experimentation.

In urban, predominantly white ethnic enclaves, often Catholic, communities like New York's Canarsie, perched at the edge of the black ghetto, the increase in street crime and the resulting experience of everyday insecurity rankled deeply and largely poisoned whatever empathy those whites might have had with blacks. In California's Orange County, it was the perceived liberal invasion in the form of the progressive school curriculum. In southern neighborhoods and some northern cities such as Detroit and Boston, it was school busing. The fact that government was seen as abetting these invasions and encroachments meant these largely blue-collar, middle-class whites felt themselves the objects of others' will – a sense of their circumstances that generated deep resentment. The resentment ensconced within tense local controversies resonated robustly with larger cultural and political tensions, especially over the Vietnam War, and created new higher-order political identities. The lack of respect and absence of moral discipline often attributed to African-Americans were ascribed in slightly different form to the anti-war movement and the youth counterculture of the 1960s. The cry for "law and order" was not just a roar about crime; it reflected a fear of the untrammeled self, let loose by the pluralistic attitude of the era. Liberal permissiveness in language, deportment, and sexuality was perceived as a threat to public space, and, crucially, to the integrity of the family. The opposition to the Vietnam War was understood not simply as a different judgment about the wisdom of U.S. foreign policy; it was felt to question America's leadership in the international order, denigrate the deaths of American soldiers, insult citizens in uniform, the style of dissent so disrespectful it smacked of treason.[129] These resentments had electoral consequences. As Jonathan Rieder put it incisively, "The upheavals of race, war, and morality did not simply create conservative temptations; rather, they exploded the Democratic container that had kept them within the party."[130]

Richard Nixon reaped the fruits of this emerging political identity of victimized producers. Nixon employed similar rhetorical strategies to Wallace, constructing a similar political identity, but moderated these and thickened the coding so that he (and presumably his supporters) could not be accused of appealing to racism. Nixon framed the racial and youth unrest of the 1960s in a way that spoke to concerned and angry whites: as a decline in respect for public authority and the rule of law. In a widely noted reflection in *Reader's Digest* in 1967, Nixon gave voice to the moral panic that accompanied the race riots, the rise in illicit drug use, and campus unrest of the 1960s. "Far from being a great society," Nixon wrote with direct allusion to the Johnson administration's slogan, America "is becoming a lawless society." How to account for this?

First, there is the permissiveness toward violation of the law and public order by those who agree with the cause in question. Second, there is the indulgence of crime because of sympathy for the past grievances of those who have become criminals. Our judges have gone too far in weakening the peace forces as against the criminal forces. Our opinion-makers have gone too far in promoting the doctrine that when a law is broken, society, not the criminal is to blame.

Nixon thus tied the social ills of the era to the tried and true conservative principle of personal responsibility and its decline into untrammeled selfhood, and to a system that had gone too far in coddling criminal and otherwise outrageous behavior. His short-term solution to social unrest? Increase the number of police, their pay, and their training.[131]

Nixon's was an anti-elitist law and order strategy, not an overtly racist one. Indeed, Nixon consciously, if duplicitously, denied that race was an issue in the problem of permissiveness and lawlessness. "The fact that whites looted happily along with Negroes in Detroit is ample proof that the affliction is not confined to one race," he wrote in "What Has Happened to America?" With his own personal loathing of the eastern establishment and the press to draw upon, Nixon's campaigns of 1968 and especially 1972 deployed a strategy of stoking white resentment toward both liberal elites and to a lesser degree the undeserving (the black poor). It is in this regard that Nixon's was less a "southern strategy," in the sense of an appeal to old-style southern racism, than it was a Sunbelt and suburban strategy, based on an appeal to the homeowner populism, class privilege, and geographically determined racial exclusion made possible in part by the success of the New Deal and the fruition of post-war subsidization of suburbanization.[132]

The success of Nixon's campaigns finally inverted the presidential electoral map in the South, bringing the South into the Republican column and beginning the peeling off of some northern white ethnics from the old New Deal coalition.[133] Although Nixon's presidency was desultorily centrist, not particularly conservative, his anti-statist, coded racial populist appeal to "Middle America" or the "Silent Majority" or the "forgotten Americans" has been the logic of the right since. Fear has always been a foundational element of the conservative playbook. In the 1950s and early 1960s, the fear of communism had central billing. By the late 1960s, it was racial fear submerged under the appeal to law and order and social stability that moved to the fore. As Garry Wills has written, "The desire for 'law and order' is nothing so simple as a code word for racism; it is a cry, as things begin to break up, for stability, for stopping history in mid-dissolution."[134] By the 1970s, the fears over race and law and order

61

were complemented by a more religiously inflected fear of moral breakdown. These anxieties and their constituencies converged in the "new right" and the Republican victory of 1980. With the election of Ronald Reagan as president, institutional change (institutional in the sense that Congress changed hands in addition to the presidency) accompanied the discursive one. The conservative era was finally born. The new right was not really new – it clearly grew from the Goldwater movement of the 1960s and the anti-New Deal businessmen before that – but the apparent dominance of what came to be called "social issues" signaled the new importance of religious conservatives in the movement.

The forces that made for conservative ascendancy, which have lasted from 1980 to the present, with a brief interregnum between 2006 and 2009 (and perhaps after the reelection of Barack Obama in 2012), were an alliance between a conservative bottom-up movement consisting of pro-capitalist, pro-property, anti-tax economic laissez-faire-cum-libertarians, joined by religious social traditionalists who wanted to stop the expansion of the Fourteenth Amendment as it moved into their institutions and secularized American society. This also helped mobilize unhappy Democrats – particularly northerners concerned about creeping ghettoes and busing to inner-city schools, and who tended to oppose abortion and sexual permissiveness – to vote for conservative Republicans. The tensions between these groups were first papered over by anti-communism, then by a shared attack on each group's bête noire: the New Class of secular humanist elitist professionals and their "liberal activist" allies in the judiciary. Neo-conservatives were crucial in providing the ideas and forging the networks that maintained the anti-establishment right-wing alliance. Institutionally, the foresight of conservative intellectual entrepreneurs such as William Baroody, Sr., William E. Simon, Lewis F. Powell, Jr., and especially Irving Kristol created an interwoven web of largely non-university scholars, policy intellectuals, media commentators and columnists, media outlets, think tanks, and the foundations that supported them. The next two chapters examine the history and nature of the alliance that re-galvanized the anti-establishment conservative movement.

— 3 —

RELIGION AND POLITICS
The Rise of the New Christian Right

By the 1970s, the New Deal political order was under severe strain. A series of social conflicts – over the war in Vietnam, the remedies designed to bring African-Americans into the mainstream of civic life, the changes in personal (particularly sexual) propriety – were felt by many to be individual manifestations of a broader, profound cultural divide brought on by the political and cultural upheaval of the 1960s. That divide, and the perception that the federal government under the leadership of the national Democratic Party sat on the wrong side of it, reinforced the longstanding wariness of white southerners toward the party on racial matters and led them to defect to the GOP. The social conflicts also gave rise to resentments outside the South among white ethnic groups and Catholics toward the political party that had historically brought them into the middle class but that now looked as if it had changed the rules of the game. With the Great Society-identified programs of affirmative action, public housing, school busing, and the like, many white northern ethnics came to believe the government had intruded into their communities, unfairly favored African-Americans at their expense, and renounced the traditional (if in part mythic) moral ethos of individual merit, self-reliance, and personal responsibility. At the same time the 1970s marked the apparent exhaustion of the New Deal economic order. Customary Keynesian fiscal and monetary policies seemed unable to deal with or even satisfactorily explain the unusual combination of high inflation and low economic growth that bedeviled the decade. The OPEC-delivered oil shocks, a primary source of the inflationary pressures, also underscored the reality that an increasingly interconnected international economy was no longer under the dominion of the United States.

With several of the constituent groups of its electoral bloc pitted against each other and its prowess at managing the economy in doubt, the New Deal coalition began to unravel. Into this breach came a resurgent anti-establishment conservatism, energized by what many considered an unlikely source: fundamentalist and evangelical Christians. It was unlikely because fundamentalist and, to a somewhat lesser extent, evangelical Protestants adhered to a religious doctrine that counseled separation from the secular world to concentrate on private morality and personal salvation. Because of this, their participation in the world of politics was assumed to be permanently low. At the broader sociological level, religion itself had been expected to diminish in importance. The widely accepted secularization thesis held that as society became more modern and prosperous, and as scientific knowledge advanced, an inexorable process of secularization would reduce the scale and scope of religion's public influence. Yet by the late 1970s, not only did a potent set of conservative Christian organizations enter and transform the political public sphere, they mobilized their congregants and co-religionists to vote en masse for Ronald Reagan in 1980. Since that time, the Christian right has become the base (or, at least, an extremely important component) of the Republican Party. How did this happen?

This chapter traces the rise of the Christian right in the 1970s and its part in anti-establishment conservatism's takeover of the Republican Party. Mapping this rise requires a close look at the changing, internally contested nature of American Protestantism and its relationship with politics over time, for conservative white Protestants have always constituted the Christian right, old and new. Reconstructing a condensed history of evangelical Protestantism in America helps us understand the split between church modernists and traditionalists, the workings beneath the supposed withdrawal of the latter from the world, and the conditions that sparked their "reemergence" to the realm of politics in the 1970s. Although I will demonstrate flaws in the standard story of conservative Christians' separation and insularity, it is clear that they did become more active in political life in the late 1970s. Their activism energized the right and helped mortally wound the New Deal political order, thereby ushering in the contemporary conservative era.

The secularization thesis

Most social theorists from the mid-nineteenth century onward viewed modernity as an inevitable process whereby religion would decline in public life, replaced by secular reason. The secularization thesis held that in the wake of economic progress and the modernist differentiation of spheres of life into the public and the private, the social importance of religion would decline and retreat to the private sphere.[1] The differentiation of spheres is not *just* that of public and private. Modernity is also characterized by separate spheres of social activity – such as law, medicine, science, the economy – operating and being judged according to standards distinctive to each sphere rather than governed and legitimated by an overall religious stamp of order, or, in the words of the sociologist of religion Peter Berger, a "sacred canopy" of meaning.[2] The basic modernist framework was encapsulated by the establishment and free exercise clauses of the First Amendment to the U.S. Constitution: "Congress shall make no law respecting an establishment of religion, or prohibiting the free exercise thereof." People are free to exercise their religion but there is to be no religious test for public office and no state religion.

For some scholars, these twin tolerations – the political freedom of elected governments from control by religious authorities and the religious choices of individuals and groups free from control by the government – marked an achievement rooted in the nature of American Protestantism itself. In Europe, democracy and religion historically were enemies. In America, founded by religiously devout Christian dissenters with republican commitments, they were allies of a particular kind. As the political scientist Hugh Heclo, following Tocqueville, puts it, "In America, organized Christianity assured its enduring influence by disassociating itself from the vicissitudes of political authority and power. The 'political' separation of church and state does not safeguard liberty by protecting secular people; rather, it safeguards liberty by protecting religion from being corrupted into something less than itself."[3] The separation of church and state meant that politics should be conducted on the basis of public reason (in principle accessible to all citizens) and not on the basis of religiously revealed truths or religiously sectarian teachings. This, too, had certain roots in the distinctive nature of American Protestantism. For most of the nineteenth century, the American Protestant worldview married a deep evangelical religiosity to republican political ideology and moral reasoning based on Scottish common-sense philosophy (rather than the acute rationalism of the continental Enlightenment). Its epistemology held that there is a world outside us, which we can know through the use of induction from facts obvious to the senses. Resting on the implicit assumption that human nature is good and educable, individuals were understood as free agents, naturally capable of understanding Scripture without priestly expertise and of exercising independent moral judgment. The capacity of individuals to read and understand the Bible meant in turn that ordinary persons in principle were capable of self-government. Science, the precise observation of the world, was the complement to the literal reading of the Bible, and science confirmed Scripture. There could be no contradiction between the deist God of the Newtonian universe and the God of the Bible, between natural and revealed religion.[4] Science was a means of realizing God's divine plan; Scripture's function was to provide inerrant facts concerning all matters, including science and history. Work in the world improved the world.

Hence the dominance of what is known as "postmillennialism," the theological doctrine that understood spiritual and cultural progress as paving the way for the thousand years of God's kingdom, after which Christ would come to earth a second time. Nineteenth-century American Protestants believed that the Holy Spirit working through Christians would so Christianize culture that Jesus could return to provide the capstone to a thousand-year reign of perfect peace. Human history reflects the ongoing struggle between the cosmic forces of God and Satan, each represented by earthly powers, but with the victory of righteousness essentially assured. Human effort can speed the advent of a perfect new world.[5] The Social Gospel, that late nineteenth-, early twentieth-century religious movement on the importance of good works and the mobilization of citizens to help the poor and do good politically, embodied the central motifs of the postmillennial Protestant worldview.[6] In this optimistic, progressive view of history, the fit between the Christian God and republican liberty was natural, even divinely ordained. America was seen as a special nation, a chosen nation even, whose self-development and encounters in the world were generally regarded as the establishment of the kingdom of God on earth. The evangelical tradition is a primary source of the idea of American exceptionalism.

The characteristic American focus on morality in this world rather than salvation in the next can be understood at least in part as the diffusion of Protestant liberalism into American culture[7] – and the reverse, as well: democratic culture diffused into Protestantism. The egalitarian drive of American culture identified by Tocqueville and the related presumptions of free will and efficacy of individual effort impacted nineteenth-century evangelical Protestantism's development. In contrast to the orthodox Calvinist doctrine of humanity's total dependence on God for salvation, nineteenth-century evangelical revivalism preached a quintessentially American version of the Arminian doctrine, influential among many European Protestant denominations, that individuals had free agency in choosing to be saved. In a complex dynamic described as "democratic evangelicalism," Protestant leaders (in part to keep up with un-churched preachers, especially in newly settled areas as white people moved west) came to embrace a religion of the heart rather than the mind, and declared morality as the essence of religion.[8]

The sociologist of religion Robert Bellah has argued that deep in the American tradition is the sense of obligation, both collective and individual, to carry out God's will on earth. This feeling of duty was present in the revolutionary founding and was associated with the creation of early Protestant denominations, but over time has become generalized no matter whose religion is referenced.[9] The deep impact of Protestantism on American values influenced politics through the diffusion of such values over the course of American history. If there was to be a continuing influence of religion in the dual commitment to religious liberty and popular self-government, it was to proceed via culture, not via politics in any direct fashion. Another sociologist, José Casanova, explains this as a double process of diffusion and secularization, involving three historical "disestablishments." The first disestablishment was the founding constitutional separation of the state from ecclesiastical institutions and the dissociation of the political community of citizens from any religious community. The second was the secularization of the life of the mind, entailing the post-Civil War secularization of higher education and diminution of Protestant hegemony over the public sphere of American civil society. Occurring in the mid-1960s and into the 1970s, the third disestablishment was the secularization of the "life-world" (the culturally grounded background environment in and through which people experience the world), involving the growth of centralized government to extend legal protection to an emerging pluralistic system of norms with regard to freedom of inquiry, thought, speech, and conduct in the public sphere.[10] This is, in brief, the secularization story in America, describing a process that unfolded over many generations. On closer look, it is more accurately the story of just the historically dominant, modernist stream of American Protestantism. This chapter chronicles the reaction *against* the development of a secularized society by the other prominent stream of American Protestantism: the traditionalists. It is this reaction that underlies the rise of the new Christian right.

Protestantism: Modernist and fundamentalist

Protestantism, by nature schismatic on account of its individualistic and democratic character and without an institutional hierarchy like Catholicism, fractured historically not just along denominational lines (e.g., Congregationalists, Lutherans, Baptists, etc.), but also within denominations over slavery and the basic view of God's word. The Civil War and Darwinism ruptured nineteenth-century evangelical Protestantism. Churches of the same denomination on different sides of the Mason–Dixon line found that they did not share the same values on the crucial issue of slavery, and, in part because of the slavery question, no longer interpreted the Bible in the same way. Pressed by abolitionist revivalist zeal, northern congregations eventually denounced slavery, finding biblical warrant in opposing the evil of the peculiar institution. Their southern counterparts likewise recited biblical passages attesting to Negro inferiority, patriarchal and Mosaic acceptance of servitude, and Saint Paul's counsels of obedience to masters, thus legitimating a slavery-based moral order. The Methodist and Baptist churches split over slavery in the 1840s, establishing distinct northern and southern branches. The Presbyterians split in 1861.[11]

Darwinism posed another fault-line. Recall that evangelical Protestantism revered science and believed there was no contradiction between science and Scripture. Faced with scientific evidence that the earth had a very long geologic history and that numerous biological species had appeared and disappeared during the eons, many Protestants came to believe that the Genesis story of creation could not be sustained. This supposition in turn opened a process of exposing Scripture to hermeneutic criticism and interpretation (the so-called Higher Criticism). These modernist presumptions caused some to doubt the inerrancy of the Bible and to accept natural science's challenge to biblical miracles. Protestant modernists began to downplay the supernatural and to view theology as no longer a fixed, God-given body of eternally valid truths. They still identified the progress of the kingdom of God with the progress of civilization, but they increasingly viewed the essence of religion as morality, not blind faith, and eventually embraced ecumenism and the pluralism of values.[12] These beliefs embodied the postmillennial approach to the world, such that the Holy Spirit was understood to work through Christians to improve the world in the here-and-now, thus allowing Jesus to return and institute a perfect peace.[13]

Modernist precepts had the effect of further dividing the Protestant denominations. Traditionalists denounced modernist (or "liberal") Protestantism's embrace of the Higher Criticism of Scripture. The Bible, they declared, was God's very word, inerrant and perfect. Darwinian theory, in their view, undermined the central biblical tenet of humanity's special creation. For traditionalists, the modernist teachings were part and parcel of the decline of civilization. Modernism and the decadence it brought represented the failure of postmillennial promises concerning the growth of God's kingdom in this age.[14] Contrary to the optimism of Enlightenment-influenced postmillennialism, some late nineteenth-century revivalists believed the world was getting worse and worse. Some of this pessimism could be tied to the splits over slavery, for alongside the southern Protestant churches' biblical justification of slavery came the loss of the impulse to transform the world and hence a weakening tie to the postmillennial worldview. The most influential anti-modern revivalist doctrine was dispensationalism, associated with the eschatological teachings of John Nelson Darby, the Anglo-Irish evangelist. Dispensationalism was a version of *pre*millennialism that provided a general theory of history. In contrast to postmillennialist Protestantism's progressive story, Darby and his followers saw history in terms of eras or "dispensations" of regression owing to the fact that human beings are by nature sinful. Historical change takes place not via human actions but through divine intervention, the details of which are revealed in Scripture. History doesn't just reflect the Bible; the Bible *is* history. In this view, the present age, marked by apostasy in the churches and the moral collapse of Christian civilization, is *prior* to Christ's kingdom; the millennium lies wholly in the future, *after* Christ returns to a very troubled world. Linking verses from the books of Revelation, Daniel, and Ezekiel, Darby described Christ's second coming as at the end of an apocalyptic period of "tribulation," a period of war, famine, and social chaos during the seven-year rule of the Antichrist. The final battle of Armageddon focuses on the Jews and takes place in the biblical land of Israel. As the "end-times" unfold, true Christian believers and innocents are pulled from earth to heaven in the "Rapture." Following Armageddon, Christ returns to establish a kingdom in Jerusalem, where he will reign for a thousand years.[15] Most, but by no means all, Protestant traditionalists (that is, those who would become known as fundamentalists) espoused some version of premillennialism.

What mattered to traditionalist Protestants in the decades just before and after the turn of the twentieth century was personal salvation through the acceptance of Christ. The legacy of revivalism inhered in their celebration of experiential truth over reasoned knowledge, of being "born again." Because the world is under Satan's rule, they scorned efforts to make the world better through social activism and politics. This is what lay behind the fierce antagonism of traditionalists toward the Social Gospel of the modernists. Traditionalists viewed the Social Gospel's emphasis on good works and serving the poor as undercutting the elemental concern for repentance from sin and the dependence on God's grace. Indeed, they considered the doctrine of human intervention in the world as just short of blasphemy; only God could so intervene. Society is not responsible for human failings. Rather, each person must find personal salvation by mastering his/her own inner soul and coming to know Jesus personally. In this way one acknowledges one's sinfulness and the need for God's grace. Hence the overwhelming emphasis was on the personal experience of God, individual prayer, reading God's true word, and saving souls by proselytizing. Political causes were to be avoided. Indeed, in the run-up to U.S. involvement in World War I, the traditionalists opposed America's military intervention, their pacifism based on the conviction that all efforts to solve the world's problems through politics were hopeless. They held that no government could receive God's blessing until the second coming of Christ. The blame for World War I was laid at the door of modernism, and especially (Social) Darwinism's doctrine of the survival of the fittest. Indeed, it was the modernists who were the war mongers and imperialists during the Great War, certain of their own rightness and superiority. This is why traditionalist Protestants fought so hard against the teaching of evolution in school – not simply because the theory violated the biblical account of creation, but also because of the Social Darwinism that stalked modernism.[16]

After a bitter struggle with their liberal co-religionists in the first two decades of the twentieth century, the traditionalists lost in various efforts to halt the spread of modernism inside the more democratically organized denominations (Baptists, Lutherans, Methodists, and, to a somewhat lesser degree, Presbyterians) and restore their churches to tradition and Scripture. The traditionalists abandoned those congregations to form their own independent churches, religious schools, Bible colleges, and missions. Allying with the Protestant liberals (and against Catholics) on alcohol and Prohibition, the traditionalists broke with them on the inerrancy of Scripture and the theory of evolution. As the standard interpretation goes, the traditionalists were defeated intellectually and publicly ridiculed in 1925 at the

Scopes trial (concerning whether laws outlawing the teaching of evolution in public schools were constitutional), after which, now labeled
"fundamentalists," they withdrew from the public arena to concentrate on institution building and personal salvation.[17] Withdrawal
was not simply a function of having lost the public relations battle
at the Scopes trial; it had a powerful theological basis. Modernism
and the theory of evolution, according to fundamentalists, had caused
the crisis of the twentieth century by undermining the biblical foundations of American civilization. After Scopes, the solution for true
Bible-believers was to separate from the evil secular world.

Terminology

At this juncture, it may be wise to take stock and register a note on
terminology. Evangelicalism is a branch of Bible-believing Protestantism deriving from the nineteenth-century revivalist movement. The
Second Great Awakening, the early nineteenth-century Arminian
revivalist movement professing that every person could be saved,
enrolled millions of new members and led to the establishment of
new denominations. The individual emotional experience of the spiritual and of personal conversion underlay the evangelical movement.
Historically, nearly all nineteenth-century Protestants were evangelicals. By the turn of the twentieth century, this evangelical root split
into two: the modernist "mainline" form (which can no longer be
considered evangelical) and the "fundamentalist" form (which sought
to maintain the old evangelical beliefs and theology). Fundamentalism can be understood as an extreme form of evangelicalism; it is
tradition made self-aware and consequently defensive.[18] It wasn't
until 1920 that the term "fundamentalist" was coined for those trying
to preserve what they took to be the fundamental truths of Christianity, including the inerrancy of Scripture and authenticity of biblical
miracles.

In the 1940s, there emerged a third general stream of Protestantism, referred to as the "New Evangelicalism." This new stream developed from more open revivalist fundamentalists: that is, those who
rejected the closed and rigid fundamentalist style in favor of a more
inclusive fellowship, but who shared fundamentalism's affinity to
biblical inerrancy and the personal experience-based spirituality of
the revivalist tradition. The New Evangelicals grew with the Youth
for Christ movement of the mid-1940s, the establishment of the
National Association of Evangelicals (NAE, the institutional umbrella

for the New Evangelicalism movement), and Billy Graham's revivalist crusade. Powered by Graham's public persona, New Evangelicalism allied with fundamentalists against the modernists but engaged the world more generously than the fundamentalists in order to lead people to Christ. What differentiates the evangelical from the mainline Protestant is the personal and devotional relationship with God, the experience of being "born again." New Evangelicals founded Fuller seminary as their training school and started the journal *Christianity Today* as their primary communication medium.[19] Since at least the 1940s, evangelical and Pentecostal denominations have grown robustly while mainline Protestant denominations have declined in membership. Approximately 51 percent of Americans are Protestants, with the evangelical Southern Baptist Convention the biggest denomination. Just under 24 percent of Americans are Catholics.[20]

To further confuse the labels and terms, fundamentalists variously refer to themselves as fundamentalists, evangelicals, and, simply, Christians. Another catchall term for evangelicals is "born-again Christians." Although it is relatively easy to distinguish between liberal (or modernist or mainline – the three terms are used pretty much interchangeably) Protestants and their conservative cousins, the line between fundamentalism and conservative evangelicalism can be hazy. To make matters more complex, Pentecostals and charismatics have some key differences with fundamentalists and evangelicals (particularly the speaking in tongues, the laying on of hands in faith-healing, and in many instances a health and wealth theology), but share the elemental doctrine of salvation and belief in the inerrancy of the Bible. In sum, where one can identify tendencies and make broad generalizations, it should be understood that the reality of categories, labels, and belief systems is fluid and complex. For the purposes of this book, it is important to understand that whereas some doctrinal and institutional differences remain between fundamentalists and evangelicals, they joined *political* forces in the late 1970s to constitute the new Christian right. For that reason, I use the term "conservative evangelicals" as a general category.

Fundamentalism's purported withdrawal from the world

The fundamentalist proscription against engaging with the secular world gained force after the traditionalists failed in their struggle to win control over the mainline denominations and suffered defeat at the Scopes trial. Historian of religion George Marsden argues that it is difficult to overestimate the impact of the Scopes trial in transforming fundamentalism. The strength of the movement in centers of national life waned. Although fundamentalism had begun as an urban and northern assemblage, after Scopes it came to embody the hostility of rural America toward modern culture and intellect, coalescing largely in local congregations in the South.[21] Fundamentalists entrenched themselves as a "cognitive minority" that, among other things, invoked the Depression as evidence of God's vindictive punishment on an apostate America.[22]

In the conventional scholarly interpretation, the intervening years did not significantly alter this dynamic of fundamentalism's separation and insularity. Even the dangers of the international situation and especially of communism did not impel conservative evangelicals toward political activism; rather they reinforced the central goal of salvation. As Heclo summarizes:

> [F]or evangelicals, the threats of atheistic communism abroad and godlessness at home served mainly as prompts to call for personal conversion and spiritual revival in the nation, not for direct engagement in politics and public policy. In the growing evangelical churches, mainline Protestantism's gospel of social reform was generally viewed as an un-Christian distraction from the ultimate value of personal salvation in the midst of a degenerating world. An emphasis on social and political activism sidetracked the Gospel.[23]

But this conventional wisdom regarding fundamentalism's withdrawal from the public arena is overstated, if not plainly inaccurate. Early on, despite their initial pacifism, fundamentalists became hyperpatriots by the end of World War I, adding bolshevism and socialism to the list of modernist forces that, in their view, had caused the decline of civilization. One of the fronts in fundamentalism's crusade was the battle for America – in Marsden's phrase, "the battle to save the nation as an evangelical civilization." While in theory this agenda conflicted with fundamentalism's pessimism about Christian civilization, in practice the two managed to coexist.[24] Fundamentalist leaders such as J. Frank Norris became heavily involved in the social movement to ban alcohol and in so doing were part of the broader Protestant effort to attack Catholic political power in big cities. As Norris declared in 1922, "[I]n the name of the American Flag and of the Holy Bible I defy the Roman Catholic machine of New York."[25] The Scopes trial itself highlighted Protestant traditionalists' public endeavors to keep the teaching of evolution out of schools. That engagement with the secular world really did not change all that much after Scopes. During the chaotic decade of the 1930s, as Leo Ribuffo and other historians have shown, various fundamentalist leaders such as Gerald B. Winrod and William Dudley Pelley blended conservative Christianity with right-wing, quasi-fascist political activities in opposition to the New Deal. Winrod formed the Defenders of the Christian Faith in 1925, a fundamentalist Christian organization that opposed teaching evolution in public schools and supported Prohibition and racial segregation. The Defenders saw Franklin Roosevelt as a devil linked with the Jewish–Communist conspiracy and believed that Adolf Hitler would save Europe from communism. Winrod's newspaper, *The Defender*, achieved a 100,000 monthly circulation by 1937. William Dudley Pelley was not a minister, but he founded the Christian Party and ran for president in 1936 to oppose FDR and the New Deal. A devotee of Hitler, Pelley earlier founded the Silver Legion, a fascist organization whose followers, known as the Silver Shirts and Christian Patriots, wore Nazi-like silver uniforms.[26]

Other fundamentalist Protestant leaders and congregations also engaged politically. The Church League of America, also known as the National Laymen's Council, formed in 1937 in opposition to the New Deal, for example, focused less on the Gospel than on the internal subversion of American institutions by liberalism, which the League considered merely a soft form of communism.[27] The Baptist preacher John R. Rice founded *The Sword of the Lord* magazine in 1934 and served as the editor of that publication of zealous religious nationalism until 1980. The *Sword* applied biblical literalism to justify and glorify capitalism, oppose the New Deal and communism, and justify modern-day and potential wars as the commands of God. Like Winrod, Rice saw Franklin Roosevelt as the Antichrist. Endorsing Senator Robert Taft in 1952, he wrote that "every Christian American" should work to free the country from "the wicked, corrupt Democratic administration."[28] Immersed in the politics of the nation in spite of the doctrine of separation from it, the *Sword* achieved a circulation of over 300,000 by the mid-1970s, and this underestimates Rice's probable influence given that the magazine reprinted his sermons and books in the tens of millions of copies.[29]

The point here is not to overstate the historic importance of these right-wing Christian leaders and groups; rather it is to show that the assumption of fundamentalism's separation and insularity from the public world is much exaggerated. This more accurate view is important because it reveals the continuities between the "old" Christian right and the "new" Christian right that emerged in the 1970s and provides clues to the emergence of the 1970s incarnation. Fundamentalists *did* create their own inward-looking institutions after Scopes in the form of schools and Bible institutes, community groups, social service agencies, bookstores, radio and television programs, and the like. Indeed, as the political scientist Rogers Smith reminds us, fundamentalist churches often sought and received access to public facilities and governmental assistance in creating their "insular" facilities.[30] They had to engage the secular world to escape from it. It was from those facilities, especially their media resources, that conservative pastoral leaders directly engaged the public world through a programmatic nationalistic anti-communism.

Richard Hofstadter called attention to the outsized role of fundamentalist leaders in right-wing anti-communist organizations of the 1950s and 1960s.[31] Although individual salvation was still primary for these pastors, gone was any isolationism of the pre-World War I variety. Probably the most significant of these religious leaders was Carl McIntire. Defrocked in 1936 along with his mentor, the theologian J. Gresham Machen, for challenging the Presbyterian foreign missions, McIntire founded a breakaway fundamentalist Presbyterian congregation. He subsequently created umbrella organizations, the American Council of Christian Churches (ACCC) in 1941 and the International Council of Christian Churches in 1948. Both organizations were formed to challenge the growing ecumenism of the mainline Federal Council of Churches and World Council of Churches. McIntire typically combined anti-communism and anti-Catholicism (the old "rum and Romanism" calumny) with attacks on liberal Protestantism. He preached that Satan's coming was imminent in the form of the worldwide communist movement, and, like many fundamentalists, he considered the mainline churches and their councils to be riddled with un-American, pro-communist traitors. McIntire and his followers cooperated with HUAC and Joseph McCarthy's staff, even fingering suspected communists within the clergy. Indeed, McIntire went so far as to denounce the National Association of Evangelicals because the association had refused to require its members to separate themselves from the modernist Federal Council of Churches.[32]

McIntire is important to understand because he shows how the inward-looking politics of individual salvation linked to public mid-century anti-communist politics writ large. Notwithstanding the doctrine of total separation from those who did not accept the Bible entirely as the word of God, McIntire and his flock were very much part of the secular world of politics. Beginning in 1955, McIntire commented directly on any number of political issues in his *Christian Beacon* monthly newspaper and on *Twentieth Century Reformation Hour*, his radio program, which by the mid-1960s reportedly reached an audience of 20 million on 600 stations. From his Pennsylvania radio station, McIntire aired innumerable attacks on civil rights, the United Nations, and UNICEF, and later called for U.S. victory in Vietnam. McIntire preached that it was imperative for a born-again believer to recognize his duty under God to be involved in politics.[33] True to his word, he served on the Young Americans for Freedom's first board of directors and joined forces with the secular right wing in the effort to elect Barry Goldwater president of the United States in 1964.[34] Associated with McIntire, but organizationally independent (grassroots anti-communism in the 1950s tended to consist of many small organizations rather than a united national movement), were several other right-wing Protestant clerical and lay activists with considerable followings: Rev. Edgar C. Bundy, who became director of the Church League of America in 1956; Billy James Hargis, an ordained minister (later disaccredited) in the Disciples of Christ Church, who latched onto Joseph McCarthy's anti-communist campaign and launched the Christian Crusade through radio; and Dr. Frederick Schwarz, an Australian émigré who set up the Christian Anti-Communism Crusade and conducted large public rallies and training seminars, with particular success in southern California. "The best way to enlist anti-Communist fighters," Schwarz claimed, "is to enlist them in the army of Jesus."[35] These groups had direct and indirect connections to the broader conservative anti-communist movement, including Senator McCarthy and military brass (particularly General Edwin Walker, who was accused of distributing right-wing literature to the soldiers of his division, and was arrested for sedition for opposing the use of federal troops to protect pro-civil rights marchers), and some loose connection to the racist right, such as the Ku Klux Klan and the John Birch Society.[36] They held particular animus for the National and World Council of Churches and the Revised Standard Version of the Bible. McIntire's ACCC declared the Revised Standard Version communistic, the work of Satan. For almost all of these right-wing preachers, broadcasting was a key resource. McIntire's radio assets were noted above. By the middle 1960s, Billy James Hargis's daily and weekly broadcasts were carried on 500 radio and 250 television stations. His Christian Crusade was a multi-million dollar enterprise, publishing pamphlets, books, and a monthly newspaper. Fred Schwarz's Christian Anti-Communist Crusade reported a gross income of $1.2 million in its peak year of 1961.[37]

Anti-communism was the ideological hub around which conservative Christians mobilized in the public arena. This included the New Evangelicals. The National Association of Evangelicals, the umbrella organization for the New Evangelicalism, founded in 1943 under the leadership of Carl Henry and Harold Okenga to unite traditionalist Protestants against the forces of Protestant liberalism, also organized anti-communist programs for member churches in the early 1960s. Much larger and more moderate than McIntire's ACCC, the still very conservative NAE member denominations had some 10 million church members and reflected the growth of mid-century urban revivalism associated with Billy Graham's crusade. Graham himself frequently preached that communism was "Satan's religion," and in the early 1950s he advocated a military as well as spiritual showdown with communism.[38] Notwithstanding the theological doctrine of personal salvation, fundamentalist and New Evangelical leaders supported a militant Cold War foreign policy. They denounced the internationalism of liberal Protestantism, its idealism, and its moralistic paeans to peace and reconciliation in favor of a muscular, militaristic anti-communism. New Evangelicalism's house organ, *Christianity Today*, directed for decades by NAE co-founder Carl Henry and backed financially by Sun Oil Company chairman J. Howard Pew, assailed communism throughout the 1950s and 1960s. (Pew was also a funder of William F. Buckley's *National Review* and Barry Goldwater's presidential candidacy.) Until the 1970s, when it moderated its tone, *Christianity Today*, in its editorials, typically linked the Christian faith with democracy, capitalism, and American culture and values, and attacked communism as a dedicated servant of the Antichrist. True to his New Evangelical roots, Henry believed Christians should be engaged with the world. It was essential to fuse social concern and personal religion, to restore supernatural religious truth in public life. In foreign policy the solution was to assume human sinful nature, knowing that peace could never come until the human spirit was regenerated through Christ. *Christianity Today* adamantly opposed the United Nations and foreign aid; it supported Chiang Kai-shek in China against the communists.[39]

Fundamentalist leaders' strident opposition to desegregation was another arena wherein the assumption of fundamentalist withdrawal from the world cannot withstand scrutiny. Carl McIntire and Billy James Hargis railed against desegregation (a "communist conspiracy"), as did the Reverend Jerry Falwell, who would become the leader of the most important Christian right organization in the 1980s, the Moral Majority. Indeed, the oft-quoted 1965 speech in which Falwell invoked biblical separation from the world was a speech in which he defended segregation, attacked the civil rights movement, and associated its leaders with communism. Just because Falwell declared, "Our ministry is not reformation but transformation . . . [t]he gospel does not clean up the outside but regenerates the inside," it seems arbitrary to find in this an example of pietistic withdrawal rather than a pointed instance of engaging the world against a looming political change. It is difficult to maintain that Falwell's public defense of segregation be understood as an *absence* of political engagement.[40] It is political engagement while asserting it is not. Finally, not to belabor the point about separation and insularity, but inasmuch as the growth of many southern independent Baptist churches reflected the growth of the New South, Falwell, for one, never interpreted the doctrine of separation to mean withdrawal from commerce and industry. As Frances FitzGerald notes aptly, Falwell's sermons typically were lessons for worldly achievement, urging not a retreat from the social order but successful participation in it.[41] The inaccurate assumption of conservative evangelicalism's separation and insularity masks the very real continuities between the "old" Christian Right and the "new" Christian right.

The new Christian right emerges

The politically mobilized Christian right that emerged in the 1970s had clear historical influences and forebears. Indeed, the old and new Christian right shared many of the same concerns and enemies, including vitriol toward liberal Protestantism. At the same time, while the standard interpretation of conservative evangelicalism's separation from the public arena is overstated, something did happen to remobilize conservative Christians toward political activity in the mid- to late 1970s. As the sociologist Robert Wuthnow notes, studies conducted between 1953 and 1974 on the relationship between conservative theological convictions and political activity consistently found that evangelicals were less inclined toward political participation than were their more modernist counterparts. In marked contrast, the studies conducted between 1976 and 1981 found just the opposite: evangelicals were the most politically involved Christians.[42] Voting data confirm this. Prior to 1980, a lower percentage of white evangelicals reported voting in presidential elections compared to non-evangelicals: 61.1 percent compared to 70.5 percent in the South; 60.8 percent compared to 73.2 percent outside the South. In the 1980 presidential election, voting turnout among white evangelicals increased significantly: 77.0 percent of evangelicals voted compared with 65.9 percent of non-evangelicals in the South; 74.6 percent of evangelicals voted compared with 73.3 percent of non-evangelicals outside the South. The white evangelical vote went strongly for Ronald Reagan in 1980 (61.2 percent in the South; 67.2 percent outside the South) and overwhelmingly to conservative Republicans thereafter.[43] Born-again Christians would make up 36 percent of the George W. Bush vote in the presidential contest of 2004 and 38.5 percent of the John McCain vote in 2008.[44] In the 2012 presidential election, 79 percent of white born-again Christians voted for Mitt Romney, accounting for roughly 38.5 percent of Romney's total vote.[45]

The voting data alone show that something happened to activate white evangelicals politically. What was it? Broadly, it was the process of secularization itself. The federal government began to secularize the life-world in response to the pluralistic cultural dynamism of the 1960s and the force of logic of judicial decisions involving the Fourteenth Amendment. Civil rights legislation expanded the rights of minorities to belong to the national community. Under the leadership of Chief Justice Earl Warren, the Supreme Court pursued a jurisprudence that embraced that expansive vision, resulting in decisions protecting the rights of racial minorities and unblocking the channels of political change.[46] As the Supreme Court moved beyond the protection of minority rights toward pluralistic positions in domains of public life that had historically embedded traditionalist Protestant values in such matters as school prayer, sexual propriety, and the discriminatory practices of religious institutions, religious conservatives felt these changes marked not only an abdication of moral responsibility but also a taking of sides. They felt their institutions were coming under threat by an intrusive government. Recall that after the Scopes trial fundamentalists engaged in extensive institution building to secure their place and status apart from the secular world and that of mainline Protestantism. They established independent congregations, Christian academies, and evangelical colleges. They used their experience in religious radio to hone revivalist techniques and fundraising practices, establishing a large number of broadcast stations and Christian programming sources, leading to the rise of what came to be called the electronic church or televangelism.[47] By the 1970s, these were among the institutions that, they believed, had come under threat by the actions of the federal government and federal judiciary.

Radio, regulation, and the rise of televangelism

One of the earliest – and somewhat bizarre – instances of institutional threat was the one to religious broadcasting. Some historical context is necessary here, as this episode underscores the importance of broadcasting as a material resource for conservative evangelicals and how intensely they would fight when they felt these institutions were imperiled. This seeming digression also has the benefit of explaining the rise of televangelism and sets the stage for understanding the critical function conservative mass media play in the current moment.

American radio has a long history of broadcasts featuring compelling preachers and inspirational church music. Religious organizations were among the earliest pioneers to be licensed by the Department of Commerce when radio broadcasting commenced in the 1920s. Enterprising evangelical and Pentecostal congregations made extensive use of the new medium of radio for outreach and institutional growth in the years prior to its regulation. Among the operators of radio stations in the mid-1920s were Aimee Semple McPherson's Echo Park Evangelistic Association, the Bible Institute of Los Angeles, and the Moody Bible Institute of Chicago. Baptist church-run stations could be found in many cities. By 1924, local churches held one of every fourteen radio licenses.[48] This changed as broadcasting came under regulation toward the end of the decade. The standard historical account is that as radio grew, the problem of signal interference intensified as well, prompting Congress after years of failed efforts to pass legislation to deal with the problems of the new communication medium. But signal interference was not the only matter to be dealt with in the Radio Act of 1927. The nature of the medium was also at issue. What should be the relationship between commercial imperatives and amateur or educational ones; between the notion of radio as a medium of general public communication and the existence of broadcasters who pursued narrow, private interests? The latter issue was not just about monetary gain, a principal subject of debate in the middle 1920s. As important to the new policy-makers of the Federal Radio Commission (FRC) was the use of radio for intemperate attacks on persons or institutions. The difficulties posed, for instance, by Joseph Rutherford's anti-Catholic sermons on his Brooklyn Jehovah's Witness station, or the Reverend Robert ("Fighting Bob") Shuler's malicious attacks on public officials, Catholics, Jews, and African-Americans on his Los Angeles station, were real and vexing.

As the FRC began formulating policy for the new mass medium of radio, it favored a commercial broadcast system, and in the spectrum reassignments of 1927–8 the Commission took back many religious and university-based licenses, forcing religious and educational stations to share frequencies, often at lower transmitting power.[49] Defining the broadcast system as public and commercial, the FRC required broadcast licensees, as part of their new mandate as trustees of the public airwaves, to cater to broad audience segments with "a well-rounded program." Religious stations were deemed "propaganda" stations precisely because they did *not* fulfil these criteria. The FRC finessed the issue by including religious programming, along with news, weather, and other types of local programs, in the category of "public service," and obligated broadcast licensees to air some unspecified amount of these.[50]

The result of the frequency reassignments and establishing a public trustee status for broadcast licensees was to reduce the radio presence of fundamentalists, Pentecostals, and evangelicals, and to elevate the broadcast profile of mainline Protestants. In the effort to meet their public service obligations, commercial radio stations tended to award free airtime, known then as "sustaining" time, to mainstream Protestant organizations, and to a lesser degree to Catholic and Jewish religious organizations. Indeed, NBC, by far the most important network in the early years of broadcasting, appointed the general secretary of the mainline Protestant Federal Council of Churches, Charles S. Macfarland, to chair the network's religious advisory council. The cooperation between NBC and the Federal Council of Churches led to several long-running mainline Protestant services on the premier radio broadcast organization's networks.[51] After all, mainline Protestants were mainline for a reason: their religious views generally held sway in dominant circles of American life and their radio programs presented these views in predictable, demure, acceptably non-sectarian and ecumenical ways. This allowed broadcasters to meet their public service obligations without attracting unwanted attention or controversy.

In contrast, fundamentalist, Pentecostal, and evangelical radio broadcasts' sectarian claims on theological truth and their direct appeals for funds rankled radio station managers and broadcast network executives. Non-mainline religious broadcasting, including that of the most famous religious broadcaster of them all, the Catholic priest Charles Coughlin, generally had to pay for airtime. The pattern for non-mainline and controversial religious broadcasters like Father Coughlin was paid commercial religious broadcasting, often on individual local radio stations that were joined in a temporary network (showing, by the way, that while they may have been anti-modernist in theology, non-mainline Christians were quite modernist in embracing new communication technologies and adept at using those technologies and popular culture genres to tie together their communities and recruit new members). More than anyone, Coughlin demonstrated the power of the new medium in garnering attention and contributions. The figure generally offered of the national audience for Coughlin's broadcasts in the early 1930s, was up to 40 million people.[52] But religious conservative radio broadcasters always felt under siege by the Protestant mainline and by the National Association of Broadcasters – and by the FCC, which viewed the inflammatory example of Father Coughlin, whose broadcasts later in the decade were increasingly marked by anti-Semitism and support for some of the policies of Hitler and Mussolini, as making a bad case for paid religious broadcasting.[53]

This pattern – mainline Protestant organizations and churches receiving free sustaining time on network-affiliated stations while non-mainline Protestants paid for airtime on small independent outlets – lasted until 1960. Recognizing that previous regulations had failed to produce sufficient public interest programming, the FCC changed course and ruled, among other things in its En Banc Programming Inquiry, that no important public interest would be served by differentiating between free airtime and commercially sponsored programming in evaluating a station's performance.[54] This policy change had important, if inadvertent, consequences for the subject at hand. Television was still early in its development in 1960. Commercial television stations, seeing the FCC's devaluation of sustaining time, began charging for the time they hitherto had set aside for free religious programming. Most mainline churches declined to take up the broadcasters' proposition or were outbid by enterprising fundamentalist, Pentecostal, and evangelical preachers. Long used to receiving free airtime, the mainline organizations had no funds allocated for the purchase of broadcast time. Moreover, mainline Protestant denominations are typically bureaucratically organized, and their broadcast units would have had to labor through the church hierarchy to obtain both permission and funding to buy airtime. In contrast, non-mainline churches are usually independent, often stand-alone, headed by a powerful preacher. Non-mainline broadcast units were organizationally nimble and were already in the habit of purchasing broadcast time. Moreover, the timing was propitious. The advent of television in the 1950s coincided with Billy Graham's New Evangelical revivalist crusade and showed the importance of the new medium for the growth of evangelical church membership and donations. Graham, Oral Roberts, and Jerry Falwell aired sermons as early as the 1950s, as, of course, did Carl McIntire and Billy James Hargis.[55] The 1960 FCC rule change thus enabled these preachers, unhampered by denominational bureaucracies, to purchase relatively cheap time on commercial broadcast stations. They were later joined by the likes of James Robison, Pat Robertson, Jimmy Swaggart, and Jim Bakker, who used radio and television time to spread their views not just on religious matters but on social and political ones as well.

As their audiences increased, and as new broadcast stations and cable channels came available when the FCC enacted a liberalized entry policy period in the 1970s, religious broadcasters began purchasing not just airtime on existing broadcast outlets, but buying stations and cable channels as well.[56] By the end of the 1970s, there were thirty religiously oriented TV stations, more than 1,000 religious radio stations, and four religious networks, all supported by audience contributions. Conservative Christian broadcast organizations became an important source both of new evangelizing and of considerable fundraising. This was the phenomenon known as televangelism. By 1980, 90 percent of all religious programming on television was commercial, almost all controlled by non-mainline Protestants.[57]

Many of the broadcast licenses obtained by religious broadcasters included frequencies reserved for educational purposes. When, in 1975, an educational group petitioned the FCC to disqualify religious affiliates and institutions from holding educational broadcast licenses, religious broadcasters and their audiences grew alarmed. The petition generated over 700,000 letters of opposition to the FCC, premised on the mistaken view the petition had been filed by the president of American Atheists.[58] The FCC quickly dismissed the petition (contradicting its 1927–8 logic that religious broadcasting constituted a kind of special, "propagandistic," rather than a general, public, educational interest). But that did not halt the flow of letters from those who believed that the Commission was considering a ban on religious broadcasting. The FCC had received more than 5 million letters by February 1977.[59] The religious right clearly believed their broadcast resources had come under threat.

Fourteenth Amendment challenges to religious resources: Evangelical victimhood

The FCC never remotely threatened religious broadcasting. But the perception among conservative evangelicals was that the federal government was on the cusp of seizing a prized resource. Although the actual, as opposed to the perceived, threat to religious broadcasting was minor, other federal agencies did clash with religious organizations over substantive issues in the mid- to late 1970s. Coming from the conceptual universe of pursuing racial nondiscrimination under the equal protection and due process clauses of the Fourteenth Amendment of the Constitution, numerous federal agencies began scrutinizing the admissions and employment practices of tax-exempt religious institutions, including schools and hospitals. In 1970, an internally divided Nixon administration ordered the Internal Revenue Service (IRS) to institute new policy denying tax exemptions to racially discriminatory private schools. Ninety percent of Christian private schools were created after the 1954 *Brown v. Board of Education* school desegregation decision, with 40 percent of such schools located in the South.[60] Whereas nationally the overall school enrollment declined by 13.6 percent between 1970 and 1980, the number of independent Christian schools grew by 95 percent.[61] To be sure, the growth of Christian academies wasn't simply a response to desegregation; it also reflected a longer-term aversion to public schools among conservative evangelicals after the Supreme Court set in motion the banning of prayer from the public schools in 1962.[62] Still, the schools were almost certainly a white refuge. The private academy operated by Jerry Falwell's Thomas Road Baptist Church in Lynchburg, Virginia, for example, enrolled only five African-Americans in its 1,147-student body, despite Lynchburg being 25 percent black.[63]

The IRS move to deny the tax-exempt status of discriminatory private academies (including, later, the fundamentalist Bob Jones University) was prompted by a series of court decisions that culminated in *Green v. Connally*, a 1971 Mississippi case in which a federal district court ruled that a segregation-practicing school did not fit the definition of a charitable institution, and thus was not eligible for tax exemption.[64] It took the IRS until 1978 to formalize the guidelines outlining the measures required for schools to avoid losing their tax exemption by proving that they did not discriminate racially in their admissions of pupils.[65] Now identified with Jimmy Carter's

Democratic administration, the guidelines set off a political firestorm, prompting strong reaction from supporters of religious schools far removed from the Mississippi segregationist private academies.[66] The IRS received more than 115,000 pieces of mail protesting the new regulations, the White House and members of Congress another 400,000. The agency was compelled to hold extended public hearings on the matter. Church school defenders, who included Catholics, claimed that IRS bureaucrats had usurped Congress and had improperly conceived of tax exemptions as federal subsidies. Under public and congressional pressure, the IRS backed off. Conservatives in Congress secured an amendment prohibiting the use of federal funds for investigating or enforcing alleged violations of IRS regulations by Christian schools.[67] The IRS threat prompted the formation of some of the earliest organizations of the new Christian right, including Christian School Action, the Christian Legal Defense and Education Fund, and the National Christian Action Coalition. The private school issue also contributed to the softening of the longstanding animosities between Catholics and evangelical Protestants.

A similar conflict involved the Equal Employment Opportunities Commission (EEOC). The EEOC filed suit in 1977 against Southwestern Baptist Theological Seminary, the largest of the six seminaries operated by the Southern Baptist Convention, to compel it under Title VII of the Civil Rights Act of 1964 to disclose the number and duties of seven categories of employees, their compensation and tenure, and their race, gender, and national origin. The EEOC routinely used such data to determine whether an organization's hiring practices were discriminatory. The seminary refused to file the form on the ground that such compulsion and potential EEOC jurisdiction violated the free exercise clause of the First Amendment.[68]

A year earlier, the IRS had proposed a regulation to implement Congress's mandate in the Tax Reform Act of 1969, that is, a definition of the term "integrated auxiliary of a church." The IRS declared that bona fide auxiliary activities would need to be exclusively religious, hence church activities such as homes for the aged, hospitals, and colleges would not come under the tax exemption of their sponsoring church.[69] This, too, generated much concern amongst a multitude of religious denominations and their associated agencies. And in another instance, in 1976 the National Labor Relations Board (NLRB) became involved in an effort by lay teachers to organize unions in Roman Catholic-operated schools in Chicago and Fort Wayne-South Bend, Indiana. The NLRB also asserted its authority to compel collective bargaining in the archdiocesan schools of

Philadelphia and Los Angeles on the ground that such schools were not "completely religious." Although the Supreme Court ruled in a five to four decision in favor of the Catholic bishops and against the NLRB on the issue of compelled collective bargaining of lay teachers in Catholic schools, here was yet another instance where religious organizations felt that the federal government had become hostile to religion.[70]

The decline of religious discrimination and discrimination in general in the 1950s and 1960s led to a more pluralistic public sphere and fed a dynamic deployment of the Fourteenth Amendment's protections, precipitating the government actions with regard to conservative evangelical institutions and in so doing triggering their resentment. The emergence of an aggrieved traditionalist Christian community thus may have been an almost inevitable reaction to increasing pluralism. Pluralism endangers committed religious faith.[71] Evangelicals interpreted the various government actions as distinctly related, and as further steps in the progression of the state's adoption and promotion of secularism. In the evangelical perception, the federal courts played a central role in the advance of secularism, having earlier prohibited prayer in the public schools, relaxed laws against pornography, and legalized abortion. Until the 1960s, fundamentalists and conservative evangelicals could safely say that Christians did not need to be involved in politics because their basic moral values were embodied in American culture. Indeed, this is why Robert Bellah's civil religion thesis – that the Protestantism of the founding generation had seeped into and had become American culture, even if the provenance of those values was no longer visible – had such salience.[72] By the 1970s, this assumption about the culture could no longer be sustained. The state's moves to act neutrally toward non-religious groups and to question religion's embedded privileges were experienced by the previously dominant social grouping as an attack on its institutions, a denial of its worldview even. These moves were then further experienced – because of the particular nature of that grouping's worldview – as abetting "bad" social behavior, even as manifestations of the work of Satan.

In short, while conservative evangelicals hitherto had always found secularism objectionable, the new course of secularization now was seen to pose a grave danger to their traditional structures and life-world. With their embedded privileges under threat, conservative evangelicals came to the realization (with robust help from political entrepreneurs of the new right, to be discussed shortly) that they could not pursue separation from the secular world. This served to intensify the evangelical critique of secularism, and led evangelicals to cast themselves as victims. They described themselves as surrounded and threatened by social decadence, seen in the various "excesses" of the 1960s – sex, drugs, rock and roll, rebellion against authority, women's rights, divorce, homosexuality, parental permissiveness. They understood these excesses as a lack of self-discipline and self-control, the decline of an ethic of personal responsibility, and the triumph of the untrammeled self.[73] Perhaps more than anything else it was the fear of subversion of the traditional family that lay at the core of the conservative evangelical anxiety about the new secularism. Conservative evangelicals evaluated nearly all symptoms of cultural crisis – especially the sexual revolution, the emancipation of women, and permissive childrearing practices – according to the effects on the family. The "vicious assault upon the American family," Jerry Falwell wrote, came from television and popular culture, pornography, abortion, the failure of parents to discipline their children, drugs, feminism, and the omission and commission of government.[74] The perceived threat to the family by permissive childrearing underlay the particular growth of what became Focus on the Family, the organization established by the right-wing child psychologist James Dobson in 1977.[75] As the sociologist Martin Riesebrodt suggests, the sense of threat to the family revolved around the role of women, and more precisely the sexual aspect of the female body. Woman as potential seducer of man into sin is an important focus of the fundamentalist worldview. Female sexuality was no longer discussed as the instrument of Satan, as it was at the beginning of fundamentalism, but the danger of sexuality – male and female – remained a force that needed to be disempowered and subdued within a patriarchal family structure.[76] Because the family also functioned as a metaphor for the nation, the assault on the family was also a threat to America itself. America's freedoms, strength, and standing were imperiled.

The source of social decadence was a particular creed: secular humanism. As Falwell inveighed, the central problem with secular humanism was that it made man, rather than God, the measure of all things.

> Humanism is man's attempt to create a heaven on earth, exempting God and His Law. Humanists propose that man is in charge of his own destiny. Humanism exalts man's reason and intelligence. It advocates situation ethics, freedom from any restraint, and defines sin as man's maladjustment to man. It even advocates the right to commit

suicide and recognizes evolution as a source of existence. Humanism promotes the socialization of all humanity into a world commune.[77]

The moral decay of society rests at the center of the conservative evangelical critique. Moral decay is the result of a turn away from divine law. And moral decay was now, in effect, government policy. Secular humanism and the unelected judges and bureaucratic elites had transformed the culture and the rules of the political game. From the institutions of political power, the secular elite acted to persecute religion, particularly traditional Christianity. The secular elite consciously excluded religion and religiously grounded values from the conduct of public business.[78]

A key theoretical statement was Francis A. Schaeffer's 1976 *How Should We Then Live?*, which was made into a film series widely popular in evangelical circles (and popularized again in *The Battle for the Mind*, a bestselling book by Tim LaHaye).[79] A student of J. Gresham Machen, the fundamentalist theologian associated with Carl McIntire, Schaeffer challenged evangelicals to engage the ideas and history of western culture with a critically Christian mind. Drawn especially to art, Schaeffer argued that the best of western culture could be traced to a Christian foundation – which was now under attack from secular elites. By the mid-1970s, he called for political engagement on the part of Christians, particularly opposition to abortion. In contrast to the Catholic hierarchy, evangelical Protestants had been late to oppose abortion, but their newly found vehemence transformed opposition into a social movement. (Randall Terry said that to understand Operation Rescue, the violent anti-abortion group that he founded, one must read Francis Schaeffer.) Schaeffer's declarations represented a McCarthy-like moment: akin to communism a generation earlier, secular humanism constituted a conspiracy to take over America.[80] Secular humanists were in government, the courts, the classrooms, the media. In LaHaye's version, secular humanists' obsessions with sex, pornography, and drugs led directly to a culture of self-indulgence, of rights without responsibilities, and disillusionment with America. The ultimate result was rebellion at God, parents, and authority, and a tragic lack in skills, self-worth, purpose, and happiness. Like the communists of decades previous, secular humanists needed to be rooted out.[81]

Books, sermons, and pamphlets began telling a story of America as a Christian nation that had "fallen." This was a chronicle about how God had promoted America to a greatness no other nation has ever enjoyed because of its heritage as a republic governed by laws predicated on the Bible. As Pat Robertson expressed these American exceptionalist sentiments in a later book:

> As we review the history of the United States, it is clear that every one of those promises made to ancient Israel has come true here [the United States] as well. There has never been in the history of the world any nation more powerful, more free, or more generously endowed with physical possessions.... We have had more wealth than the richest of all empires. We have had more military might than any colossus. We have risen above all the nations of the earth.... But these things did not happen by accident, nor did they happen somehow because the citizens of America are smarter or more worthy than the citizens of any other country. It happened because those men and women who founded this land made a solemn covenant that they would be the people of God and that this would be a Christian nation.[82]

While the Founding Fathers may have metaphorically separated church and state, they never intended to establish a government devoid of God. But the liberals and secularists had managed to do just that, Robertson claimed. They had gained control over the government and sin now permeated the land, seen in pornography, abortion, divorce, feminism, homosexuality, and so on. Because of secular amorality, America has grown weak and decadent. It had lost its course and teetered at the edge of defeat from world communism. Only a return to God could save the nation.[83]

The symbolic importance of Watergate and Jimmy Carter's apostasy

The anguish of conservative Christians was understandable. But what prompted their political mobilization in the late 1970s? There is no automatic or immediate connection between changes in the social environment and any particular response. Here a suggestion by the sociologist Robert Wuthnow is helpful. His analysis moves beyond the material threat to evangelical institutions and resources to a more symbolic level. Wuthnow suggests that conservative Christians were galvanized by two events that blurred the distinction between private morality and public institutions: Watergate and *Roe v. Wade*, the Supreme Court decision legalizing abortion. The Watergate scandal and the behavior of White House officials, President Nixon foremost among them, challenged the hitherto assumed separation between personal, private morality and public institutions. The reigning (secular) cultural assumption was that private morality among political figures was mostly a personal matter, largely irrelevant to their leadership of public institutions. Conservative evangelicals had never shared this assumption, of course; they always believed that private conceptions of morality posed serious repercussions for public morality and for the society as a whole.[84] The bad behavior of the Nixon White House found the evangelical view being expressed in the culture generally and articulated pointedly by Democratic presidential candidate Jimmy Carter, himself a born-again whose public witnessing of his evangelical faith was new and noteworthy. Wuthnow's argument is not quite correct, in the sense that Nixon's lies concerned his *public* not his private behavior. Still, Watergate stunned evangelicals.[85]

Jimmy Carter gained traction among evangelicals because of the contrast of his promises of sincerity with Nixon's dissembling. "I will not lie to you" was a staple of Carter's campaign against Republican candidate Gerald Ford in the 1976 presidential campaign. Calling for "a government as good as its people," Carter affirmed the virtue of the American public and the need for morality in its leaders. This, Wuthnow suggests, allowed the forging of a symbolic link between the identity of evangelicals and that of the larger society, giving them a sense of political entitlement that made it more conceivable to speak out on moral and political issues. Historically, evangelical Christians always conceived themselves as the moral custodians of American culture. Watergate permitted their reentry into public life in a direct way. A large number of evangelical churches and organizations were drawn toward and into the Carter campaign, even though many parted company with the campaign in the end because of Carter's desultory position on abortion, another issue that challenged the presumed separation between public and private morality.[86]

If the symbolism of Watergate and candidate Jimmy Carter's open born-again faith allowed many evangelicals to enter the political arena, it was the threat to their institutions – specifically the Christian schools – that brought together conservative Christians and created the foundation for a politically effective movement. The perceived attacks on conservative evangelical institutions by the courts and government agencies discussed earlier were set in motion well before Carter occupied the White House. But because the initiatives came to fruition during his administration, he was seen as their cause. Because Carter was himself an evangelical who had promised better, governmental "attacks" on conservative evangelicals were seen as apostasy and betrayal on his part. Carter, of course, was a Democrat.

In sum, as secularization proceeded through the life-world, particularly via government action, conservative evangelicals were motivated by feelings that their way of life was under attack. They saw themselves as victims of governmental and judicial overreach, realizing their political identity on the basis of victimhood. As victims of the liberal secular agenda, conservative Christians in the mid- to late 1970s became receptive to entreaties from former Goldwater movement operatives, figures such as Richard Viguerie, Phyllis Schlafly, Howard Phillips, and Paul Weyrich. Having helped build the web of conservative political institutions discussed at the end of the previous chapter, these leaders operated as political entrepreneurs for the conservative political renaissance that was being called the "new right."[87]

Building a Christian political movement: The importance of political entrepreneurs

It was Paul Weyrich who saw political opportunity in the IRS initiative on Christian schools after years of unsuccessful attempts to politicize evangelicals. Weyrich helped form Christian School Action, recruiting James Dobson, Jerry Falwell, Pat Robertson, and Jim Bakker to the cause. Recall that some years earlier Weyrich and Edwin Feulner had taken the lead role in establishing the Heritage Foundation. Heritage produced policy analyses against the IRS private academies policy, establishing a connection between Heritage and conservative evangelical churches, and legitimizing Weyrich in those circles. In an interview with the sociologist William Martin, Weyrich asserted emphatically that it was the Christian schools/IRS conflict that really launched the relationship between conservative evangelicals and the new right.

> What galvanized the Christian community was not abortion, school prayer, or the ERA [Equal Rights Amendment]. I am living witness to that because I was trying to get those people interested in those issues and I utterly failed. What changed their mind was Jimmy Carter's intervention against the Christian schools, trying to deny them tax-exempt status on the basis of so-called de facto segregation.

The IRS threat, according to Weyrich,

> enraged the Christian community and they looked upon it as interference from government, and suddenly it dawned on them that they were not going to be able to be left alone to teach their children as they pleased. It was at that moment that conservatives made the linkage between their opposition to government interference and the interests of the evangelical movement, which now saw itself on the defensive and under attack by the government. That was what brought those people into the political process. It was not the other things.[88]

An important strain in the sociology of social movements emphasizes the importance of the resources available to groups as they become organized and mobilize for collective action. A social movement must have robust, able leadership and sufficient resources – be they moral, material, or organizational – to be successful. The political system must be vulnerable to challenge and present opportunities for movements to exploit. Such political opportunities may stem from conflict between elites or access to elite allies or increased ability to affect political decisions.[89] But "resource mobilization" and "political opportunity" theories have tended to neglect the grievances or bases for solidarity that give life to group consciousness. Conservative evangelicals had to mobilize specific resources to become a group capable of political action, of course. But they had to see themselves as a group capable of action first, and this emerged from their sense of themselves as both victims of secularism and government policies, and politically entitled, in Wuthnow's phrase, to rectify secularism's evils. This is where the mobilization of resources plays out, *after* a sense of focused (rather than diffuse and abstract) grievance. Evangelicals felt aggrieved about the general state of society; Watergate shocked them. Still, according to Paul Weyrich, evangelical leaders typically blanched at becoming directly involved in the political process.[90] What changed that reticence was the perception of a specific, palpable threat to the material resource of Christian schools and, by way of extension, the existential challenge it posed to the conservative evangelical way of life. The very government that had helped evangelicals finance their private schools and obtain their broadcast licenses was now threatening to withdraw that assistance and in the process embroil these Christians in the evil secular whirlwind. The brilliance of the new right political entrepreneurs, Paul Weyrich perhaps foremost among them, lay in their ability to bring those Christians who were frustrated and angry about the culture into conservative political organizations. The prior existence of vibrant conservative organizations meant that the religious right emerged in an already open political opportunity structure blessed with all manner of institutional resources.

It is perhaps foolish to fix one event or conflict as *the* key to the formation of the Christian right. Obviously, in addition to the Christian schools/IRS conflict the opposition to abortion played a major role in the making of the movement (although, as many have pointed out, the anti-abortion struggle was led initially by Catholics, and it took several years before evangelicals took heed of the issue). And the national movement against the Equal Rights Amendment in the early to middle years of the 1970s was surely another moment when conservative evangelicals, particularly women, began to shift from an internal, family-based orientation to an external agenda of acting to halt or transform public policies. With the ERA, the nascent leaders of the religious right became convinced that they would have to go on the political offensive in order to win their defensive battles against the threats of feminism, gay rights, and state interference in the domestic sphere. The anti-ERA movement mobilized religious conservatives as victims who were now fighting back against the secular humanist tide. Indeed, the anti-ERA movement united major elements of the conservative critique of American politics. As the political scientist Jane Mansbridge writes, if the primary cause of the ERA's defeat was the fear that it would lead to major changes in the roles of men and women, a major subsidiary cause was backlash against "progressive" or "activist" Supreme Court decisions, starting with the 1954 school desegregation decision.[91]

The growth of these single-issue campaigns – the ERA, religious schools, abortion, and so on – revealed the skills and importance of new right entrepreneurs: that is, the Phyllis Schlaflys, the Richard Vigueries, the Paul Weyriches, most of whom had long histories in anti-establishment conservatism and intensive experience in the 1964 Goldwater campaign.[92] Long considered a brilliant, intemperate organizer on the far right of the GOP, it was Schlafly, more than any other figure, who breathed life into the campaign against the ERA.[93] Viguerie, who worked for the Christian anti-communist crusader Billy James Hargis in his early career, discovered his direct mail prowess in service as executive secretary of the Young Americans for Freedom as that organization was mobilizing for Goldwater. Weyrich, too, had been active in the Goldwater campaign. After Goldwater's defeat and the purge of his followers from Republican Party positions, these activists returned to the political trenches and began looking for new issues and new ways to reenergize the conservatives who had mobilized for the Arizona senator. They eventually found those in the "social" issues that so exercised the conservative evangelicals. Just as the success of the conservative mobilization for Goldwater had lain in the ability of gifted organizers to weave an otherwise inchoate web of resentments and criticisms of the post-war liberal order into a coherent political movement by naming them and finding them an articulator in the Arizona senator, so, in the late 1970s, Goldwater veterans helped add a new set of resentments – and constituencies – to the old. Schlafly, Viguerie, Weyrich et al. were a part of the link between the anti-establishment Goldwater right, the "new" right, and the Christian right. They brokered the intellectual affinities and institutional and financial contacts. Weyrich's Committee for the Survival of a Free Congress was a case in point. Established in 1974 with, like the Heritage Foundation, a grant of money from beer magnate Joseph Coors, it trained and mobilized conservative activists, reaching into evangelical churches for recruits.

This is not to say that there was some direct line from the Goldwater campaign to Jerry Falwell's Moral Majority. But the differences were less about ideologies and principles than they were about style, tactics, and organization. The new right called *itself* the new right to distinguish its leadership from what it believed to be the effete, overly moderate Republican leadership of the East Coast, and the polite politics of established conservative organizations – in other words, it was a new label for the old anti-establishment conservatism.[94] The overly moderate leadership that the new right vilified came to include, rather astonishingly, the intellectual leaders of the earlier generation of anti-establishment conservatism, including William F. Buckley, Jr. and the old *National Review* leadership. One new right strategist dismissed the brand of conservatism represented by Buckley and the *National Review* crowd as "a surviving High-Church religion" struggling to remain "uncontaminated by mass culture and politics."[95] In that combative spirit, a new right effort by Viguerie and Weyrich, with financial backing from Coors, battled traditional conservatives for control of the old American Conservative Union and the newer American Legislative Exchange Council. The new right influenced the GOP through a quasi-insurgency strategy, setting up hard-line anti-establishment conservatives to run against establishment Republicans in congressional primaries, and roiling the waters through direct mail attacks on Republican moderates.[96] New right operatives even attacked Barry Goldwater himself as too compromising and undependable when the former standard-bearer declined to back

Ronald Reagan's challenge of Gerald Ford for the 1976 Republican presidential nomination.[97]

The organizational coming together of the new Christian right in the late 1970s centered on four main groups that built on local actions and organizations: the National Christian Action Coalition (NCAC), the Religious Roundtable, Christian Voice, and the Moral Majority.[98] The NCAC, as we saw, was launched in 1978 in response to the Internal Revenue Service's attempts to revoke the tax-exempt status of private schools believed to practice racial discrimination. The Religious Roundtable was the brainchild of Ed McAteer (field director for the Christian Freedom Foundation and called by some the "godfather of the religious right") and formed in 1979 among other reasons to recruit conservative ministers into politics, with the expectation they would bring their congregations with them. The televangelist James Robison was vice-president of the Religious Roundtable. Christian Voice, launched in 1978, published the original "Congressional Report Card" assessing how congressional representatives had voted on key issues of concern to conservatives. Paul Weyrich in particular tried to steer a middle course between the new right and the Christian right, recasting the "social" issues in terms of a general cultural conservatism, with the intention of bringing on board other religious denominations – even in principle culturally conservative atheists.

But the alliance between the new right and the Christian right wasn't fully cemented until the birth of the Moral Majority in 1979. The most important organization of the right-wing alliance, the Moral Majority came out of a series of Jerry Falwell-led rallies called "I Love America." The rallies, a mix of patriotism and religion, were staged in 1976 to celebrate the country and attack the ills threatening to bring it down: pornography, homosexuality, abortion, and the Equal Rights Amendment. They marked Falwell's transition from preaching theology to speaking publicly against secular evils. In the context of those rallies, Falwell was approached by the new right entrepreneurs. Viguerie, Howard Phillips, McAteer, and Weyrich were convinced that if they could create a religious umbrella under which all of the hot button, single-issue groups would gather, they could mold the new conservative thrust into a very powerful political force. The idea was to unite the groups concerned with school curricula and pedagogy, birth control, sex education, abortion, homosexuality, the Panama Canal treaty, gun rights, and so on, and bind them to the old anti-establishment conservative organizations dedicated to lowering taxes on corporations and the wealthy, reducing the size of the federal government, and suspending government regulations. The Conservative Caucus, under Phillips's leadership, had the goal of bringing the single-issue groups under one roof in preparation for the 1980 presidential election. Viguerie's National Conservative Political Action Committee brought several smaller single-issue groups for planning conferences.[99] The new right entrepreneurs approached Falwell to establish and lead the umbrella organization, the Moral Majority.

Falwell, it should be noted, early on exemplified a version of fundamentalist insularity – with a racist tinge. His Thomas Road Baptist Church founded the Lynchburg Christian Academy in 1966. In the plain words of the *Lynchburg News*, it was "a private school for white students." Segregation was a biblical mandate, in Falwell's view. He was initially reluctant to move beyond that fundamentalist comfort zone. The abortion question, which so fed Francis Schaeffer's theological and political rage, was not on Falwell's agenda until later in the 1970s. Falwell's decision to lead the Moral Majority signaled a move from a race-based, but muted enmity toward government to a more generalized political hostility that put a moral spin on the broad new right agenda. The Moral Majority transformed the old libertarian concern that governmental power would undermine individual initiative at the economic level into a concern that federal power was the source of the decline of individual responsibility and family authority, religiosity, and morality. This broad socio-moral program marked the ascendance of the traditionalist strain in anti-establishment conservative fusionism and distinguished the Moral Majority-led right-wing alliance from the older anti-establishment conservatism. It would be a mistake, however, to conclude that the new "social conservative" or traditionalist orientation departed widely from economic conservatism. As Falwell declared:

> The free-enterprise system is clearly outlined in the Book of Proverbs in the Bible. Jesus Christ made it clear that the work ethic was a part of His plan for man. Ownership of property is biblical. Competition in business is biblical. Ambitious and successful business management is clearly outlined as a part of God's plan for His People. Our Founding Fathers warned against centralized government power, concluding that the concentration of government corrupts and sooner or later leads to abuse and tyranny.[100]

After paying obeisance to the conservative economist Milton Friedman, Falwell continues in *Listen, America!*, "More and more today, we are seeing our government run by thousands of bureaucracies that destroy the productive institutions they supervise."[101]

A brief aside on Catholics and the right

Unlike fundamentalist and conservative evangelical Protestants, it can reasonably be argued that there really was no Catholic right until the 1970s. Father Coughlin had been the most visibly engaged, inflammatory Catholic in the public arena in the 1930s. Notwithstanding his support among many Catholics and despite some claims that the Coughlin phenomenon was a dangerous example of irrational, antidemocratic mass behavior (especially by 1938, when he mounted radio attacks on the New Deal for its "dictatorial" and "communistic" policies), Coughlin's support among Catholics was mixed, and his appeal more populist than right wing per se.[102] Although Coughlin was protected by the bishop under whose ecclesiastical authority he operated, there was no clear sense that the Church hierarchy supported him generally. As a voting bloc, Catholics remained decidedly in the Democratic camp.[103] Coughlinism did not represent any right-wing Catholic movement.

A similar assessment can be made of Catholics and McCarthyism. The Catholic Church long condemned communism as an atheistic and materialist doctrine. In some church circles, communism was said to represent the Antichrist. Of course, Catholicism had its own version of collective obligations, including the papal encyclical calling on Catholics to oppose unjust economic conditions and the exploitation of labor. Catholic doctrine called for the protection of the social fabric and help for the poor. Unlike conservative Protestants, Catholics never supported strict laissez-faire capitalism. But they did share strong anti-communist sentiments. The suffering endured by the Catholic Church in eastern European countries under Soviet domination after World War II only stoked the animosity of the church and its adherents against communism. Moreover, the combination of Catholic hatred of communism and Joseph McCarthy's Catholic upbringing meant that the senator's following included a great many in that church. However, while McCarthy's anti-communism may have had roots in his Catholic faith, he tended not to tie the two together in any public way. And though Catholic anti-communism may have been a way for Catholics to demonstrate their fundamental Americanism,[104] McCarthy's Catholic support was not that much higher than his support among Protestants, and there was no sense that his anti-communist crusade was a Catholic movement.[105] Despite the senator's various charges of treason against Democratic leaders, Catholics did not depart the New Deal coalition. The political positioning of American Catholics made it unlikely that they would develop a right-wing political movement. They were constantly under siege by Protestants for the authoritarianism of the church hierarchy and accused of "dual loyalty." In part because Protestants dominated the Republican Party, Catholics tended to be dependable Democrats. Catholics began departing the Democratic Party only in the 1970s, when the Great Society programs and court-mandated rulings on busing and affirmative action began affecting their communities. Catholics voted for Ronald Reagan in 1980 and 1984. Since then the Catholic vote has become a swing vote.[106]

To the extent that there is a Catholic right wing, its roots lie with the liberalization of the abortion laws in the late 1960s. Catholic conservative political action took off after the *Roe v. Wade* decision. The National Conference of Catholic Bishops (NCCB) declared it would not accept the Supreme Court's judgment and called for a major legal and educational battle against abortion. The NCCB put together a strategy for the church's anti-abortion campaign, and used the parishes to mobilize a political machine to influence national and local elections to change the abortion laws. Still, as the political scientist Rosalind Petchesky argues, the organized anti-abortion movement was distinct from the new right. "Unlike the National Right to Life Committee (NRLC) or the Catholic bishops, the individuals, organizations, publications, and political action committees that define themselves as the new Right are not ultimately concerned with fetal souls or moral purity but with achieving state power."[107] For the most part, Catholics wanted to end abortion; anti-abortion Protestants wanted to change the political system that sanctioned abortion rights.

The mobilization of resources

The mobilization of what became the Moral Majority depended on the tight linkages and personal networks among church leaders, particularly independent Baptist clergymen connected through the Baptist Bible Fellowship.[108] They were buttressed by sizeable contributions of seed money from right-wing businessmen such as Nelson Bunker Hunt, Joseph Coors, Amway Corporation founder Richard DeVos, and, following those, direct-mail donations and televangelist appeals.[109] Direct mail and religious broadcasting constituted powerful resources that expanded the Moral Majority's appeal beyond the churches. Pioneered by Richard Viguerie, direct mail used computer technology to target conservative households with specific political appeals.[110] Collecting contributions from small donors, direct mail became especially important after the Watergate-inspired campaign finance laws limited large campaign donations. Viguerie saw direct mail as a way to break through the power of the "liberal media," which, in conservative eyes, had long thwarted the conservative message.[111] Radio broadcasting, as we know, was important in certain kinds of religious appeals in twentieth-century America. Broadcasting became a contribution cash cow when revivalist-style preachers transformed religious television into an electronic ministry in the 1970s. Television preachers found a formula to cater to their audiences' religious needs and bring in immense numbers of cash donations. It is no accident that many of the preachers most active in the new Christian right were conservative evangelicals and Pentecostals who were able to transform small ministries into mega-church organizations in part through the use of television. Falwell's *Old-Time Gospel Hour*, the videotaped recording of his 11 am Sunday service, was a key element in the rise of the several ventures aligned to his Thomas Road Baptist Church.[112] James Robison's Evangelistic Association established a large television apparatus to preach the word about public morality in the late 1970s before he ceased speaking publicly about politics.[113] Pat Robertson's signature television program, *700 Club*, and his Christian Broadcast Network laid the basis for his run for the presidency in 1988. Later, in a kind of squaring the circle, Robertson shared his direct-mail presidential campaign list with Viguerie and new right organizations.

An interlocking network of activists and groups bound the new Christian right to the less overtly religious new right, coordinated by select forums for otherwise independent conservative organizations and serviced by a comprehensive set of think tanks, media watchdog groups, and organizations devoted to proposing legislation and the training of candidates and recruitment of future leaders. Sharing issues, leaders, and members were the National Christian Action Coalition, the Religious Roundtable, Christian Voice, and the Moral Majority, as well as the American Family Association, Focus on the Family, the Family Research Council, the Council for National Policy, the Christian Freedom Foundation, Concerned Women for America, and the Traditional Values Coalition, among others. The networks had myriad ideological and financial connections. For example, Rousas Rushdoony, the founder of Christian Reconstructionism, was able to get his Chalcedon think tank and the creationist Discovery

Institute bankrolled by the southern California billionaire Howard Ahmanson. Ahmanson also funded James Dobson's Focus on the Family, the Institute for Religion and Democracy, and the conservative intellectual Claremont Institute. Another example of the network is the Council for National Policy (CNP), which functioned as one of several important gathering points for a variety of powerful leaders, whether religious (Pat Robertson, Rousas Rushdoony, Jerry Falwell, James Dobson), corporate (Nelson Bunker Hunt, Robert Perry, Richard Mellon Scaife, Joseph Coors, Howard Ahmanson), military (John K. Singlaub, Daniel O. Graham), think tank (Edwin Feulner, John Bolton, Grover Norquist), or political entrepreneurial (Paul Weyrich, Howard Phillips, Ed McAteer). Founded by Tim LaHaye in 1981 and operating largely below the public radar, the CNP continues to act as a policy and funding conduit for anti-establishment conservative projects, both political and religious.[114] The American Legislative Exchange Council, which has brought together conservative activists, corporate leaders, and state legislators to rewrite state laws under a cloak of non-partisan discussion since 1973, is another fruit of conservative networking.[115]

Conservative networks of intellectual affinity and organizational interpenetration coalesced in the Religious Roundtable-sponsored August 1980 National Affairs Briefing of religious leaders. This was the setting where Bailey Smith, president of the Southern Baptist Convention, opened with the pronouncement that "God Almighty does not hear the prayer of a Jew," and candidate Ronald Reagan famously declared his endorsement of the efforts of the 15,000 assembled religious luminaries.[116] The creation of interlocking and umbrella coalitions, mobilization of material resources, and articulation of a powerful political ideology of victimhood coalesced around Reagan's candidacy. Reagan, from his pro-business, anti-union work at General Electric, to his electrifying nomination speech for Barry Goldwater, through his counterculture-bashing California governorship and his anti-government and pro-family candidacies for president, became the fount of the hopes of the religious and economic right.

Religious ideology and political action

There is one final piece to this puzzle: religious ideology. Recall that evangelical Christians divided roughly into two camps: post- and premillennialism. Postmillennials believed in intervening in the world through good works. Premillennials saw the world as evil and counseled separation from it. Why would premillenialist Protestants become politically engaged if they view the secular world as Satan's and biblical prophecy assures that things are going to get worse until Armageddon? Indeed, witnessing the reaction of religious leaders at the famous National Affairs Briefing addressed by candidate Reagan and from which emerged a politically passionate Christian voting bloc, the *post*millennialist Gary North observed:

> Here were the nation's fundamentalist religious leaders . . . telling the crowd that the election of 1980 is only the beginning, that the principles of the Bible can become the law of the land. . . . Here was a startling sight to see: thousands of Christians, including pastors, who had believed all their lives in the imminent return of Christ, the rise of Satan's forces, and the inevitable failure of the church to convert the world, now standing up to cheer other pastors, who also have believed this doctrine of earthly defeat all their lives, but who were proclaiming victory, in time and on earth. . . . Thousands of people were cheering for all they were worth – cheering away the eschatological doctrines of a lifetime, cheering away the theological pessimism of a lifetime.[117]

North was crowing for good reason. In his view all these premillennialists had jettisoned their doctrine and come over to the postmillennial position. What happened to their pessimism, their separation from the secular world? Often neglected by scholars, this is addressed quite brilliantly by the anthropologist Susan Harding. Harding points out that in addition to inevitable doctrinal disputes and disagreements within the premillennialist tent, including the Rapture's timing, the free play in the interpretive zone between current events and biblical imagery creates an opening for alternative views of Christians' role in their world. Did the 1967 Arab–Israel Six-Day War, for example, confirm Book of Revelations prophecies? How should one interpret the fall of the Soviet Union vis-à-vis the expected future attack on Israel by Revelations' "armies of the north"? The heterogeneity, instability, and partiality of narrative framings of current events, Harding argues, undermine the absolute futurism of Bible prophecies. Premillennial doctrine posits that the tribulation is a time when God will judge the Jews according to immutable, irreversible, biblical prophecy. But by 1980, major national evangelical preachers and writers such as Hal Lindsey, Billy Graham, Jerry Falwell, and Tim LaHaye were postulating new narrative frames on the end-times, writing of a "pretribulational judgment" that would precede the tribulation, during which God would judge Christians, not Jews. After denouncing the evils of secular humanism for an entire book, in the last few pages of *The Battle for the Mind* Tim LaHaye writes:

> The seven-year tribulation period will be a time that features the rule of the anti-Christ over the world. . . . It originates with the signing of a covenant between Israel and the anti-Christ, which he breaks after three and one-half years. That tribulation is predestined and will surely come to pass. But the pretribulation tribulation – that is, the tribulation that will engulf this country if liberal humanists are permitted to take total control of our government – is neither predestined nor necessary. But it will deluge the entire land in the next few years, unless Christians are willing to become much more assertive in defense of morality and decency than they have been during the past three decades.[118]

In the pretribulation, God's judgment is not fixed by biblical prophecies. If Christians respond to God's call through holy living and moral action, God will spare them and the American nation. As Harding writes, "Thus, with this little tribulation, bible prophecy teachers opened a small window of progressive history in the last days, a brief moment in time when Christians could, and must be, agents of political and social change."[119]

Jerry Falwell's great achievement was to moderate fundamentalism such that its adherents could maintain their religious integrity and engage the world by calling for a fusion of morality and politics. Indeed, the pretribulationist theological opening created a compulsion to do so. As Harding puts it, unless born-again Christians acted politically, they would lose their religious and moral freedom, which was what enabled them to spread the good news and fulfill Bible prophecy. Unless they acted politically, they might even lose their status as God's "elect." If fundamentalism's traditional critique of the world abandoned it to Satan, the new appraisal argued forcefully that the whole world belongs to God. This was a powerful instance of what the sociologist Bennett Berger called "ideological work."[120] With the pretribulation, the task of good Christians was not to avoid the world, but to enter it, even infiltrate it.[121] In this regard, Carl McIntire was the unacknowledged model.

And infiltrate they did. Although the claims are difficult to document with accuracy, it seems clear that evangelicals registered millions of co-religionists to vote.[122] Under the leadership of Pat Robertson and Ralph Reed, the Christian Coalition of America, the more-or-less successor organization to the Moral Majority fashioned on the coattails of Robertson's 1988 run for the presidency, claimed to have distributed 45 million "voter guides" between 1990 and 1994, promoting the candidacies of conservative Republican candidates for federal office and attacking their opponents. These voter guides presented single-phrase statements of complex problems with "supports/opposes" comparisons of candidate positions on issues of concern to the Coalition. Robertson received almost 1.1 million votes in the 1988 GOP primaries, 9 percent of the vote. By 1995, the Christian Coalition claimed to dominate the Republican Party in eighteen states and exercise significant influence in thirteen others. Even if these numbers are self-serving, the perception has consequences. The national Republican Party is now loath to antagonize its religious base. Indeed, the perceived power of conservative evangelicals is such that all Republican presidential candidates must essentially make pilgrimage to the fundamentalist bastions of Bob Jones University and Falwell's Liberty University (including 2008 Republican presidential nominee John McCain, who in 2000 had pointedly denounced Jerry Falwell and Pat Robertson as "agents of intolerance").[123] Republican candidates for high office seek the endorsement of Focus on the Family's James Dobson or Family Research Council's Tony Perkins, the heirs to Falwell's influence in the evangelical community.[124]

An associated trend has seen new Christian right efforts to capture local political offices, particularly school boards. To some degree these efforts are informed by doctrines known as Dominionism and Christian Reconstructionism (the dominant form of Dominionism), which hold that America is a Christian nation, and that Christians need to reassert control over political and cultural institutions. Pat Robertson was instrumental in promoting elements of Dominionism through his books and especially his Christian Broadcasting Network. Derived from Genesis 1:26, in which God gives mankind dominion over the animals of the earth, Dominion doctrine holds that Christians are commanded to bring all societies under the rule of God's word. As Rousas Rushdoony, the founder of Christian Reconstructionism, declared, the only answer to rampant social problems is for Christians to capture and occupy elected offices.[125] (As a postmillennial doctrine, Dominionism doesn't have to jump through theological hoops in justifying its intervention in the world.) Rushdoony had a particular fixation on public education. Government-based education is offensive to God because it usurps family authority.

Reconstructionist thinking informs (if in a largely hidden way) the general right-wing Christian passion for home schooling and the efforts to re-traditionalize public education through the capture of school boards.

To counter what it sees as the prevailing anomie of American society, this faction of the new Christian right offers an eternally valid order of divine salvation, now no longer as a distant historical ideal but as an immediate political program. The "Christian economics" coming out of Reconstructionism finds warrant in the Bible against inflation, welfare, and labor unions, and in favor of a gold standard for money. The publications of Gary North, Reconstructionism's post-Rushdoony leader and one-time speechwriter for Texas Congressman Ron Paul, are influential in the intellectual world of the new Christian right and reveal how and where its social moralism meets up rather effortlessly with a biblically sanctioned economic libertarianism.[126] Reconstructionism's basic positions resound throughout the anti-establishment right: capitalist self-reliance, personal responsibility, opposition to welfare, denunciation of the "nanny state."

For the most extreme of the politically engaged Christian right, the ideal order in the future is the theocratic republic. The ultimate aim is to apply to America the alternative Christian legal system that evolved in the shadow of the Roman Empire. The model is Calvin's Geneva or Puritan Massachusetts: cleanse the land of sin by seizing the reins of government and (re)establish divine law.[127] Dominionism marries the historic understanding of the Bible (in fact, primarily the Old Testament) as a blueprint for every area of life with a politics of theocracy – hence its theory of "theonomy" (the state of being governed in accord with divine law). What theorists such as Gary North pose is in some essential respect an almost exact obverse of Marxism, or of any totalitarian doctrine that insists that modernity's differentiation of spheres must be dissolved. This is even true of Francis Schaeffer, although Schaeffer was no proponent of theonomy. If Marxism insisted that everything is politics, that political inflection and judgment were to be inserted into all spheres of human activity, so Schaeffer et al. substitute the Christian worldview and Christian morality for politics. For Schaeffer, the problem with historical Christianity in America was its tendency toward pietism, and the division of the world into the spiritual and the material. He believed that Christianity "is true to total reality. . . . True spirituality covers all of reality . . . In this sense there is nothing concerning reality that is not spiritual."[128] This is a religious messianism no less utopian than its

Stalinist secular counterpart. Indeed, borrowing from the philosopher Leszek Kolakowski, both derive from the framework of religious eschatology – descent into Hell, absolute break, the arrival of a "new time."[129] Granted, this is an extreme version of the new Christian right; most talk or worry about theocracy is overwrought, and the mainstream of conservative evangelicalism mobilized by the Moral Majority and its subsequent organizational manifestations declares obeisance to the Constitution and disclaims any theocratic intention. Still, a utopian anti-modern impulse to dissolve the separation of spheres, to obliterate the distinction between public and private, is an essential feature of the new Christian right as a whole.

The new Christian right, foreign policy, and rationality

The sociologist Steve Bruce posts a warning to scholars trying to understand the new Christian right. Breaking with the old "status anxiety" paradigm associated with Richard Hofstadter and Seymour Martin Lipset, Bruce writes:

> [L]ike Hofstadter and Lipset I want to identify a discrepancy between the actual social forces which threaten the world of fundamentalists and their perceptions of that threat, but I do not want to conceptualize the thinking of those who believe they are threatened by a conspiracy of secular humanists as being radically different from styles of thought found in "institutionalized" patterns of social action. Nor do I want to overlook a cultural explanation for them thinking like that. Where others see conspiracy thinking as a reasoning disorder brought on by status anxiety or structural strain, I see it as being at least partly a simple continuation of a style of thought which lies at the heart of most traditional religions.[130]

Bruce provides a compelling corrective to scholarship that fails to take at face value what evangelicals say about what worries them, imputes the root of those concerns to hidden or unconscious material or class- or status-based interests rather than an open clash about values, and, finally, judges their beliefs and actions as irrational.[131] Fair enough. Still, when one moves to the realm of religion and foreign policy, the question of irrationality is harder to ignore or dismiss. And because the decision to invade Iraq in 2003 was so consequential for American foreign policy, attention must be paid to the support for war on the part of the new Christian right.

105

The new Christian right got involved in foreign policy issues via its general anti-communism and the globalized extension of its concern over secularization's threat to the family. Signature issues included halting U.S. underwriting for abortions abroad and protecting Christian populations that were perceived as under threat. Christian right opposition to President Jimmy Carter in part orbited around the perception that his weak-kneed foreign policy permitted the spread of communism to countries such as Angola, Mozambique, and Nicaragua. The Christian right thus sided with the general conservative demand in the 1970s to rebuild the American military and halt the Soviet Union's depredations in the Third World.

With Reagan administration operations in Central America a motivating introduction to foreign affairs activism, the support of "freedom fighters" absorbed a noteworthy part of the new Christian right's attention during the 1980s, as evidenced in publications, broadcasts, rallies, and fundraising efforts. Indeed, the network of religious right groups associated with the Reagan administration policy in this area was extensive. As Sara Diamond revealed through Hoover Institution papers, more than fifty religious right and neoconservative groups met secretly with White House personnel on a regular basis to coordinate media and lobbying activities on behalf of the Nicaraguan Contras.[132] They also gave much support, including impressive amounts of money, to private groups that aided the evangelical General Efrain Rios Montt in the Guatemalan dirty war, anti-guerilla forces in El Salvador, and the mujahideen in Afghanistan, as well as the Contras. They aided Reagan administration covert operations by distributing "humanitarian" supplies to paramilitary forces in Central America. In 1984, Pat Robertson alone raised $3 million for the Nicaraguan Contras. Religious right leaders provided theological justifications, as well. The conservative Catholic intellectual George Weigel, for example, devoted much of his energies in the 1980s to defending Reagan's foreign policy using concepts derived from the Catholic "just war" tradition.[133] The Christian right also opposed the nuclear freeze movement. In 1986, U.S. evangelical broadcasters engaged in a pro-apartheid South Africa publicity campaign.[134] In many respects these stances represented a continuation of the long-ongoing battle of conservative evangelicals against the Protestant mainline churches. The latter typically espoused positions critical of American policy in Central America and southern Africa. Some of the more liberal mainline churches signed on to the movement giving sanctuary to Central American refugees and supporting the corporate divestiture of assets in apartheid

South Africa. Conservative evangelicals attacked these positions with gusto.

The above stances of the new Christian right could be integrated easily enough into a normal, "rational" conservative foreign policy paradigm of supporting American interests against leftist gains in the Third World. Less able to be integrated in a rational metric were their efforts to lobby for nuclear build-up in the 1980s and, later, their support of U.S. wars in the Middle East. New Christian right support for nuclear build-up was not just for the purpose of protecting the United States from Soviet aggression, but because of the connection of nuclear bombs to the end-times. Jerry Falwell used a television appeal to raise funds for pro-nuclear newspaper ads and circulated a pamphlet in 1983, *Nuclear War and the Second Coming of Jesus Christ*, linking the two events to belief in the Rapture. The pamphlet could be read as welcoming, or at least not condemning, a nuclear war: " 'Nuclear War and the Second Coming of Jesus Christ' – the one brings thoughts of fear, destruction, and death, while the other brings thoughts of joy, hope, and life. They almost seem inconsistent with one another, yet they are indelibly intertwined."[135]

Likewise, new Christian right support for the U.S. wars in the Middle East derived in some significant measure from the belief in the end-times. If not the Antichrist himself, suggested conservative evangelical organizations and preachers, Saddam Hussein could well be a forerunner of the "Evil One." During the 1991 Persian Gulf War, for example, Jews for Jesus took out full-page newspaper adver- tisements declaring that Saddam "represents the spirit of Antichrist about which the Bible warns us."[136] For premillennialists, the Euphra- tes River in Iraq represents the eastern border of what God intends to be the state of Israel, hence support for the 2003 invasion of Iraq was tied to the belief in the fulfillment of biblical prophecy.[137] In many evangelical readings, the return of Christ to earth requires first that Jews return to the biblical boundaries of ancient Israel. This in part underlies the Christian right's strident support of Israel. As the promi- nent evangelical activist Ed McAteer declared, "I believe without any reservation whatsoever that every grain of sand on that piece of property called Israel belongs to the Jewish people. It's not because I happen to think that. It's not because history gives a picture of them being in and out of there. It's because God gave it to them." And "[w]hen the nations gather against Israel, I believe at that time the Scriptures will be fulfilled."[138] To point to another example, the Christian Coalition's Road to Victory conference of 2002 was orga- nized around the evangelical right's support of Israel. Keynote speaker

Ehud Olmert, then Jerusalem mayor, later the Prime Minister of Israel, was joined in person or through videoconference by a parade of luminaries on the Christian and new right, among others, Pat Robertson, Jerry Falwell, former House Majority Leader Dick Armey, former chair of the Senate Foreign Relations Committee Jesse Helms, Oliver North, Alan Keyes, former Alabama Chief Justice Roy Moore, and former Israeli Prime Minister Benjamin Netanyahu. Robertson, who said his support for Israel was longstanding, cited the Book of Genesis, in which God granted Abraham and his descendants the ancient land of Canaan, now believed to be modern Israel.[139] In the name of the Bible and the premillennialist view of the end-times, Christian Zionists and their fellow travelers in the conservative evangelical movement routinely exercised their lobbying muscle and connections inside the George W. Bush administration to object to even the slight diplomatic pressure the United States occasionally applied to Israel.

What to make of this? In a discussion of evangelicals and foreign policy in the respected journal *Foreign Affairs*, the foreign policy expert Walter Russell Mead revived the distinction between fundamentalism and evangelicalism, arguing that evangelicals constitute a middle path between fundamentalism and liberal Protestantism. Sharing common roots with fundamentalism but moderated by endemic American optimism, evangelicalism comprises churches such as the Southern Baptist Convention, the National Baptist Convention, USA and National Baptist Convention of America, and the Lutheran Church-Missouri Synod, and parachurch organizations such as the Campus Crusade for Christ and the Promise Keepers. Mead reminded readers that evangelicals, less pessimistic than fundamentalists, believe that the benefits of salvation are potentially available to everyone, and that God gives everyone just enough grace to be able to choose salvation if he or she wishes.[140] In Mead's view, these evangelicals in some ways hark back to their nineteenth-century co-religionists, who fought slavery and supported humanitarian and human rights policies on a global basis. Their moderate beliefs aren't changing U.S. foreign policy in any drastic manner.

But Mead's view does not comport with the complexity of the reality. It is true that when Richard D. Land, president of the vital Ethics and Religious Liberty Commission of the Southern Baptist Convention, backed the Bush administration's Iraq policy, he did so on the basis that using military force against Iraq would fit the theological definition of a "just war" – that is, because it would amount to a defensive action against a biological or nuclear strike from

Saddam Hussein – rather than on the basis of end-times prophecy.[141] But many leading conservative evangelicals long advocated war in the Middle East because they saw Saddam as the Antichrist or held that war would restore Israel's biblical boundaries and bring about the second coming of Jesus.[142] Even when they did not directly allude to Revelations or end-times, evangelical pastors claimed God in their support of the Iraq War. Encapsulating the union of theological certitude and militant nationalism that could be said to typify the foreign policy agenda of the Christian right since the late 1970s, Jerry Falwell stoutly defended the U.S. invasion of Iraq in a baldly entitled article, "God is Pro-war." Falwell called attention to where Scripture sanctions war and where God strengthens individuals for war:

> President Bush declared war on Iraq to defend an innocent people. This is a worthy pursuit. In fact, Proverbs 21:15 tells us: "It is joy to the just to do judgment: but destruction shall be to the workers of iniquity." One of the primary purposes of the church is to stop the spread of evil, even at the cost of human lives. If we do not stop the spread of evil, many innocent lives will be lost and the kingdom of God suffers.[143]

Likewise, Charles Stanley, pastor of the First Baptist Church of Atlanta and former president of the Southern Baptist Convention, declared in a sermon in support of the Iraq War, "The government is ordained by God with the right to promote good and restrain evil. . . . [G]overnment has biblical grounds to go to war in the nation's defense or to liberate others in the world who are enslaved." Moreover, in a strong warning to the war's opponents, Stanley intoned, "God battles with people who oppose him, who fight against him and his followers." These are hardly the moderate beliefs to which Walter Russell Mead refers. Nor were they unrepresentative of evangelicals in general: 87 percent of white evangelical Christians in the United States supported Bush's invasion decision in April 2003, compared to 62 percent of the U.S. population as a whole.[144]

While it is always difficult to speak in general terms about the new Christian right, its pervasiveness, who belongs to it, and who speaks for whom, the dominant trend – contrary to Mead's analysis – has been the re-enfranchisement of fundamentalism to political activism and its largely successful effort to bring other evangelicals into *its* ideological tent. The new Christian right represents an alliance struck between fundamentalist and conservative evangelical traditions. There still exists an extreme fundamentalism that separates from the world, exemplified by Bob Jones and his namesake university. But that is no longer the fundamentalist norm. That Falwell and others were able, in Susan Harding's words, to stitch together rhetorics and styles across the old fundamentalist–conservative evangelical divide was not an accident.[145] Harding relates a crucial meeting in 1982 at the home of Carl Henry, founding editor of *Christianity Today* and among the most eminent evangelical spokesmen in the United States, at which Falwell, Francis Schaeffer, and other top pastors and professors from Falwell's community met with the heads or former heads of various church associations and theological seminaries. The purpose and result of the meeting were to acknowledge that there was little difference theologically between fundamentalists and evangelicals, act to erase any lingering tensions or divisions, and secure a promise that they would defend each other.[146] The new Christian right is part fundamentalist, part Pentecostal, part charismatic, and part evangelical. Jerry Falwell was a premillennial Baptist fundamentalist; Carl Henry was a New Evangelical who helped launch the National Association of Evangelicals; Pat Robertson is an eclectic postmillennial Pentecostal; Francis Schaeffer was a Presbyterian traditionalist with some sympathies toward Christian Reconstructionism. Far from the differences Mead sees between fundamentalists and evangelicals, for the most part the rise of a new Christian right over the past thirty-five years or so has brought together those once-divided religious movements. And the politics of that coalition tend to be far less moderate, and are infused with a far more eschatological bent, than the evangelicals Mead commends. The new Christian right's organizational takeover of the two main conservative Protestant denominations, the Southern Baptist Convention and the Missouri Synod of the Lutheran Church, in the 1980s, is testament to the power of the radical right.[147]

There may be good reasons to increase the American nuclear arsenal. But a rational justification is not that it will hasten Armageddon and the second coming.[148] Wondering whether and how U.S. policies may have contributed to the al-Qaeda attacks of September 11, 2001 is necessary and important. But declaring the attacks as God's judgment on America owing to its domestic moral decay by secular humanism simply does not qualify as thoughtful argument.[149] The United Nations may be a largely ineffective broker of international understanding. But a legitimate position opposing the U.N. is not that the international body is the institutional base of the Antichrist.[150] There may be reasons to support Israel and be wary of Palestinian statehood. But one reason should not be the conviction that God promised all of the biblical land of Canaan to the Israelites, and Christ's second coming first requires the ingathering of Jews to Israel and Jewish supremacy over all of Jerusalem.[151] There may be good reason to have supported the Bush administration's proclaimed "global war on terror," but a rational basis for such support cannot be the belief that George W. Bush was chosen by God to lead the United States in that effort (a belief held in 2006 by at least 29 percent of Republicans and perhaps as many as 57 percent[152]). There may be good reasons to have considered an invasion of Iraq, but rational justifications cannot be because Saddam Hussein is the Antichrist or that redrawing a defeated Iraq's borders would restore Israel's biblical boundaries or that a larger conflagration in the Middle East confirms the second coming of Jesus Christ.[153] Whether self-identified as evangelical or fundamentalist, belief continues to trump rational, fact-based policy-making among members of the Christian right. How, then, did this belief-based thinking find an ally in the neoconservative intellectual elite? That is the subject of the next chapter.

— 4 —

TWO GENERATIONS OF NEOCONSERVATISM
From the Law of Unintended Consequences to the Cleansing Fire of Violence

The anti-establishment conservative movement that helped bring Ronald Reagan to power in 1980 was a coalition whose constituent parts shared considerably overlapping agendas, but there were differences. With its moralistic preoccupations, the new Christian right, which had reinvigorated the movement, paid most notice to those issues that focused on the family and dealt with what became known as "social conservatism": abortion, homosexuality, pornography, gender roles, school curriculum, childrearing practices. True to their roots in business and the Goldwater cause, the new right's proclivities tended toward economic libertarianism. In this respect the Reagan electoral coalition replicated the old anti-establishment fusion between traditionalism and libertarianism, now under new historical conditions. To be sure, the new Christian right also cared deeply about taxes and regulation and a too intrusive federal government. All the issues of concern to anti-establishment conservatism were united by the underlying, primary concepts of personal responsibility and virtue. Still, each part of the coalition had its priorities. And while the clever Reagan lent rhetorical attention to the issues dear to the social conservatives during his presidency, at the end of the day his administration didn't actually enact much policy in that domain. What Reagan did do was revive anti-establishment conservatism's old "rollback" agenda: of the federal government and of international communism.

Rollback was the preoccupation of the final element in the reinvigorated anti-establishment conservative movement: neoconservatism. Neoconservatism was an influential intellectual persuasion that entered the public arena in the 1970s with a forceful critique of government overreach and the unintended consequences of public policy. The first generation of neoconservatives, who began on the political left and moved to the right, provided anti-establishment conservatism with a new set of intellectual hooks for the political struggles in the domestic arena. In their diagnosis of Great Society programs as governmental overreach by a self-serving "New Class," neoconservatives provided a non-religious explanation for the political ills of the 1960s and 1970s that complemented and thus legitimized the conservative evangelical critique of secular humanism. The crisis of American society was too much government and a culture out of control.

In the foreign policy arena, the neoconservatives brought new fervor to the debates of the post-Vietnam era, arguing for a bold restoration (one could say a re-masculinization) of American political and military dominance in the world. In this respect, too, the militancy of the neoconservatives resonated with the new Christian right's belief in American exceptionalism, that God had assigned the United States a mission to extend its values to the other peoples of the world. Neoconservatives did not speak of God; rather, they spoke of "history." It was history that bequeathed to America the universalizing status upon which it must act, calling to mind the originally religious proclamation of Manifest Destiny, that "Providence" had given the United States a mission to spread "the great experiment of liberty."[1] Forcefully endorsing the theme of America's historical mission, the neoconservatives were probably the most important constituency in formulating American foreign policy after the attacks of September 11, 2001, including the decision to invade Iraq. This chapter traces the development of neoconservatism and how its distinctive ideological positions linked to the new Christian right and helped forge a new and ascendant anti-establishment conservatism. Particular attention is paid to foreign policy inasmuch as neoconservatives were so important in that realm.

The first generation: Anti-communism, the lessons of Tocqueville and Burke, and "the law of unintended consequences"

The first generation of neoconservatives, largely New York Jews who were the sons and daughters of Russian and Eastern European immigrants, cut their teeth in the debates of the Marxist left in the 1930s and 1940s.[2] Affiliated with the Trotskyist anti-Stalinist left, after

World War II their anti-Stalinism became anti-communism per se. They found themselves part of the liberal anti-communist wing of the Democratic Party, mainstays of the post-war liberal consensus. The writers and editors Irving Kristol, Norman Podhoretz, and Midge Decter, the academics Sidney Hook, Nathan Glazer, Daniel Patrick Moynihan, and like-minded others, championed liberal social reform at home and vigilant anti-communism abroad.[3] Fierce debaters and tempestuous polemicists, some neoconservatives articulated the position that Soviet communism was morally indistinguishable from Nazism. In the heated intellectual politics of the 1950s, Irving Kristol especially, in his capacity as a prolific essayist and editor of the influential intellectual magazine *Encounter* (and later *The Public Interest*, with a stint as managing editor of *Commentary*), vilified those who believed that the real enemy of the United States was McCarthyism rather than communism. The failure of liberals to understand the true foe lay at the root of Kristol's loathing. In his eyes, liberals demonstrated excessive tolerance toward communism and a cowardly unwillingness to make imperative moral distinctions. As Kristol wrote in 1952, the essence of communism is a conspiracy to subvert every social and political order it does not dominate; yet liberals extended tolerance to those who gave voice to the evil ideology.[4] Communism was "the most powerful existing institution which opposes such changes and reforms as liberalism proposes. . . . Why, then, should not liberals and liberals especially, fear and hate it?"[5] Liberals were to be counted among the naïve "children of light," in the theologian Reinhold Niebuhr's phrase, committed to a belief in human goodness and incapable of recognizing evil, particularly the evil of communism.[6] Yet unlike liberal cold warriors such as Niebuhr and the historian Arthur Schlesinger, Jr., along with the diplomats George Kennan and Hans Morgenthau – men who grasped the evil of communism but counseled a foreign policy of containment – Kristol and some of his intellectual compatriots argued for the rollback of communism. Liberal*ism* was largely betrayed by liberals, the neoconservatives thought. Liberal institutions needed defenders, and the first generation of neoconservatives saw themselves as liberalism's fierce and hard-headed guardians.

Many members of the first generation of neoconservatives quietly came to disagree with American policy in Vietnam, but they all found themselves appalled at the violence, social disorder, and hot-headed attacks on American institutions that accompanied the anti-war movement and the associated politics of the new left, black militancy, and the counterculture of the 1960s. Although American involvement

114

in Vietnam was, for some neoconservatives, a mistake, for them it did not represent an indictment of the American system as it did for the new left. As in the 1950s, neoconservatives saw the primary threat to liberalism as coming from the left. This time, in the 1960s, the danger came from the new left's "mindless assault on the civic and social order," in Daniel Patrick Moynihan's phrase.[7] Used to the thrust and parry of learned and intricate policy debate, neoconservative intellectuals were aghast at the new left's essential lack of interest in this level of discussion. "Whenever I have mentioned [Social Security and Medicare] legislation in conversation," Irving Kristol wrote of his dealings with new left leaders in 1965, "I have received an icy stare of incomprehension and disdain, as if I were some kind of political idiot who actually believed what I read in the *New York Times*."[8] This is what prompted the neoconservatives to conceptualize the new left as an anti-intellectual, anti-liberal cultural movement, populated by true believers and masquerading as a political movement. As such, they believed it to be a movement without political responsibility.[9]

Apart from the civil rights struggle, which they supported more or less unreservedly, the politics of the 1960s, with its concern for all-embracing social justice and assertion of unconditional individual rights and private autonomy, its political and cultural intemperance and more than occasional violence, shocked the neoconservatives deeply. Professors Allan Bloom and Nathan Glazer, among others, railed against the takeovers of university campuses by student radicals and at what they saw as the radicals' attacks on academic freedom. They thought that campus radicals' justifications of their actions were alarmingly shallow and duplicitous.[10] And they seethed that older, established liberal intellectuals refused to defend such liberal principles as freedom of speech in the face of attack by campus activists. The neoconservatives were shaken by the new left's turn against Israel following the 1967 war, and were equally distressed by the increasing anti-Semitism of the black power movement. These factors prompted Jeane Kirkpatrick, the neoconservative professor turned diplomat, to conclude that it was the counterculture that created neoconservatism. The movement's "passionate rejection – less of what the U.S. did than of what it was – constituted a wholesale assault on the legitimacy of American society," she wrote, looking back in 2004. "I believe this assault became the foundation of the opposing neoconservative position."[11]

The new left saw the crisis of the 1960s as a crisis of American institutions – soulless capitalism, a runaway military-industrial complex, institutional racism, a neo-imperialist national security state

115

operating by technocratic rationality, a shallow advertising-driven and sexually repressed culture, a narrow and restricted form of democracy. The early new left rejected the liberal consensus as hypocritical: the country had not lived up to its promise to recognize equal rights. The later new left and black power movements went further: the liberal consensus was tainted by an original, essential racism and imperialism.[12] Neoconservatives judged these criticisms to be pure cant. To them, the real crisis of America was a crisis of authority and the decline of values and morals. New left radicals and the counterculture were judged to be both symptoms of a culture dangerously out of kilter and agents of its decline. Indeed, among others, Midge Decter assailed the parents of her own generation for pandering to such a spoiled and undisciplined cohort of over-privileged, ungrateful youth whose stock in trade was self-indulgence and the performance of a mindless "adversary culture."[13]

Jeane Kirkpatrick's observation was that neoconservatives, unlike the new left and black militants, were not fundamentally alienated from American life and society. Neoconservatives' trust in liberal institutions meant, as a general proposition, that they favored stability over any far-reaching change. Although they were distrustful of religious fundamentalism and political populism, neoconservatives came to appreciate the value of religion as a basis for virtue and morality, an imperative source of social cohesion. By contrast, they saw in radicalism, especially cultural radicalism, a threat to the liberal democratic order. Of course, some understood that this cultural radicalism was a consequence of the very success of the capitalist order, whose emphasis on consumption could not help but undermine the ascetic Protestant worldview and discipline that originally constituted that order.[14]

Although many neoconservatives developed their intellectual chops in discussions about Marxism, it was the republican virtue tradition associated with Alexis de Tocqueville toward which they gravitated. In that intellectual tradition, freedom and community are not in contradiction; rather, individual freedom is nourished and exercised in communities that, in turn, are created and maintained by the voluntary commitments of individuals.[15] Committed to moderation (even as in debate they engaged in heated, even vitriolic polemics), neoconservatives came to champion the intermediary institutions so dear to Tocqueville – the family especially, and the voluntary associations such as churches, neighborhoods, labor unions, universities. These are the settings wherein liberal democratic commitments, values, and behaviors are bred, where virtue is cultivated. These are the institutions that also serve to restrain the state. As it was for Leo Strauss, the University of Chicago political theorist who is often linked to neoconservative thought, individual moral virtue was a key concept and value. Virtue is the basis of the polity.

Many commentators have pointed to the Straussian origins of neoconservatism. Although there are many points of intersection, both at the level of persons and ideas between Strauss and neoconservatism, they are, however, hardly identical. Prominent first-generation neoconservatives who focused on foreign policy, such as Norman Podhoretz and Jeane Kirkpatrick, had little use for Strauss and his preoccupation with ancient and classical political theory. Still, some resonances are strong, and Strauss made a considerable impact on Irving Kristol. Strauss upheld the classical idea of a natural, hierarchic order and derided the modern, liberal idea of rights. The focus on rights, Strauss held, led to a culture of unlimited tolerance and nihilism. The trouble with modernity lay in its denial of truth, particularly moral truth. For these reasons, Strauss and neoconservatives shared an antipathy toward liberals. For neoconservatives, particularly of the second generation, Strauss's appeal lay in his sense of moral absolutism, which was not tied to any particular religious tradition.[16] Strauss's influence on foreign policy decision-making is usually discussed in terms of his tendency to view the world as a place where isolated liberal democracies live in constant danger from hostile elements abroad, and face threats that must be confronted vigorously and with strong leadership. And because ideas are hard for the common person to understand, philosophers must exercise strong leadership, and, in the words of one Strauss critic, need to "tell noble lies not only to the people at large but also to powerful politicians."[17]

Despite their ethnic resentments against the American white Anglo-Saxon Protestant establishment – Norman Podhoretz, for example, spoke disparagingly of the "WASP patriciate"[18] – neoconservatives paradoxically admired the traditional English Anglo-Saxon virtues that they saw as having defeated the Nazis: duty, honor, patriotism. Winston Churchill was a star in their firmament. But first-generation neoconservatives were decidedly not traditional, "small government" American conservatives. This was one of the features that made them "neo." They always accepted the New Deal and defended the welfare state as a legitimate means to stem the socio-economic instability and cultural disenchantment that inevitably accompanied industrial capitalism; they considered labor unions a legitimate and important counterweight to the power of the business corporation. They pointedly did not consider the growth of the state, as did the libertarian Friedrich Hayek, to be "the road to serfdom." Indeed, neoconservatives believed that government must act to promote the good life, and coercion sometimes must be exercised to ensure the triumph of the good. Neoconservatives tended to view hardcore libertarianism as essentially vapid. They shared with classical European conservatism an admiration for Edmund Burke's notions of historical continuity and the importance of habit, the idea that tradition embodies the wisdom of generations. Public signals through law, custom, and tradition are the key to getting people to behave well.[19] In this regard, neoconservatives aligned with the traditionalist strain of post-World War II conservative fusion of libertarianism and traditionalism: society was a community woven into a web of values and obligations binding individuals to one another. But neoconservatives had no patience with traditionalism's sometime agrarian nostalgia for the antebellum South. Neoconservatives were unabashed modernists. Thus, although the first generation of neoconservatives occasionally entered into debate with the political right, among other things supporting its anti-communism and condemning its ingrained anti-Semitism, its argument was really with the left.

In keeping with the intellectual pedigree associated with Tocqueville and Burke, neoconservatives came to harbor grave doubts about the welfare state programs of Lyndon Johnson's Great Society. In response to burgeoning anti-poverty programs created in the 1960s, Irving Kristol and Daniel Bell in 1965 launched *The Public Interest* to study the outcomes of the programs through empirical social science. (Nathan Glazer replaced Bell as Kristol's co-editor in 1973.) Typically, the studies published in the journal found that the majority of well-intentioned social programs had outcomes rather startling to their architects (if anticipated by more level-headed social scientists like the editors). Mostly, the programs had failed to achieve their goals of poverty reduction and racial integration. Worse, *The Public Interest* claimed that in their overreach the Great Society programs designed to feed, house, educate, and employ the disadvantaged often exacerbated existing problems or created new ones through unintended consequences. Indeed, governmental overreach and "the law of unintended consequences" of social policy became the watchwords of neoconservatism.

Although Daniel Patrick Moynihan's famous report on the African-American family did not appear in *The Public Interest*, it was emblematic of the kinds of studies that did appear in the journal, and Moynihan himself was a leading member of the neoconservative

118

intellectual universe. "The Negro Family: The Case for National Action" was a report written for the Department of Labor in 1965. It noted very high rates of illegitimate births, welfare participation, and single-parent families among African-Americans. Moynihan argued that the rise in single-mother families was due not to a lack of jobs but rather to a destructive trend in ghetto culture that could be traced back to slavery and Jim Crow discrimination. These had produced a "tangle of pathology" of delinquency, joblessness, school failure, crime, and, most devastating, fatherlessness.[20] To the extent that government policy provided welfare payments to families with fatherless dependent children, the policy added to the undermining of the basic socializing function of the family. Moynihan suspected that the risks were magnified in the case of African-Americans owing to the history of slavery and discrimination. "In essence," he wrote, "the Negro community has been forced into a matriarchal structure which, because it is so out of line with the rest of the American society, seriously retards the progress of the group as a whole, and imposes a crushing burden on the Negro male, and in consequence, on a great many Negro women as well." The Burkean baseline conception of the fundamental importance of the family was plain, as was the sense of the burden of history and the unintended consequences of social policy. The report triggered a furor. Moynihan was denounced in liberal circles for "blaming the victim," his warning about "family stability" an example of subtle racism. The uproar added greatly to the disgust with which neoconservatives regarded the report's left-liberal detractors.[21]

A slew of studies of other Great Society programs confirmed for neoconservatives the persistence of habit and settled mores, and the limits of what some began calling the "social engineering" associated with hubristic liberalism. Nathan Glazer and Thomas Sowell diagnosed affirmative action programs not only as a perversion of the original philosophy of nondiscrimination in favor of racial quotas, but as not working because they stigmatized their purported beneficiaries and erected perverse incentives for social advancement. State intervention on behalf of social equality must stop at the point of securing the equality of opportunity, they declared.[22] Earlier, in *Beyond the Melting Pot*, Glazer and Moynihan had argued that because of the continuing hold of racial and ethnic identity in American life, the liberal conception of integration was unlikely to be realized.[23] James Q. Wilson, showing how the role of the police in American cities had changed from maintaining order to fighting crimes, suggested that the forgotten link between order maintenance and crime prevention lay behind the great rise in urban crime in the 1960s.[24] In a famous follow-up article written with George L. Kelling, Wilson argued it was imprudent to believe that social policy could get at the alleged root causes of crime (poverty and racism). Rather, effective crime-fighting policies had to reestablish order by attending to short-term symptoms like fixing broken windows and removing graffiti.[25] Reflecting basic neoconservative tropes, Wilson argued that criminality is, at bottom, a function of character and socialization: people who acquire a decent degree of self-restraint and a fundamental regard for others tend not to engage in criminal behavior. "But for most social problems that deeply trouble us, the need is to explore, carefully and experimentally, ways of strengthening the formation of character among the very young. In the long run, the public interest depends on private virtue."[26] Again, virtue emerged as a central theme among neoconservatives, one that would bridge its first and the second generations.[27] Moynihan's oft-quoted 1986 aphorism on the relationship between culture and politics captured the intellectually serious, hard-headed approach of the first generation of neoconservatives. "The central conservative truth is that it is culture, not politics, that determines the success of a society. The central liberal truth is that politics can change a culture and save it from itself."[28]

The critique of the "New Class"

If the Great Society social programs didn't work as planned, what they did do, according to the neoconservatives, was generate a surfeit of experts and college-educated professionals employed in the public sector to devise them and carry them out. Convinced of their own goodness and efficacy and that of the programs they administered, these professionals became a powerful constituency for yet more programs and ever-larger government outlays. They advanced a perilous culture of entitlement. Indeed, the public sector and welfare state were, in the eyes of many neoconservatives, the liberal community's means to power. This move, from a serious questioning of liberalism's well-intentioned overreach to a variety of cheap, anti-intellectual populist critique, was pioneered by Irving Kristol. Drawing on his old Trotskyism, Kristol took as his basis Max Schachtman's theory of Stalinism as the ideology of a parasitic bureaucratic class that had corrupted socialism, channeling this into a critique of American liberal professionals. He labeled them "the New Class."[29] New Class theory didn't simply reflect a hidden, transformed Trotskyism, of course. The left-leaning populist tradition had long lauded virtuous "producers": that is, those who create tangible goods against the depredations of a white-collar elite that sponges off the producers' self-reliant efforts.[30] By the 1960s, moreover, distrust of the technocrats and the military and political elites who ran the Vietnam War was widespread among the left. The distrust on the left of experts reflected the broad cultural revolt against authority in the 1960s and was observable in egalitarian-based challenges to established authority in nearly every area of social practice.[31] What is curious was how the populist anti-elitist impulse migrated by the 1970s from the political left to the political right. The new manifestation of virtuous producers consisted of business and the (primarily white) working class, who were being victimized by a counterculture-influenced anti-capitalist elite cadre of public sector professionals, lawyers, teachers and academics, union officials, mass media, and liberal think tanks and foundations. It was the New Class that took over the Democratic Party under the banner of 1972 presidential nominee George McGovern, transforming liberalism, in Jeane Kirkpatrick's phrase, into "an ideology of the privileged."[32] The New Class oppressed virtuous producers from above; the recipients of the entitlements created by New Class-engineered government programs oppressed virtuous producers from below.

In his skewering of the New Class, Irving Kristol also attacked the idea of disinterested social science in the service of the national interest, a principle that had rested at the core of the post-World War II liberal consensus. The liberal consensus required an ethic of public duty on the part of America's elite, of securing the common good through disinterested government service.[33] But when New Class professionals and experts presented themselves as defenders of objective social science and champions of universal principles such as equality, they were disguising their true intentions, in Kristol's view.

This "new class" consists of scientists, lawyers, city planners, social workers, educators, criminologists, sociologists, public health doctors, etc. – a substantial number of whom find their careers in the expanding public sector rather than the private. The public sector, indeed, is where they prefer to be. They are, as one says, "idealistic," i.e., far less interested in individual financial rewards than in the corporate power of their class. Though they continue to speak the language of "progressive reform," in actuality they are acting upon a hidden agenda: to propel the nation from that modified version of capitalism we call "the welfare state" toward an economic system so stringently regulated in detail as to fulfill many of the traditional anti-capitalist aspirations of the Left.[34]

The New Class' "zealotry" for environmental protection and worker safety and the strict regulation of business revealed its true interests, wrote Robert L. Bartley, editor of the *Wall Street Journal* editorial page:

> In the midst of this kind of zealotry, it is not hard to locate the interests of the New Class, whose members populate, draw economic support from, and above all wield power in the name of the "public interest" groups and regulatory agencies. Indeed, when activists advocate a "no-growth economy," one in which the power of the business class would necessarily fall, and anyone with an upper-middle class income would be secure from the threat of social mobility, their intentions are quite clear: a society in which rewards would no longer be distributed in wealth, but in power and status, to be won by precisely those skills (abstraction, moralistic rhetoric, manipulation of symbols) in which the highly educated New Class excels.[35]

What began as sober empirical social science assessment of the outcome of specific public policies slipped into a broad, fairly malicious ideological critique not only of the efficacy of government in general, but also of the devious, self-serving nature of those who design, advocate, and carry out such policies. In their critique of the New Class, Kristol et al. ended up disparaging the entire edifice of progressive public policy since the Social Gospel, in effect exposing it as a fraud. Social science and liberal public policy had no objective basis, they insinuated; "expertise" was simply a mask for the elitist will to (leftist) power. Of course this attack on certain kinds of intellectuals and their so-called expertise couldn't be confined. The New Class critique fueled what became the anti-establishment conservative war on expertise and, eventually, in some hands, a war on evidence-based inquiry, including science itself.[36] The roots, in our time, of, for example, the climate change deniers, those who denounce the science of climate change as a political hoax, in no small measure lie in the neoconservative critique of the New Class.

The New Class thesis formed an intellectual bridge to other targets of conservative criticism that bubbled up in the 1970s. It piggybacked effortlessly onto the attack on the growth of government (particularly the federal government), as well as the hazards, futility, and outsized costs of the regulation of business.[37] The New Class critique not only rebuked the public sector and the culture of entitlement, it also channeled a new appreciation for businessmen and the virtues of market capitalism. For, unlike New Class spongers and welfare recipients, business and businessmen created value.[38] All these tropes were part of a broader narrative of recuperation of capitalism's reputation. Business had been put on the defensive in the late 1960s and early 1970s, criticized by the civil rights and public interest and consumer movements for racial discrimination, environmental pollution, unsafe products and workplaces. The increase in the number of regulatory agencies and the broader purview of regulatory oversight of business were testaments to this liberal democratic, if not anti-corporate, political mobilization.[39] By the mid-1970s, business was engaged in a counter-offensive through new lobbying organizations and the funding of new organs of intellectual production, including distinctly conservative legal foundations.[40] The formation of the Business Roundtable and a reinvigorated Chamber of Commerce, the new conservative think tanks and political lobbies described in chapter 2, were a major part of this business counter-offensive.

The alliance with the religious right

Another strain of the counter-offensive focused on the New Class's permissiveness in the arenas of culture and personal behavior. The cultural excess of the New Class, its narcissism, its unbounded pleasure seeking – all features of the "untrammeled self" that exposed the New Class's overall lack of virtue – tainted virtually all the areas of the culture touched by its members.[41] Ultimately, neoconservatives began to blame the "crisis of the 1960s" on the adversarial, decadent, subversive, and fundamentally naïve New Class. For the neoconservatives, the crisis of contemporary America – and to neoconservatives the United States since the 1960s seemed *always* to be in crisis – was a crisis of values, morals, and manners. America's liberal capitalist order was precarious, threatened by the nihilism of the counterculture. It was natural, then, that neoconservatives, Irving Kristol foremost, began sidling up to the religious right. This alignment was perhaps initially more for strategic political purposes than true intellectual ones, but eventually it became so on the merits. Kristol's longstanding wariness of populist movements vanished by the 1980s. Because he saw religion as an indispensable constraint to antisocial impulses, and thus a utilitarian foundation for liberal democracy, he

123

and others began to view the religious right with favor. Kristol found in contemporary conservative movements, including the new Christian right, an expression of the "common sense – not the passion, but the common sense" of the American people against the "unwisdom of its governing elites – whether elected, appointed, or (as with the media) self-appointed."[42] Lending support to conservative evangelicals' objection to the teaching of evolution in the public schools, Kristol echoed its canard that Darwinism was simply a "theory," far from an established scientific fact.[43] Joining with the Moral Majority and its allies in conservative Catholic circles (the author Michael Novak and the priest and writer Richard John Neuhaus most prominently), Kristol agreed that secular humanism was the real danger to the United States.[44] He came to champion conservative evangelicals because, in his view, they "see, quite clearly and correctly, that statism in America is organically linked with secular liberalism – that many of the programs and activities of the welfare state have a powerful antireligious animus."[45] Kristol thus echoed the charge that religion was subject to discrimination in contemporary America, that the religious were victims of secularism. Like the progressivism of the New Class, secularism was simply another self-serving belief system – but a devious one because it rested on claims of universality.

Conservative evangelical support of Israel was another important element in winning the allegiance of many neoconservatives. A pro-Israel *Realpolitik* found Kristol defending the public anti-Semitic remarks of preachers Bailey Smith and Jerry Falwell in 1984. "After all, why should Jews care about the theology of a fundamentalist preacher when they do not for a moment believe that he speaks with any authority on the question of God's attentiveness to human prayer? And what do such theological abstractions matter as against the mundane fact that this same preacher is vigorously pro-Israel?"[46] Other neoconservatives adopted Kristol's reasoning. Norman Podhoretz and Midge Decter, for example, posted apologies for Pat Robertson's anti-Semitism, claiming it was unimportant, trumped by his and the Christian Coalition's support for Israel.[47]

Kristol was hardly alone in allying with the new Christian right agenda. *Commentary*, for decades a serious magazine dedicated to probing contemporary politics and culture, also began to reflect the increasing ideological convergence between neoconservatives and the new Christian right. Transformed under longtime editor Norman Podhoretz into a vehicle of neoconservative thought, *Commentary* consistently published pieces "exposing" the left and

political correctness, attacking feminism, and savaging the homosexual lifestyle. Homosexuals, exclaimed *Commentary*, were intent
on destroying the family and, with it, western civilization. The magazine featured articles on religion as underpinning freedom and
extolling the vital role of religion in the blessed American ethos.
Contributing writers railed against pornography and homosexuality,
reviled the critics of Israel, and blamed AIDS victims for their condition. These were nothing if not hot buttons in the culture war pressed
by the new Christian right. In short, neoconservative polemics on
values and virtue echoed the positions of the religious right. The
public discourse of both the neoconservatives and the intellectuals of
the religious right evinced a similar lacerating rhetorical style of
attack and, increasingly, similar content.

If the linkages between the new Christian right and neoconservatives began as intellectual affinities, the groups soon began to share
material resources, including funding sources and institutional networks. Among other organizations they formed the well-funded
Washington-based Institute on Religion and Democracy (IRD),
whose stock in trade was the slashing media-savvy attack on the
foreign policy positions and foreign mission programs of mainline
Protestant denominations. The IRD was especially vicious about
mainline Protestant objections to Reagan administration policies in
Central America, including administration support for the Nicaraguan Contras. The IRD's attacks were designed to delegitimize mainline criticism of American foreign policy – in many respects a
continuation of the decades-long conservative evangelical denunciation of mainline liberalism in the foreign policy arena.[48] One
informed commentator called the IRD's particular combination of
Christianity and democracy an effort to "baptize Reaganism."[49]
Established in 1981, the IRD received almost $5 million between
1985 and 2005 from the same conservative foundations (Sarah
Scaife, Bradley, Olin, Carthage) that bankrolled the conservative
think tanks.[50]

The IRD was just one of the more visible organizations in a broad
effort by the right to undermine liberal institutions in the political
sphere and take them over in the religious sphere. Steven Tipton's
Public Pulpits provides an in-depth account of the effort of conservative evangelicals to take over the leadership of the United Methodist
Church.[51] Damon Linker traces the many connections – intellectual
and material – among the circle of the religious intelligentsia and
neoconservative-affiliated magazines and think tanks, and the foundations that supported both groupings.[52] A prominent figure in both

camps was Richard John Neuhaus. Neuhaus fashioned himself a bridge between the religious right and neoconservatives, on one hand, and between conservative Catholics and right-wing Protestant evangelicals, on the other. He and his Catholic intellectual compatriot Michael Novak began their intellectual journeys as religious supporters of the new left. They shifted to a religious political conservatism in the 1970s. Novak's *The Spirit of Democratic Capitalism* was an effort to show that the system of American capitalism embodied biblical precepts and was an expression of divine beneficence.[53] Neuhaus's *The Naked Public Square* was a bold manifesto condemning the fact that public discourse in the United States had been shorn of religious reason. The fundamental mistake, Neuhaus declared, is the assumption that the United States is a secular society. Secularism poses the gravest of dangers to the country. *The Naked Public Square* essentially put in more moderate, acceptably scholarly form the arguments proffered by new Christian right stalwarts Jerry Falwell and Tim LaHaye.[54] A seemingly reasonable, quiet extremism was Neuhaus's particular talent, which he played out regularly in his journal, *First Things*. With former Watergate felon-turned-prison evangelical Charles Colson, Neuhaus initiated the high-level consultation between Catholics and evangelical Protestants that resulted in "Evangelicals and Catholics Together – The Christian Mission in the Third Millennium" (1994), pledging to pass laws against abortion, euthanasia, and pornography. Neuhaus's Institute on Religion and Public Life provided intellectual heft for the religious right agenda, especially through *First Things*.[55] Between 1989 and 2005, the Institute on Religion and Public Life received over $8 million from the conservative foundations.[56]

Foreign policy: The tough anti-communist realism of neoconservatism's first generation

The neoconservative orientation toward foreign policy was usually coupled to its diagnosis of the domestic crisis in the United States. Radicalism at home undermined the pivotal struggle against communist expansionism abroad. Communism, and particularly the Soviet Union, posed an existential threat to freedom. As Norman Podhoretz put it in his 1980 book, *The Present Danger*, "[T]he Soviet Union is not a nation like any other. It is a revolutionary state, exactly as Hitler's Germany was, in the sense that it wishes to create a new international order in which it would be the dominant power and whose character would be determined by its national wishes and its ideological dictates."[57] If Irving Kristol was the leading voice in domestic affairs for the first generation of neoconservatives, Podhoretz was that voice in foreign policy. Podhoretz, too, began on the political left. During his first years as editor of *Commentary*, the magazine reflected his interest in the left avant-garde, featuring articles by the likes of Paul Goodman, Michael Harrington, Staughton Lynd, and James Baldwin. By the late 1960s, Podhoretz broke with the left, and *Commentary* reflected his rightward shift. *The Present Danger* expressed in more measured tones the heated foreign policy positions – diatribes even – which he had expounded for many years in *Commentary* and other publications.[58]

The Present Danger provides a window on neoconservatism's foreign policy outlook. Podhoretz's text constructs a succinct overview of post-war American foreign policy and the rise of a weak and dangerous policy of "appeasement." The book begins with praise for President Harry Truman's policy of containment and its early manifestation in the establishment of NATO. Truman and Eisenhower's commitment of American troops to repel North Korea was also commended – but for the fact that their administrations stopped at containment rather than a rollback to liberate subject peoples under communist oppression. American entrance into Vietnam under President Kennedy was consonant with containment policy. Podhoretz believed that containment policy derived from the "lesson" of Munich: never appease aggression. But the containment of communism in Vietnam, according to Podhoretz, was rendered problematic by the overlay of the Vietnamese fight against French imperialism. America's involvement in Vietnam was not discolored by the stain of imperialism, however; U.S. intervention stemmed from the sincere, altruistic desire to repel communism.[59] For Podhoretz, the grievous American defeat in Vietnam was due to circumstance (not the least of which was the domestic anti-war movement), not from bad motives or morals.

It was the aftermath of the Vietnam War that preoccupied Podhoretz. In the face of eventual defeat in Vietnam, the Nixon administration initiated a policy of "strategic retreat" – not just from Vietnam but from containment policy in general, in Podhoretz's view. Nixon and Kissinger championed détente with the Soviet Union. Détente meant cooperation, rather than confrontation, between the two superpowers. In Podhoretz's interpretation, Nixon believed – or hoped – that a linkage of surrogate force and positive economic and political incentives would be enough to restrain Soviet adventurism.

But this hope was desperately naïve, for the Soviet Union had entered into a period of imperial dynamism and was building up its arms and lining up its proxies to engage in subversion all over the globe. The United States, plagued by post-Vietnam syndrome, was recklessly cutting its military arsenal and entering into arms limitation treaties that favored the Soviet Union. By the time Jimmy Carter occupied the White House, containment policy was a relic, according to Podhoretz. The absence of American reaction to Soviet military interventions in the horn of Africa in the mid- to late 1970s confirmed to neoconservative critics that the United States was making too many concessions in order to safeguard détente. The Soviet invasion of Afghanistan and the fall of the Shah in Iran (which Podhoretz intimated would end with Iran allying with the Soviet Union) confirmed the bankruptcy of post-Vietnam foreign policy: "[T]he United States had lost its nerve and could now be taken on with impunity."[60]

Podhoretz's unyielding support of U.S. policy in Vietnam differed from some of his neoconservative compatriots, but his savage critique of the anti-war movement and his disgust with former Cold War liberals who found themselves chastened by the Vietnam debacle resonated strongly with most neoconservatives and others on the political right. In Podhoretz's view, the domestic anti-war (and later nuclear freeze) agenda had triumphed, instantiating in the political culture a malevolent combination of pacifism, anti-Americanism, and isolationism. This represented a "culture of appeasement." It meant the essential capitulation of the United States in the face of Soviet expansionism. In characteristically overheated prose, Podhoretz wrote in *The Present Danger*:

> Soon enough, perhaps by the date chosen by [George] Orwell's pro-phetic soul – when to their political ambition to dominate the West would have been added the Soviets' own economic need for Middle Eastern oil – the President of the United States, whoever he might be, would have to choose between nuclear war or Soviet control over the oil supply of the West. By then the vulnerability of our missiles to a Soviet first strike would automatically dictate surrender – checkmate by telephone, as someone has called it.
>
> [W]e would know by what name to call the new era into which we have entered (though it would be an essential feature of that era that we would be forbidden to mention its name aloud): the Finlandization of America, the political and economic subordination of the United States to superior Soviet power.[61]

Podhoretz articulated the key lesson that neoconservatives drew from the history of American foreign policy: bad things happen because of American weakness. The post-Vietnam culture of appeasement reflected and reinforced the enormity that America had lost faith in itself and its values. This theme recycled a central premise of Barry Goldwater's 1960 campaign book, *Conscience of a Conservative*, and thus began to reveal that on some key foreign policy principles there was increasingly little ideological distance between neoconservatives and Goldwater conservatives. Anxious about its role in the world and insecure in the use of its military, the United States was beset by cowardice; it had become the "pitiful, helpless giant" that President Nixon had warned about in 1970.[62] The culture of appeasement was not simply the result of the influence of the new left and the peace wing of the Democratic Party. The reviled culture of appeasement was due – again, the familiar trope – to the failure of liberals to defend liberalism. Neoconservatives disparaged liberal intellectuals such as Arthur Schlesinger, Jr. and John Kenneth Galbraith, whose support of the anti-war wing of the Democratic Party was seen as apostasy.

The Vietnam War, of course, exploded the liberal foreign policy consensus that had married liberal internationalism with balance-of-power realism in the paramount aim of containing communism. The presumed "capture" of the Democratic Party by George McGovern's anti-interventionist peace wing led neoconservatives to conclude that Democrats had gone soft and now shrank from the duty to confront Soviet aggression. Some neoconservatives abandoned their historic loyalty to the Democratic Party and supported Richard Nixon for president in 1972. Many eventually defected to the GOP permanently. The perceived weakness of the United States was highlighted by the maddening and cynical diplomacy that took place at the United Nations. Neoconservative writing in the 1970s and 1980s displayed exasperation at the anti-American and anti-Israel posturing in U.N. forums by communist and Third World governments. No instance more exercised neoconservatives than the 1974 U.N. resolution condemning Zionism as a form of racism, a campaign led by Ugandan strongman Idi Amin. Such appalling resolutions were adopted because, in the absence of a clear U.S. foreign policy after Vietnam, duplicitous communist and Third World dictators could successfully manipulate the diplomatic process. In this respect, Soviet and Third World manipulation of diplomacy was, again, a consequence of the inability or unwillingness of American liberals to defend liberal, realist principles. As Irving Kristol lamented, the problem with American diplomacy was that it had taken a "global point of view" rather than an American one. That perspective, he argued, was the legacy of "a debased and vulgarized Wilsonianism" wedded to "the utopian notion that the ultimate and governing purpose of American foreign policy is to establish a world community of nations all living amiably under the rule of law."[63] As Kristol put it, "We are a strong nation, and they [Third World nations] will respect our strength, as well as our loyalty to our own political and social ideals, when we behave in a self-respecting way."[64] Capitulating to bad people and bad nations via diplomatic blandishments simply emboldens them.

Implacably anti-communist and realist in foreign policy orientation, the first generation of neoconservatives battled détente and arms control agreements throughout the 1970s and formed organizations calling for the massive rebuilding of the American military. Three organizations in particular reflected neoconservative aims to beat back the culture of appeasement and restore American fortitude: the Coalition for a Democratic Majority (CDM), the Committee on the Present Danger (CPD), and "Team B." The Coalition for a Democratic Majority was a group formed under the leadership of Senate Armed Services Committee Chairman Henry M. "Scoop" Jackson to take back the Democratic Party from its peace wing.[65] Jackson had long served as a hawkish focal point within the Democratic Party for the continuance of Cold War liberal anti-communism. Several young neoconservatives such as Richard Perle, Paul Wolfowitz, Elliott Abrams, and Douglas Feith – the second generation of the neoconservative movement – got their start in Washington politics working in Jackson's offices over the years, toiling against détente and arms control. The Committee on the Present Danger, formed to warn that America's defenses were disintegrating in the face of strong Soviet threat, revived a moribund organization begun in the 1950s. Founding members were Deputy Defense Secretary Paul Nitze and former Under Secretary for Political Affairs Eugene Rostow, and included Donald Rumsfeld, Richard Perle, William Casey, Richard Allen, Norman Podhoretz, Lane Kirkland, Richard Pipes, and Max Kampelman, representing an alliance of realist hawks, neoconservatives, and a smattering of Cold War anti-communist liberal internationalists who opposed arms limitation agreements with the Soviet Union. The CPD contended that like Nazi Germany, the Soviet Union was by nature expansionist, and thus arms control only hindered the ability of the United States to protect itself.[66] Détente only served to legitimize Soviet communism, and allowed the USSR to keep itself on a military par with the vastly more economically productive United States.

The revitalization of the Committee on the Present Danger grew out of the creation of an independent group authorized in 1976 by President Gerald Ford to develop an independent judgment of Soviet capabilities and intentions. The same political environment propelled the formation of "Team B." Team B was organized by then CIA Chief George H.W. Bush to review charges leveled by Albert Wohlstetter, the RAND Corporation and University of Chicago military intellectual who in the late 1950s had been part of an effort warning the Eisenhower administration of a "bomber gap" and "missile gap" vis-à-vis the USSR. Wohlstetter accused the CIA in 1974 of systematically underestimating Soviet missile deployment.[67] Bush tasked an independent set of analysts ("Team B") to check the research of the CIA ("Team A"). Headed by Harvard historian and détente critic Richard Pipes, the group included several hard-line military policy and hawkish arms negotiation veterans, including retired Army Lieutenant General Daniel O. Graham, former Deputy Defense Secretary Paul Nitze, and defense staffer Paul Wolfowitz. Team B argued that the CIA had assumed a fundamentally false mirroring of motives of the United States and the Soviet Union, whereas in fact the USSR had never altered its long-held goal of world domination. Unlike the United States, the Soviet Union planned to fight and win a nuclear war.[68] Team B's finding that the Soviets were moving ahead of the United States in military capabilities, and its recommendation for the immediate massive build-up of American armed forces, reflected much of what defense hawks and neoconservatives had been arguing for years. In fact, Team B's projections of Soviet military strength turned out to be vastly exaggerated. The report projected that by 1984 the Soviets would have 500 Backfire bombers; they built 235. Team B predicted that by 1985 the Soviets would have replaced 90 percent of their long-range bombers and missiles; they replaced less than 60 percent. Despite warnings of huge Soviet military outlays, in fact the growth in Soviet military spending slowed in the mid-1970s and was flat for the next decade.[69]

The Committee on the Present Danger, the Coalition for a Democratic Majority, and Team B duly reflected the hawkish realist position on military strategy since the end of World War II – that the Soviet Union, evil and expansionist, was outstripping America's military, particularly its nuclear arsenal. In response, neoconservatives and other hawks maintained, the United States had to increase its arsenal and plan counterforce measures, including possible first-strike capability. The latter policy was rooted in the conviction that a nuclear war could be limited and was winnable. This position, based on the abstract game theory modeling championed by the RAND Corporation and on self-serving and grossly exaggerated estimates of Soviet strength by the Air Force and the Navy, justified massive increases in military spending.[70]

Together, these groups constituted a conservative policy echo chamber and an influential shadow defense establishment during the Carter years. The Team B report was released a month after Jimmy Carter won the 1976 election, and the Republican right used it against him throughout his presidency.[71] Conservatives of all stripes objected to the Carter administration's liberal internationalist focus on human rights and its drift from foreign policy realism. Carter's insistence on human rights as a central plank in American foreign policy represented an intrusion of religious sensibility into the usually cold, calculating, amoral realist foreign policy paradigm, and was met initially with outrage and scorn from neo- and other conservatives. First-generation neoconservatives saw Carter as having a leftist hidden agenda that dangerously skewed foreign policy in ways that penalized America's allies and thus undermined vigilance against Soviet expansion. They judged both foolish and perilous Carter's conceptual shift in foreign policy from East–West superpower rivalry to North–South economic development issues. The most prominent exemplar of this stance was Jeane Kirkpatrick. Her essay "Dictatorships and Double Standards," about the fundamental difference between authoritarian and totalitarian regimes and published in *Commentary* in 1979, brought her to the attention of Ronald Reagan and was responsible for her subsequent appointment as U.S. Ambassador to the United Nations.

A foreign policy based on human rights lost us Iran, wrote Kirkpatrick, and was about to lose us Nicaragua. Both the Shah of Iran and Nicaraguan president Anastasio Somoza were traditional rulers of traditional societies, corrupt but fiercely anti-communist and friendly toward the United States. Their fates fit a distinctive political pattern, Kirkpatrick lamented. The pattern went roughly like this: internal subversion, usually by communists, and the repressive reaction to it by the government in power, results in widespread violence in a moderately authoritarian, pro-U.S. country. In the wake of this violence, the absence of an opposition party prompts American liberals to question the morality of continuing aid to the rightist dictatorship. U.S. aid and backing are now seen as inconsistent with our support for democracy and human rights. Aid is withheld, weakening the leader, but efforts at engineering a moderate replacement come to nothing. Anarchy reigns and the insurgents take over. In sum, liberal misunderstanding of the situation inadvertently leads it to assist in deposing an erstwhile friend and ally and installing a proto-communist government hostile to American interests.[72]

In Kirkpatrick's eyes, President Carter and his foreign policy team failed to understand the fundamental truth that communism is different. *Authoritarian* regimes may be corrupt, but they permit the rudiments of civil society, including, nominally, political parties, an independent press, and voluntary associations. But because *totalitarian* regimes by nature are in the utopian business of remaking human beings, they destroy civil society and the independent institutions that form the foundations for democracy. In Kirkpatrick's view, "Only intellectual fashion and the tyranny of Right/Left thinking prevent intelligent men of good will from perceiving the *facts* that traditional authoritarian governments are less repressive than revolutionary autocracies, that they are more susceptible of liberalization, and that they are more compatible with U.S. interests."[73] Communist and left-leaning regimes are never held to the human rights principles the United States applies to right-wing authoritarian regimes – hence the "double standard." Irving Kristol opined similarly, "It would also be nice if the Carter administration would disengage itself from the double standard, whereby left-wing governments are given the benefit of every doubt as concerns human rights while right-wing regimes are continually indicted. Nothing could more effectively make a mockery of the entire issue."[74] The Carter administration's naïve commitment to a foreign policy outlook of liberal internationalism led it to accept at face value the claim of revolutionary groups to represent "popular" aspirations and "progressive" forces – and thus deliver troubled U.S. allies into the hands of the Soviets.

In point of fact, Carter's foreign policy still rested on the time-honored view that the United States had a responsibility to spread liberal democracy and American values. He just didn't trumpet the overt military commitment of his predecessor exceptionalists. But Carter reconsidered the wisdom of détente late in his presidency and, under the influence of his National Security Adviser, Zbigniew Brzezinski, began increasing military spending and supporting groups that opposed Soviet proxies in Africa and Asia.[75] Nonetheless, his right-wing critics had defined him, and Carter's late hawkishness was not enough to dispel the perceptions of his own weakness and the weakness of the United States under his guidance. For a variety of reasons, not least the ramifications of the 1979 Iranian revolution and hostage crisis, and the widespread belief that the Soviet Union's interventions in the Third World (especially the invasion of Afghanistan in late 1979) had to be stopped, Ronald Reagan trounced Carter in the 1980 election.

Neoconservatives now had a say in Washington. Podhoretz's *The Present Danger* was reputed to have been influential in the new Reagan White House, and several *Commentary* contributors and other neoconservatives became high-level functionaries in that administration. In the account of one scholar, thirty-two members of the Committee on the Present Danger were appointed to key posts in national security-related portfolios.[76] Reagan had long been a determined critic of détente and of the Soviet Union, and he set confronting Soviet expansion in the Third World as a top foreign policy priority. But, although they lauded Reagan's presidency and tried to claim his mantle later, many neoconservatives complained about Reagan almost as much as they did Jimmy Carter. They adored Reagan's build-up of the American military, his administration's campaign to destroy leftist movements in Central America, its wariness of the nuclear freeze movement, and the president's occasional oratorical bluster about the "Evil Empire" (a signature speech given to the 1983 annual convention of the National Association of Evangelicals).[77] But as the historian John Patrick Diggins and others argue, Reagan was a shrewd politician whose hard-line rhetoric often masked a foreign policy pragmatism. Reagan actually believed in arms control; he employed the soft diplomacy of dialogue to this end. His administration's military build-up served to better position the United States in arms control negotiations with the Soviets – which was always the goal, and not, as neoconservatives wanted, the rollback of communism.[78]

Through much of the 1980s, neoconservatives fretted, wrung their hands, and declared disappointment with Reagan. Norman Podhoretz in particular lamented that among other disappointments Reagan had failed to commit troops to battle against Soviet expansionism in Latin America and Africa, did not establish an economic embargo against Poland and the Soviet Union in support of the Solidarity Trade Union uprising in the Polish crisis of 1981–2, and had condemned Israel's settlement policy in occupied Palestinian territory.[79] When Reagan began negotiating with Soviet leader Mikhail Gorbachev over reductions in nuclear arsenals and possibly sharing missile defense technology, neoconservatives veritably blanched in horror. They were appalled at Reagan's naïveté. The Soviet Union was irredeemably evil and supremely powerful; Gorbachev was a cunning Leninist who had figured out how to strengthen the Soviet empire and psychologically disarm the West.[80] As Diggins notes, although neoconservatives questioned the use of state power in the domestic sphere, they never thought to question it in foreign affairs. Reagan did, to their great chagrin. It was only with the surprise demise of the Soviet Union in 1991 (largely as a consequence of Gorbachev's efforts to reform the Soviet system from within) that neoconservatives changed their tune on Reagan and clamored to anoint themselves his heirs.[81] In their revised view, Reagan not only had always been a stalwart in the effort to demolish the Soviet Union, it was his administration's tough actions that accomplished the monumental deed. This was encapsulated in the triumphal motto that "Reagan won the Cold War." This shorthand embodied Jeane Kirkpatrick's fallacious conclusion that communist regimes were incapable of internal change and that only American will and steadfast coercion could have transformed the Soviet Union.

The post-Cold War neoconservative rift: Reserved realism vs. crusading internationalism

The disintegration of the Soviet bloc and the implosion of the USSR created a generational rift within neoconservatism. With the end of the Cold War, the first generation of neoconservatives, relentlessly and unbendingly anti-communist, drifted back to a more reserved foreign policy realism and began to advocate a more modest American presence in the world. Jeane Kirkpatrick wrote in 1990 that America's purposes are "mainly domestic." "It is not within the United States' power to democratize the world.... The time when Americans should bear unusual burdens is past. With a return to 'normal' times, we can again become a normal nation.... Most of the international obligations that we assumed were once important are now outdated."[82] Nathan Glazer argued similarly. "In promoting and recommending those universal principles to which we are attached," he wrote, "it is now time to withdraw to something closer to the modest role that the Founding Fathers intended."[83] American foreign policy should now identify vital national interests, pay nominal attention to other matters and events, and give up its crusading moralism, Irving Kristol opined.[84] To the extent that the administration of Bill Clinton followed the human rights-based liberal internationalism begun under Jimmy Carter, the first generation of neoconservatives criticized it as simply more crusading Wilsonianism, captured perhaps best in the contemptuous phrase of Michael Mandelbaum (not a neoconservative), "foreign policy as social work."[85]

But for the second generation of neoconservatives, figures such as Richard Perle, William Kristol (Irving's son), Douglas Feith, Paul Wolfowitz, Joshua Muravchik, Carl Gershman, Ben Wattenberg, Zalmay Khalilzad, Francis Fukuyama, Robert Kagan, Lawrence Kaplan, and Daniel Pipes (Richard's son), to name the most visible, the human rights-based interventionism of Clinton's foreign policy was a feature to be applauded. Against the foreign policy establishment realists and, for that matter, most of their own neoconservative forebears, the second generation advocated moralism and idealism in foreign policy. It was foreign policy that preoccupied them. Domestic politics seemed almost an afterthought for them, a subject worthy of attention only to the extent that it put the right people in office.

Francis Fukuyama's 1989 essay, "The End of History?" set the tone. With the fall of the Berlin Wall and the emergence of marketization of the economy in China, the end of the twentieth century marked the triumph of the West. Fukuyama labeled it "the end of history": that is, the unabashed victory of economic and political liberalism that marked the conclusion of the long struggle between rival ideological systems. This outcome was definitively not the result of any deterministic materialism or the material superiority of capitalism. Rather, paying homage to the nineteenth-century German philosopher Hegel, Fukuyama argued that this outcome was the result of victory in the realm of consciousness and values. He was careful to state that the triumph of liberalism did not mean the end of conflict. Religious fundamentalism and nationalism still had punch and could foment terrorism and wars of national liberation. Still, large-scale conflict was now a thing of the past because the great states necessary for it were passing into "post-history."[86] And implicitly, because the dangers of large-scale conflict were disappearing, U.S. foreign policy could be geared toward calming international hot spots purely on the basis of liberal values.

This second generation of neoconservatives, who had none of the lingering attachment to the Democratic Party of their forebears and no ambivalence identifying with the right, paradoxically tended to support Bill Clinton over George H.W. Bush in the presidential election of 1992. Bush hewed to a classic realist foreign policy. Whereas he had galvanized the international community to invade Iraq in the 1990–1 Gulf War, his administration refused to march American troops to Baghdad to overthrow Saddam Hussein or provide backing to the Kurdish and Shiite rebellions against Saddam's regime. Bush administration realists had no truck with calls to intervene in Somalia or Bosnia, or tangle with China in response to the 1989 Tiananmen

Square massacre. Their cautious realism was anathema to the emerging vision of neoconservatism's second generation, which displayed an expansive faith in American power.[87] U.S. global leadership had to "challenge regimes hostile to our interests and values" and "promote the cause of political and economic freedom abroad," according to the Project for the New American Century (PNAC), perhaps the most important umbrella group of the new muscular, post-Cold War orientation. PNAC's Statement of Principles married some of the main tenets of liberal internationalism to neoconservative goals. Now the sole superpower at the end of the Cold War, the United States should permit no military rival, and needed to remain the "unipolar" power. The United States had "a unique role in preserving and extending an international order friendly to our security, our prosperity, and our principles."[88] In practical terms, this translated into calls for substantial increases in the military budget, support for missile defense systems, and a foreign policy dedicated to transformation, not coexistence; for "regime change," not mere stability and containment; for an aggressive unipolar internationalism rather than a balance of power realism. The fall of the Soviet Union created the possibility of a unipolar peace, a Pax Americana.[89] Because American interests were tied inextricably to universal liberal values, any transformation of bad political regimes was a blessing to the world as well as a benefit to the United States.

This view had surfaced publicly for a brief moment in 1992 in the form of the Defense Department Planning Guidance (DPG) document, written by a team under the imprimatur of then Secretary of Defense Dick Cheney during the George H.W. Bush presidency. The document stressed that the United States should not allow the emergence of a new rival power and should be prepared to strike unilaterally and preemptively at any nation's capacity to produce weapons of mass destruction (WMD). The DPG paper further maintained that the United States no longer needed alliances and should build a Strategic Defense Initiative (missile defense) system. In other words, the document dumped the post-World War II policy of collective internationalism in favor of a policy of unipolarity and ("benevolent") domination by the United States. The classified document circulated for several weeks at senior levels in the Pentagon, but controversy erupted after it was leaked to the *New York Times* and the *Washington Post*, and the White House ordered Defense Secretary Cheney to rewrite it.[90] The congruity between PNAC's Statement of Principles and the DPG report was not accidental. The DPG report was drafted principally by Undersecretary of Defense for Policy Paul Wolfowitz with strong input from I. Lewis Libby and Zalmay Khalilzad – all of whom later signed the PNAC document (and all of whom, with Cheney, went on to positions of high responsibility in the administration of George W. Bush).

One specific expression of the distinctively neoconservative combination of moralist idealism and unipolar militarism was the demand to topple Iraqi strongman Saddam Hussein. Second-generation neoconservatives judged unpardonable the senior Bush's decision not to send troops to Baghdad to take out Saddam Hussein at the close of the Gulf War. Saddam's murderous regime was so discredited, deceptive, and dangerous, wrote Richard Perle among others, that it no longer could be considered a legitimate government. Long-term stability in the region required an American strategy to bring down Saddam and rid the Middle East of his weapons of mass destruction.[91] The failure to do so during the Gulf War was a missed opportunity. Indeed, younger neoconservatives judged it the worst feature in a "squandered decade." The United States could have shaped the international system in the 1990s in ways that would advance its values and interests without opposition from a powerful, determined adversary, but had failed to do so.[92] It wasn't that Democrats and liberals didn't also cleave to the hoary messianic chestnuts of American exceptionalism and the transformative power of democracy. The Clinton administration recognized the sole superpower status of the United States after the fall of the Soviet Union – Secretary of State Madeleine Albright spoke often of the United States as the "indispensable nation."[93] But in the eyes of the neoconservatives, Clinton did not follow through on the proper implications of unipolarity. His foreign interventions were both anemic and fatally flawed because they relied on international institutions. Paul Wolfowitz, a future architect of the Iraq War, was scathing in his criticisms of Clinton's vacillating policy toward Iraq and the former Yugoslavia, and condemned Clinton's failure to deploy the American military in those situations.[94]

Second-generation neoconservatives called for intervention in the Balkans to stop Serb aggression. In this they shared the moral motivations of liberal internationalists but rejected the latter's stance of working through multilateral institutions. In effect, neoconservatives drew sustenance from the human rights-based policy of military intervention pursued desultorily by the Clinton administration, even as they savaged Clinton's actual practice of it. The failure of NATO and the United Nations to halt Serb aggression and ethnic cleansing in the Balkans was, to second-generation neoconservatives, an object lesson in why the United States had to exercise military power on its own. The neoconservatives felt utterly vindicated after the Balkan wars ended. The international institutions such as UNPROFOR and NATO had presided over a series of disasters. Only the U.S. military, with its unambiguous command structure and precision-guided bombs capable of inflicting heavy damage with limited civilian casualties, had proved capable of deterring the Serbs.[95] Further, the lesson about precision bombs proved correct the theories of Albert Wohlstetter, who had mentored several of the younger neoconservatives. Wohlstetter, the hugely influential defense analyst, had consistently argued over the years that Mutually Assured Destruction nuclear policy made for insufficient protection. Genuine safety lay in always finding more effective ways to use force. It was the new military capability of smart bombs that reinforced the idea among second-generation neoconservatives that the exercise of American military power was a policy option of the first order (and that later convinced Secretary of Defense Donald Rumsfeld that the United States could conquer Iraq quickly, with limited military forces, and on the cheap).[96]

The Balkan experience's confirmation of the uselessness of international institutions, in turn, reinforced neoconservative beliefs in U.S. unipolarity and the rightness of the American rebuff of old European allies. Robert Kagan's *Of Paradise and Power* best captured this sentiment (although his articulation was far milder than the often pejorative neoconservative denunciations of Europe). In this view, Western Europe is a "free rider," comfortably benefiting from the U.S. military umbrella after a horrific century of bloody conflict. Europe has generated a set of beliefs and multilateral institutions that play down conflict and protect its social democratic prosperity and quiet. Increasingly, Europe and the United States find themselves in conflict over international relations and the perception of dangers. Europe sees the United States as high-handed, unilateralist, and unnecessarily belligerent; the United States sees Europe as spent, unserious, and weak – a legacy of its free riding since World War II.[97] In neoconservative eyes, the European worldview reflects a nihilism characteristic of late modernity or postmodernity, of the soft, effete, and effeminate strain in contemporary western culture. To the extent that the Clinton administration looked to the world community and its institutions as the ultimate source of international legitimacy, it partook of this unserious, feminine European worldview. In the judgment of young neoconservatives, Clinton's foreign policy demonstrated an immature mistrust of military power and a parallel quixotic, legalistic faith in the shibboleths of "collective security" and the liberalizing influence of commerce and technology to accomplish strategic ends. War, in contrast, focuses the mind, rids the body politic of softness, and restores the manly virtues.[98] Second-generation neoconservative preoccupation with manly virtue, physical and philosophical courage, and the personal and national assertion of risking lives in order to save lives was in keeping with a prominent strain of conservative theory.[99] Of course, none of the second generation of neoconservatives had ever been to war or had even served in the military. Their manliness played out in a realm of theory, rhetoric, and fantasy. War, for them, was no longer a last resort against the worst evils but an instrument of human progress, a fast way to improve the world – a stance some labeled "Jacobin," after the French Revolution's conviction that the past could be left behind in an all-encompassing transformation of society.[100]

For the second generation of neoconservatives, then, liberal internationalism properly adopted human rights as a basic principle of foreign policy. The internal nature of other states matters profoundly. But in embracing multilateral institutions, especially the United Nations, the liberal internationalist approach embraced weakness. And, because it forswears the use of military force if at all possible, the approach ultimately results in retreat and isolationism. Realism, historically viable but hard-hearted and selfish, no longer works in the post-Soviet (let alone the post-9/11) world. Realist suppositions about deterrence always depended on the assumption that (Soviet) leaders were fundamentally rational actors – rational in the sense of a foe that would respond rationally to the threat of overwhelming force. Rational opponents do not want their country laid waste in a nuclear exchange and will adjust their strategies accordingly. This logic underlay the long-held policy of Mutually Assured Destruction. But the assumption of rationality cannot apply to rogue states such as Saddam's Iraq and non-state actors such as al-Qaeda. The "just war" tradition requires that proper authority declare war only as a last resort to defend against imminent armed threats with the clear promise of proportionality in protecting against even greater harm.[101] But, neoconservative theorists retorted, weapons of mass destruction wielded by non-rational actors blur the distinction between immediate and looming threats. When dealing with non-rational actors under such conditions, military preemption is thus warranted. It is justifiable to preempt rogue states and terrorists because, as irrational actors, they do not respond to threat of their destruction. Again, in the neoconservative intellectual universe, correct foreign policy doctrine returns to Munich, not Vietnam, as the cautionary lesson: enemies must be met with quick and unrelenting force. The purpose of American foreign policy should be to preserve America's dominance.

But the world should not fear that dominance, insisted second-generation neoconservatives, because the United States seeks no empire. America's interests and values are identical, and in fact are universal. The United States is a model for the world because, as Lawrence F. Kaplan and William Kristol put it in their 2003 book, *The War over Iraq*, "[f]aith in the universal ideal of freedom, not a blood-and-soil nationalism, is what defines the American ideal."[102] The United States, in this logic, is at one and the same time exceptional and universal, its values shared and cherished by all (well-meaning) peoples, its power both awesome and benevolent. Because of these characteristics, *withholding* America's transformative power would both be selfish and dangerous.

> [U]nlike past imperial powers, if the United States has created a Pax Americana, it is not built on colonial conquest or economic aggrandizement. As George Bush put it in a 2002 speech, "America has no empire to extend or utopia to establish." Rather, what upholds today's world order is America's benevolent influence – nurtured, to be sure, by American power, but also by emulation and the recognition around the world that American ideals are genuinely universal. As a consequence, when the world's sole superpower commits itself to norms of international conduct – for democracy, for human rights, against aggression, against weapons proliferation – it means that successful challenges to American power will invariably weaken those American-created norms. Were we – through humility, self-abnegation or a narrow conception of the national interest – to retreat from the position that history has bequeathed us, the turmoil that would soon follow would surely reach our shores.[103]

Other neoconservatives acknowledged American actions as imperialist, but benevolently imperialist.[104]

Bush, neoconservatism, and 9/11: Ideas, networks, and resonant historical tropes

George W. Bush, though insistently unilateralist in foreign policy orientation, echoed the realism of his father's administration during

141

the 2000 presidential campaign. On the campaign trail, the junior Bush emphasized the need for the United States to conduct a "humble" foreign policy based on American interests, navigating between isolationism and the exercise of dominance. It was a vision pointedly to avoid the "Clintonian" assertion of values through humanitarian interventions, such as those in Somalia and Haiti, and the use of the U.S. military for nation-building, as in the Balkans.[105] Recall the distinction in foreign policy between interests and values. Interests refer to the defense of nation and the hard-headed expansion of national power and influence in the international competition between states. Interests are usually associated with the realist school of foreign policy, in which the internal nature of a particular foreign government is far less important than its power and its ability to help or thwart U.S. national aims. But America has also understood itself as a nation that stands for particular values – freedom, democracy, and humanitarianism foremost – and should conduct its foreign policy according to these high-minded principles. Values are usually associated with the foreign policy school of liberal internationalism. Interests and values are usually understood to be in tension, if not mutually exclusive. Bush began his presidency with a foreign policy of unilateralist realism. His administration pulled the United States out of the Kyoto protocols on climate change and the agreements on the International Criminal Court. Then came September 11, 2001. "Everything" didn't change after the attacks on the World Trade Center and the Pentagon, but the approach to foreign policy surely did.

Barely a week after the attacks, a large group of prominent neoconservatives (and others who may not have so identified) outside government sent an open letter to the White House. Endorsing the war on terrorism that the president had announced after the attacks, the letter demanded that Bush bring Osama bin Laden to justice. But the letter went much further. The signatories charted an entire Middle East foreign policy. They urged the president to pressure Syria and Lebanon to sever ties with the Lebanese militant group Hezbollah, suspend assistance to the Palestinian Authority if it did not move decisively against terrorism, and strike Iraq to overthrow Saddam Hussein – even if evidence did not link Iraq directly to the 9/11 attacks.[106] Bush didn't need much prodding with regard to the latter. The day after 9/11, he pressed counterterrorism coordinator Richard Clarke to find a connection between Saddam and the attacks.[107] It has become conventional wisdom that after 9/11 the Bush administration adopted much, if not most, of the neoconservative foreign policy agenda. As we have seen, that program asserted the ability – even the moral duty – of the United States to attack evil states and terrorists preventively. It seemed to go beyond unilateralism – that the United States will act on its own without hindrance by the U.N. or other international bodies – to embrace the "unipolar" doctrine that America will act to prevent the rise of any possible competing superpower. The 2002 National Security Policy of the United States, which encoded in precise terms the foreign policy doctrine that emerged in the wake of 9/11, put the matter plainly:

> The gravest danger our Nation faces lies at the crossroads of radicalism and technology. Our enemies have openly declared that they are seeking weapons of mass destruction, and evidence indicates that they are doing so with determination. The United States will not allow these efforts to succeed. We will build defenses against ballistic missiles and other means of delivery. We will cooperate with other nations to deny, contain, and curtail our enemies' efforts to acquire dangerous technologies. And, as a matter of common sense and self-defense, America will act against such emerging threats before they are fully formed. We cannot defend America and our friends by hoping for the best.[108]

The policy mirrored neoconservative debating points. Facing a dangerous world of rogue states run by irrational dictators, and of failed states wherein terrorists fester, the United States will act both preemptively and preventively against immediate security threats. *Preemptive* military action seeks to eliminate an immediate and credible threat of grievous harm; *preventive* military action is undertaken when a state believes that war with a potential adversary is possible or likely at some future date – even though the threat is not imminent or even certain to materialize.[109] The doctrine of preventive action for the most part was new (although it harkened back to the ideas of the anti-communist preventive "rollback" conservatives of the 1950s).

Post-9/11 national security policy denied any conflict between interests and values. When the United States acts in its interests in the international arena, its actions ineluctably unleash and satisfy the universal yearning for the freedom long denied oppressed peoples. And because democracy both taps into the inherent longing of all people's will to freedom and serves as a barricade against terrorism, the United States will act to champion aspirations for human dignity and foster a new era of global economic growth through privatization, free markets, and free trade. In the words of the 2002 National Security Policy document,

> The U.S. national security strategy will be based on a distinctly American internationalism that reflects the union of our values and our national interests. The aim of this strategy is to help make the world not just safer but better. Our goals on the path to progress are clear: political and economic freedom, peaceful relations with other states, and respect for human dignity.

This was the position that neoconservatives had been pushing for years.

Nothing better captured the identity of neoconservative doctrine and the foreign policy of George W. Bush's administration better than Bush's second inaugural address, four years after 9/11:

> We have seen our vulnerability – and we have seen its deepest source. For as long as whole regions of the world simmer in resentment and tyranny – prone to ideologies that feed hatred and excuse murder – violence will gather, and multiply in destructive power, and cross the most defended borders, and raise a mortal threat. There is only one force of history that can break the reign of hatred and resentment, and expose the pretensions of tyrants, and reward the hopes of the decent and tolerant, and that is the force of human freedom.
>
> We are led, by events and common sense, to one conclusion: The survival of liberty in our land increasingly depends on the success of liberty in other lands. The best hope for peace in our world is the expansion of freedom in all the world.
>
> America's vital interests and our deepest beliefs are now one. From the day of our Founding, we have proclaimed that every man and woman on this earth has rights, and dignity, and matchless value, because they bear the image of the Maker of Heaven and earth. Across the generations we have proclaimed the imperative of self-government, because no one is fit to be a master, and no one deserves to be a slave. Advancing these ideals is the mission that created our Nation. It is the honorable achievement of our fathers. Now it is the urgent requirement of our nation's security, and the calling of our time.
>
> So it is the policy of the United States to seek and support the growth of democratic movements and institutions in every nation and culture, with the ultimate goal of ending tyranny in our world.[110]

In short, Bush seemed to have become a dyed-in-the-wool neoconservative. His administration had hijacked liberal internationalism's preoccupation with values and ethical appeals and married them to realism's fixation on interests, which meant not only justifiable war against Iraq, but also potentially war without end inasmuch as "[t]he survival of liberty in our land increasingly depends on the success of liberty in other lands."

How did this come to be? After all, for the first year of his presidency, Bush followed a realist foreign policy line. Neoconservatives had gained a number of appointments in the new Bush administration, but their influence wasn't inordinate; none occupied the highest tier of government positions.[111] Here circumstance – the shock of 9/11 – and the extensive, embedded networks of neoconservatism were propitious and reinforcing. The realist foreign policy paradigm did not appear capable of addressing suicidal terrorism; liberal internationalism in the end would merely coddle it; paleoconservative isolationism would just force the United States to sit back and wait to be attacked. Neoconservatism's new influence followed the recalibration of risk in the aftermath of 9/11. Neoconservative positions claimed to address the heightened perception of risk, especially from seemingly irrational adversaries. All-important were the climate of fear and the projection of neoconservative efficacy in that context.

The invasion of Afghanistan in October 2001 marked the first instantiation of the new neoconservative-inspired foreign policy doctrine. The stated goal of destroying al-Qaeda and ending its use of Afghanistan as a base of operations was joined by the aim to remove the Taliban from power and create a democratic Afghan state. But this was not yet the full realization of neoconservative policy. As a response to the 9/11 attacks, the invasion of Afghanistan was not preventive war. Rather, the 2003 invasion of Iraq represented the real triumph of the neoconservative vision.

It is important to probe the nature of neoconservatism's foreign policy vision, inasmuch as it ties back to broader neoconservative themes that also link to the new Christian right. Although neoconservatives had a bold, detailed set of foreign policy positions, especially with regard to the Middle East, there was a sense that the deepest focus of their attention was not other countries or world affairs but rather the United States itself. The underlying agenda was about rescuing the United States from its own effete, "postmodern" liberalism. Decadent liberalism is both frail and perilous – even treacherous – because it undermines the mission of America. As

Kagan and Kristol put it, "The main threat the United States faces now and in the future is its own weakness. American hegemony is the only reliable defense against a break-down of peace and international order."[112] Thus, for all of the horrors of 9/11, the terrorist attacks had a silver lining for the neoconservatives and the religious right. September 11 marked the restoration of "moral clarity," of a serious attitude to life. As Leon Kass, a neoconservative who usually writes about medical ethics, intoned after 9/11, "In numerous if subtle ways, one feels a palpable increase in America's moral seriousness, well beyond the expected defense of our values and institutions so viciously under attack. . . . A fresh breeze of sensible moral judgment, clearing away the fog of unthinking and easy-going relativism, has enabled us to see evil for what it is . . . ."[113] This sentiment was echoed by the "theocon" Richard John Neuhaus. The September 11 attacks, Neuhaus wrote, would "inaugurate a time of national unity and sobriety in a society that has been . . . on a long and hedonistic holiday from history."[114] September 11 thus revived the Manichaean worldview in which America embodies the good in a "clash of civilizations" with evildoers.[115] The plane attacks solved a problem posed by the end of the Cold War: they provided the United States with a clear-cut enemy around which to mobilize its exceptionalism.

For American exceptionalists, whether of religious or secularist inclination, the United States is always the embodiment of the spirit of freedom. The form of nationalism that the religious right and neoconservatism share is one that locates the messianic future greatness of the country in an idealized national past. America is the exceptional nation, innocent of the ills that beset other nationalisms.[116] From Governor John Winthrop's characterization of the Massachusetts Bay colony as a "city on the hill," transformed by later politicians as America's "manifest destiny" to perfect and extend civilization around the globe, to William McKinley's assertion that war against Spain conferred "the blessings of liberty and civilization upon all the rescued peoples," to Woodrow Wilson's belief that the United States served the common welfare of mankind rather than its own imperial ends, to Harry Truman's conviction that God had graciously given America a second chance "to get the right sort of peace in the world," the assertion that God chose America as the agent of His special purposes in history is a longstanding, powerful theme in the nation's ideological narrative.[117] Recent survey data confirm these historic inclinations. Among white evangelicals, 84 percent believe that God has granted a special role for the United States in human history.[118] It was the perceived departure from and denigration of that idealized national past that fueled the vehemence of the shared religious right–neoconservative perspective. Thus for all of the myriad reasons articulated to justify the invasion of Iraq, for neoconservatives the war was not really about terrorism per se; rather it was about the pivotal relationship between Saddam Hussein and the assertion of American power. Saddam provided the opportunity to clarify the United States' global objectives and moral obligations. Between the senior Bush administration's too-cautious realism and Clinton's wishful, feeble liberal internationalism, Saddam's continued survival in power was a metaphor for all that had gone wrong with American foreign policy since the fall of the Soviet Union. Saddam had rejected American liberal values; Iraq was the arena in which to demonstrate the crucial tenets of neoconservative doctrine.

Invading Iraq

The George W. Bush administration invaded Iraq in order to project and consolidate American power in the Middle East. Overthrowing Saddam and bringing democracy to Iraq through military means – a Jacobin version of Joseph Schumpeter's economics-based concept of "creative destruction" – would, the administration believed, change the political culture of the Arab world and bring it under the sway of American values. These aims represented the dearest dreams of second-generation neoconservatives, and constitute the most persuasive explanation for why the United States went to war on Iraq. Other explanations for the war in Iraq are simply not convincing, at least as primary accounts. Bush's idiosyncratic (some said Oedipal) obsession with Saddam Hussein is not a plausible explanation for the war.[119] Removing Saddam had been a considered foreign policy option since the Gulf War, and when Bush pushed for war in 2002 most of the foreign policy establishment and politicians of both parties backed his bid. That the war was fought at Israel's direct behest is also not a serious proposition.[120] While the U.S. foreign policy establishment has long committed itself to the protection of Israel's security, and Saddam did pose a threat to Israel, the benefits of ridding the region of Saddam were surely outweighed in Israel's strategic calculations by the risk of generating an out-of-control regional conflagration. Moreover, the Israel explanation makes the United States a simple agent of, even patsy to, Israel – and thus violates the fundamental realist tenet that states pursue their own self-interest and do so rationally.

147

The war-for-oil thesis, that the war was designed to bring control of Iraq's vast oil reserves to American oil companies and alleviate the U.S. national security problem of declining access to the essential resource, is powerful, but is not a plausible explanation at least as a single, direct cause.[121] While the United States is of course critically concerned about oil supply, the government is not the mere agent of oil companies; power at the level of the U.S. government is rarely if ever exercised that easily, directly, or simply. Moreover, whereas Iraq had large reserves, its actual petroleum industry was in shambles; it would take a decade just to double its 3 percent of world production. As one long-time oil policy scholar argued, "No U.S. administration would launch so momentous a campaign just to facilitate a handful of oil development contracts and a moderate increase in supply – half a decade from now."[122] For neoconservatives and the Bush administration in general, oil wasn't an overt and distinct goal; it was more an assumption that American access to Middle Eastern oil was a given and hence was woven into the broader national security agenda of a strong America. The United States, by force of its importance as a great democratic power and guarantor of world security, must, by right, have and maintain access to the vital energy resources. As Norman Podhoretz wrote in *The Present Danger* in 1980, American access to Middle Eastern oil is essentially a given. Almost unstated was the assumption that part of America's belligerence toward the Soviet Union in the 1980s was to make sure the communist superpower could not hold the West hostage by cutting off its access to Middle Eastern oil. Hence, yes, a central goal of the American invasion of Iraq was the control of Iraq's oil reserves. But that was simply one objective, as was the protection of Israel's security. And war would also likely have a side benefit in domestic politics of keeping the country on a war footing, rallying the electorate around the flag and current administration, and thus ensure an indefinite period of Republican control. These were all ancillary factors in the overarching explanation: the utopian ambition to remake the Middle East through the apocalyptic cleansing fire of violence, to spread democracy and markets and thus make a new world, and, in so doing, fulfill America's sacred mission. That this ambition aligned with what many saw as Israel's interests, U.S. access to oil, and Republican electoral control were added bonuses.[123]

Needless to say, the main publicly stated reason for the invasion, Saddam Hussein's possession of weapons of mass destruction, was largely a smokescreen. The intelligence on Iraq's WMD was cooked to fit the predetermined war policy, despite what Donald Rumsfeld claims in his autobiography.[124] The secret Downing Street Memo of July 23, 2002 from British foreign policy aide Matthew Rycroft to the most important members of Tony Blair's government revealed conclusively that the Bush administration decided to overthrow Saddam Hussein in the summer of 2002 – *before* there was any claim of WMD in Iraq. Sir Richard Dearlove, the head of Britain's foreign intelligence agency, MI6, gave an assessment of his talks in Washington: "Bush wanted to remove Saddam, through military action, justified by the conjunction of terrorism and WMD. But the intelligence and facts were being fixed around the policy."[125] Dearlove's assessment was ratified by Baroness Manningham-Buller, former director-general of Britain's domestic intelligence agency, MI5, in testimony before a 2010 panel investigating the events leading to the invasion of Iraq in 2003. "There was no credible intelligence to suggest a connection" linking the government of Saddam Hussein to the terrorist attacks in the United States on September 11, 2001, "and that was the judgment, I might say, of the CIA. . . . It was not a judgment that found favor with some parts of the American machine. . . . That is why Donald Rumsfeld started an alternative intelligence unit in the Pentagon to seek an alternative judgment."[126] Rumsfeld's alternative intelligence unit was the Office of Special Plans, headed up by the redoubtable neoconservative Douglas Feith (labeled, memorably, "the fucking stupidest guy on the face of the earth" by General Tommy Franks).[127] The modus operandi of the unit was, in effect, to reject the empirical evidence accumulated by the CIA and the Defense Intelligence Agency in favor of unverified information provided by sources connected to the favored exile group, the Iraqi National Congress (INC), headed by Ahmad Chalabi. Of course the lifeblood of the INC, in a tight, self-serving circle, rested on providing a picture of Iraq that suited Bush administration presumptions. The information provided by INC-affiliated sources proved fabricated.[128] The Office of Special Plans can only be described as a gambit within the executive branch, reminiscent of the decades-earlier hawkish claims of bomber gaps and missile gaps, to justify war on Iraq. But why was WMD presented as the reason for war? Because of the administration's calculation that the fundamental policy goal, regime change in Iraq (and beyond) in accordance with the doctrine of preventive war, needed a concrete *causus belli*. Without it, preventive war was still too controversial and too thin a reed to rally Congress, other foreign policy elites, and the American people.[129]

The influence of the neoconservatives lay in the fact that they were organized, institutionally potent, and had in place a set of policies that addressed the fear and the new risk calculus after 9/11. They in effect called up the shadow defense establishment instituted during the Carter presidency and evolved during the Clinton years across a number of think tanks, policy institutes, and media. This shadow establishment over the years developed a notable neoconservative cast, in terms of both discourse and personnel. A large number of second-generation neoconservatives with histories in government policy-making bureaucracies in the Defense or State departments, such as Paul Wolfowitz, Richard Perle, and Douglas Feith, had been housed as analysts and commentators in high-level conservative think tanks, notably the American Enterprise Institute and the Heritage Foundation. They came back into government with the victory of George W. Bush in the 2000 election. Others, such as Charles Krauthammer, David Frum, and William Kristol, were high-profile columnists in elite print and broadcast media. The connections among these think tanks, government, and media were key, as was the funding that facilitated these networks. The Washington think tanks and lobbying shops, including the Project for a New American Century, received funding from conservative foundations such as Olin, Bradley, Scaife, and Smith Richardson, and functioned to employ neoconservative analysts and functionaries in years when the Republicans were out of political power.[130]

Indeed, neoconservatives had done so well that the paleo-conservatives complained the neocons had stolen away their conservative funders. The *Weekly Standard*, founded by William Kristol, became the flagship publication of the neoconservative movement when it was launched in 1995. Underwritten by News Corp CEO Rupert Murdoch, the editors and writers for the *Weekly Standard*, as well as fellows at the American Enterprise Institute, Heritage, and other like-minded think tanks, had become mainstay contributors and interviewees on Fox News and the right-wing radio talk shows by the mid-1990s. Even the *National Review*, since the mid-1950s the showplace journal of anti-establishment conservatism, by 1997 moved over to the neoconservative camp. Gary Dorrien notes that by the 1990s neoconservatives controlled most of the right's advocacy and policy organizations: *Weekly Standard, Policy Review, Commentary, The Public Interest, First Things, National Interest, National Review, American Spectator, Claremont Review of Books, American Enterprise, Journal of Democracy, Public Opinion, Orbis*, the editorial page of the *Wall Street Journal*, the American Enterprise Institute, the Hoover Institution, the Manhattan Institute, the Jewish Institute for National Security Affairs, the Center for Security Policy, the

Center for Strategic and International Studies, and, off and on, *The New Republic*.[131] And although neoconservatives did not occupy the highest positions in the Bush administration, either they converted the defense hawks who had not been strongly identified with the discourse, such as Dick Cheney and Donald Rumsfeld, or the latter found that their unipolar interventionist stance overlapped enough with neoconservatism that any differences were trivial.[132]

We see here an intricate, intimate relationship between ideas and institutions. It is perhaps of no great theoretical moment to suggest that the triumph of a set of ideas rests upon a confluence of factors beyond the salience of the ideas in and of themselves. Ideas and the people propagating them need institutional supports and responsive reverberations inside and outside the formal institutions of political power. Mass media and think tanks, "shadow" cabinet posts and the legitimacy to comment and declaim publicly – all of which require considerable financial resources – very often are the factors that give life to ideas in a liberal democracy and sustain them when their bearers are out of power. Here lay the signal importance of Irving Kristol, intellectual-political entrepreneur par excellence. Kristol's skill lay in establishing the intellectual networks, guiding the connections among intellectuals, politicians, and big conservative contributors, cultivating talented young neoconservatives and securing their employment first within his association of journals and then at the think tanks that he helped grow – a kind of neoconservative vanguardism. The other great visionaries of the conservative counter-revolution, mentioned in chapter 2, were Wall Street mogul and Nixon Treasury Secretary William E. Simon and Supreme Court justice-to-be Lewis F. Powell, Jr. Simon helped establish and reorient conservative foundations to sow the conservative think tanks that, in turn, created conservative centers of intellectual life and media intervention in the public arena. Powell can be seen as a father of the conservative legal movement. Corporate gifts to conservative foundations, think tanks, and conservative media helped create a potent network of institutions, largely outside of academia, to recruit, house, succor, and eventually place in government a stable of conservative intellectuals and publicists. Scott McConnell, a former contributor to *Commentary* and editor at the *National Interest*, offered an astute observation on the structure and reach of the neoconservative Washington network:

> With the fledgling Fox News network, the [*Weekly*] *Standard* soon emerged as the key leg in a synergistic triangle of neoconservative

argumentation: you could write a piece for the magazine, talk about your ideas on Fox, pick up a paycheck from Kristol or from AEI. It was not a way to get rich, but it sustained a network of careers that might otherwise have shriveled or been diverted elsewhere. Indeed, it did more than sustain them, it gave neocons an aura of being "happening" inside the Beltway that no other conservative (or liberal) faction could match.[133]

Michael Lind, another former insider, reveals much the same:

The neocon network orchestrated by the foundations resembled an old-fashioned political patronage machine, or perhaps one of the party writers' or scholars' guilds in communist countries. A shared pool of right-wing writers and scholars in receipt of foundation grants from the same program officers was established into which conservative journals like *Commentary, American Spectator, Policy Review, Public Interest, National Interest, New Criterion,* and *Wall Street Journal* regularly dipped. Washington had come to resemble Hollywood, with the foundations playing the role of the big studios, the program officers acting as producers, editors playing directors, and the talent – policy wonks, publicists – divided between a few well-paid superstars and legions of poorly paid wannabes.[134]

This is not to claim that a cabal of highly networked policy activists somehow took control of American foreign policy and steered it in ways that were anathema to the general tide of American history. As American conservatives have always insisted, ideas matter. But the ideas that matter must have both institutional supports and resonance with contemporary challenges and historically laden tropes. The crusading moralism embedded in neoconservative Iraq policy and neoconservative insistence that America's interests and values are one and the same, as we have seen, constitute an entirely recognizable strain in the history of American foreign policy and American self-understanding. It means that the United States' exercise of military power is by definition in the service of liberty. What was new – again, set in motion by the attacks of September 11 – was the doctrine approving *preventive* wars against more distant threats and legitimating the policy not simply by tweaking the just war doctrine, but with recourse to American exceptionalism and the unique, triumphalist mission of the United States to spread political and economic freedom. The strength of the institutional base of neoconservative presence in the elite debates over foreign policy allowed neoconservatives to seize the discourse after 9/11.

A final observation in this regard. Implicit (and sometimes explicit) in much neoconservative policy analysis and prescription in the aftermath of 9/11 was the utopian, ultimately Jacobin, notion that violence can create a new world. This is a central observation of the British political philosopher John Gray.[135] The Jacobin urge of the French Revolution is but a secular version of Christian eschatological thought: violence can be an instrument for perfecting humanity. Underscoring Gray's point, various neoconservatives compiled competing lists of the countries the United States should invade and the regimes ripe for overthrow beyond President Bush's "axis of evil" inventory of Iraq, Iran, and North Korea.[136] Lists included, beyond the evil troika, Syria, Lebanon, Libya, the Palestinian Authority, Hezbollah, even Saudi Arabia and Egypt.[137] As the political scientist Kenneth Jowitt suggested, such lists revealed neoconservatism to be an American form of Leninism, which formulated a vanguardist foreign policy designed to speed history along through military action, legitimized by the benevolence of American values.[138] And the historical endpoint? A new, harmonious democratic capitalist world under the beneficent umbrella of the United States. Suffice it to say that this neoconservative vision was entirely consonant, in both structure and endpoint, with the premillennialist evangelical Protestant vision of the end-times. Neoconservatism's design to remake the Middle East through the cleansing fire of violence paralleled premillennialist Protestantism's focus on Armageddon as a clearing away of the evil of this world in order to speed Christ's second coming.

A second order of paradoxes, unintended consequences, and limits to social engineering: The debacle of Iraq

The Bush administration and the neoconservatives pictured democracy as a default condition to which societies would revert once liberated from dictators.[139] Overthrowing Saddam would rid Iraq of a murderous dictator and a threat to the region. A conquered Iraq represented the best hope for a democratic model in an Arab country. Richard Perle articulated this view plainly:

> I think there is a potential civic culture in Arab countries that can lead to democratic institutions and I think Iraq is probably the best place to put that proposition to the test because it's a sophisticated educated

population that has suffered horribly under totalitarian rule, and there's a yearning for freedom that, you know, I think we find everywhere in the world but especially in subject populations.[140]

To the extent that there was a theoretical basis to the democracy claim in this context, it rested in large part on the scholarly work of Princeton historian Bernard Lewis. Although some of his writings cast doubt on the ability to impose democracy on Islamic nations, in others Lewis argued that the violent, retrograde condition of Arab countries was a result of the failure of their leaderships to modernize. The model of success for Lewis was Turkey and Kemal Atatürk's imposition of modernity and secularism from above. With Lewis's understanding of Atatürk as the guide, the Bush administration inferred that the West could sow democracy in the Middle East.[141]

But, of course, the record of jump-starting democracy is problematic, and impressing it on other countries has proved fairly dismal. Herein lies the great irony that the second-generation neoconservatives violated the cardinal principle of their first- generation forebears: the overreach of policy, the law of unintended consequences, the dangers and ultimate failure of social engineering. This is not the place to engage in a detailed history of Iraq or enter the debate over whether colonial boundary determinations can make a modern, viable nation-state. The point rather is to highlight how inappropriate was Saddam's Iraq as a potential model of democracy and how fanciful, extravagant, even preposterous were neoconservative aspirations for the "liberated" country. According to Kanan Makiya (writing under the pseudonym Samir al-Khalil), a prominent anti-Saddam exile intellectual, the Iraqi Ba'ath Party was most akin to Stalinism, the Iraqi state a police state in service to Saddam's personal power. All vestiges of civil society – even personal trust – had been extinguished in the effort to prevent the rise of political rivals. "The Ba'ath turned fear into the precondition for their legitimacy. . . . This is a polity whose ideal is the transformation of everybody into an informer," Makiya wrote in 1989.[142] That Saddam's Iraq was a ghastly totalitarian state was among the reasons why neoconservatives urged its overthrow by the American military. But a police state defeated by an external force does not leave the society with the institutions and social capital upon which to construct a viable democracy. To the extent that it is permissible to generalize, police states that have a chance for democracy usually must be defeated from *within*, for it is in the indigenous groups willing to resist the former regime that one locates (potentially, and certainly not always) the seeds of democratic values and institutions.[143] Indeed, a case can be made that the neoconservatives planning for the Iraq War and its aftermath, Deputy Secretary of Defense Paul Wolfowitz in particular, either had some inkling about the weakness of domestic Iraqi civil institutions or demonstrated closet contempt for the actual process of instituting democracy. This can be seen in the Defense Department's effort to install the exile millionaire Ahmad Chalabi and his Iraqi National Congress in power in post-invasion Iraq as a latter-day Iraqi Atatürk. But with no institutional base or legitimacy in Iraq, the Chalabi provisional government gambit proved a quick failure.[144]

The importance of civil society and the difficulty of establishing democracy are basic principles of political science taught to undergraduates in western universities. These truisms concerning democracy were watchwords for the first generation of neoconservatives. Here's Jeane Kirkpatrick in her famous "Dictatorships and Double Standards" article discussed earlier:

> Although most governments in the world are, as they always have been, autocracies of one kind or another, no idea holds greater sway in the mind of educated Americans than the belief that it is possible to democratize governments, anytime, anywhere, under any circumstances. This notion is belied by an enormous body of evidence based on the experience of dozens of countries which have attempted with more or less (usually less) success to move from autocratic to democratic government. Many of the wisest political scientists of this and previous centuries agree that democratic institutions are especially difficult to establish and maintain – because they make heavy demands on all portions of a population and because they depend on complex social, cultural, and economic conditions.[145]

Needless to say, Kirkpatrick's admonitions applied to Iraq – in spades. As detailed in chapter 1, the direct American combat role in the Iraq War proceeded for nearly nine years, with high casualties, immense long-term costs, and secured barely a fragile political accommodation in Iraq itself. Inter-community violence has never really abated and could spark the resurrection of civil war or partition. A weakened Iraq is no longer a counterweight to Iran; indeed, many analysts point to Iran's influence on Iraq's ruling parties. Intelligence agencies concluded that the Iraq conflict was a prime source of recruitment for the global jihadist movement. The Iraq war was a fiasco, a colossal drain on American and Iraqi lives and treasure, and a dreadful monument to the "laws" of overreach and unintended consequences.

As we have seen, neoconservatism and the Christian right share many specific features and preoccupations. More deeply, they share a utopian, dogmatic approach to the world: an insistence on the palpable, embodied existence of evil, a tendency to demonize Islam as an inherently violent religion, an unquestioning support of Israel, a hatred of liberals, an insistence on American exceptionalism, a conviction that American power can positively remake the Middle East, and an embrace of military force that reflects reverence for a particular version of masculinity and an impatience with ideas or positions that feel feminine. But these features are anathema to the give and take of democratic politics.

— 5 —

RICHARD HOFSTADTER'S "PARANOID STYLE" REVISITED
The Tea Party, Past as Prologue

The Bush presidency ended in 2008. It left the country with two long-running, unfinished wars on its hands, a colossal rise in the federal debt, and the worst economic crisis since the Great Depression. Bush's failed presidency gave rise to ennui among elements of the Christian right, precipitating some reconsideration of the Bush Doctrine and the commitment to the anti-establishment conservative agenda generally. In 2007, for example, in an overt critique of one facet of the Bush administration's national security doctrine, the board of the National Association of Evangelicals issued a declaration against torture.[1] And a few prominent evangelical megachurch pastors began to distance themselves from the Moral Majority/Christian Coalition old guard. Rick Warren, for one, leader of Saddleback Church in southern California, announced that he had left the domestic culture wars behind in an effort to reorient his flock toward the fight against AIDS, poverty, and malaria in the Third World. Even the neoconservatives, in the wake of the Iraq War debacle, let their public profile slip below the radar just a bit, although they continued, when pressed, to insist how correct they had been about Iraq all along. The post-invasion disaster, they maintained, was due to the failed efforts of incompetents such as Defense Secretary Donald Rumsfeld and Administrator of the Coalition Provisional Authority of Iraq Paul Bremer.[2] Indeed, neoconservatives insisted it was they who rescued the war effort by their formulation of and insistence on the "surge," the plan that placed an additional 20,000 troops in Iraq in January 2007.[3] Although they might have lowered their public profile a notch, neoconservatives also demanded that U.S. military force be used against *Iran* – showing that, unlike some of their conservative evangelical compatriots, the Iraq debacle hadn't altered

157

their outlook at all. For the most part, anti-establishment conservative political sensibilities remained pretty much intact.

Following the election of Barack Obama to the presidency, the quieting of anti-establishment conservatives changed quickly, with the noisy emergence of the Tea Party in early 2009 marking their brisk resurgence. An acronym for "Taxed Enough Already," the Tea Party name was a deliberate evocation of the colonial American patriotic revolt against oppressive, centralized government. President Obama's Keynesian-inspired $787 billion stimulus package, the American Recovery and Reinvestment Act of 2009, sparked a few locally organized protests against government spending. The local events were picked up by conservative media, which served to encourage similar protest actions in more communities.[4] Tea Party lore has it that the movement took off when deep, but still inchoate, political unhappiness was tapped into by an intemperate on-air outburst from Rick Santelli, a futures-trading-floor television correspondent for CNBC television. Upon hearing reports of possible government programs to rescue homeowners who had taken on unrealistic mortgages and now, with recession and the collapse of home prices, faced foreclosure, Santelli went ballistic on the air, declaring that "the government was rewarding bad behavior." He asked heatedly, "How many of you people want to pay for your neighbor's mortgage that has an extra bathroom and can't pay their bills?"[5] The video went viral on the Internet, promulgated by right-wing bloggers and Fox News. Tea Partiers-to-be testified that "Santelli's rant" set them in motion. The people who participated in various tax protests organized themselves as locals of the emerging Tea Party movement. In addition to challenging Obama's economic stimulus, they began attending and disrupting congressional town hall meetings in the summer of 2009, particularly those devoted to discussion of health care reform. Irate protesters displayed signs depicting President Obama in whiteface[6] and shouted down officials touting the Democratic health care bill. Thereafter, local Tea Party groups, assisted by longstanding national conservative advocacy organizations, dove into the 2010 midterm elections, challenging Republican incumbents from the right and working hard to elect Tea Party-identified candidates.

What the Tea Party protesters shared was a visceral anxiety about President Obama and the Democratic political agenda, an antipathy to taxes and government spending, and apprehension about what they saw as the increasing control by the federal government over virtually all aspects of American life. They stood for limited government and constitutional originalism – getting back to what they saw as the basic role of government as outlined by the Founding Fathers. They scrutinized taxes and government spending not just in economic terms, but in moral ones: taxes and spending not only skewed the performance of the economy, they were also for all intents and purposes evil because they rewarded irresponsible individual behavior and punished virtuous behavior.[7] These are, of course, familiar conservative tropes, longstanding components of the critique of modern liberalism. What startled was the Tea Partiers' *style*: the fury that accompanied their otherwise substantive critique of government spending; the rage at feeling they were not in control of their lives; the bizarre, blind fixation on President Obama's citizenship status and religious affiliation, often accompanied by overtly racist rhetoric; the vehement condemnation of the president's "palling around" with terrorists and his "apologizing" for America; the certainty, *sans* evidence, that Keynesian economic policies were bankrupt, indeed, the source of America's ills; claims that the Democratic-sponsored health care reform bill called for "death panels"; the charge that the scientific consensus on climate change was a politicized hoax on the part of leftist elites. "We want our country back!" roared Tea Partiers at meetings and rallies. The Tea Party appeared to represent not just the resurgence of anti-establishment conservatism, but the revival of that set of beliefs in an extreme, enraged form.

Although it was young and its longevity was unclear, the Tea Party's successes in the 2010 midterm elections and its muscular shove of the GOP to the right were striking. Sixty-three House seats, five Senate seats, and six governorships swung from the Democrats to the Republicans. The GOP won around 700 seats in state legislatures. One must be careful not to over-interpret and attribute this political change to the Tea Party movement alone. After all, there is a well-known pattern in midterm elections wherein the party in power loses seats – especially during bad economic times. Moreover, in the 2010 elections some prominent Tea Party candidates lost their bids. But the Tea Party movement does seem responsible for moving political and ideological goalposts well to the right internally within the GOP and in the public arena in general. Within the party, the rollback of New Deal institutions and programs is back on the table as a serious political option. More broadly, the Tea Party movement abruptly halted the Obama agenda. No longer were citizens and policy-makers debating the range of government stimulus programs, the plight of the unemployed, and extending medical insurance to all;

rather, discussion turned to the dreaded socialism of the Obama administration, the catastrophe of federal debt, and the tyrannical power of government elites.

The Tea Party's sudden impact cried out for analysis. Some intellectuals turned to the ideas of the historian Richard Hofstadter. Hofstadter, as we know, introduced the analytical concept of the "paranoid style" in an effort to understand the mid-twentieth-century movements around Joseph McCarthy and Barry Goldwater. Hofstadter's new relevance was based on the perception that in many ways the Tea Party looked like those earlier movements. References to Hofstadter or the paranoid style appeared in Tea Party news coverage or political commentary by the score.

Hofstadter and the paranoid style

One of the most influential historians of the post-World War II era, Richard Hofstadter wrote on the nineteenth-century Populist movement, the Progressive movement of the early twentieth century, and the conflicted nature of American liberalism. The implicit and occasional explicit backdrop of Hofstadter's scholarship was a defense of the New Deal order.[8] As he expanded his scholarly purview to the analysis of McCarthyism and the popular movement tied to the 1964 candidacy of Barry Goldwater, Hofstadter displayed uneasiness about the durability of New Deal liberalism in the face of right-wing mass movements. After a brief youthful dalliance with the Communist Party in the 1930s, he grew suspicious of populist mass democracy by the 1950s. Always critical of the Progressive historiography that had depicted the downtrodden, noble democratic people rising successfully against the evil corporate trusts, Hosftadter shifted the analytical focus of reform movements from the economic dimension to the ethno-cultural. He discerned in nineteenth-century agrarian Populism a distinctive nativism and anti-Semitism that other historians had glossed over. Dispelling the myth of the democratic yeoman farmer, Hofstadter crafted an analytical difference between "old" and "new" liberalisms. He categorized the agrarian ideal of opportunity, laissez-faire capitalism, and the removal of government-induced barriers to investment as "old liberalism." Fundamentally different, the "new liberalism" of the New Deal was the product of a modern, urban movement that championed government intervention to revitalize markets and establish a social safety net to compensate for the failings of capitalism.

160

This distinction underlay one of Hofstadter's main scholarly contributions. Previously, most historians had understood Progressivism as the natural lead-in to the New Deal, and, in a parallel historical move backward, the Populists as proto-Progressives – thus drawing a generally straight line of reform from Populism to Progressivism to New Deal liberalism. Hofstadter would have none of this. In his estimation, the reformers of the Progressive Era had not been radicals at all. Rather, they were old-stock middle-class Protestants worried about their diminishing status in the wake of immigration, the horrors of "race-mixing," and threatened by new ethnic groups seeking place and power in a bewildering modernizing America. The key to Progressivism and Populism was not declining economic fortunes but "status anxiety," or "rank in society." Thus the most important issue for the old Protestants of the Progressive Era and the most revealing of their politico-cultural inclinations was Prohibition, with its intrinsic moralism and manifestly anti-immigrant, anti-Catholic overtones. The New Deal, in contrast, marked a striking departure from the Populist–Progressive heritage, in Hofstadter's view. If the old liberalism had been Protestant and ideological, rooted in a backward agrarian ideal, the new liberalism was urban, ethnic, hospitable to non-Protestants, forward-looking, and results-oriented.[9]

Hofstadter saw in the McCarthyism of the 1950s and in the Goldwater juggernaut of the 1960s a threat to the legacy of the new liberalism of the New Deal. He understood the right-wing movements as manifestations of a periodic gush of anti-intellectualism in American life that harked back to the prejudiced agrarianism of Populist–Progressive old liberalism. Hofstadter identified three historical pillars of American anti-intellectualism: evangelical religion (which privileged faith and emotion over the skeptical mind), practical-minded business (which valued instrumental know-how over intellectual depth), and the populist political style (enraged, accusatory, uncompromising). These combined to foster a political culture hostile to complexity, to cosmopolitanism, to intellectuals (denigrated as "eggheads"), and to the life of the mind in general.[10] Sensitive to the popular roots of authoritarianism, Hofstadter sought a deeper understanding of the historical phenomenon. He turned to the social sciences for help in illuminating the underlying psychological motivations of right-wing movements and actors. His lodestar was Theodor W. Adorno et al.'s *The Authoritarian Personality*. Published in 1950, this influential study scrutinized the nature of anti-Semitism by identifying the cluster of personality characteristics said to underlie racial or religious prejudice. Based on extensive survey and interview data rooted in a psychoanalytic theoretical model, the brilliant, flawed *Authoritarian Personality* theorized that the children of authoritarian fathers project their deep-seated, unresolved conflicts onto others, particularly onto safe-to-stigmatize ethnic, political, and religious minorities.[11]

Hofstadter thus joined the circle of scholars, primarily sociologists, who sought to understand the nature of McCarthyism against a backdrop of unease over presumed, though usually latent, fascist tendencies in America. His essay "The Pseudo-Conservative Revolt – 1954" was collected in the widely noted 1955 volume edited by Daniel Bell called *The New American Right*.[12] In it, Hofstadter acknowledged his debt to Adorno by labeling McCarthyism a "pseudo-conservative" movement. Pseudo, because rather than hewing to the principled but temperate and compromising spirit of "genuine" conservatism, Hofstadter argued that McCarthy and his followers displayed a deep, restless dissatisfaction with the direction of American life and institutions. Feeling unsettled and insecure in the post-war period, McCarthy's supporters believed themselves to be living in a world in which their liberties were arbitrarily and outrageously invaded. They felt "spied upon, plotted against, betrayed, and very likely destined for total ruin," Hofstadter wrote.[13] Their enemy was communism and its putative defenders. McCarthyism set the tone of the political life in the 1950s and fostered a dangerous, punitive assault not only against communists but also against those of elite status – the "striped-pants diplomats," Ivy League graduates, high-ranking generals, college presidents, intellectuals, the Eastern upper classes, Harvard professors, and members of Phi Beta Kappa, who were understood to be the source of the nation's difficulties and failings.[14] Hofstadter interpreted the broad vilification of elites as an attack on New Deal liberalism and on the intelligent mind per se.

Consistent with the status-based analytical framework of his earlier work, Hofstadter suggested that McCarthyism was born in part of the rootlessness and heterogeneity of American life in the period just after World War II. Of key salience was its adherents' fall from status and the peculiar form taken by their search for secure identity. Followers of McCarthy were agitated by fears of the cosmopolitan society that was emerging around them. Why was this? Hofstadter theorized that "interest-based" politics are dominant in periods of hard economic times; "status-based" politics are dominant in prosperous times. The 1950s, a time of rising prosperity, were characterized by the intense status concerns of persons in two main groups: old-family white Anglo-Saxon Protestants (WASPs), whose immediate ancestors had been Populists and Progressives, and, secondarily, Germans and Irish immigrant Catholics. The anxiety of the WASPs was rooted in their cultural decline. The anxiety of the German and Irish immigrant groups derived from their unease about their newfound prosperity and need to demonstrate their fundamental Americanism. With Irish and German immigrants, the politics of religion was a factor. Protestants for decades had bashed Catholics as politically untrustworthy because of their allegiance to the Vatican hierarchy. Declaiming their true Americanism through support of McCarthy was a way for Irish and German Catholics to counter the Protestant charge. In the end, Hofstadter veered toward the kind of social psychology found in Adorno and the scholars whose work appeared in *The New American Right*. Hofstadter suggested that the hyper-patriotic, hyper-conformist pseudo-conservatives about whom he was concerned were usually the same kinds of people as the anti-Semites whom Adorno examined in his opus. They had the same obsession with authority. "The mechanisms at work in both complexes are quite the same," Hofstadter wrote.[15]

> For pseudo-conservatism is among other things a disorder in relation to authority, characterized by an inability to find other modes for human relationship than those of more or less complete domination or submission. The pseudo-conservative always imagines himself to be dominated and imposed upon because he feels that he is not dominant, and knows of no other way of interpreting his position. He imagines that his own government and his own leaders are engaged in a more or less continuous conspiracy against him because he has come to think of authority only as something that aims to manipulate and deprive him. It is for this reason, among others, that he enjoys seeing outstanding generals, distinguished Secretaries of State, and prominent scholars brow-beaten.[16]

Hofstadter revisited the topic eleven years later in the wake of the popular excitement surrounding the presidential candidacy of Barry Goldwater. Somewhat less social psychological and more historical in presentation, "Pseudo-Conservatism Revisited – 1965" still rested on the concept of status anxiety. But whereas the followers of Joseph McCarthy had come from mixed class and mixed religious backgrounds, Hofstadter claimed that the demographic profile of the John Birch Society and other typical Goldwater backers revealed them to be well-educated, middle- and upper-status Republican Protestants who carried into secular affairs the Manichaean, apocalyptic style of thought prevalent in the fundamentalist religious tradition. The result, Hofstadter wrote, was a curiously crude form of anti-communism, one that deprecated presidents as men of wholly evil intent who conspired against the public good, and that denounced New Deal-inspired economic policies as a grave danger to the fabric of free society.[17] By 1963, when he wrote his capstone essay on the topic, "The Paranoid Style in American Politics," Hofstadter had come to the conclusion that the anti-intellectual conspiratorial style was a steady, ineradicable feature of American life that surfaced periodically in waves of varying intensity.

The mid-twentieth-century paranoid style was similar to older conspiracy theories about the Masons and the Illuminati, in Hofstadter's view. Like the narrative structure of the religious millenarian formula from which it borrowed – rankest betrayal, then constancy and redemption – the paranoid politics of the mid-twentieth-century pseudo-conservative offered salvation if true Americans stood firm and fought the evil enemy to the finish.[18] What was distinctive about the modern right wing in contrast to its nineteenth-century forebears lay in its conviction that "America has been largely taken away from them and their kind."[19] In the eyes of the Goldwater right, liberals had brought the economy under the direction of the federal government to pave the way for socialism or communism. Many Goldwater supporters believed the government and other key social institutions to be infiltrated by a network of communist agents. They interpreted every instance of public incompetence as a deliberate act of treason.

But the paranoid style of the mid-twentieth century was different from earlier incarnations in one central respect. The mass media altered the calculus because, typically, they intensified paranoid movements.

Important changes may be traced to the effects of the mass media. The villains of the modern right are much more vivid than those of their paranoid predecessors, much better known to the public; the contemporary literature of the paranoid style is by the same token richer and more circumstantial in personal description and personal invective. For the vaguely delineated villains of the anti-Masons, for the obscure and disguised Jesuit agents, the little-known papal delegates of the anti-Catholics, for the shadowy international bankers of the monetary conspiracies, we may now substitute eminent public figures like Presidents Roosevelt, Truman, and Eisenhower, Secretaries of State like Marshall, Acheson, and Dulles, justices of the Supreme Court like Frankfurter and Warren, and the whole battery of lesser but still famous and vivid conspirators headed by Alger Hiss.[20]

Hofstadter's social psychological approach is descriptively arresting. It also holds some theoretical appeal when trying to understand the Tea Party phenomenon. After all, the heat and invective, the heavy dose of persecution and victimhood, the sudden leap to wild, conspiratorial conclusions are rather astonishing and beg explanation. Many, in Hofstadter's time and today, comment on right-wing rage and resentment. But what is the basis of this fury and umbrage? The Hoftstadter thesis at least hazards an explanation: status anxiety, angry bewilderment over the sense of loss of group rank. What distinguishes the Hofstadter thesis is the effort to link political orientation to social structure (which, in fact, was typical of older sociological approaches to the study of social movements). The problem with the social psychological approach, as we noted in chapter 1, is that it makes it easy to label as irrational and reactionary those political actors and behaviors with which the researcher happens to disagree. Perhaps, skeptics argue, we should just take people at their word rather than try to read the deep, subconscious reasons that lay beneath what they say they believe. Moreover, formulaic conspiratorial readings of events are not just the property of the right wing, as Hofstadter's critics noted. All kinds of irrationality can be found in political life. Conspiracy theories can be found on the left, as well as on the right. In our time, for example, many believe that the Bush administration or rogue elements of the U.S. military had prior knowledge of or carried out the September 11 attacks, and have devoted years of intense effort to prove this. Other critics found Hofstadter's historical evidence thin and thus his central thesis flawed.[21] The worry of the contributors to *The Radical Right*, including Hofstadter, always harked back to Nazism: that is, whether this or that mass movement portended the advent of fascism in America – a fear that seemed somewhat overwrought. Perhaps the most consequential scholarly critique, that of Michael Paul Rogin, was that Hofstadter's central empirical presumption was simply wrong. The groups that sided with McCarthy had *not* historically been associated with the Populist or Progressive movements. McCarthyism's roots were in traditional conservatism, not agrarian radicalism.[22]

Hofstadter revived: Anti-intellectualism and the new paranoid style

Notwithstanding these criticisms of the Hofstadter thesis, observers found a replay of key elements of his central notions of anti-intellectualism and the paranoid style in the political climate of the new millennium. Media treatment of the 2000 presidential campaign tended to depict the irritating and smarmy egghead city slicker Al Gore against the intellectually incurious and lazy, but winsome country boy George W. Bush. As Todd Gitlin, for one, commented, invoking Hofstadter,

> In the eyes of half the population, the vice president [Gore] fell prey to a suspicion that he was not only preachy but also a sharpie. In the media's campaign story line, the standard charge against Gore, shared by the Bush campaign and the comedians, was that, like the traditional confidence man, Gore – too smart for his own good – lied, while Bush was the amiable common man.[23]

Indeed, candidate Bush's educational mediocrity and affected anti-intellectual, good-old-boy persona seemed to energize his supporters. Trying to make sense of this phenomenon, commentators noted the heavy presence of southern and midwestern evangelical Protestants in Bush's electoral base and returned to Hofstadter's concepts of status anxiety and the paranoid style for explanatory guidance. As the victorious Bush took up the process of governing, many saw evidence of the anti-intellectualism Hofstadter had described decades earlier. Commentators noted the administration's previously described contempt for science in the debates over climate change and environmental protection, its blithe ignoring of inconvenient contrary evidence with regard to Iraq's alleged weapons of mass destruction and the supposed link between Iraq and al-Qaeda, and so on. As the historian Jon Wiener observed after giving partial due to Hofstadter's scholarly critics, Hofstadter may have been wrong about yesterday's populists, but he was right about today's Republicans.[24]

The rise of the Tea Party in the wake of the economic crisis and the election of Barack Obama prompted a further revisit of Hofstadter. Some Tea Partiers' baffling pronouncements on Obama's purported non-citizenship, Islamic faith, and treasonous Kenyan socialism were seen by many as the latest display of the paranoid style in American politics. To be sure, these kinds of claims did not

166

emerge simply with Obama's election and his response to the economic crisis. After all, fears of U.N. storm-troopers taking over America circulated widely during the Clinton years; charges that the Federal Emergency Management Agency had built camps that could detain citizens were rampant after Hurricane Katrina in 2005 – not to mention the belief that the 9/11 attacks were not perpetrated by al-Qaeda operatives but were the result of an "inside job" by some element of the U.S. government. But that was Hofstadter's point: there is a constant undercurrent of conspiracy and paranoia in American political culture. Yet it clearly did seem to be the case that the number, frequency, and intensity of paranoid outbursts increased markedly after Obama's election.[25] The preoccupation among at least some significant elements of the Tea Party with Obama's birth, race, and religion (and therefore the legitimacy of his election victory) belied the movement's claims that its anxieties were solely over economic matters. Race and national identity were also of major concern.

The Hofstadter revival thus rests on the fact that despite the scholarly problems inherent in the social psychological analysis of a paranoid style, Hofstadter's succinct oeuvre provides a set of tools for help in grasping some of the most baffling features of contemporary American politics. The overweening conservative discourse in the period following Obama's election was one of a particular kind of restoration, captured in the ubiquitous Tea Party slogan, "We want our country back!" The slogan echoed Hofstadter's wording on the feeling of dispossession characteristic of earlier conservative revolts. Again, in the historian's words, describing followers of Joseph McCarthy, "America has been largely taken away from them and their kind." In the Tea Party political moment, the right wing sees the country as having departed from an original (almost holy) consensus expressed in the Constitution.[26] As *New York Times* columnist David Brooks and others claimed, the Tea Party articulates a fundamental complaint shared by many Americans: the distrust of experts, especially government experts, and the feeling of being controlled by them. The Tea Party movement is made up of people who "are against the concentrated power of the educated class. They believe big government, big business, big media and the affluent professionals are merging to form a self-serving oligarchy – with bloated government, unsustainable deficits, high taxes and intrusive regulation."[27] That governmental control is unconstitutional, the Tea Party declares. Indeed, many Tea Partiers carry copies of the Constitution on their persons and consult and refer to the document, citing it in a rote originalism akin to how Christian fundamentalists carry and quote the inerrant Bible.[28]

After the 2008 election, local Tea Party chapters appeared to proliferate and well-funded national advocacy organizations – a few new, most longstanding – endeavored to put their stamp on the movement and lay claim to its intellectual basis. Although there are no comprehensive data on how many Tea Party groups were constituted, some research has been conducted. According to an October 2010 *Washington Post* study, many Tea Party organizations may have been essentially virtual, consisting of a person or two with an Internet address. Only 647 local Tea Party groups could be verified of the 2,300 to 3,000 affiliates claimed by the Tea Party Patriots (the national umbrella organization most closely linked to local Tea Party groups). And 70 percent of the groups said they had not participated in any political campaigning in 2010. At the same time, the research also revealed a great deal of genuine grassroots localism underlying the Tea Party movement. These were *not* "Astroturf" groups: that is, made to appear as if they were grassroots but in actuality created by existing national advocacy organizations.[29]

At the core of the movement were hundreds of active local Tea Party chapters and several national organizations: Tea Party Patriots, Tea Party Express, Tea Party Nation, FreedomWorks, Americans for Prosperity. These groups held the public protests and rallies widely covered by the news media, and devoted time and large amounts of cash to the 2010 midterm elections. Although there was no official platform, Tea Party-backed candidates stood united on tax-related issues. They advocated the continuation of the Bush tax cuts, the repeal of the estate tax, and the replacement of the progressive income tax with a flat tax or a national sales tax. Many expressed willingness to allow Social Security withholding to be diverted into private investment accounts and Medicare into a voucher system. Invoking the Tenth Amendment, they called for the repeal of the health care and financial regulatory legislation passed by the Democratic-controlled Congress, and insisted that many government social programs, even entire Cabinet departments, were unconstitutional.[30] Some advocated eliminating or lowering the federal minimum wage, others the elimination of the Seventeenth Amendment's direct election of senators by popular vote in favor of the pre-1913 system under which senators were elected by state legislatures. Many called for a balanced budget amendment. The idea of a cap-and-trade system for carbon emissions was anathema because such a system would entail further government control of private enterprise, not to mention the fact that Tea Partiers judged claims and evidence of climate change a liberal hoax.[31] Those political candidates who did not stand fast with these positions – even reliable hard-line conservative Republican incumbents – were treated with contempt by the Tea Party movement.

But note that the above summary of Tea Party-linked positions was largely the effort of outsiders to make coherence of them. When articulated by Tea Partiers themselves, in rallies or on the stump or on websites, the positions often were muddled, accompanied by false empirical data and outlandish historical claims. Here again, Hofstadter had relevance. His description of the intensely rationalistic mode of paranoid "scholarship" of earlier historical periods – an obsessive accumulation of facts and evidence and the marshaling of these toward a "proof" that required curious leaps of imagination and an ability to incorporate, thus explain away, conflicting information[32] – was also descriptive of much Tea Party and right-wing intellectual work in the 2000s. Indeed, in keeping with their anti-intellectual bent, Tea Partiers often displayed an extraordinary, almost defiant, ignorance of the nature of government and policy, as in the oft-repeated demand articulated during the health care bill debate: "Keep the government out of my Medicare!" Some Tea Party-aligned candidates for the 2010 midterm elections seemed almost to revel in their lack of specific knowledge of policy issues. It was as if ignorance was a badge of authenticity, of being one of the people and not of the reviled expert elite. One's values were far more important than one's command of policy details. To underscore this dynamic, the popular stock of Sarah Palin, GOP vice-presidential candidate in the 2008 election and Tea Party heroine, continued to rise despite resignation from office, public gaffes and untruths, and family scandals – in large part because, to supporters, her foibles and apparently unadorned lifestyle trappings made her seem genuine, un-elite.[33]

Who are these anti-elitists, these Tea Partiers? According to a widely cited 2010 CBS News/*New York Times* demographic survey, Tea Party supporters – not necessarily the activists – are older, better educated, and wealthier than the average American. They appear to be majority male; they are overwhelmingly white; they are mostly Protestant, and, of those, substantially evangelical. The basic demographics are these: 89 percent of Tea Partiers are white; 59 percent are men; 75 percent are 45 years of age or older; 56 percent have an annual household income of over $50,000 and 20 percent over $100,000; 61 percent are Protestant, 39 percent evangelical; 22 percent are Catholic, and 39 percent report attending religious services weekly; 54 percent identify as Republicans and 41 percent as Independents. More Tea Party supporters live in the South and West than in the Northeast and Midwest. Many are or were small business owners. Unlike their media portrayal as political neophytes, many have political experience, interestingly, in the Goldwater campaign.[34] Like the southern California Goldwater activists chronicled by Lisa McGirr in her study *Suburban Warriors*, women are rather prominent in the visible leadership of the local Tea Party groups.[35] The leadership and staff of the national, Washington DC-based organizations such as Americans for Prosperity and FreedomWorks – the longstanding ultra-free-market advocacy organizations established with funding from billionaire energy industrialists Charles and David Koch – tend to be long-term political operatives (like former House Majority Leader Dick Armey), including lobbyists and young former congressional staffers along with Internet-savvy communication consultants.[36] Surprisingly, most Tea Party adherents are not personally affected by the policies they hate. They have not lost jobs and do not feel particularly threatened by the decline of their retirement investments and/or drop in the value of their homes. Seventy percent of Tea Party adherents in the survey reported that their own economic situation is "fairly good," and only 14 percent testified to experiencing "hardship." Thus it is reasonable to conclude that their rage may be primarily ideological, not narrowly interest based. Their older age, whiteness, and class position would seem to comport with Hofstadter's notion of status decline. The "we want our country back" lament conveys a nostalgic loss for "the America we grew up in," an America in which people like themselves and their old-fashioned values were dominant. Note, however, that the Tea Party's status anxiety takes place during a period of economic decline, not, going by Hofstadter's usual historical pattern, during a period of economic prosperity.

The most important stated issue of concern for Tea Party supporters is the size and role of the federal government. Of course, the CBS News/*New York Times* poll also confirms at least in part the old saw that Americans tend to be ideologically conservative but operationally liberal: Tea Partiers want the big federal programs that benefit them (Medicare, Social Security) largely maintained and defended. And, when pushed, even the supposedly all-important issue of federal deficits yields, at least a bit, to self-interest: ninety-two percent of Tea Partiers support smaller government, but if smaller government would require cuts in Social Security, Medicare, education, or defense, the number drops nearly 20 percentage points. Granted, 73 percent support of smaller government is huge. Still, the drop could be read to show that Tea Partiers' concern is not simply the state of the economy as a whole but also their own economic conditions and, importantly, the sense of their deservingness. They are sanguine enough to have government assist *them* – "libertarianism with benefits," as the historian Ronald Formisano cleverly labels it[37] – but they oppose the expansion of government to assist others whom they consider undeserving.

Here it is important to delve a bit deeper. Just who are the undeserving? They are those who at least ostensibly are without an ethic of personal responsibility. Despite the purported animosity toward elites writ large, most of the Tea Party's anger is directed far less at Wall Street brokers and mortgage lenders than toward, on the one hand, those much lower in the class system, including the overextended foreclosed homeowners reviled in Rick Santelli's rant, and, on the other hand the "credentialed" – that is, those with higher educations who assume the role of experts and policy-makers. This points to the "producerist populism" examined in the previous chapter as underlying the Tea Party revolt and informing its implicit petit bourgeois class appeal.[38] Presumably caught between the personally irresponsible freeloaders below and subject to the government-backed whims and cultural snobbery of the liberal educated elite above, Tea Party followers tend to see themselves as the oppressed middle, the people who work hard, pay taxes, find themselves "regulated to death," and suffer discrimination because of unfair, unconstitutional affirmative action for (undeserving) minorities. Indeed, Tea Partiers discern a nefarious alliance between the credentialed elite and the undeserving.

Despite Tea Party disavowals of racism, racial minorities count heavily in the "undeserving" category. In a November 2010 poll, 61 percent of Tea Party supporters said that discrimination against whites was a major problem. Indeed, the occasional sign at Tea Party rallies equated the Obama presidency to "white slavery." Fifty-seven percent of white evangelicals echoed this sentiment, as did 56 percent of Republicans. (Forty-four percent of all people surveyed responded this way.)[39] Tea Party rallies often feature racial minorities as speakers in order to show that racism is anathema to the movement. But the heavy inclusion of racial minorities, including Hispanic illegal immigrants, in the category of the undeserving underscores that the Tea Party's racial attitudes are simply more subtle than overt racism; they define race as a cultural, rather than a biological, category. Racial minorities tend to be undeserving because they tend to want handouts. Young people, who demographically are now far less white than Tea Partiers, also tend to be included in the undeserving category – especially young people asking for help on student loans. And public sector workers, also often more racially diverse than Tea Partiers, are included in the undeserving category because their overly generous benefits and pensions come at taxpayers' expense.

The political subjectivity which the Tea Party appeals to – and, in turn, produces – is the victimized, dictated-to, predominantly white middle. Big government, referred to by one Tea Party author as "the Leviathan," à la Thomas Hobbes, irresponsibly funnels tax dollars to "losers."[40] As one typical online responder to the CBS News survey wrote, "One thing that seems apparent though, the real reason you jerks hate them is because they are the very people you lie-berals despise. Hard working, small business owning, tax paying people that make the country work."[41] This is nothing if not a restatement of the 1970s neoconservative critique of the New Class, and confirmation that victimhood is among the most powerful identity positions in American politics – for the left as well as the right. For the Tea Party the oppressor is not the familiar historic demons of left-wing populism, to wit, Wall Street, unfeeling corporations, and the malefactors of great wealth. Rather, the oppressor is the federal government and the smug educated elite that inhabits its swollen bureaucratic ranks. In assigning blame for the economic crisis, Tea Partiers generally pointed to Congress and the Obama administration rather than Wall Street or the Bush administration. Wall Street took some rhetorical hits here and there, but at the end of the day it mostly received a pass from the Tea Party.[42] In the final analysis, Tea Partiers' concern about the U.S. deficit is enveloped within their fear of tax hikes: big government will redistribute their hard-earned dollars to the undeserving. And the Tea Party's solution to the economic crisis? Cut back government drastically and return to tried-and-true free-market principles.

The ostensible sins of the Obama administration were embodied in three big government initiatives: (1) the $700 billion Troubled Asset Relief Program (TARP), which addressed the Great Recession by bailing out financial institutions (including the insurance company AIG, and certain large, troubled industrial corporations, notably General Motors and Chrysler, through bankruptcy and the government taking large, even if temporary, ownership positions); (2) the $787 billion dollar economic stimulus package known officially as the American Recovery and Reinvestment Act; and (3) the health care reform bill (The Patient Protection and Affordable Care Act), which amplified Tea Partiers' anxiety over the federal government's intrusive, costly, unconstitutional control over the everyday lives of Americans. The Tea Party denounced these actions as "socialism." A variation on the socialism charge was "corporatism," that the Obama administration was merging big government and big corporations into one unholy apparatus of social control. Conservatives of a libertarian bent, including people dear to the Tea Party movement such as Congressman Ron Paul and Fox News host Glenn Beck, articulated variations of this view. One of the clearest statements came from Steven Malanga of the Manhattan Institute:

> If [Obama's] agenda harks back to anything, it is to corporatism, the notion that elite groups of individuals molded together into committees or public–private boards can guide society and coordinate the economy from the top down and manage change by evolution, not revolution. It is a turn-of-the 20th century philosophy, updated for the dawn of the 21st century, which positions itself as an antidote to the kind of messy capitalism that has transformed the Fortune 500 and every corner of our economy in the last half century. To do so corporatism seeks to substitute the wisdom of the few for the hundreds of millions of individual actions and transactions of the many that set the direction of the economy from the bottom up.

The condemnation of Obama economic policy was that it undermined the dynamic nature of the free-enterprise system in favor of "a world managed by the few, the elect, through the state."[43] With the charge of corporatism, the animosity toward corporate CEOs and Wall Street was mostly shifted to the government. Hence the link again to producerist populism's anger about elites, experts, the New Class: expertise as a hidden, insidious form of liberalism. Obama betrayed laissez-faire entrepreneurial capitalism through dangerous and unconstitutional state interventionism. Bankers surely were not beloved by the Tea Party movement, but in the final analysis even the bankers were pawns in the Tea Party view: liberal government policies coerced banks to award sub-prime mortgages to undeserving minorities.[44] At the far rhetorical end of the accusation, Obama's corporatism was called "crony capitalism," even "Hitlernomics." Progressivism is fascism.[45]

Thus the continued relevance of Hofstadter's paranoid style analysis. In the 1950s some people needed an explanation as to why America wasn't winning the Cold War. Here was the most powerful country on earth losing the international struggle to its communist foes. Joseph McCarthy's explanation was: internal betrayal.

America's political leaders, if not themselves communists, protected and coddled the communist enemy and, in so doing, betrayed America. In the first decades of the twenty-first century, the Tea Party movement demanded an explanation as to why America, the greatest country in world history, found itself beset by a financial crisis and cruel economic recession. The Tea Party explanation was, at least in part: internal betrayal. The current domestic enemy is not communists but elitists, including the privileged, exotic, strangely named "Kenyan socialist" who is perhaps "the most anti-business president" in American history.[46] How else to understand the peculiar, undying preoccupation with Barack Obama's birth and whether he is secretly a Muslim?

Elements of Tea Party ideology and their intellectual roots

The Tea Party harangue about Obama's socialism underscores the apparent shift in the post-World War II conservative fusionist coalition from dominance by its traditionalist wing back to its libertarian wing – just at the moment when the capitalist economy ran into deep trouble. The traditionalists or social conservatives, as we have seen, came to the fore in the late 1970s when evangelical Christians became politically mobilized by the perception of threats to their institutions and values. Their entrance en masse into the world of electoral politics helped make the Reagan Revolution. Social conservatives held sway within the conservative coalition until the 2006 midterm elections. At the intellectual level, conservative political engagement in the wake of the Great Recession and the election of Barack Obama is in large part a re-fight over the New Deal. It is the libertarians who provide the intellectual firepower in the critique of the current situation and it is they who counsel the restoration of an "authentic" capitalism. Just as Richard Hofstadter has been revived on the left, on the right the sales of the decades-old books by Friedrich Hayek and Ayn Rand are once again on the rise, as is the long obscure 1850 text, *The Law*, by Frederic Bastiat, which denounced taxes on behalf of schools or roads as "theft."[47] FreedomWorks and Americans for Prosperity, the established ultra-free-market national advocacy organizations ardent to gather Tea Party activism under their ideological aegis, help provide Tea Party groups with arguments about taxation and deficits. When Tea Partiers protest Obama's policies as socialistic they are, at bottom, denouncing the level, perhaps even the principle, of taxation, for taxation beyond some very restricted level of collective security is, to them, illegitimate, theft even, which makes the entire thrust of twentieth-century progressive politics essentially criminal. In this regard the Tea Party is heir to the post-World War II exemption of military spending from the conservative denunciation of the state, as well as heir to the state-based tax revolts of the late 1970s, when California voters first rolled back state property taxes.[48] To be sure, this is complicated. Tea Partiers do support government entitlements such as Social Security and Medicare – but for themselves: the deserving, the responsible. But in the abstract, this is an attack on the New Deal and the New Deal institutions that have become so much a part of contemporary American life. Indeed, the right-wing intellectual attacks on the Obama administration from the likes of Jonah Goldberg, Amity Shlaes, Ron Paul, and Glenn Beck are simply new (and intellectually shabbier) versions of the 1940s critiques of the New Deal.[49]

Another conservative intellectual linkage, if only barely acknowledged, is the legacy of the political philosopher Leo Strauss. The "progressivism is fascism" charge stemmed in part from the identification of preexisting and timeless natural rights in America's founding documents, and the (reprehensible) rejection of these by liberals. Franklin Roosevelt's renegotiation of the social contract to include economic rights was a particular piece of perfidy. Because government, rather than God or nature, bestowed these economic rights, this precipitous act was said to undermine and repudiate the earlier timeless and universal rights. And that is because, as Strauss and others argued, the basis of political order is acceptance of moral constraints that lie outside the human sphere.[50] The consequence of the rejection of natural law is the elevation of the state over and against the citizen, the "progressive" planner/expert over the autonomous individual.

A peculiar, conspiratorial version of this thesis is found in the work of the Mormon anti-communist theorist W. Cleon Skousen. Championed by then Fox News host Glenn Beck and a primary source of the television commentator's on-air political lectures, Skousen's *The 5000 Year Leap* argues that the Constitution was rooted not in the Enlightenment but in the devout, Bible-based Christianity of the Founding Fathers. The founders, according to Skousen, rejected European collectivist philosophies in favor of divinely inspired principles of limited government. God-given natural law is the only reliable basis for sound government and just human relations.[51] Much along the lines of John Birch Society scholarship, Skousen's earlier works, *The Naked Communist* (1958) and *The Naked Capitalist* (1971), held forth on the worldwide communist threat and the betrayal of America by the "Ivy League Establishment."[52] Some Tea Party leaders, Glenn Beck prominent among them, lay the origin of progressive apostasy at the feet of Woodrow Wilson, the "original elitist," who, it is said, believed that university intellectuals should decide how the world should be run. It is the hubristic violation of natural law that aligns liberalism with fascism. Under the tutelage of Beck, a latter-day would-be Father Coughlin, the resurrected understanding of timeless, original rights is joined to the attack on elites and the government institutions championed by those elites. It was under Woodrow Wilson, for example, that the loathed Federal Reserve System and the graduated income tax came to be. Hating Woodrow Wilson is a maxim among intellectually inclined Tea Partiers.[53]

Glenn Beck has become a leading Tea Party public intellectual, supplementing his lectures on both television (for several years on the Fox News Channel, now on Glenn Beck TV) and radio (distributed to 400-plus stations by Premiere Radio Networks) with an online, for-profit Beck University. Among other things, Beck discusses serious books on the air, sketching diagrams and conceptual maps, and establishing particular interpretations of historical context. His lectures and courses recycle themes from the works of conservative thinkers W. Cleon Skousen, Frederic Bastiat, and others, and condemn the American history taught in schools and universities as false. The conventional version of American history, according to Beck and his mentors, is the result of a conspiracy by ideologically driven liberals. In this, Alexander Zaitchik and Sean Wilentz each have noted, Beck has revived the ideas circulated some fifty years ago by the John Birch Society.[54]

The turn to Skousen as an intellectual authority for the Tea Party underscores the fact that the apparent dominance of the libertarians in the current version of conservative fusionism is, in the end, not all that significant, for accompanying the Tea Party plea to restore genuine capitalism is also a call to restore genuine Christianity. Skousen's *The 5000 Year Leap* is one of many tracts in a decades-long campaign among conservative evangelicals to make clear that the Founding Fathers explicitly intended the United States to be a Christian nation, and that America's laws and school curricula ought to reflect that historical and genealogical fact. A central figure in this particular effort is David Barton, another Glenn Beck favorite, and a principal textbook is *America's Providential History* by Mark A.

Beliles and Stephen K. McDowell.[55] Presented in large format with many illustrations, *America's Providential History* ties biblical passages to the writings and practices of the Founding Fathers. The Constitution, divinely inspired, rests on bedrock notions of individual salvation and individual freedom; liberty is a matter of following the Spirit of the Lord.[56] The book's claim that government-bestowed rights and entitlement programs elevate government over God and thus constitute idolatry is widely held among Tea Partiers. As Sharron Angle put it in a radio interview during her unsuccessful 2010 campaign as GOP candidate for the Nevada U.S. Senate,

> Entitlement programs . . . make government our God. And that's really what's happening in this country is a violation of the First Commandment. We have become a country entrenched in idolatry, and that idolatry is the dependency upon our government. We're supposed to depend upon God for our protection and our provision and our daily bread, not for our government.[57]

Note the elision of First Amendment to First Commandment. It is not simply un-American to rely on government; it is un-Christian, as well. The linkage of this perspective to American exceptionalism also is clear and direct: What makes the United States the greatest nation in the history of the world and its values universal is the fact that America is based on private enterprise, which is itself the fruit of Christian (specifically Protestant) concepts of individual freedom and responsibility.[58] These motifs, by the way, are not very far removed from the religious and political fundamentalism articulated by Carl McIntire in the 1950s. In sum, although there exist some political differences between libertarians and social conservatives on questions regarding the extent of civil liberties, the current Christian right and the libertarians have the identical long-term political goal – to shrink support for government. The new twenty-first-century culture war is waged over the role of government.[59]

To be sure, certain evangelical leaders expressed some dismay about Tea Party politics early in 2010.[60] The Tea Party is funded largely by persons and organizations closely tied to pro-business, ultra-free-market conservatism, not to church-linked social conservatism. But talk of a rift between libertarians and social conservatives is clearly overblown. The ethnographic part of Skocpol and Williamson's study of local Tea Party organizations revealed that social conservative members generally ran the meetings and propelled the intellectual agenda, and the libertarian members overwhelmingly tended to go along.[61] This cooperation extends to the national conservative conversation, as well. At the Values Voter Summit, a key conference where contemporary conservatives meet, debate, recruit, posture, and establish their policy orientations and positions, the religious right fully embraced the Tea Party movement at the September 2010 confab. The announced foci of the summit represented an effort to bridge libertarians and traditionalists: "Protect Marriage; Champion Life; Strengthen the Military; Limit Government; Control Spending; Defend Our Freedoms." The summit featured many of the old social conservative hands, from Family Research Council's Tony Perkins to American Values president Gary Bauer, who, while embracing the economically inflected themes of the horror of massive government deficits and Obama's class warfare, tied these effortlessly to old stances on abortion and human rights for the unborn, judicial activism, and the danger of the homosexual agenda.[62] Glenn Beck may have become more dubious of the threat of the homosexual agenda, but his call for a "third Great Awakening" surely fused a social libertarian agenda with that of the religious right.[63]

In terms of policy, an insistent focus of Republican office-holders at state and federal levels after the 2010 elections was to pare back abortion rights and defund Planned Parenthood, even changing the category of rape covered under the abortion exceptions to "forcible rape."[64] Likewise, political figures usually identified as economic conservatives, such as Paul Ryan, leader of the GOP House majority on budget matters, couched proposed cuts to government "entitlements" in the personal responsibility language common to both social conservatism and libertarianism: "[W]e don't want to turn the safety net into a hammock that lulls able-bodied people to lives of dependency and complacency, that drains them of their will and their incentive to make the most of their lives."[65] The raucous 2012 GOP primaries revealed an ideological temper that wedded economic conservatism to social conservatism through the culture war on elites and entitlements. The unexpected ascension of the Catholic ultra-traditionalist Rick Santorum as serious challenger to Mitt Romney from the right was due to Santorum's channeling of the social concerns evangelical conservatives hold dear. Romney, who styled himself as a business conservative, won the GOP nomination, but he was forced to embrace many of the positions of the evangelical bloc. And in choosing Paul Ryan as his running mate for the 2012 GOP ticket, Romney tapped a hard-line conservative, a passionate devotee of Ayn Rand, who bridged both the evangelical and libertarian right. In an interview on the Glenn Beck program, Ryan paraded his fusionist bona fides: "[Progressivism] is really a cancer because it basically takes the notion that our rights come from God and nature and turns it on its head and says, no, no, no, no, no, they come from government, and we here in government are here to give you your rights and therefore ration, redistribute and regulate your rights."[66]

In short, this remains the fusionist conservatism of traditionalism and libertarianism described in previous chapters, now embodied in the Tea Party movement. Any who argue that the Tea Party's influence had run its course by 2012 need only consider its central role in several important GOP primary elections, including the defeat of six-term moderate Richard Lugar in the Senate primary in Indiana and the easy victory of Tea Party challenger Ted Cruz in the Senate primary in Texas.[67] Mitt Romney himself articulated a version of Tea Party producerist ideology in a closed-door speech to wealthy donors during the presidential campaign, in which he declared that 47 percent of the people would vote for President Obama "no matter what," because they are "dependent upon government . . . believe that they are victims . . . believe that government has a responsibility to care for them . . . [and] believe that they are entitled to health care, to food, to housing, to you name it." The 47 percent were takers, as opposed to makers, of wealth.[68] Although Romney moderated his self-presentation during the campaign, he essentially restated the "47 percent 'takers'" declaration in a post-election conference call with fundraisers and donors, attributing his loss to President Obama in part to big policy "gifts" that Obama had bestowed on loyal Democratic constituencies, including young voters, African-Americans, and Hispanics.[69]

Connections to violent groups?

To the extent that the Tea Party movement reflects the fear of the strong state and the rage at feeling controlled, like its historic predecessor movements on the right it hovers between "legitimate" conservative populism and proto-violent conspiracy. The dispersed nature of most Tea Party organizations means that the groups can be quite different, from truly local grassroots newcomers, to essentially GOP front organizations such as the Tea Party Express and market advocates FreedomWorks and Americans for Prosperity, to allies of a reinvigorated John Birch Society and the Patriot and Militia movements. These latter movements, hard to classify clearly, have hovered at the fringes of anti-establishment conservatism for decades. Since the 1970s, Patriot and Militia groups have wrapped themselves in a discourse of reaction and violence in an effort to renegotiate masculinity in the wake of the U.S. defeat in Vietnam and the challenge posed to traditional culture by minority and feminist political activism.[70] The groups were reenergized by the election to the presidency of an African-American man with a foreign-sounding name and suspected Muslim ties. The Patriot and Militia groups hew to an anti-government, anti-tax strict constitutionalism and are sometimes organized along paramilitary lines. They reputedly accumulate weapons and engage in military-type training exercises. A few of their members have engaged in racist violence. Timothy McVeigh, the domestic terrorist responsible for the bombing of the Oklahoma City federal building in 1995, traveled in Patriot movement circles.

Patriot and Militia groups now operate websites that offer their conspiratorial analysis of current events. In their view, reminiscent of Phyllis Schlafly's *A Choice Not an Echo*, governments and economies are controlled by a network of shadowy international elites. The United States itself is on the cusp of a "New World Order" of socialist tyranny. Harking back to an old anti-Semitic canard, the Patriot movement views the "Jewish-controlled" Federal Reserve as the ultimate symbol of New World Order power. Perhaps the greatest concern of Patriot and Militia groups is the perceived campaign of the federal government to confiscate guns and impose martial law. In their view, the government orchestrated the 9/11 attacks on the World Trade Center and the Pentagon in order to pursue those diabolical aims.[71]

The connections between the Patriot and Militia movements and the Tea Party are anecdotal and subject to exaggeration, but the groups engage in some of the same analysis, and share a certain amount of the same rhetoric. Without the intervention of good patriots, declares the Friends for Liberty, a fairly typical Tea Party affiliate based in northern Idaho/eastern Washington, "Those who wish to impose collectivism and tyranny on this nation could prevail."[72] As such, some Tea Party supporters speak of resorting to their guns to meet the threat of tyranny.[73] But this may be posturing for reporters and symptomatic of the weird romance of parroting the rhetoric of the fringe groups that float at the boundaries of many populist political movements.[74] Other journalists who report on Tea Party rallies speak of their "festive and friendly" atmosphere notwithstanding the tough rhetoric from the stage.[75] Whether or not the Tea Partiers have knowledge of William F. Buckley's historic move to purge the John Birch Society from the conservative movement in the 1960s, some of the larger Tea Party organizations try similarly to police their more wayward members or allies. To the degree that there is an official Tea

Party, it dismisses those who dispute President Obama's citizenship (the "Birthers") and tries to discipline or create distance from those who display protest signs of Obama as Hitler at Tea Party events (see the billboard photo in chapter 1). And in another nod to earlier political battles on the right, the Tea Party tries to keep its distance from the Republican Party. Much like the Goldwater activists of the early 1960s, Tea Partiers work within the Republican Party but display hostility toward its "establishment" wing and declaim the intention to take it over. Thus Tea Party members may seem in thrall at public rallies to Republican Party celebrities such as GOP vice-presidential candidate Sarah Palin or Congresswoman Michele Bachman, but within Tea Party councils they are protective of the independence of the movement from Republican Party takeover. Indeed, many Tea Party locals endeavor to keep their distance from the national organizations that claim to speak for the Tea Party movement.[76] The old worry of being absorbed by the establishment runs very deep.

In short, the Tea Party displays characteristics of a collection of generally like-minded, enraged groups rather than a tightly controlled political movement. Indeed, the Tea Party grassroots fashion themselves as leaderless, decentralized, and flexible, patterned after the distributed intelligence of the Internet, or, perhaps closer to their ideological predispositions, the decentralized genius of the market. The Tea Party movement is held together – by design – not by a top-down structure or through centralized leadership, but by commitment to a common set of values.[77] The movement's strength at this historical juncture has lain in its ability to galvanize people to political action outside the customary structures of big-time, established, moneyed politics; again, the local Tea Party organizations often resist being co-opted into those structures. That said, at the same time, the Tea Party has provided a grassroots connection to the Washington, DC Republican-based policy-making organizations that have touted low taxes and reduced government spending, and have denounced regulation for more than thirty-five years. (We might call the latter "established" anti-establishment conservatism.) As noted earlier, the national organizations provide important technical, organizational, and logistic support to the local organizations; they help fund the big rallies and offer speakers and materials and website advice.[78] Finally, to return for a moment to the William F. Buckley–John Birch Society story, it is noteworthy that the JBS is now back in the legitimate conservative fold. As for the Patriot and Militia movements, they may influence some Tea Party rhetoric, but they remain at the margins of the movement. Still, in the nebulous and fluid political imagination, the Patriot and Militia groups hover like a bad omen, as if to warn that should the peoples' righteous anger not be heeded, the groups will descend with force of violence upon the body politic to "refresh . . . the tree of liberty . . . with the blood of patriots and tyrants" – a quote from Thomas Jefferson that Tea Partiers are very fond of repeating.

Foreign policy (or the lack thereof)

An important and curious feature of the Tea Party is the absence of substantive concern in the vital area of foreign policy. The Tea Party movement's focus, at least for the time being, is almost entirely domestic. This represents the most notable break from the pattern of post-war conservative fusionism, which, recall, made its mark by distancing itself from traditional right-wing isolationism and instead embraced the Cold War crusade against international communism. Indeed, what characterized the original fusion was its obsession with the two "rollbacks": of the New Deal and of international communism. Yet there is barely any talk among Tea Party adherents about foreign policy. To the extent that there is, suggests David Brooks, it is in reaction to what the "elite" believes. Because the educated class is internationalist, isolationist sentiment is now at an all-time high. Because the educated class believes in multilateral action, so the number of conservative Americans who believe we should "go our own way" has risen sharply.[79] In this regard, the Tea Party looks like a throwback to the pre-fusionist era. Tea Party thinking on foreign policy perhaps defaults to the libertarian Congressman Ron Paul (and Patrick Buchanan before him), who essentially articulates a paleo-conservative, isolationist view of the world, including opposition to the wars in Iraq and Afghanistan. Glenn Beck has been inching toward this position.[80] But while Ron Paul has appeal to libertarians, his condemnation of America's wars makes many in the Tea Party movement (not to mention the GOP) nervous. Indeed, always keen to "support the troops" and display their patriotism, the Tea Party tends not to make public pronouncements on foreign policy lest those cast aspersions on the armed forces and their missions.

Thus the assumption of a default paleo-conservatism is probably too definitive. Tea Party-affiliated leaders, as they climb the political ladder and are forced to comment on foreign policy matters, seem to be all over the map. Sarah Palin and Marco Rubio, Florida's 2010 elected U.S. Senator and Tea Party favorite, endorse aspects of George

W. Bush's aggressive neoconservative foreign policy. Palin believes the United States must take the fight to international terrorism (and has sidled up to Israel in order to facilitate that fight, which may also reflect her aim to appeal to the Christian right's Zionism), but she also offers a variation of the old John Quincy Adams warning, "We don't go looking for dragons to slay."[81] Rubio more fully echoes the forthright neoconservatism of the recent Republican past, pressing on the Senate floor for still more military intervention against still more enemies in the Middle East. Mitt Romney, characteristically all over the map, articulated both neoconservative and realist foreign policy views during the 2012 presidential campaign. But one thing he reiterated constantly was the Tea Party charge that President Obama had gone around the world "apologizing" for America.[82]

Perhaps the one common foreign policy article of faith among the Tea Party is the aversion to international organizations.[83] In this they continue the legacy of their Bush administration neoconservative forebears. But the neoconservatives are largely in eclipse in the current Tea Party moment. Indeed, neoconservatives are more than occasionally denounced in Tea Party broadsides. A Pew poll found that the share of conservative Republicans agreeing that the United States should "pay less attention to problems overseas" increased from 36 percent in 2004 to 55 percent in May 2011.[84] Hence some Tea Party-affiliated congressmen do not blanch with horror at the prospect of budget cuts to the Pentagon, not only because of their overweening commitment to cut federal spending, but also because they don't mind pulling back on American military commitments abroad. Clearly, the ennui engendered by George W. Bush's wars and the influence of the Tea Party movement have served to expand the numbers of Republicans returning to the party's historic Robert A. Taft foreign policy isolationism and quietism.

This neglect of foreign affairs, of course, has consequences. The Tea Party's (and, it seems, most everybody else's) preoccupation with the domestic agenda means that the Iraq foreign policy debacle has essentially disappeared from view and its essential failure remains unexamined. And, crucially, that failure is not just a foreign policy failure. The Iraq War was and continues to be an important factor in domestic economic difficulties. Although the tax cuts that favored the wealthy were a Bush administration priority in and of themselves, it is arguable that war deficit spending hid the true cost of the tax cuts and the Middle East wars – transferring the financial burden of the wars from the present onto later generations – and thus made the wars (particularly Iraq) easier to pursue politically. One should not discount the possibility that this was not serendipity but rather a conscious strategy to hide costs, thought through by Bush operatives from the outset. After all, it was the only time in recent American history that taxes were cut during time of war. Moreover, as professors Joseph Stiglitz and Linda Bilmes argue, the war contributed indirectly to disastrous monetary policy and regulations.

> The Iraq war didn't just contribute to the severity of the financial crisis, though; it also kept us from responding to it effectively. Increased indebtedness meant that the government had far less room to maneuver than it otherwise would have had. More specifically, worries about the (war-inflated) debt and deficit constrained the size of the stimulus, and they continue to hamper our ability to respond to the recession.[85]

Recent foreign policy and domestic policy remain inextricably linked. Tea Party and conservative ire at Obama's spending ignores the fact that the Bush tax cuts added over $2 trillion to the national debt in the first decade of the twentieth century.[86] Deficit spending for the Bush wars at the very least ran over $1 trillion and, as estimated by Stiglitz and Bilmes, between $3 and $4 trillion over the long term, with nary a peep from the right. These numbers dwarf the deficits under Obama.

A middle level of analysis: The importance of institutions

There is a legitimate and important debate to be had about the limits of federal deficit spending, the efficacy and size of economic stimulus, how much taxation is enough, the dangers of corporatism, and the like. But Richard Hofstadter was concerned with the *style* of populist revolt in the mid-twentieth century in large part because it made reasoned debate impossible. As such, in the current period, it is the style of Tea Party anxieties, gripes, and claims that spurs the Hofstadter revival.

Can we use the insight of Hofstadter's paranoid style to understand the Tea Party movement without succumbing to the reductionist social psychology it inevitably becomes? Hofstadter's analysis entailed the description of a political style, tied to a grand social psychological theory. A central flaw, I have suggested, is the absence of a middle level of analysis to connect the two. Hofstadter presented a macro argument (social structural conditions that produce status anxiety) and a micro argument (the paranoid style), with nothing in between.

Here I suggest a middle level of institutions that work in and through three key contexts. At the broad theoretical level, an institution is a well-established and structured pattern of behavior or of relationships that is accepted as a fundamental part of a culture. At a more concrete level, the organizations that facilitate that pattern are also identified as institutions. Institutions create meaning for individuals, and shape human behavior through rules, norms, and other frameworks. A middle level of institutions permits us to better connect political style, in Hofstadter's terms, with social structure. It also enables us to grant the existence of a paranoid style while acknowledging the legitimate elements of the political critique that underlay the rage, for it is important to concentrate not just on what is false and worrisome about Tea Party ideology, but also on what it gets right.[87]

Institutions operate in distinct historical and cultural contexts. The first context to consider in an analysis of the Tea Party is structural: that is, the nature of political power in a two-party liberal democracy built on a mixed capitalist economy and a powerful bias in favor of capitalist institutions. The second context is cultural. Here, appreciating the strength and appeal of particular kinds of political culture characteristic of the American tradition, specifically individualism and suspicion of the state, is crucial. The third context is political and hinges on the decline of the liberal left. For the last few decades preoccupied with identity politics – equity issues concerning race, gender, and sexuality, to name the most prominent – the left no longer effectively addresses fundamental issues with regard to class and political economy. The crucial middle level, then, consists of the institutions that channel anger, anxiety, and critique in particular directions, with kinds of analysis that draw on particular historical resonances, and that produce specific kinds of political subjectivities. As conservatives have always maintained, ideas matter. But that argument, by itself, falls short. For ideas to matter, they must be channeled effectively in and through institutions. At that institutional level, the concrete networks of money, media, and political organizations are key.

The structural nature of political power within a mixed capitalist economy

The "We want our country back" anthem, punctuated by rally posters of President Obama in whiteface or alongside photos of Hitler or

Lenin, may very well express both a racist shock that a black man is now the president of the United States and a fundamental misunderstanding of the nature of socialism.[88] But other aspects of the Tea Party critique of current American politics are rooted in reality. On the one hand, Washington politicians, Democrats nearly as much as Republicans, *did* do the bidding of Wall Street and the banking institutions over the last three decades, what with financial deregulation and the refusal to extend banking rules to "shadow banks," the repeal of the Glass–Steagall separations between insurers, investment banks, and commercial banks, and legislation forbidding government oversight of derivatives and similar financial instruments.[89] The credit default swaps and insurance schemes that repackaged junk mortgages and uncollateralized loans as prime-rated instruments, earning brokers millions in easy fees and a leading source of the financial meltdown of 2007–8, were unregulated – by design.[90] Institutionalized bank lobbying and political contributions, buttressed by ideological campaigns extolling globalization, the virtues of deregulation, and market fundamentalism, quite obviously helped grease the favorable legislative and regulatory treatment of financial institutions and speculative practices over many years. The revolving door and web of personal relationships that tied Goldman Sachs, Citigroup, Fannie Mae and Freddie Mac, the Federal Reserve, and the Treasury are empirical facts.[91] In this regard, the populist sense that Washington and Wall Street have been in bed together reflects political reality. The Tea Party protests registered a genuine hatred for the financial bailout and the politics that underlay it. The Tea Party's political vocabulary condemning the class bias and unfairness of the bailout had broad political resonance.

On the other hand, the Tea Party critique entailed a flawed understanding of the nature of the structure of institutions and power. The government's reaction to the financial crisis of 2008, in a classic instance of Keynesian-derived crisis management, resulted in a massive infusion of federal money into the economy via the rescue of banks and Wall Street. To the degree that the state bailed out financial institutions while common people lost jobs and homes, the Tea Party at least in part properly discerned the bias of the state in favor of capitalist institutions. But that bias was reductively and misleadingly characterized as favoring "the elite," thus *personalizing* what is a structural relationship. The built-in bias inheres in the fact that banking institutions constitute a crucial part of the economic infrastructure – the institutions and mechanisms and procedures of value, credit, and trust that underlie the American economy. The state is structurally and historically disposed to maintain that infrastructure and, typically in the American case, protect its private nature, not supplant it. In general, the state provides the supports for private capital accumulation and for some level of social welfare, and depends on taxes and borrowing to fund these programs. Occasionally the state needs to step in to protect the infrastructure from itself. Even the George W. Bush administration recognized this. After all, the massive state interventionist Troubled Asset Relief Program (TARP) was initiated during the final months of office of a stridently conservative administration. The error of the Tea Party and its fellow travelers on the right is to mistake governmental actions to rescue the financial infrastructure as "socialism." In fact it is anything but. President Bush's $700 billion TARP and Obama's $787 billion dollar economic stimulus package were instances of the state engaging in crisis management to rescue capitalism from its periodic failures. A government that fails to engage in crisis management under these circumstances hazards economic depression and corresponding peril to civil order, not to mention the loss of its political legitimacy.[92]

Of course there was no inevitability as to the specific content of the state's crisis management. The government could have required banks to take a "haircut": that is, receive only a percentage of what they were owed by insurers such as AIG. The government could have required the banks' agreement on new regulatory authority in exchange for getting bailed out. In principle the government could have taken over major banks, for example, and directed their lending practices. The government could have replicated the famous Pecora hearings that investigated the Wall Street crash in 1932, and clawed back corporate bonuses and even prosecuted certain traders and bank executives.[93] Had the government gone this route, the Tea Party's accusation of socialism would at least be a bit more plausible. But upending the structural bias toward large capitalist institutions would have required a remarkable, and hence unlikely, challenge to corporate power, customary political expectations, and legal authority. Still, President Obama, if we can believe Ron Suskind's *Confidence Men*, did advocate the restructuring of many of the large, troubled banks, starting with Citigroup, but was overruled by his economic advisers (some of whom had been associated with the deregulatory policies of the past).[94] Various parties have disputed Suskind's account. Notwithstanding, the Obama administration's unwillingness to go this tough, confrontational route served to cement the outraged sense that Washington and Wall Street continued to sleep together. After its initial broad condemnation of the bailout, the Tea Party moved quickly toward the conventional libertarian critique that capitalism was good and big government was the problem; that corporations and the rich were " job creators" hamstrung and corrupted by parasitic political elites; and, finally, that, absent corrupt government intervention, America could return to the simple, small heroics of individual entrepreneurial initiative and the timeless free-enterprise verities of supply and demand. This is where the default small business/petit bourgeois sentiments of many Tea Party members were colonized by the ultra-free-market, stridently anti-tax positions of the plutocrat-funded FreedomWorks, Americans for Prosperity, and Club for Growth advocacy organizations. The national organizations largely succeeded in guiding the Tea Party movement back to a conventional libertarian critique.

American political culture

The bias of the state toward capitalist institutions is both structural and a mainstay of political culture. Political culture can be one of those slippery terms that explain too much and hence not much at all. But the concept does have its uses. It can be defined as the reigning beliefs on how political, governmental, and economic life should be carried out and the behavioral norms associated with those beliefs. And America *does* have a distinct political culture. It has always been characterized by individualism and suspicion of the strong state. Indeed, Richard Hofstadter's "old liberalism," rooted in the legacies of Presidents Jefferson and Jackson, championed small producers against the statism of the Hamiltonian elites. The central thesis of Louis Hartz's *The Liberal Tradition in America*, that most Americans are essentially Lockean liberals committed to a worldview limiting the state's role to protecting property relations among equal producers, is not to be taken lightly.[95]

This longstanding political culture inspires the interpretation proffered by observers such as Mark Lilla. The powerful tropes of individualism and suspicion of the state lie beneath both the anti-authoritarianism of the 1960s and the anti-government populism of the Tea Party, Lilla suggests. For him, the Tea Party is the latest efflorescence of the wave of populist libertarianism that started on the left in the 1960s as the celebration of private autonomy. The new, Tea Party version betrays a key difference. Historically, populist movements use the rhetoric of class solidarity to seize political power so that "the people" can exercise it for their common benefit. Tea Party populist rhetoric does something different. It fires up emotions by appealing to individual opinion, individual autonomy, and individual choice, all in the service of neutralizing, not using, political power. It gives voice to those who feel they are being bullied. They want to be left alone.[96] Following the Hofstadter logic through, the current political style of conservative rage reflects not just status anxiety, but a broader, more disturbing sense of the dependence of Americans on government action, a dependence that eats at the longstanding and deeply held American belief in individual autonomy.[97] Paradoxically, of course, the very individualism the Tea Party promotes was a principal contributing factor to the current economic and cultural crisis. On the one hand, the no-holds-barred, individualistic "rent-seeking" behavior of the bankers, traders, and mortgage lenders was central to the Great Recession. The financial deregulation that allowed such unaccountable speculative practices embodied, in part, the idea that regulations stifled individual entrepreneurial effort.[98] On the other hand, the politics of victimhood endemic to Tea Party rhetoric in the end generates a beggar-thy-neighbor dynamic that undermines the notion of a collective life. The broader point is that in times of grave economic stress, during which the state acts to protect the socio-economic order through an unusual degree of intervention on behalf of capitalist institutions, some significant portion of the American citizenry becomes unnerved about individual autonomy – even when that intervention guards against further economic instability and even depression. Now, pointing out the strength of particular historical tropes does not really prove anything about why the Tea Party would choose one set over others. But the strength of American individualist political culture does, I think, indicate how and why certain tropes have more salience and resonance than others – especially when they are so effectively referenced, appropriated, and channeled by networks of institutions over long periods of time.

The decline of a left alternative

The noisy arrival of the Tea Party and its successes in the 2010 midterm elections underscore a hard question about the politics of the moment: why was the popular response to the worst economic crisis since the Great Depression a distinctly conservative one? This is as important as it is a difficult question to answer. The popular reaction to the Great Depression of the 1930s was generally liberal, even left wing. It was the widespread discontent of the people,

189

manifest in political agitation, protests, and strikes, which pushed the Roosevelt administration to experiment with state intervention in the economy in ways that so departed from the previous laissez-faire orthodoxy.[99] In the 1930s the left was energetic, its analyses acute, the movement was not yet discredited by Soviet totalitarianism, and its influence was vital in the popular discontent of the time. But, of course, the communist movement was destroyed in American politics, and destroyed itself as a viable ideology owing to its connection to Soviet despotism under Stalin. The power of trade unionism as a social movement – and hence as the agent of progressive activism – declined in the post-World War II period, initially owing to Taft–Hartley, and subsequently as the manufacturing sector and union density declined and unions' endeavors shrunk largely to the servicing of their members' delimited economic needs. It may be an overly harsh judgment, but labor's political horizons narrowed after, in effect, it got its piece of post-war prosperity. And as the American intellectual left drifted from concern with class and economic policy to concern about culture, group stigma, and identity – and as traditional Keynesianism seemed less able to deal with the drift of the economy by the 1970s – liberalism's political hegemony came under challenge, its allegiance to and loyalty from the working class weakened, its solutions to socioeconomic dilemmas viewed as problematic. Indeed, in our current period it is the institutions of the New Deal that are the status quo, now subject to the vagaries of bureaucratization and corruption, and hence subject to pointed criticism. Unlike the 1930s, left solutions to the endemic problems of advanced capitalism and the fiscal crisis of the state appear problematic, if not exhausted.

Politically, the embrace of the African-American struggle for equality by the liberal left in the 1960s – a righteous, necessary embrace – had serious political consequences, some foreseen, some unforeseen. The electoral departure of the white South from the Democratic Party was understood as virtually inevitable. And when the federal government began to enforce civil rights in the north through school busing and affirmative action, the result was antagonism on the part of white ethnics toward interventionist government in general and disaffection from the Democratic coalition. The unforeseen drift of the intellectual left from the struggle for political-economic reform to what has come to be known as identity politics largely sundered its historic connection with the working class and the critique of structural power, and diminished the left's historic project defending the common good and expanding universal values.[100] As one commentator put it, liberals "lost sight of the essential element that had made the coalition possible in the first place: the sense that liberalism stood with the common man and woman in their struggle against economic forces too large and powerful to be faced by individuals on their own."[101] Into that breach came a strong conservative critique, which claimed for conservatism the mantle of common sense and commonly held values. Tea Party author John O'Hara encapsulates the critique thus:

> In modern times, . . . the Left has taken the fight for racial equality to be a Good Housekeeping Seal of Approval for all their protests. They claim to be fighting for equality, but what the nanny-state proponents want is to legislate everything from your car's mileage, despite safety concerns, to whether you can smoke in your own home, allegedly *due* to safety concerns, and much more. Where will it end? What's worse, the Left does not merely want to inhibit others, it wants to enrich itself while manufacturing consent. While the Right wants to be left alone, the Left wants to take, control, and distribute as it sees fit when it sees fit. Leftists are moochers who depend on the fruits of a harvest carved out by secretive, niche legislation, government mandates, and union dues – force and fraud rather than the successes or failures of individual attempts at productivity.[102]

The point is that it is impossible to talk about why the Great Recession garnered a conservative political response without acknowledging the weakness of any left alternative. This judgment may itself be provisional in light of the "Occupy Wall Street" phenomenon of late 2011, which reintroduced to the political arena basic questions about inequality and the political power of corporations. But Occupy has hitherto kept its distance from conventional politics.

Institutions: Networks of money, media, and political organizations

The middle level of analysis – highlighting the important institutional role of networks of money, media, and political/intellectual organizations in supporting, directing, and energizing political movements – received some treatment in previous chapters. Recall that in the early 1970s, leading neoconservatives and some corporate leaders called on business to defend itself by entering directly into the realm of public ideas. Since then, conservatives have wielded their muscle through tight networks of foundations, think tanks, and partisan media. The Tea Party movement has benefited from those previous networks and has expanded them. The movement is networked internally and externally, connected through right-wing mass media (particularly Fox News Channel and talk radio), a plethora of Internet sites and blogs, tutored by longtime conservative political entrepreneurs, and bankrolled in part by right-wing billionaires and their foundations. Anti-establishment *éminence grise* Richard Viguerie dutifully leads Tea Party workshops and offers sage advice. Dick Armey lends his political expertise as former House Majority Leader through FreedomWorks.[103] Many Tea Party and ideologically affiliated organizations receive significant funding from Koch-affiliated foundations and other right-wing funding sources. One must be careful here and acknowledge the reality of the social movement's values and positions. As mentioned earlier, the Tea Party is not a "manufactured" movement; it is not "Astroturf." It is a grassroots manifestation of genuine anxiety and deeply held political values fueled in particular by opposition to the policies of President Obama and profound unease about his identity.

But one also must understand the movement's resource base and how its media and corporate backers pursue both material and ideological advantage. The increasingly tightly bound networks of anti-establishment conservative institutions – right-wing mass media and websites, plutocratic right-wing entrepreneurs, foundations, advocacy organizations, and think tanks described in previous chapters – feed the Tea Party, draw upon its vitality, and try to channel its grassroots activist energy. The money from wealthy entrepreneurs that now flows into the Tea Party is from the same sources that have sustained conservative political ideas and organizations for decades. Extensive and largely impossible to track, Tea Party-directed funds were primed to defeat moderate Republicans and Democrats in the 2010 midterm elections.[104] Rupert Murdoch's Fox News gives the Tea Party immense media coverage and its commentators act to orchestrate the movement. And Murdoch, through his News Corporation umbrella, directly engages in sizeable political contributions. The Koch brothers have bankrolled conservative organizations over many years to the tune of many tens of millions of dollars, and pledged hundreds of millions toward the defeat of Barack Obama in 2012. Bob Perry, the Houston homebuilder and key benefactor of the Swift Boat Veterans for Truth, the group that attacked Democrat John Kerry in the 2004 presidential campaign, gave $7 million to American Crossroads, the conservative group founded by former George W. Bush chief adviser Karl Rove. Las Vegas tycoon Sheldon Adelson single-handedly bankrolled Newt Gingrich's presidential primary campaign. After Gingrich faltered, Adelson donated scores of millions to Mitt Romney or the campaigning groups ("Super PACS") supporting him.[105] And these are the contributions that are known. Under the virtually unregulated campaign finance world set by the Supreme Court in the 2010 *Citizens United* case, it is as if Frank Capra's chilling 1941 comedy drama *Meet John Doe*, in which a proto-fascist newspaper owner finances a naïve, well-meaning social movement in order to hijack it and propel him to political power, has become reality.[106] Only in our moment the Kochs, the Murdochs, the Scaifes, the Perrys, the Adelsons have no need themselves to capture political office; their bankrolling of the Tea Party and the GOP means that any nationally prominent conservative Republican will do. Again, money does not create a movement, but it is a key material resource that can shape its positions and talking points, which, in turn, affect the general political discourse.[107]

The latter point underlies one more crucial change in political context, hinted at in chapter 2: polarizing dogmatism. Until into the 1980s, adherents of most ideological stripes – conservatives, moderates, even liberals – could be found in both political parties. Recall that the old pre-World War II conservative opposition to the New Deal crossed party lines. Because of the Civil War, Reconstruction, and the politics of race, the "solid South" was Democratic but largely conservative, certainly with regard to matters of race and organized labor. For much of the twentieth century, Republicans, of the party of Abraham Lincoln, could be liberal on race and other matters, such as protecting the environment and opposing corporate power, and retain their conservative credentials. Conservation, after all, was a Republican issue from the time of Theodore Roosevelt. The passage of the National Environmental Policy Act in 1970 was a bipartisan affair. Strong antitrust policy was the watchword of western and upper Midwest progressive Republicans in the mold of Wisconsin Senator Robert LaFollette. Many Republicans from the Northeast were moderates, some even liberal (which, as we know, is why they were vilified by the anti-establishment conservative movement). In short, for much of the twentieth century, intra-party factions blurred ideological differences. This began to change when the national Democratic Party under the leadership of Lyndon Johnson pursued the civil rights agenda. The Civil Rights Act and Voting Rights Act initiated a long process of shifting ideological proclivities by political party. Although the transformation was not completed for a few decades, there was a clear shift of conservatives into the Republican

Party by the early 1980s. The Democratic Party still retains a certain ideological catholicity, but the Republican Party has become a bona fide conservative political party. The Tea Party movement has accelerated that trend, its electoral activism helping to wipe out more moderate Republicans in the 2010 and 2012 primaries. Republican elected officials, closely monitored by Tea Party activists and right-wing media, find themselves having to behave with unparalleled intransigence toward Democrats – or suffer electoral consequences. A study of congressional voting patterns by the *National Journal* showed that the 2010 voting record of the most liberal Senate Republican lay to the right of the most conservative Senate Democrat. The 2012 election did not alter this dynamic; indeed, it may have exacerbated it. The GOP lost two Senate seats and eight seats in the House of Representatives. The losers in the congressional races tended to be *moderate* Republicans, leaving the House GOP caucus positioned even further to the right.[108] Now that conservatism is centered in a single party, the GOP can and does exercise tight discipline, engendering breathtaking ideological dogmatism, polarization, and political brinkmanship.[109]

Contributing to polarization and dogmatism are the media. In the "Paranoid Style" essay, as noted above, Richard Hofstadter posted an observation about the amplifying effects of the mass media. Mass media appeared to exacerbate or expand paranoid tendencies, Hofstadter believed, lending vividness and added invective to the depiction of political villains. If this was true in the early 1960s, it can only be more the case today. Indeed, Fox News and right-wing talk radio are less news operations than they are political advocacy enterprises whose media outlets produce ideological echo chambers.[110] Fox and talk radio commentators have positioned themselves as the ideological testing ground for positions designed to move the general political discourse rightward. They have become the ideological driver of conservative politics. They say things and articulate opinions most elected politicians won't until Fox makes it safe for them to do so. By giving extensive coverage to Tea Party events even prior to the events themselves, they function as recruiters as well as cheerleaders. Fox News hosts have even helped lead Tea Party rallies.[111] These same hosts, along with other right-wing media, hold Republican office-holders to account for perceived deviations from the correct political line. It's not for nothing that David Frum, conservative author and former speechwriter for George W. Bush, remarked ruefully in 2010, "Republicans originally thought that Fox worked for us and now we're discovering we work for Fox."[112] Yet Fox and conservative talk radio are not the whole picture. They hold down just one anchor of the right-wing media universe. With audiences in the scores of millions, Christian radio and television broadcasting hold down another anchor. Both of these wings benefited from the deregulation of electronic mass media, to which we now turn.

To make proper sense of right-wing media as the ideological driver of contemporary conservatism, the political-economic and regulatory context of contemporary communications needs to be understood. Deregulation was not just a phenomenon affecting the banks, of course; it was a powerful movement affecting many American industries and economic sectors. One effect of the deregulation of electronic mass media in the 1970s and 1980s was to open up the airwaves to niche programming. Although fundamentalist religious programming has a long history in American broadcasting, incendiary *political* opinion and overtly politically partisan news programming had been largely muted because of the longstanding conditions of the regulatory environment: limited broadcast frequencies and the resultant public trusteeship regulatory model, and the vague, veiled, mostly unimplemented regulatory threats of the Federal Communications Commission (FCC). The public trusteeship model of broadcast licensing in general, and the Fairness Doctrine specifically, obligated broadcasters to air programs of interest and controversy and be balanced in their presentation of such. This generally inculcated a broadcast culture of playing it safe, even of diffidence, with regard to political programming. In those instances when a broadcast licensee engaged in frowned-upon practices, which included politically unbalanced programs, the FCC let its displeasure be known. The offending broadcaster's license was almost always renewed, but the broadcaster might encounter hassle and expense during license renewal time.[113] And left unsaid was the "nuclear" option: the FCC in principle had the power to strip the broadcaster of the license and in rare, extraordinary instances had done so. In fact, the few instances in which the FCC revoked licenses involved small right-wing radio stations that had violated the Fairness Doctrine-related personal attack rules – including Carl McIntire's WXUR and the small radio station that aired Billy James Hargis.[114]

With deregulation, entry into electronic media got easier and the public trusteeship model of broadcasting was correspondingly weakened. The deregulation impulse began before Ronald Reagan came to power in 1981, but his administration quickened its momentum and altered its course.[115] Under Reagan, the FCC abandoned its policy preventing the quick turnover and sale of broadcast stations (known as trafficking or station-flipping) and determined not to enforce the Fairness Doctrine (the commission formally rescinded the doctrine in 1987).[116] These developments helped lead to a new niche of partisan programming primarily on the right side of the political spectrum in the form of talk radio.[117] The remarkably raw programming that ensued went unchecked by the FCC, with the exception of a flurry of concern around "indecency": that is, references to sex and sexuality. But it became clear that no penalty would be paid for general program outrageousness.[118] Rush Limbaugh, the leading figure in the slashing, mocking invective style of right-wing talk radio, began his local Sacramento show in 1984 and commenced nationally in 1988. Although precise numbers are hard to come by, Limbaugh's show has become the most listened-to radio program in the United States, with an audience that ranges from 14 to 25 million.[119] The other important beneficiary of deregulation was Fox, the first new television network in decades. In 1996, in the wake of talk radio's success, Fox launched a news operation that in many respects aped the conventions of right-wing talk radio: highly opinionated, short on facts, quick to engage in partisan attacks. The formula brought audiences. Of course, talk radio and Fox News did not inaugurate broadcast programming that gave voice to the resentments of aggrieved actual and would-be suburbanites. That was pioneered by the legendary broadcaster Paul Harvey, whose idiosyncratic radio show ran from the late 1940s until his death in 2009.[120] But Rush Limbaugh et al. sharpened the pitch and invective immeasurably.

Deregulation fostered additional changes in the news. For a variety of political and legal reasons, cable television, which grew significantly in the 1970s, largely escaped FCC regulatory controls. New entry and competition in broadcast and cable set in motion forces that pushed hard at traditional journalistic professional norms of newsworthiness, objectivity, proper sourcing, and balance. Network television news had long served as a loss-leading brand for the three major television networks. But in the wake of competitive pressures and the merger spree set off by deregulation, the television networks cut back their news operations dramatically. By the mid-1980s, NBC, ABC, and CBS all had new corporate owners highly leveraged from these purchases and facing unexpected competition from new media sources. The new corporate owners saw no great benefit in loss-leading news organizations. In addition to cutting news budgets, they imposed profitability requirements on each television program, news programs included. This, in turn, put considerable strain on the traditional norms of broadcast journalism. Critics and scholars lamented the new profitability requirements on news programs and the resulting heightened emphasis on entertainment over journalism in the broadcast media.[121] Finally, the advent of the World Wide Web and the practice of easy copying and linking set in motion the deterioration of the traditional newspaper business model and thus amplified the challenge to traditional journalistic professional norms. Following in the pathway of talk radio and Fox News, the Internet and World Wide Web facilitated an explosion of partisan websites and blogs – and a concomitant challenge to professional journalistic editing and vetting.

What is different now, in the aftermath of the deregulation and liberalization of American electronic media and the subsequent growth of the Internet, is that conservative movements have their *own* media; they do not have to rely, as social movements did previously, on their treatment by "mainstream media" wedded to conventional, professional notions of newsworthiness, objectivity, balance, and the like.[122] There is no Fairness Doctrine to compel broadcast stations to hew to the norms of cordial, middle-range debate. The torrent of new partisan electronic media has resulted in an informational universe in which partisanship and position-taking, along with panic-mongering, rumor, invective, and outright falsehoods, compete with and sometimes overrun facts and considered opinion. Professional journalism hasn't disappeared in the new media environment; it has simply become one (declining) niche among many. Increasingly, some considerable percentage of the populace is able to occupy insular informational silos, reflecting the behavioral phenomenon that people tend to gravitate toward media that confirm and fortify their perspectives.[123] This phenomenon can be exaggerated, and I certainly do not want to claim the inordinate power of mass media. Still, it has important, if difficult to specify and impossible to quantify consequences for the shaping of political subjectivity. The importance of talk radio, religious broadcasting, and Fox News to contemporary conservatism is considerable: they advocate and lead ideologically in the guise of news media operations.

Viral conservative media can stoke, in Hofstadteran fashion, ginned-up paranoid campaigns that unite many of the elements of the current right wing in spasms of self-righteous anger and victimhood. One example of this phenomenon was the summer 2010 opposition to the construction of an Islamic community center two blocks from the World Trade Center in New York – but this is just one of innumerable incidents of frenzy that explode regularly and achieve "media event" status for a few days or sometimes weeks, to be replaced by the next item that generates comparable rage. In the case of the Islamic community center, right-wing media stoked anger that the "mosque" would dishonor the hallowed ground of "Ground Zero." This explosive media-amplified rage is one of the ways that politics are now conducted in the United States. Right-wing talk radio and Fox News are master practitioners of the practice. Seizing upon an incident or the blog of a partisan ranter, talk radio and Fox News repeat an item of outrage so often and in so hyped a fashion that its audiences seethe with anger as their prejudices are confirmed and amplified. Those audiences then become indignant that the mainstream media have ignored the issue – at which point the mainstream media usually do cover it. In this manner, right-wing media manage to force issues into the public sphere that wouldn't necessarily have the conventional news value to be addressed in the first place. This is an important way they shape the news agenda. Conservative talking heads are then given airtime, followed by responses and further rounds of response. Right-wing media organizations typically act to intensify the controversy while mainstream news outlets are compelled, by their professional norms, to treat the issue in something approaching a "balanced" manner, according neutral credence to both sides. In the mosque controversy, former House Speaker and presidential aspirant Newt Gingrich compared the Muslims wishing to build the center at Ground Zero to allowing Nazis to put up a sign next to the Holocaust museum in Washington.[124] The evangelical leader Franklin Graham, who continues to assert that President Obama is Muslim, justified his opposition to the center with the assertion that "[t]he teaching of Islam is to hate the Jew, to hate the Christian, to kill them; their goal is world domination."[125]

The mosque controversy highlights how a news explosion can connect to other political meanings and maneuverings. Just as the Tea Party's stance toward the Constitution is one of (re)sacralization, the mosque controversy served to confirm the claim that September 11 and the ruined site of the World Trade Center have become the political equivalent of a holy day and place of martyrdom, of crucifixion, a communion around the mystical body of a wounded, but avenging republic.[126] The mosque controversy coincided with a spike in the number of Americans who said they believed President Obama to be Muslim (from 12 percent in 2008 to 18 percent in 2010), a belief fanned by radio demagogues such as Rush Limbaugh, who constantly refers to the president as "Imam Obama, America's first Muslim president."[127]

Fox News and talk radio steer anti-establishment conservative ideological politics through a dynamic of stoking victimhood and rage. Indeed, they have managed to embed a powerful class-and race-based resentment in the style of their address of their audiences. Glenn Beck takes the process further, in the sense that he doesn't simply highlight any particular incident that offends particular conservative sensibilities. Rather, the purpose of his history lessons and lectures is to frame the offense in a way that creates a self-reflexive, coherent, if paranoid, worldview.

Illiberal democracy

Hofstadter's error was to engage in a social psychology that was analytically unsatisfactory, largely because the approach was so prone to reductionism. In the end, social psychology is too problematic a causal explanation because of its tendency to try to decipher unconscious motivation rather than taking people's political arguments at face value. Whether or not Hofstadter meant to, his approach tended to stigmatize followers of Joseph McCarthy and Barry Goldwater as fanatical, atavistic paranoids. But if we use Hofstadter's analysis to talk about political culture rather than the mental defects of right-wingers, the insights of the paranoid style analysis can be utilized without the social psychology baggage.

We have already laid the basis for this. It is clear that Tea Party members and sympathizers responded to the genuine economic travails and political difficulties associated with the Great Recession. Their critique of what they labeled socialism or corporatism or crony capitalism displayed an accurate, if skewed, perception that the system favors certain institutions and elites to the exclusion of common people. The older, very conservative white people who populate the Tea Party also in actuality are becoming demographically fewer in contemporary America; at some point in the near future they are likely to be less dominant in the polity. Older white Americans are generally not on a downward economic slope, but they perceive themselves and their children to be, and probably are, becoming less influential in defining or setting the terms of American culture. Thus the demographic data on Tea Party membership can be seen to support elements of Hofstadter's status anxiety thesis. But it doesn't really help to label people who are losing their status as paranoid crazies; indeed, the perception of status loss fuels genuine consternation and anger. Rather, legitimate fear and anxiety are channeled to reinforce a particular kind of political culture, one characterized by victimhood, resentment, and anger about the perceived loss of individual autonomy. Paradoxically, at the same time, Tea Party and other conservative institutions push policies of mythic cultural resonance that in practical terms primarily serve the interests of corporate capitalism and the very wealthy. This can be seen in constant GOP efforts to extend the Bush tax cuts for the wealthiest 2 percent of the population. After all the hue and cry in the 2010 midterm elections about the budget deficit being the most important issue facing America, the issue that congressional Republicans pushed hardest in the 2010 lame-duck session was an item that added $81.5 billion to the deficit.[128] And after losing the presidential race and failing to retake the Senate in the 2012 election, high-level Republican office-holders concluded that the problem was not their policies, but rather their "tone." Meeting to talk about the results of the election and the path ahead for their party, GOP governors concluded that they had lost on "strategy," not on the issues, and vowed, together with Congressional Republicans, to hold the line against President Obama in his second term, especially on taxes. Anti-establishment conservatism lives on.[129]

Key, here, is understanding how fear and anger are channeled by conservative institutions to create a particular kind of political culture. In this regard, long-established networks of right-wing money, idea-generating political organizations, and mass media have been able to "canalize" the anxieties triggered by economic crisis and the sense of dependence and political inefficacy in a distinctly conservative direction. These networks have been successful in tapping into a particularly powerful strain of American political culture – that is, the fear of the strong state and the need to preserve individual autonomy. In personalizing the structural capitalist bias of the state into the resentment of certain kinds of political elites, conservatives have managed to channel resentment into an attack on government per se.[130] As this book has shown, this development is largely the result of a long series of strategic attacks on liberal institutions, be they political or religious, since the 1970s. Liberal institutions were vulnerable to such attacks because liberal-left economic policies were no longer seen to work, and because for complicated reasons the liberal left, after supporting the civil rights struggle, found its politics diverted from the fight for the common good and the expansion of universal values that had made it the champion of social progress since the 1930s. The left's support of identity politics allowed the right to label it as the party of special interests. One important consequence is that the liberal left's politics were challenged as elitist and a masquerade for power. Confronting the left, indeed claiming that its own agenda is more universal and true to American tradition, was anti-establishment conservatism.

Truth be told, the Tea Party may be a short-lived political phenomenon, tied more than anything else to the depth of the economic crisis, and particularly the high unemployment woes accompanying the Great Recession. What is of moment is how the Tea Party movement both reflects and reinforces a kind of conservatism and a corresponding Republican political style that has become deeply dogmatic. We can call this style of anti-establishment conservatism "illiberal democracy." Introduced by the public intellectual Fareed Zakaria in a 1997 article in *Foreign Affairs*, the concept of illiberal democracy tried to capture the incompleteness of the democratization movement in the former Soviet bloc and in many parts of the Third World, and the shallow nature of freedom under many putative democratic regimes. For Zakaria, an illiberal democracy holds regular elections, but citizens are distanced from knowledge about the activities of those who exercise real power because of the lack of civil liberties.[131] Zakaria edged toward applying his concept to the United States, suggesting in his Tocquevillean way that the democratic urge had begun to undermine the liberal institutions that lie beneath democracy. Under such conditions, politics itself becomes dysfunctional.[132] I see little reason to edge or hedge. Notwithstanding the reelection of Barack Obama in the 2012 election, it seems eminently reasonable to consider the United States, still under the sway of anti-establishment conservatism, an example of illiberal democracy.

— 6 —

DOGMATISM, UTOPIANISM, AND POLITICS

As it emerged in the early post-war period, the fusion of traditionalism and libertarianism I have labeled anti-establishment conservatism embodied a politics of double rollback: of the New Deal and of international communism. Its grievance was not just with the liberals it so reviled but with the moderate, "me-too" apostates who constituted the Republican Party establishment and who practiced a more modest version of New Deal tyranny. Anti-establishment conservatives found in the New Deal and communism a common betrayal of individual freedom and a deification of the state power they so feared. The evil of the despotic, bloated American state was absolved, however, when it came to national security. The anti-establishment conservative cause was premised on halting socialist tendencies and restoring the free market and traditional values, while expanding the military-industrial complex and taking the fight to the Soviet foe. In the early 1960s, anti-establishment conservatives found their voice in Senator Barry Goldwater. When Goldwater's defeat in the 1964 election removed anti-establishment conservatives from GOP centers of power, they went into a quiet rebuilding mode. Over the ensuing decades, they constructed the early intellectual, media, charitable, and political institutions that since have played such a critical role in channeling and shaping discontent with the post-war liberal consensus.

Anti-establishment conservatism surged again in the 1970s, its ranks enlarged by the new Christian right, neoconservatives, and the bloc of big business that defected from the liberal consensus. A litany of factors underlay the resurgence. Accompanying the drive for African-American civil rights, a judicial expansion of Fourteenth Amendment protections, coupled with the decline of religious discrimination and discrimination in general in the 1950s and 1960s, led to a more pluralistic public sphere – backed by law. Fundamentalist and evangelical Protestants reacted negatively to these changes. Having long dominated American culture indirectly, in the form of the civil religion, conservative Christians experienced the growing pluralism of the culture as a direct attack on their institutions and life-world. This aggrieved sense of threat led them to denounce secular humanism and judicial activism and brought them into the circles of longtime Goldwater-bred political entrepreneurs who helped organize their discontent. The national Democratic Party's championing of civil rights and remedies led to the eventual loss of the white South to the GOP and the defection of many northern ethnic and Catholic voters as well. The old conservative theme of the intrusive state found resonance in these constituencies. Neoconservatives were "reformed" liberals with strong misgivings about Johnson administration social programs and the perceived decline of American international standing in the wake of the United States' defeat in Vietnam. They came to share with conservative evangelicals a disgust with the counterculture and the permissive direction of American culture under its sway. They, too, joined the anti-establishment conservative ranks, bemoaning the loss of traditional values of authority, restraint, virtue, and personal responsibility. Indeed, if the Christian right swelled anti-establishment conservatism's electoral ranks, the neoconservatives expanded its intellectual reach, particularly with its critique of the New Class. Neoconservatives blamed liberals and Democratic administrations for fostering a culture of entitlement in domestic affairs and a culture of appeasement in international affairs. Finally, with the slowdown of the economy and the seeming inability of Keynesian tools to solve stagflation, business deserted the liberal consensus and demanded union concessions, lower taxes, leaner federal budgets, and the end of regulatory "despotism." Certain businessmen and corporations funded the anti-establishment conservative institutions generously, providing a sound institutional base for the resurgent movement. The election of Ronald Reagan in 1980 was in no small measure due to the movement's efforts.

Since the Reagan victory, the anti-establishment conservative movement has come to challenge the establishment Republican Party, if not mostly displace it. As this process has unfolded, the GOP, which historically had been relatively heterogeneous ideologically, by the mid-1990s began to look like a bona fide, disciplined, conservative political party and, arguably, a religious one. As such, it increasingly displays utopian and dogmatic features, about which many have commented.[1]

Outside of academic circles, utopianism signifies unrealistic, naïve, even foolish, if good-hearted belief. But in American intellectual circles, utopianism has long been a pejorative. At least since the post-World War II period, utopianism has signaled danger. The scholarly analysis and denunciation of totalitarianism – particularly communist totalitarianism – moved seamlessly into a critique of utopianism. Totalitarianism's sacrifice of means in the service of abstract ends was characteristic of utopian thinking. According to the political philosophers Karl Popper, Jacob Talmon, Isaiah Berlin (and, to a lesser degree, the early Hannah Arendt), who helped establish the scholarly theoretical underpinnings of Cold War anti-communist liberalism, the search for perfection wasn't an innocent exercise in unrealistic dreaming; it was a recipe for bloodshed.[2] As the sociologist Karl Mannheim suggested several years prior, the utopian mentality was characterized by a closed system of deductive procedure, with an internally balanced equilibrium of motives comprised in a body of axioms capable of ensuring inner coherence, and hence, in many instances, isolation from the world.[3] For the Cold War liberal political theorists, this characterization of utopian thinking fit their understanding of the communist movement – and, because that movement was very much *in* the world, had chilling and disastrous consequences. Communist utopianism imposed a black-and-white model on a gray world, and thus instilled a frightening moral absolutism in its followers.

What we find now in the United States is a shift of utopianism from the left to the right. The Christian right's utopianism lay in an anti-modern impulse to dissolve the separation of spheres, to obliterate the distinction between public and private – in the sociologist Max Weber's terms, to "re-enchant" the world under some semblance of a sacred canopy. If in the recent past the process of secularization meant the ambiguous withdrawal of Christian fundamentalists and conservative evangelicals from the secular world to concentrate on saving souls within their own insulated institutions, since the 1970s they have re-engaged with the world in order, if not to destroy secularism outright, then at the very least to re-instill Christian values in American public life, to recapture the civil religion. Always stridently anti-communist and nationalistic, the Christian right's effort to reaffirm Christian values in American society also has meant the assertion of American values in international affairs. Indeed, fundamentalists' longstanding, vociferous anti-communism was one of the reasons to have doubted the standard story of their withdrawn status from the secular world. The Christian right believes profoundly in American exceptionalism, that God has granted a special role for the United States in human history.

The religious dimension of anti-establishment conservatism, particularly in the last several years, underscores one aspect of the underlying dogmatism of the movement and its uncomfortable relationship with democracy. This, again, is evidenced in the flight from science, the denunciation of expertise as self-serving elitism, of policy-making as a matter of conviction and faith. The most telling instance, of course, was the decision-making around the Iraq War. As some have suggested, the great, unexamined issue of the George W. Bush presidency was the extent to which Bush's unwavering commitment to Middle East militarism was rooted in theological and religious convictions, not in pragmatic or geopolitical concerns.[4] Because the Bush administration's foreign policy decision-making was grounded in absolute moral and theological convictions, it was immune from re-examination or change. Bush himself said that he sensed a "Third [Great] Awakening" of religious devotion in the United States that has coincided with the nation's struggle with international terrorists, a war he depicted as "a confrontation between good and evil."[5] Bush's post-9/11 public theology is described as having shifted from a Wesleyan theology of "personal transformation" to a Calvinist "divine plan" laid out by a sovereign God for the country and himself. At the 2003 National Prayer Breakfast, for example, he said, "We also can be confident in the ways of providence, even when they are far from our understanding. Events aren't moved by blind change and chance. Behind all of life and all of history, there is a dedication and purpose set by the hand of a just and faithful God, and that hope will never be shaken."[6] It was his theological conviction that allowed Bush his commitment, his calm, his dismissal of bad news and opposition, his imperviousness to change. Bush knew God and he knew what was right. Revealingly, journalist Kurt Eichenwald reports a telephone conversation in which Bush, trying to persuade Jacques Chirac to support a U.N.-backed invasion of Iraq, and appealing to the French president's Christian (Catholic) faith, declared: "Gog and Magog are at work in the Middle East. . . . Biblical prophecies are being fulfilled. . . . This confrontation is willed by God, who wants to use this conflict to erase His people's enemies before a new age begins."[7] This, at bottom, is the reason we must understand the religious basis of the Iraq War and, more broadly, the Republican dismissal of science; and, further, grapple with the fundamental issue about whether and how religious arguments can and should play a role in the public sphere in a democracy. It is the certainty of belief, embedded inside and fostered by the cultivation of religious awe, itself wrapped around traditions, rituals, and ceremonies, that can make religion dogmatic and possibly anathema to a democratic politics.

To be sure, I do not suggest that religion can play no role in politics – that would be both historically inaccurate and normatively untenable. Religious motives and motifs are inextricably woven into the American experience, and religion informs not only the way in which many, perhaps most, Americans understand their everyday lives and identities, but their political inclinations and commitments as well. Religious belief has animated any number of consequential political stances in American history, from the abolition of slavery to Prohibition to civil rights to efforts to reduce poverty.[8] No one can gainsay the importance of religion to political experience, and of religious perspective to political perspective. But religious argument is not political argument. That is, religious argument ultimately is based on some form of revelation or revealed truth, and thus is not "argument" per se. Rather it is a foundationalist, pre-rational appeal not amenable to counterclaims outside of its faith-based framework. A democratic political public sphere is in principle the space for *reasoned* communicative exchange, wherein we exchange reasons in public in order to assess validity claims that have become problematic. Religious claims are not of this character, because they are true not through argument; they are true through revelation or faith and thus not accessible to those outside the revelatory framework. It is in this sense that the reasons offered by religious argument are not really "public." Political argument in a democracy must be open to everyone at both participatory and epistemic levels; hence political claims must in principle be accessible and fallible, subject to evidence and counterclaims. Because of this, religious claims per se cannot pass for *legitimate* political argument in a democracy; they can only be legitimate if presented in terms of secular – hence, public – rationales. Even the conservative theologian Richard John Neuhaus concurred with the claim that religious arguments must be cast in public reason.[9]

Of course, religious convictions can comprise the very identity of persons. We cannot expect religious individuals to split their essential beings into public and private components as soon as they participate in public debates. Indeed, as we have seen in this book, the bifurcation of identity is one of the features of modernity that has so incensed conservative Christians. But, as the social theorist Jürgen Habermas suggests, every citizen must know that only secular reasons count beyond the institutional threshold that divides the informal public sphere – that is, the sphere of public opinion formation – from parliaments, courts, ministries, administrations, and the decisions and policies that emanate from these political institutions. Democracy ensures that people can practice religion freely; democracy must require the separation between church and state to *be* a democracy. That is the balance that must be struck in a democratic system: individuals can articulate religious arguments in the informal political public sphere, but as those arguments move into the formal institutional political realm they must be translated into secular, reasoned terms, in language and epistemic structure that are in principle accessible to all citizens.

It is here where the religious right and the Bush administration breached this balance. Bush appointed large numbers of conservative evangelicals to public positions high and low, and even among non-evangelicals in the White House there was a general affinity for religious faith. Bible study groups permeated the administration and federal agencies. The linkage between Republican public officials and Christian right organizations during the Bush years was extensive, including weekly closed-door meetings of the Values Action Team (representing Focus on the Family, the Family Research Council, Eagle Forum, the Traditional Values Coalition, Concerned Women for America, among others) and the Arlington Group (run by Paul Weyrich).[10] One cannot conclude any prima facie causal relationship between religion and public policies from the fact that conservative evangelicals served in the government and engaged in broad contacts with Christian right organizations. But we know from the notorious episode when a number of U.S. Attorneys were summarily fired in 2006 that young evangelicals and fundamentalists recruited straight out of law schools such as Pat Robertson's Regent University to serve in bureaucratic positions had bearing on how that fiasco played out.[11] We also know that political allegiance and religious credentials, rather than experience or particular competence, determined the hiring for various bureaucratic positions in the Coalition Provisional Authority in occupied Iraq, with occasionally disastrous consequences.[12] And, finally, we know that the Bush-created Office of Faith-Based and Community Initiatives channeled billions of federal dollars to groups such as the National Right to Life and Christian organizations running drug and pregnancy clinics and abstinence-only school programs not accountable to independent oversight.[13]

The reasons for the Iraq War and Middle East policy were articulated publicly in both religious and secular registers, but with the religious largely underpinning the secular. Indeed, it was the pervasive religious attitude that so suffused the Bush administration that helps clarify the plethora of disturbing instances in which facts and evidence – not just regarding the Middle East, but in the realms of science, environmental protection, and public health policy as well – were deemed dispensable, irrelevant, even irritatingly inconvenient. For the Bush administration what mattered was the predetermined dogmatically held policy. What was of consequence was Bush's conviction in the rightness of his policies – not as a matter of evidence, but as a matter of faith. But dogmatism, particularly religious dogmatism, should be out of bounds in a democracy as a matter of principle.[14] For all its frustrations, politics must be a process of continual negotiation – an ethic of responsibility rather than an ethic of convictions or "ultimate ends," in Max Weber's terms.[15]

In fact, although Weber's notion of an ethic of responsibility is helpful, his equation of an ethic of convictions with that of ultimate ends is not. One can possess practical political commitment without holding to an ethic of ultimate ends, even if the latter informs the former. As the mid-twentieth-century Protestant theologian and public intellectual Reinhold Niebuhr expressed so perceptively in *Moral Man and Immoral Society*:

Religion, in short, faces many perils to the right and to the left in becoming an instrument and inspiration of social justice. Every genuine passion for social justice will always contain a religious element within it. Religion will always leaven the idea of justice with the ideal of love. It will prevent the idea of justice, which is a politic-ethical ideal, from becoming a purely political one, with the ethical element washed out. The ethical ideal which threatens to become too purely religious must save the ethical ideal which is in peril of becoming too political. Furthermore there must always be a religious element in the hope of a just society. Without the ultrarational hopes and passions of religion no society will ever have the courage to conquer despair and attempt the impossible; for the vision of a just society is an impossible one, which can be approximated only by those who do not regard it as impossible. The truest visions of religion are illusions, which may be partially realized by being resolutely believed. For what religion believes to be true is not wholly true but ought to be true; and may become true if its truth is not doubted.[16]

Utopianism, religious or otherwise, often animates political courage and action. Utopianism marshals a vision of the future that can transform the dreary, stuck politics of today. But it must be contained within democratic values and norms or it threatens to become dogmatic and crush them.

The neoconservative intellectuals who attacked the New Class, challenged the bona fides of expertise, and championed the Iraq War did adhere to the church–state balance, but they offered arguments in a dogmatic spirit parallel to their comrades of the religious right. They, too, were utopians. Neoconservatism began as an intellectual movement with a distinctly anti-utopian approach to the world. It recognized the "crooked timber of humanity" and demonstrated a corresponding skepticism of progress and social engineering – the features usually taken as the hallmarks of liberal hubris.[17] But as Irving Kristol and his compatriots grew closer to the new Christian right and their war on the counterculture and secular humanism, the neoconservative attack on the New Class morphed into an attack on the basis for scientific claims writ large. And as neoconservatism evolved into its second generation, it moved precipitously toward a utopian mode of analysis and advocacy. Second-generation neoconservatives' utopianism lay in a vision of the United States as the exceptional nation whose national interests are identical to its deep-seated democratic values, and hence whose actions in the world are *ipso facto* benevolent. America's values are universal. By nature innocent, the United States can never truly be imperialist. Because of its special historical provenance, America's proper mission is to assert its values. In so doing, the exceptional nation brings the blessings of freedom to the world and rectifies the world's problems.[18] Because of the ways of the world and the existence of evil actors, the principal means to carry out America's mission is military force. War is not only the right tool in the international arena, it has beneficial consequences at home, as well, for war and its preparation restore private virtue and public spirit.[19] The Iraq War was nothing if not a utopian project, revealing that current anti-establishment conservatism is not conservative at all; it is a movement of redemptive reaction or Jacobinism in which the cleansing fire of violence is mobilized to create a new world.

Neoconservative dogmatic utopianism may be best revealed in the recent demand that the United States deal harshly with Iran, on account of that nation's lack of cooperation with nuclear non-proliferation. In a June 2007 essay in *Commentary*, Norman Podhoretz, advocating the bombing of Iran, wrote of Iranian president Mahmoud

Ahmadinejad: "Like Hitler, he is a revolutionary whose objective is to overturn the going international system and to replace it in the fullness of time with a new order dominated by Iran and ruled by the religio-political culture of Islamofascism."[20] The language is virtually identical to what Podhoretz wrote of the USSR thirty-seven years earlier (see pp. 126–7). And that's for a reason. The world is always endangered by Hitlers, and it is the task of patriotic American Podhoretzes to rouse a sluggish United States against them.

Neoconservative utopianism is rational, in the sense that it offers reasons for its positions, while, as we have seen, the dogmatism of the Christian right is not, in the sense that its positions ultimately are based on some form of revelation or of reason not accessible to those outside of that religious tradition. But the deep structure of both approaches is similar. As Leszek Kolakowski suggests in an exploration of religion and ideology:

> What is common to both ideological and religious belief systems is that they both purport to impose an a priori meaning on all aspects of human life and on all contingent events, and that they are both built in such a way that no imaginable, let alone real, facts could refute the established doctrine. I refer here to the classic Popperian frame of interpretation. Religious and ideological doctrines are both immune to empirical falsifications, and they are able to absorb all the facts while surviving intact.[21]

Absolutism and certitude – the dogmatic approach to thinking and acting – are anathema to the give and take of democratic politics.[22] The Tea Party movement is simply the latest incarnation of dogmatic anti-establishment conservatism, buoyed by the economic collapse of 2008 and the strength of the institutions of right-wing media, money, and idea-generating organizations. The Tea Party movement currently polices the GOP's ideological boundaries with a rage and dogmatism that calls to mind Richard Hofstadter's paranoid style.

Writing in 1944, Reinhold Niebuhr warned of the Soviet Union's threat to the peace of the world, "not because it is communistic or materialistic; but rather because it is informed by a simple religion and culture which makes self-criticism difficult and self-righteousness inevitable."[23] How ironic that Niebuhr's observation is a spot-on description of anti-establishment conservatism's dogmatic and messianist America. And because anti-establishment conservatism has succeeded in taking over one of America's two political parties, utopianism and dogmatism are not going away anytime soon.

NOTES

Chapter 1   Introduction

1 At various rallies and town hall meetings in 2009, Tea Party supporters displayed protest signs and made statements about keeping the government out of Medicare. A national poll conducted in August of that year asked if respondents thought the government should "stay out of Medicare." Thirty-nine percent said "yes." An additional 15 percent were "not sure." Public Policy Polling, "Obama's Approval . . . Increases" (August 19, 2009), at *http://www.publicpolicypolling.com/main/2009/08/obamas-approvalincreases.html#more* as of September 2012.

2 Clinton Rossiter, *Conservatism in America: The Thankless Persuasion* (New York: Knopf, 1955); Louis Hartz, *The Liberal Tradition in America: An Interpretation of American Political Thought since the Revolution* (New York: Harcourt, Brace, 1955); Barry Goldwater, *The Conscience of a Conservative* (Shepherdsville, KY: Victor Publishing Co., 1960); George H. Nash, *The Conservative Intellectual Movement in America since 1945* (Wilmington, DE: ISI, 1996).

3 Robert Green McCloskey, *American Conservatism in the Age of Enterprise, 1865–1910: A Study of William Graham Sumner, Stephen J. Field and Andrew Carnegie* (New York: Harper & Row, 1951).

4 John Locke, *Two Treatises of Government* [1690], Peter Laslett, ed. (Cambridge: Cambridge University Press, 1988).

5 Edmund Burke, *Reflections on the Revolution in France* [1790], J.C.D. Clark, ed. (Stanford, CA: Stanford University Press, 2001).

6 Frank S. Meyer, *In Defense of Freedom: A Conservative Credo* (Chicago: Regnery, 1962).

7 Ron Suskind, "Without a Doubt," *New York Times Magazine* (October 17, 2004), at *http://query.nytimes.com/gst/fullpage.html?res=9C05EF D8113BF934A25753C1A9629C8B63&pagewanted=all* as of September 2012.

8 Richard Hofstadter, "The Paranoid Style in American Politics," in *The Paranoid Style in American Politics, and Other Essays* (New York: Knopf, 1965), pp. 6, 23.

9 Hofstadter, "Pseudo-Conservatism Revisited – 1965" and "Goldwater and Pseudo-Conservative Politics," in *The Paranoid Style in American Politics, and Other Essays*, pp. 66–92 and 93–141, respectively.

10 Hofstadter, "The Paranoid Style in American Politics," p. 4.

11 John B. Judis, *The Paradox of Democracy: Elites, Special Interests, and the Betrayal of Public Trust* (New York: Pantheon, 2000).

12 Cited in Jeffrey K. Hadden and Anson Shupe, *Televangelism: Power and Politics on God's Frontier* (New York: Henry Holt, 1988), p. 28.

13 David Harvey, *A Brief History of Neoliberalism* (New York: Oxford University Press, 2005).

14 John Patrick Diggins, *Ronald Reagan: Fate, Freedom, and the Making of History* (New York: Norton, 2007); Sean Wilentz, *The Age of Reagan: A History, 1974–2008* (New York: Harper, 2008); Joshua Green, "Reagan's Liberal Legacy: What the New Literature on the Gipper Won't Tell You," *Washington Monthly* (January/February, 2003).

15 Paul Boyer, *When Time Shall Be No More: Prophecy Belief in Modern American Culture* (Cambridge, MA: Harvard University Press, 1992), p. 328.

16 Peter Baker, "Bush Tells Group He Sees a 'Third Awakening'," *Washington Post* (September 13, 2006).

17 David Brooks, "Heroes and History," *New York Times* (July 17, 2007).

18 Evan Lehman, "Retired General: Iraq Invasion was Strategic Disaster," *The Lowell Sun* (September 30, 2005), at *http://www. informationclearinghouse.info/article10488.htm* as of September 2012; George F. Will, "Inoculated for Exuberance?" *Washington Post* (November 10, 2006); Matthew Bigg, "Iraq Worst Disaster for U.S. Foreign Policy: Albright," *Reuters* (February 22, 2007).

19 The conservative 100,000 figure for Iraqi casualties comes from confirmed casualty reports via Iraq Body Count, *http://www. iraqbodycount.org/database/* as of September 2012. That number was revised upward to 120,000 in the aftermath of the release of classified Pentagon information by WikiLeaks in October 2010. A far higher figure of 655,000 Iraqi casualties as of the end of 2006, published in *The Lancet*, includes deaths from worsening health and environmental conditions as well as violence. David Brown, "Study Claims Iraq's 'Excess' Death Toll Has Reached 655,000," *Washington Post* (October 11, 2006), at *http://www.washingtonpost.com/wp-dyn/ content/article/2006/10/10/AR2006101001442.html* as of September 2012. The cost figure comes from Joseph E. Stiglitz and Linda J.

Bilmes, "The $10 Trillion Hangover: Paying the Price for Eight Years of Bush," *Harper's* (January 2009). The Iraq internal displacement and exile figures come from the Brookings Institution Iraq Index (November 30, 2010), at *http://www.brookings.edu/iraqindex* as of September 2012.

20 U.S. Office of Director of National Intelligence, Declassified Key Judgments of the National Intelligence Estimate, "Trends in Global Terrorism: Implications for the United States" (April 2006), at *http://www.dni.gov/files/documents/Special%20Report_Global%20 Terrorism%20NIE%20Key%20Judgments.pdf* as of September 2012.

21 Stiglitz and Bilmes, "The $10 Trillion Hangover."

22 Americans for Tax Reform's Grover Norquist (see epigraph above) is the source of the notorious quip, "I don't want to abolish government. I simply want to reduce it to the size where I can drag it into the bathroom and drown it in the bathtub."

Chapter 2 Anti-statist Statism: A Brief History of a Peculiarly American Conservatism

1 Alan Brinkley, "The New Deal and the Idea of the State," in Steve Fraser and Gary Gerstle, eds., *The Rise and Fall of the New Deal Order, 1930–1980* (Princeton: Princeton University Press, 1989), pp. 85–121.

2 William E. Leuchtenberg, *Franklin D. Roosevelt and the New Deal* (New York: Harper & Row, 1963); Robert B. Horwitz, *The Irony of Regulatory Reform: The Deregulation of American Telecommunications* (New York: Oxford University Press, 1989); Jerome L. Himmelstein, *To the Right: The Transformation of American Conservatism* (Berkeley: University of California Press, 1990).

3 Everett Carll Ladd, with Charles D. Hadley, *Transformations of the American Party System: Political Coalitions from the New Deal to the 1970s* (New York: Norton, 1978).

4 John Quincy Adams, Speech of July 4, 1821, at *http://rcocean. blogspot.com/2009/06/adams-american-does-not-go-abroad-in.html* as of October 2012.

5 E.H. Carr, *The Twenty Years' Crisis, 1919–1939* (London: Macmillan, 1939); Francis Fukuyama, *America at the Crossroads: Democracy, Power, and the Neoconservative Legacy* (New Haven: Yale University Press, 2006).

6 Sallie Pisani, *The CIA and the Marshall Plan* (Lawrence: University of Kansas Press, 1991).

7 Odd Arne Westad, *The Global Cold War: Third World Interventions and the Making of Our Times* (Cambridge: Cambridge University Press, 2005).

8 Harry S. Truman, Speech to Federal Council of Churches (March 6, 1946), at *http://www.trumanlibrary.org/publicpapers/index.php?pid=1494&st=&st1=* as of October 2012.

9 George F. Kennan, "Long Telegram," U.S. Department of State, Foreign Relations of the United States: Eastern Europe; the Soviet Union, Vol. VI, 1946 (Washington, DC: GPO, 1969), pp. 696–709; Kennan, "The Sources of Soviet Conduct," *Foreign Affairs*, Vol. 25, No. 4 (1947), pp. 566–82.

10 Fred Kaplan, *The Wizards of Armageddon* (New York: Simon & Schuster, 1983).

11 Arthur M. Schlesinger, Jr., *The Imperial Presidency* (Boston: Houghton Mifflin, 1973); Garry Wills, *Bomb Power: The Modern Presidency and the National Security State* (New York: Penguin Press, 2010).

12 Mark L. Kleinman, *A World of Hope, a World of Fear: Henry A. Wallace, Reinhold Niebuhr, and American Liberalism* (Columbus: Ohio State University Press, 2000).

13 Karl Mannheim, "Conservative Thought" [1953], in Kurt H. Wolff, ed., *From Karl Mannheim*, 2nd edition (New Brunswick, NJ: Transaction Publishers, 1993), p. 290.

14 Frederick Rudolph, "The American Liberty League, 1934–1940," *American Historical Review*, Vol. 56, No. 1 (October 1950), pp. 19–33; George Wolfskill, *The Revolt of the Conservatives: A History of the American Liberty League, 1934–1940* (Boston: Houghton-Mifflin, 1962).

15 Ludwig von Mises, "Economic Calculation in the Socialist Commonwealth," in F.A. von Hayek, ed., *Collectivist Economic Planning: Critical Studies on the Possibilities of Socialism* (London: Routledge & Kegan Paul, 1935); Mises, *Human Action: A Treatise on Economics* (New Haven: Yale University Press, 1949); Friedrich Hayek, *The Road to Serfdom* (Chicago: University of Chicago Press, 1944); Hayek, *The Constitution of Liberty* (Chicago: University of Chicago Press, 1960); Edmund Burke, *Reflections on the Revolution in France* (London: J. Dodsley, 1790); Alexis de Tocqueville *Democracy in America* (London: Saunders and Otley, 1835).

16 Kim Phillips-Fein, *Invisible Hands: The Businessmen's Crusade against the New Deal* (New York: Norton, 2009).

17 George W. Mowry, *Another Look at the Twentieth Century South* (Baton Rouge: Louisiana State University Press, 1973), p. 66.

18 Cited in James T. Patterson, *Congressional Conservatism and the New Deal: The Growth of the Conservative Coalition in Congress, 1933–1939* (Lexington: University of Kentucky Press, 1967), p. 13.

19 John Robert Moore, "Senator Josiah W. Bailey and the 'Conservative Manifesto' of 1937," *Journal of Southern History*, Vol. 31, No. 1 (February 1965), pp. 21–39.

20 Alan Brinkley, *Voices of Protest: Huey Long, Father Coughlin, and the Great Depression* (New York: Knopf, 1982).

21 National Bureau of Economic Research, Real Gross Domestic Product and Gross National Product, NBER Series 08166, at *http://www.huppi.com/kangaroo/GDPreal.htm* as of October 2012.

22 Richard Hofstadter, "Goldwater and Pseudo-Conservative Politics," in *The Paranoid Style in American Politics, and Other Essays* (New York: Knopf, 1965), p. 119.

23 Felix M. Morley, *Freedom and Federalism* (Chicago: Regnery, 1959); Frank Chodorov, *Out of Step: The Autobiography of an Individualist* (New York: Devin-Adair, 1962); Ayn Rand, *Capitalism: The Unknown Ideal* (New York: Penguin, 1967).

24 National Security Act of 1947 (Public law 253, 61 Stat. 495, enacted July 26, 1947).

25 Labor – Management Relations Act (Public law 80–101, 61 Stat. 136, enacted June 23, 1947).

26 Robert A. Taft, *A Foreign Policy for Americans* (Garden City, NY: Doubleday, 1951), p. 6.

27 Joseph McCarthy, *America's Retreat from Victory: The Story of George Catlett Marshall* (New York: Devin-Adair, 1951); Freda Utley, *The China Story* (Chicago: Regnery, 1951).

28 Taft, *A Foreign Policy for Americans*, p. 12.

29 Ibid., p. 118.

30 President Harry S. Truman, Address to Congress (March 12, 1947), at *http://millercenter.org/scripps/archive/speeches/detail/3343* as of October 2012.

31 Cathal J. Nolan, "The Last Hurrah of Conservative Isolationism? Eisenhower, Congress, and the Bricker Amendment," *Presidential Studies Quarterly*, Vol. 22, No. 2 (Spring 1992), pp. 337–49.

32 William Henry Chamberlin, *Beyond Containment* (Chicago: Regnery, 1953); James M. Burnham, *Containment or Liberation? An Inquiry into the Aims of U.S. Foreign Policy* (New York: John Day, 1953).

33 Barry M. Goldwater, *Why Not Victory? A Fresh Look at American Foreign Policy* (New York: McGraw-Hill, 1962).

34 Himmelstein, *To the Right*, p. 42; Jeffrey Hart, *The Making of the American Conservative Mind: National Review and Its Times* (Wilmington, DE: ISI Books, 2005).

35 John T. Flynn, *The Road Ahead: America's Creeping Revolution* (New York: Devin-Adair, 1949); Whittaker Chambers, *Witness* (New York: Random House, 1952); James M. Burnham, *Containment or Liberation?*; Burnham, *Suicide of the West; An Essay on the Meaning and Destiny of Liberalism* (New York: John Day Co., 1964).

36 Hofstadter, "The Pseudo-Conservative Revolt – 1954," in *The Paranoid Style in American Politics*, p. 46.
37 Harry S. Truman, Executive Order 9835 (March 21, 1947), at *http:// teachingamericanhistory.org/library/index.asp?document=930* as of October 2012.
38 Joseph McCarthy, Speech at Charleston, West Virginia (February 1954), at *http://www.nndb.com/people/490/000051337/* as of October 2012; McCarthy, speech at Wheeling, West Virginia (February 9, 1950), at *http://www.h-net.org/~hst306/documents/mccarthy.html* as of October 2012.
39 Niels Bjerre-Poulsen, *Right Face: Organizing the American Conservative Movement, 1945–65* (Copenhagen: Museum Tusculanum Press, 2002), p. 75.
40 Ann H. Coulter, *Treason: Liberal Treachery from the Cold War to the War on Terrorism* (New York: Crown Forum, 2003).
41 George H. Nash, *The Conservative Intellectual Movement in America since 1945* (New York: Basic Books, 1976).
42 Philip Mirowski and Dieter Plehwe, *The Road from Mont Pelerin: The Making of the Neoliberal Thought Collective* (Cambridge, MA: Harvard University Press, 2009).
43 Hayek, "The Use of Knowledge in Society," *American Economic Review*, Vol. 35, No. 4 (September 1945), pp. 519–30; Ayn Rand, *The Fountainhead* [1943] (New York: New American Library, 1971); Rand, *Atlas Shrugged* (New York: Random House, 1957).
44 Jennifer Burns, *Goddess of the Market: Ayn Rand and the American Right* (New York: Oxford University Press, 2009).
45 Burke, *Reflections on the Revolution in France; Thomas Paine, The Rights of Man* (Garden City, NY: Dolphin Books: 1961), pp. 59, 64, 73, 110–16.
46 Ibid., p. 213.
47 Ibid., p. 73. A personal rumination. Notwithstanding its importance as a key statement of conservatism, upon rereading *Reflections on the Revolution in France* after thirty-five years I found it to be a tedious book punctuated by a few intellectual gems, and deeply flawed by a constant anti-Semitism that made me wonder about the real limitations to Burke's "public affections." It is perhaps not for nothing that his reference to the "swinish multitude," although directed at French revolutionists, utterly enraged English radicals at the time.
48 The key articulation of post-war traditionalism can be found in two books, Richard Weaver, *Ideas Have Consequences* (Chicago: University of Chicago Press, 1948), and Russell Kirk, *The Conservative Mind: From Burke to Santayana* (Chicago: Regnery, 1953). The work of political philosopher Leo Strauss was also important to

traditionalism. Strauss, *The Political Philosophy of Hobbes* (Chicago: University of Chicago Press, 1952) and *Natural Right and History* (Chicago: University of Chicago Press, 1953).

49 William F. Buckley, Jr., *God and Man at Yale: The Superstitions of Academic Freedom* (Chicago: Regnery, 1951); Buckley, Jr., *Up from Liberalism* (New York: McDowell, Obolensky, 1959); John B. Judis, *William F. Buckley, Jr., Patron Saint of the Conservatives* (New York: Simon & Schuster, 1988).

50 Karl Marx and Friedrich Engels, "Manifesto of the Communist Party" [1848], in *Selected Works* (New York: International Publishers, 1974), p. 38.

51 Peter Berkowitz, Review of Patrick Allitt, *The Conservatives: Ideas and Personalities throughout American History*, in *Policy Review*, No. 156 (August/September, 2009), at *http://www.hoover.org/publications/policyreview/51579192.html* as of October 2012.

52 Louis Hartz, *The Liberal Tradition in America: An Interpretation of American Political Thought since the Revolution* (New York: Harcourt, Brace, 1955).

53 Clinton Rossiter, *Conservatism in America: The Thankless Persuasion* (New York: Knopf, 1955), p. 201.

54 Carl McIntire, "What is the Difference between Capitalism and Communism?" at *http://www.carlmcintire.org/booklets-capitalism Vcommunism.php* as of October 2012; McIntire, "What is the Difference between Marxism and Christianity?" at *http://www.carlmcintire. org/booklets-mVc.php* as of October 2012.

55 Frank S. Meyer, ed., *What is Conservatism?* (New York, Holt, Rinehart & Winston, 1964). Belief in God was pretty much de rigueur for conservative fusionism, at least at the institution of its intellectual articulation, *National Review*. Hart, *The Making of the American Conservative Mind*, pp. 109–24.

56 Cited in Hofstadter, "Goldwater and Pseudo-Conservative Politics," p. 117.

57 Barry Goldwater, *New York Times Magazine* (September 17, 1961), cited in Lisa McGirr, "A History of the Conservative Movement from the Bottom Up," *Journal of Policy History*, Vol. 14, No. 3 (July 2002), p. 337.

58 Cited in Hofstadter, "Goldwater and Pseudo-Conservative Politics," p. 117.

59 See, for example, the exchange between L. Brent Bozell and Frank Meyer over conservative fundamentals. Taking aim at libertarianism, Bozell championed the concept of virtue over that of freedom. Meyer's response held that the freedom of the individual person was the decisive foundation of a good political order. L. Brent Bozell, "Freedom or Virtue?" *National Review* (September 11, 1962); Frank Meyer, "Why Freedom," *National Review* (September 25, 1962). But atheism

was anathema at *National Review*. William F. Buckley, Jr. constantly attacked Ayn Rand over her hostility to religion.

60 James M. Burnham, *Congress and the American Tradition* (Chicago: Regnery, 1959).

61 Patrick Allitt, *Catholic Intellectuals and Conservative Politics in America, 1950–1985* (Ithaca, NY: Cornell University Press, 1993). Perhaps more than any other factor, Catholic anti-communism may have eased Catholicism's way into the American religious and cultural mainstream. The pre-war old right, primarily Protestant, had been associated with anti-Catholicism and anti-Semitism. The fact that Joseph McCarthy was Catholic, as were many of the most prominent intellectuals forging the new post-war conservatism, began to contribute to the easing of the old accusation against Catholics of "dual loyalty" to America and to the Vatican. Bjerre-Poulsen, *Right Face*, p. 73.

62 William F. Buckley, Jr., Letter to the Editor, *The Freeman*, Vol. 5, No. 7 (January 1955), p. 244.

63 Cited in Louis Fisher, "Invoking Inherent Powers: A Primer," *Presidential Studies Quarterly*, Vol. 37, No. 1 (March 2007), pp. 1–22.

64 The most visible public proponent of this view is former Vice-President Dick Cheney. The key intellectual works are those of John Yoo, *The Powers of War and Peace: The Constitution and Foreign Affairs after 9/11* (Chicago: University of Chicago Press, 2005); Yoo, *Crisis and Command: The History of Executive Power, from George Washington to George W. Bush* (New York: Kaplan Publishing, 2009). The unitary executive has resonances with the Nazi-linked political theorist Carl Schmitt. In Schmitt's *The Concept of the Political*, human relationships reduce to friend or foe, and the leader who embodies the nation effectively assumes the authority of Hobbes's Leviathan. Garry Wills maintains that the actual concentration of power began with the secrecy of the Manhattan Project and in the vesting of control over the atomic bomb in the Office of the President. This moved almost inexorably into the president controlling virtually all foreign policy. In the name of the national security state, the president amalgamated an ever-growing range of powers that are not actually constitutionally granted. The war on terrorism intensifies an already permanent constitutional crisis into a kind of permanent state of emergency in which presidential power is virtually supreme and barely challengeable. Note the irony that Wills has in effect resurrected the mid-twentieth-century conservative arguments of Robert A. Taft that liberals at the time denounced as "demonstrably irresponsible." Cheney and Yoo have elevated the old liberal advocacy of strong, sometimes labeled "heroic," presidential power to the near-fascistic plane of Carl Schmitt. Carl Schmitt, *The Concept of the Political*, George Schwab, trans. (New Brunswick, NJ: Rutgers University Press, 1976); Schmitt, *The Leviathan in the*

State Theory of Thomas Hobbes: Meaning and Failure of a Political Symbol, George Schwab and Erna Hilfstein, trans. (Westport, CT: Greenwood Press, 1996); Wills, *Bomb Power*; Giorgio Agamben, *State of Exception*, Kevin Attell, trans. (Chicago: University of Chicago Press, 2005). Jack Goldsmith's review of the Wills and Yoo books provides a particularly succinct overview of the changing ideological positions on presidential power. Jack Goldsmith, "The Accountable Presidency," *The New Republic* (February 18, 2010), pp. 33–9.

65 Rossiter, *Conservatism in America*.

66 Arthur M. Schlesinger, Jr., "The Politics of Nostalgia" [1955], in Schlesinger, *The Politics of Hope* (Boston: Houghton Mifflin, 1963), pp. 76, 77.

67 Mannheim, "Conservative Thought," p. 263.

68 See Phillips-Fein, *Invisible Hands*.

69 "Taking Hayek Seriously," at *http://hayekcenter.org/?p=* as of October 2012; "The Road to Serfdom as a Comic Book," *American Digest*, at *http://americandigest.org/mt-archives/enemies_foreign_domestic/the_road_to_serfdom_in_ca.php* as of August 2012. Likewise Hayek's rival in mid-century libertarianism, Ayn Rand. The initial press run of Rand's *The Fountainhead* was 7,500 copies, but by 1950 half a million copies were circulating the country. *Atlas Shrugged* had an initial press run of 100,000 copies. Three days after the publication date of October 10, 1957, the novel appeared on the *New York Times* best-seller list at number six. It remained on the list for twenty-one weeks, peaking at number four for a six-week period beginning December 8, 1957. Net sales of the book were nearly 70,000 copies in the first twelve months. The initial press run for the first paperback edition by New American Library in 1959 was 150,000 copies. It, too, had net sales of nearly 70,000 copies in the first twelve months. Rand's novels evoked widespread and sometimes intense intellectual conversions. They remain popular to this day, a staple of adolescent rebels and conservative activists. Their popularity was renewed again with the Great Recession of 2008. "History of *Atlas Shrugged*," at *http://atlasshrugged.com/book/history.html* as of October 2012; Burns, *Goddess of the Market*.

70 Rick Perlstein, *Before the Storm: Barry Goldwater and the Unmaking of the American Consensus* (New York: Hill and Wang, 2001).

71 Robert Caute, *The Great Fear: The Anti-Communist Purge under Truman and Eisenhower* (New York: Simon & Schuster, 1978).

72 Federal Bureau of Investigation, *Communist Target: Youth: Communist Infiltration and Agitation Tactics* (Washington, DC: U.S. Government Printing Office, 1960); HUAC, *Operation Abolition* (1960), at *http://www.youtube.com/watch?v=AVQnFpzU5h8* and *http://www.youtube.com/watch?v=l00IAGwKjDE&feature=relmfu*, as of October 2012.

73 Perlstein, *Before the Storm*, p. 149; Sara Diamond, *Roads to Dominion: Right-Wing Movements and Political Power in the United States* (New York: Guilford Press, 1995), pp. 37–65.

74 Perlstein, *Before the Storm*; Lisa McGirr, *Suburban Warriors: The Origins of the New American Right* (Princeton: Princeton University Press, 2001).

75 Robert H. Welch, *The Politician* (Belmont, MA: Belmont Publishing Co., 1963). The John Birch Society's publication, *American Opinion*, issued an annual "Scoreboard" edition. In the 1965 "Scoreboard" the percentage of the country the Society declared was communist-dominated drifted up from 40–60 to 60–80. Cited in "The John Birch Society and the Conservative Movement," *National Review* (October 19, 1965), at *http://www.nationalreview.com/nroriginals/?q=YzM0O Dg0YTEyNzhkM2RjNGQzOTY5ODI5MWVkZjk3NWI=&w =MQ==* as of October 2012.

76 Robert Welch, *May God Forgive Us* (1952), cited in Hofstadter, "The Paranoid Style in American Politics," p. 30.

77 Hart, *The Making of the American Conservative Mind*, pp. 153–60.

78 Michael Paul Rogin, *The Intellectuals and McCarthy: The Radical Specter* (Cambridge, MA: MIT Press, 1967).

79 Daniel Bell, "The Dispossessed," in Bell, ed., *The Radical Right: The New American Right Expanded and Updated* (Garden City, NY: Anchor Books, 1963), p. 16.

80 Richard Hofstadter, *Anti-intellectualism in American Life* (New York: Vintage, 1962); Hofstadter, *The Paranoid Style in American Politics*; Seymour Martin Lipset, *Political Man: The Social Bases of Politics* (Garden City, NY: Doubleday, 1960); Lipset, with Earl Rabb, *The Politics of Unreason: Right-Wing Extremism in America, 1790–1977* (Chicago: University of Chicago Press, 1978); Bell, ed., *The Radical Right*. Much of the analysis rested ultimately upon social psychological models rooted in Erich Fromm and Theodor W. Adorno's studies of authoritarianism. Erich Fromm, *Escape from Freedom* (New York: Rinehart, 1941); T.W. Adorno, Else Frenkel-Brunswik, Daniel J. Levinson, and R. Nevitt Sanford, *The Authoritarian Personality* (New York: Harper, 1950). This intellectual move was resuscitated in John Dean's analysis of the conservatism of the George W. Bush administration. John W. Dean, *Conservatives without Conscience* (New York: Viking, 2006). Gunnar Myrdal's influential volume on white racism did not partake of Frankfurt School social psychology, but it, too, helped set the agenda that racism was the irrational reaction of the uneducated, and that the solution to the oppression of African-Americans was the education of poor whites. Gunnar Myrdal, *An American Dilemma: The Negro Problem and Modern Democracy* (New York: Harper & Brothers, 1944).

81 Michael Rogin found that backers of Joseph McCarthy came from higher status groups in *The Intellectuals and McCarthy*. According to Arnold Forster and Benjamin R. Epstein, over 50 percent of Fred Schwarz's Christian Anti-Communism Crusade supporters were businessmen or professionals, and over half were college graduates with good incomes. Forster and Epstein, *Danger on the Right* (New York: Random House, 1964), pp. 58–9. Lisa McGirr found that most of the members of the John Birch Society and those active in highly conservative causes in Orange County, California in the 1960s were solidly middle class, including businessmen, engineers, and physicians. McGirr, *Suburban Warriors*, pp. 54–110.

82 From 1951 to 1965, $67.2 billion or about 20 percent of all the Department of Defense's prime contracts for supplies, services, and construction went to California. When veterans' benefits are added to this sum, DOD spending from 1946 to 1965 accounted for nearly 11 percent of personal income in California and was the principal cause of the large population growth in southern California in particular. NASA, the space agency, also played a role. From 1961 through 1965, an estimated additional $5.3 billion was spent by NASA in California, amounting to 41 percent of its total expenditures during those years. When indirect income is added in, defense spending probably accounted for $100 billion in California by 1965. James L. Clayton, *The Economic Impact of the Cold War: Sources and Readings* (New York: Harcourt, Brace & World, 1970), pp. 65–81.

83 Ibid., p. 78.

84 Bruce J. Schulman, *From Cotton Belt to Sunbelt: Federal Policy, Economic Development, and the Transformation of the South, 1938–1980* (Durham, NC: Duke University Press, 1994); Kenneth T. Jackson, *Crabgrass Frontier: The Suburbanization of the United States* (New York: Oxford University Press, 1985).

85 McGirr, *Suburban Warriors*; McGirr, "A History of the Conservative Movement from the Bottom Up."

86 Burns, *Goddess of the Market*.

87 McGirr, *Suburban Warriors*, pp. 56–9, 71–110.

88 On the heavily southern, independent Baptist and Pentecostal origins of Depression-era migrants to southern California, see Darren Dochuk, *From Bible Belt to Sunbelt: Plain-Folk Religion, Grassroots Politics, and the Rise of Evangelical Conservatism* (New York: Norton, 2011).

89 It is too strong an argument to claim a *necessary* connection between post-war suburbanization and conservative political tendencies. Still, the basic pattern of post-war suburbanization – white middle-class abandonment of urban cores to cheap single-family housing in the outlying areas beyond the city's political jurisdiction – exacerbated racial and class segregation in ways that accelerated the deterioration

of the city and abetted suburban political conservatism. Housing innovations from Washington, including the Federal National Mortgage Association (Fannie Mae) and the Government National Mortgage Association (Ginnie Mae), made possible the easy transfer of savings funds out of the cities of the Northeast and Middle West and toward the new developments of the South and the West. Jackson, *Crabgrass Frontier*, pp. 190–219.

90 Nicol C. Rae, *The Decline and Fall of the Liberal Republicans from 1952 to the Present* (New York: Oxford University Press, 1989).

91 Michael E. Kazin, *The Populist Persuasion: An America History* (New York: Basic Books, 1995), pp. 19–22.

92 Perlstein, *Before the Storm*, pp. 4–16, 43–52.

93 F. Clifton White, with William J. Gill, *Suite 3535: The Story of the Draft Goldwater Movement* (New Rochelle, NY: Arlington House, 1967), p. 37.

94 Perlstein, *Before the Storm*; Donald T. Critchlow, *Phyllis Schlafly and Grassroots Conservatism: A Woman's Crusade* (Princeton: Princeton University Press, 2005). Goldwater received campaign contributions from almost two million individuals, according to former Young Americans for Freedom stalwart John Andrew. By contrast, just 40,000 gave money to the party in the 1960 election. John A. Andrew, III, *The Other Side of the Sixties: Young Americans for Freedom and the Rise of Conservative Politics* (New Brunswick, NJ: Rutgers University Press, 1997), p. 210.

95 William F. Buckley, Jr. and L. Brent Bozell, *McCarthy and His Enemies: The Record and Its Meaning* (Chicago: Regnery, 1954).

96 Barry Goldwater, *The Conscience of a Conservative* (Shepherdsville, KY: Victor Publishing Co., 1960), p. 12.

97 Goldwater himself may have believed that the cause of African-American civil rights was just but federal preemption of states' rights wrong. As a Phoenix businessman he had hired African-Americans and contributed to the local National Association for the Advancement of Colored People. Kazin, *The Populist Persuasion*, p. 226. But he duly voted against the Civil Rights Act of 1964. For many conservatives at mid-century, however, the claim of states' rights was mostly cover for racism and white supremacy. To the degree that Richard Weaver's *Ideas Have Consequences* was a key founding text of post-war conservatism, it is important to underscore that its southern agrarianism could easily be read as an apology for white supremacy. Even the usually sophisticated William F. Buckley, Jr. was not immune from the fundamental assumption of black inferiority. In a 1957 *National Review* editorial on civil and states' rights he wrote: "The central question that emerges . . . is whether the White community in the South is entitled to take such measures as are necessary to prevail,

politically and culturally, in areas in which it does not predominate numerically. The sobering answer is *Yes* the white community is so entitled because, for the time being, it is the advanced race. . . . *National Review* believes that the South's premises are correct. If the majority wills what is socially atavistic, then to thwart the majority may be, though undemocratic, enlightened." Buckley, *National Review* (August 24, 1957), partially quoted in John B. Judis, *William F. Buckley, Jr.: Patron Saint of the Conservatives* (New York: Simon & Schuster, 1988), pp. 138–9.

98   Goldwater, *The Conscience of a Conservative*, p. 41.
99   Ibid., p. 91.
100 William F. Buckley, Jr., *Flying High: Remembering Barry Goldwater* (New York: Basic Books, 2008), pp. 147–8.
101 Phyllis Schlafly, *A Choice Not an Echo* (Alton, IL: Pere Marquette Press, 1964).
102 C. Wright Mills, *The Power Elite* (New York: Oxford University Press, 1956). Publication figures from Critchlow, *Phyllis Schlafly and Grassroots Conservatism*, p. 125.
103 The Ripon Society, *From Disaster to Distinction: A Republican Rebirth* (New York: Pocket Books, 1966).
104 William A. Rusher, *The Rise of the Right* (New York: William Morrow, 1984).
105 Sidney Blumenthal, *The Rise of the Counter-Establishment: From Conservative Ideology to Political Power* (New York: Times Books, 1986).
106 Andrew, *The Other Side of the Sixties*, pp. 215–220; Niels Bjerre-Poulsen, "The Heritage Foundation: A Second-Generation Think Tank," *Journal of Policy History*, Vol. 3, No. 2 (April 1991), pp. 152–72.
107 Cited in Phillips-Fein, *Invisible Hands*, p. 63.
108 Blumenthal, *The Rise of the Counter-Establishment*, pp. 32–45; Donald T. Critchlow, *The Conservative Ascendancy: How the GOP Right Made Political History* (Cambridge, MA: Harvard University Press, 2007), pp. 118–22; Thomas Medvetz, *Think Tanks in America* (Chicago: University of Chicago Press, 2012).
109 William E. Simon, *A Time for Truth* (New York: Reader's Digest Press, 1978).
110 Ibid., pp. 215–16, 221. Published by Reader's Digest, *A Time for Truth* featured a preface by Milton Friedman and a foreword by Friedrich Hayek.
111 Lewis F. Powell, Jr., "Confidential Memorandum: Attack of American Free Enterprise System," to Eugene B. Sydnor, Jr., Chairman, Education Committee, U.S. Chamber of Commerce (August 23, 1971), at *http://www.reclaimdemocracy.org/corporate_accountability/powell_memo_lewis.html* as of October 2012.

112 F.A. Hayek, "The Intellectuals and Socialism," *University of Chicago Law Review* (Spring 1949), pp. 417–33.

113 Franklin Foer, "Ideas Rule the World," *The New Republic* (April 7, 2011). Supply-side economic theory, with roots in the Austrian economics of Mises and Hayek, is typically attributed to the libertarian Arthur Laffer and was popularized by the economic journalist Jude Wanniski.

114 The Heritage Foundation, at *http://www.heritage.org/About/35thAnniversary.cfm* as of October 2012. After just ten years of existence, Heritage commanded an annual budget of more than $10 million and a staff of 105. In parallel, the AEI's budget grew ten times between 1970 and 1980, to $10.4 million with a staff of 135. Robert K. Landers, "Think Tanks: The New Partisans?" *Editorial Research Reports*, Vol. 1, No. 23 (June 20, 1986), pp. 455–72.

115 Jane Mayer, "Covert Operations: The Billionaire Brothers Who Are Waging a War against Obama," *The New Yorker* (August 30, 2010).

116 *Brown v. Board of Education*, 347 U.S. 483 (1954).

117 Earl Black and Merle Black, *The Rise of Southern Republicans* (Cambridge, MA: Belknap Press of Harvard University Press, 2002), pp. 53–4.

118 Charles Wallace Collins, *Whither Solid South? A Study in Politics and Race Relations* (New Orleans: Pelican Press, 1947), pp. ix–x, cited in Joseph E. Lowndes, *From the New Deal to the New Right: Race and the Southern Origins of Modern Conservatism* (New Haven: Yale University Press, 2008).

119 Ira Katznelson, "Was the Great Society a Lost Opportunity?" in Fraser and Gerstle, eds., *The Rise and Fall of the New Deal Order*, pp. 185–211; Lowndes, *From the New Deal to the New Right*, pp. 34–9, 48–54.

120 Black and Black, *The Rise of Southern Republicans*, p. 207.

121 Ibid., pp. 24–7, 206–40.

122 Lowndes, *From the New Deal to the New Right*, pp. 79–80; Kazin, *The Populist Persuasion*, pp. 222–42.

123 George C. Wallace, *Stand Up for America* (Garden City, NY: Doubleday, 1976), pp. 86–7.

124 Irving Kristol, *Two Cheers for Capitalism* (New York: Basic Books, 1978), pp. 3–70; Norman Podhoretz, "The Adversary Culture and the New Class," in B. Bruce-Briggs, ed., *The New Class?* (New Brunswick, NJ: Transaction Books, 1979), pp. 19–32.

125 Matthew D. Lassiter, *The Silent Majority: Suburban Politics in the Sunbelt South* (Princeton: Princeton University Press, 2006).

126 Ibid. McGirr, *Suburban Warriors*; Jonathan Rieder, *Canarsie: The Jews and Italians of Brooklyn against Liberalism* (Cambridge, MA: Harvard University Press, 1985); J. Anthony Lukas, *Common Ground:*

A Turbulent Decade in the Lives of Three American Families (New York: Knopf, 1985).

127 Kazin, *The Populist Persuasion.*

128 Jefferson Cowie, *Stayin' Alive: The 1970s and the Last Days of the Working Class* (New York: The New Press, 2010).

129 Rieder, *Canarsie*; Cowie, *Stayin' Alive*; Lukas, *Common Ground.*

130 Jonathan Rieder, "The Rise of the 'Silent Majority,'" in Fraser and Gerstle, eds., *The Rise and Fall of the New Deal Order*, p. 253.

131 Richard Nixon, "What Has Happened to America?" *Reader's Digest* (October 1967), pp. 49–54.

132 For a comprehensive account of Nixon's career and how he narrated and fed white resentment, see Rick Perlstein, *Nixonland: The Rise of a President and the Fracturing of America* (New York: Scribner, 2008).

133 Kevin Phillips, *The Emerging Republican Majority* (New Rochelle, NY: Arlington House, 1968).

134 Garry Wills, *Nixon Agonistes: The Crisis of the Self-made Man* (Boston: Houghton Mifflin, 1970), pp. 51–2.

Chapter 3 Religion and Politics: The Rise of the New Christian Right

1 José Casanova, *Public Religions in the Modern World* (Chicago: University of Chicago Press, 1994), pp. 11–39.

2 Peter L. Berger, *The Sacred Canopy: Elements of a Sociological Theory of Religion* (Garden City, NY: Anchor Books, 1969). The overall thrust of the differentiation of spheres argument derives from Max Weber's concept of the "disenchantment" of the world. Weber, *Economy and Society: An Outline of Interpretive Sociology* [1922], Guenther Roth and Claus Wittich, eds. (Berkeley: University of California Press, 1978).

3 Hugh Heclo, *Christianity and American Democracy* (Cambridge, MA: Harvard University Press, 2007), pp. 15, 20.

4 Henry F. May, *The Enlightenment in America* (New York: Oxford University Press, 1976).

5 This summary is drawn from George M. Marsden, *Fundamentalism and American Culture: The Shaping of Twentieth-Century Evangelicalism, 1870–1925* (New York: Oxford University Press, 1980); Jack Rogers, *Claiming the Center: Churches and Conflicting Worldviews* (Louisville, KY: Westminster John Knox Press, 1995); Walter A. McDougall, *Promised Land, Crusader State* (Boston: Houghton-Mifflin, 1997); Mark A. Noll, *America's God: From Jonathan Edwards to Abraham Lincoln* (New York: Oxford University Press, 2002).

6   Ronald C. White, Jr., *Liberty and Justice for All: Racial Reform and the Social Gospel, 1877–1925* (San Francisco: Harper & Row, 1990).

7   Will Herberg, *Protestant, Catholic, Jew: An Essay in American Religious Sociology* (New York: Doubleday, 1955).

8   Alexis de Tocqueville, *Democracy in America* [1835], Arthur Goldhammer, trans. (New York: Library of America, 2004); Sydney E. Ahlstrom, *A Religious History of the American People* (New Haven: Yale University Press, 1972), pp. 386–509. By 1850, the "upstart" democratic and emotional Baptist and Methodist sects far outpaced the more hierarchical and intellectual Episcopalian and Congregationalist denominations that had dominated religious life in the colonial period. Roger Finke and Rodney Stark, *The Churching of America, 1776–1990: Winners and Losers in Our Religious Economy* (New Brunswick, NJ: Rutgers University Press, 1992), pp. 54–108.

9   Robert N. Bellah, "Civil Religion in America," *Daedalus*, Vol. 96, No. 1 (Winter 1967), pp. 1–21.

10 Casanova, *Public Religions in the Modern World*, pp. 11–39, 135–57.

11 Noll, *America's God*, pp. 386–438; Ahlstrom, *A Religious History of the American People*, pp. 648–73.

12 Ahlstrom, *A Religious History of the American People*, pp. 429–54.

13 Rogers, *Claiming the Center*, pp. 16, 139.

14 Marsden, *Fundamentalism and American Culture*, pp. 24–5, 53.

15 Ibid., pp. 62–3; Victoria Clark, *Allies for Armageddon: The Rise of Christian Zionism* (New Haven: Yale University Press, 2007), pp. 27–144.

16 William Jennings Bryan, *Prince of Peace* (Independence, MO: Zion's Printing and Pub. Co., 1925); Edward J. Larson, *Summer for the Gods: The Scopes Trial and America's Continuing Debate over Science and Religion* (New York: Basic Books, 1997); Michael S. Evans and John H. Evans, "Arguing against Darwinism: Religion, Science and Public Morality," in Bryan Turner, ed., *The New Blackwell Companion to the Sociology of Religion* (New York: Blackwell, 2010), pp. 286–308.

17 Joel A. Carpenter, *Revive Us Again: The Reawakening of American Fundamentalism* (New York: Oxford University Press, 1997); Susan Friend Harding, *The Book of Jerry Falwell: Fundamentalist Language and Politics* (Princeton: Princeton University Press, 2000); Heclo, *Christianity and American Democracy*.

18 Malise Ruthven, *Fundamentalism: The Search for Meaning* (Oxford: Oxford University Press, 2004).

19 Jack Rogers, personal letter to author (October 2009); George Marsden, *Reforming Fundamentalism: Fuller Seminary and the New Evangelism* (Grand Rapids, MI: Eerdmans, 1987); Marsden,

"Introduction," in George Marsden, ed., *Evangelicalism and Modern America* (Grand Rapids, MI: Eerdmans, 1984), pp. vii–xix.

20 Finke and Stark, *The Churching of America*, pp. 237–75; Pew Forum on Religion and Public Life, "U.S. Religious Landscape Survey" (2012), at *http://religions.pewforum.org/reports/* as of October 2012. The percentage of people without religious affiliation has grown in recent years, to 16 percent of the population.

21 Marsden, *Fundamentalism and American Culture*, pp. 184–8.

22 James Davison Hunter, *American Evangelicalism: Conservative Religion and the Quandary of Modernity* (New Brunswick, NJ: Rutgers University Press, 1983).

23 Heclo, *Christianity and American Democracy*, p. 110.

24 Marsden, *Reforming Fundamentalism*, p. 5.

25 Cited in Bill J. Leonard, "Independent Baptists: From Sectarian Minority to 'Moral Majority,'" *Church History*, Vol. 56, No. 4 (December 1987), p. 513.

26 Leo P. Ribuffo, *The Old Christian Right: The Protestant Far Right from the Great Depression to the Cold War* (Philadelphia: Temple University Press, 1983); James C. Juhnke, *A People of Two Kingdoms: The Political Acculturation of the Kansas Mennonites* (Newton, KS: Faith and Life Press, 1975).

27 Sara Diamond, *Roads to Dominion: Right-Wing Movements and Political Power in the United States* (New York: Guilford Press, 1995), pp. 101–2; Frank P. Mintz, *The Liberty Lobby and the American Right: Race, Conspiracy, and Culture* (Westport, CT: Greenwood Press, 1985).

28 Cited in Leonard, "Independent Baptists," p. 513.

29 Warren L. Vinz, *Pulpit Politics: Faces of American Protestant Nationalism in the Twentieth Century* (Albany: State University of New York Press, 1997), pp. 109–20.

30 Rogers Smith, "An Almost Christian Nation? Constitutional Consequences of the Rise of the Religious Right," in Steven Brint and John Reith Schroedel, eds., *Evangelicals and Democracy in America*, Vol. I: *Religion and Society* (New York: Sage, 2009), pp. 329–55.

31 Richard Hofstadter, "Pseudo-Conservatism Revisited – 1965," in Hofstadter, *The Paranoid Style in American Politics, and Other Essays* (New York: Knopf, 1965), pp. 74–6.

32 Joel A. Carpenter, "From Fundamentalism to the New Evangelical Coalition," in Marsden, ed., *Evangelicalism and Modern America*, pp. 3–16.

33 Heather Hendershot, *What's Fair on the Air? Cold War Right-Wing Broadcasting and the Public Interest* (Chicago: University of Chicago Press, 2011), p. 109.

34 Gary K. Clabaugh, *Thunder on the Right: The Protestant Fundamentalists* (Chicago: Nelson-Hall, 1974), pp. 83–92.

35 Cited in Allan J. Lichtman, *White Protestant Nation: The Rise of the American Conservative Movement* (New York: Atlantic Monthly Press, 2008), p. 197.

36 Diamond, *Roads to Dominion*; Daniel Bell, "The Dispossessed," in Bell, ed., *The Radical Right: The New American Right Expanded and Updated* (Garden City, NY: Anchor Books, 1963), pp. 1–45; Ribuffo, *The Old Christian Right*.

37 Donald T. Critchlow, *The Conservative Ascendancy: How the GOP Right Made Political History* (Cambridge, MA: Harvard University Press, 2007), pp. 33–6; Hendershot, *What's Fair on the Air?*, pp. 170–205.

38 K.A. Courdileone, *Manhood and American Culture in the Cold War* (New York: Routledge, 2005), p. 82; Stephen P. Miller, *Billy Graham and the Rise of the Republican South* (Philadelphia: University of Pennsylvania Press, 2009), p. 22.

39 Miller, *Billy Graham and the Rise of the Republican South*, pp. 137–57; William Inboden, *Religion and American Foreign Policy, 1945–1960: The Soul of Containment* (Cambridge: Cambridge University Press, 2008), pp. 81–9.

40 Jerry Falwell, "Ministers and Marches," sermon delivered March 21, 1965, subsequently published in booklet form (Lynchburg, VA: Thomas Road Baptist Church, 1965), pp. 3, 10.

41 Frances FitzGerald, *Cities on a Hill: A Journey through Contemporary American Cultures* (New York: Simon & Schuster, 1981), p. 170.

42 Robert Wuthnow, "The Political Rebirth of American Evangelicals," in Robert C. Liebman and Robert Wuthnow, eds., *The New Christian Right: Mobilization and Legitimation* (New York: Aldine Publishing, 1983), pp. 167–85.

43 Corwin Smidt, "Born Again Politics: The Political Behavior of Evangelical Christians in the South and the Non-South," in Tod A. Baker, Robert P. Steed, and Laurence W. Moreland, eds., *Religion and Politics in the South: Mass and Elite Perspectives* (New York: Praeger, 1983), pp. 27–56.

44 Steven Waldman, "Evangelicals Made Up a BIGGER Part of the Republican Coalition This Time," *beliefnet* (November 10, 2008), at *http://blog.beliefnet.com/stevenwaldman/2008/11/evangelicals-made-up-a-bigger.html* as of October 2012.

45 "How the Faithful Voted: 2012 Preliminary Analysis," The Pew Forum on Religion and Public Life (November 7, 2012): *http://www.pewforum.org/Politics-and-Elections/How-the-Faithful-Voted-2012-Preliminary-Exit-Poll-Analysis.aspx* as of November 2012.

46 Rebecca E. Zietlow, "The Judicial Restraint of the Warren Court (and Why It Matters)," *Ohio State Law Journal*, Vol. 69, No. 2 (2008), pp. 255–94.

47 Jeffrey K. Hadden and Anson Shupe, *Televangelism: Power and Politics on God's Frontier* (New York: Henry Holt, 1988).

48 Matthew Avery Sutton, *Aimee Semple McPherson and the Resurrection of Christian America* (Cambridge, MA: Harvard University Press, 2007); Quentin J. Schultze, *Christianity and the Mass Media in America: Toward a Democratic Accommodation* (East Lansing: Michigan State University Press, 2003), pp. 145, 382.

49 Philip T. Rosen, *The Modern Stentors: Radio Broadcasters and the Federal Government, 1920–1934* (Westport, CT: Greenwood Press, 1980).

50 Federal Radio Commission, In the Matter of the Application of Great Lakes Broadcasting Co., 3 FRC *Annual Report* 32 (1929).

51 Tona J. Hangen, *Redeeming the Dial: Radio, Religion and Popular Culture in America* (Chapel Hill: University of North Carolina Press, 2002), pp. 23–6.

52 Alan Brinkley, *Voices of Protest: Huey Long, Father Coughlin, and the Great Depression* (New York: Knopf, 1982), pp. 89–120.

53 Hangen, *Redeeming the Dial*; Schultze, *Christianity and the Mass Media in America*; Arthur H. Matthews, *Stand Up, Standing Together: The Emergence of the National Association of Evangelicals* (Carol Stream, IL: NAE, 1992), p. 47.

54 Federal Communications Commission, Report and Statement of Policy Re: Commission En Banc Programming Inquiry, 44 FCC 2303 (1960).

55 Ben Armstrong, *The Electric Church* (Nashville: Thomas Nelson, 1979).

56 Robert B. Horwitz, *The Irony of Regulatory Reform: The Deregulation of American Telecommunications* (New York: Oxford University Press, 1989), pp. 244–63; Hadden and Shupe, *Televangelism*, pp. 47–52.

57 FitzGerald, *Cities on a Hill*, pp. 124–5.

58 Federal Communications Commission, In the Matter of Revisions of Rules Permitting Multiple Ownership of Non-Commercial Educational Radio and Television Stations in Single Markets, et al., Memorandum Opinion and Order, 54 FCC 2d 941 (1975).

59 Janis Johnson, "Mail Protests Alleged Religious Broadcasts Ban," *Washington Post* (February 17, 1977).

60 *Brown v. Board of Education*, 347 U.S. 483 (1954); Smith, "An Almost Christian Nation?" p. 334.

61 James Davison Hunter, *Evangelicalism: The Coming Generation* (Chicago: University of Chicago Press, 1987), p. 6.

62 *Engel v. Vitale*, 370 U.S. 421 (1962).

63 Daniel K. Williams, "Jerry Falwell's Sunbelt Politics: The Regional Origins of the Moral Majority," *Journal of Policy History*, Vol. 22, No. 2 (April 2010), pp. 125–47; David Nevin and Robert E. Bills,

The Schools That Fear Built: Segregationist Academies in the South (Washington, DC: Acropolis Books, 1976).

64 *Green v. Connally*, 330 F. Supp. 1150 (D.D.C.) *aff'd. sub nom. Coit v. Green*, 404 U.S. 997 (1971).

65 U.S. Department of Treasury, Internal Revenue Service, Proposed Revenue Procedure on Private Tax-Exempt Schools, *Federal Register*, Vol. 43, No. 163 (August 22, 1978), p. 37296.

66 Joseph Crespino, *In Search of Another Country: Mississippi and the Conservative Counterrevolution* (Princeton: Princeton University Press, 2007).

67 Editorial, "Bureaucratic Government Regulation of Churches and Church Institutions," *Journal of Church and State*, Vol. 21, No. 2 (Spring 1979), pp. 195–207; Peter Skerry, "Christian Schools versus the IRS," *The Public Interest* (Fall 1980), pp. 18–41; U.S. House of Representatives, Committee on Ways and Means, Subcommittee on Oversight, Hearings on Proposed IRS Revenue Procedure Affecting Tax-Exemption of Private Schools (February 20, 21, 22, 26, 28; March 12, 1979), Serial 96–11.

68 Editorial, "Bureaucratic Government Regulation of Churches and Church Institutions," pp. 205–6.

69 U.S. Department of Treasury, Internal Revenue Service, Integrated Auxiliary of a Church, *Federal Register*, Vol. 42, No. 2 (January 4, 1977), p. 767.

70 *National Labor Relations Board v. Catholic Bishop of Chicago*, 440 U.S. 490 (1979); Editorial, "Bureaucratic Government Regulation of Churches and Church Institutions," pp. 201–4.

71 Berger, *The Sacred Canopy*.

72 Bellah, "Civil Religion in America."

73 Martin Riesebrodt, *Pious Passion: The Emergence of Modern Fundamentalism in the United States and Iran*, Don Reneau, trans. (Berkeley: University of California Press, 1993).

74 Jerry Falwell, *Listen, America!* (Garden City: NY: Doubleday, 1980).

75 Focus on the Family grew rapidly in the 1980s and 1990s, with Dobson achieving the kind of influence in conservative circles on a par with Jerry Falwell and Pat Robertson. At its height in 2002, Focus on the Family employed 1,400 people. It had an operating budget of $160 million in 2008. Dobson's daily radio show had an audience of 1.5 million listeners a day on about 1,000 stations by the end of 2009. Dan Gilgoff, *The Jesus Machine: How James Dobson, Focus on the Family, and Evangelical America Are Winning the Culture War* (New York: St. Martin's Press, 2007); Max Blumenthal, *Republican Gomorrah: Inside the Movement That Shattered the Party* (New York: Nation Books, 2009); Laurie Goodstein, "Founder of Focus on the

Family is Starting a New Radio Show," *New York Times* (January 17, 2010).

76 Riesbrodt, *Pious Passion*, p. 64. An important line of Christian popular culture marketed to women explores how female submission within the patriarchal family is both God's will and – in an unacknowledged adoption of the transformational politics of the 1960s – a form of female empowerment. Linda Kintz, *Between Jesus and the Market: The Emotions That Matter in Right-Wing America* (Durham, NC: Duke University Press, 1997).

77 Falwell, *Listen, America!*, pp. 65–6.

78 Richard John Neuhaus, *The Naked Public Square: Religion and Democracy in America* (Grand Rapids, MI: Eerdmans, 1984).

79 Francis A. Schaeffer, *How Should We Then Live? The Rise and Decline of Western Thought and Culture* (Old Tappan, NJ: Fleming H. Revell, 1976); Tim LaHaye, *The Battle for the Mind* (Old Tappan, NJ: Fleming H. Revell, 1980).

80 In a later Schaeffer tract, highly influential in galvanizing anti-abortion activism to a more radical stage, a list of three key books appears on the page prior the introductory chapter: *The Communist Manifesto* (1848), *Humanist Manifesto I* (1933), *Humanist Manifesto II* (1973). Schaeffer, *A Christian Manifesto* (Westchester, IL: Crossway Books, 1981).

81 LaHaye, *The Battle for the Mind*, p. 136. LaHaye's history demonstrates the fluidity of the movement of ideas and persons within right-wing circles. He received his BA from the fundamentalist Bob Jones University, was active in Christian Voice, one of the early Christian activist groups around school issues, and helped found the politically influential, publicity-shy Council for National Policy in 1981. LaHaye is a conspiracy theorist with historic ties to the John Birch Society. Besides his premillennial dispensational publications, including the immensely popular *Left Behind* novels, he has written on the global conspiracy of the Illuminati and other groups – such as the NAACP, the ACLU, and Planned Parenthood – to destroy Christianity. Other subjects of LaHaye's ire include Catholicism. A Christian educator and psychologist, LaHaye uses his writings on personality and temperament to help fund his ministry. At *https://timlahaye.com/* as of October 2012.

82 Pat Robertson, *The Turning Tide: The Fall of Liberalism and the Rise of Common Sense* (Dallas: World Publishing, 1993), pp. 293–4.

83 Falwell, *Listen, America!*; LaHaye, *The Battle for the Mind*; Robertson, *The Turning Tide*.

84 Wuthnow, "The Political Rebirth of American Evangelicals."

85 William Martin, *With God on Our Side: The Rise of the Religious Right in America* (New York: Broadway Books, 1996), pp. 144–54.

86 Ibid.; Kristin Luker, *Abortion and the Politics of Motherhood* (Berkeley: University of California Press, 1984).

87 Alan Crawford, *Thunder on the Right: The "New Right" and the Politics of Resentment* (New York: Pantheon, 1980); Gillian Peele, *Revival and Reaction: The Right in Contemporary America* (Oxford: Clarendon Press, 1984), pp. 51–79.

88 Cited in Martin, *With God on Our Side*, p. 173.

89 John D. McCarthy and Mayer N. Zald, "Resource Mobilization and Social Movements: A Partial Theory," *American Journal of Sociology*, Vol. 82, No. 6 (May 1977), pp. 1212–41; McCarthy and Zald, *Social Movements in an Organizational Society: Collected Essays* (New Brunswick, NJ: Transaction Books, 1987); Doug McAdam, John D. McCarthy, and Mayer N. Zald, eds., *Comparative Perspectives on Social Movements: Political Opportunities, Mobilizing Structures, and Cultural Framings* (New York: Cambridge University Press, 1996); David S. Meyer, "Protest and Political Opportunities," *Annual Review of Sociology*, Vol. 30 (August 2004), pp. 125–45.

90 Martin, *With God on Our Side*, pp. 171–2.

91 Jane J. Mansbridge, *Why We Lost the ERA* (Chicago: University of Chicago Press, 1986), pp. 5, 174; Matthew D. Lassiter, "Inventing Family Values," in Bruce J. Schulman and Julian E. Zelizer, eds., *Rightward Bound: Making America Conservative in the 1970s* (Cambridge, MA: Harvard University Press, 2008), pp. 13–28; Marjorie J. Spruill, "Gender and America's Right Turn," Schulman and Zelizer, eds., *Rightward Bound*, pp. 71–89.

92 Rick Perlstein, *Before the Storm: Barry Goldwater and the Unmaking of the American Consensus* (New York: Hill and Wang, 2001).

93 Donald T. Critchlow, *Phyllis Schlafly and Grassroots Conservatism: A Woman's Crusade* (Princeton: Princeton University Press, 2005).

94 Richard A. Viguerie, *The New Right: We're Ready to Lead* (Falls Church, VA: The Viguerie Co., 1981).

95 Kevin Phillips, quoted in John B. Judis, *William F. Buckley: Patron Saint of the Conservatives* (New York: Simon & Schuster, 1988), p. 378.

96 Critchlow, *The Conservative Ascendancy*, pp. 128–31.

97 Richard A. Viguerie and Lee Edwards, "Goldwater: Leader or Legend?" *Conservative Digest* (January 1976), pp. 6–8; William A. Rusher, "What's Happened to Barry?" *Conservative Digest* (April 1976), p. 16. Goldwater, who hewed toward the libertarian pole of conservative fusionism, objected to much of the new right's social agenda. He was pro-choice on the abortion question, supported Planned Parenthood, and endorsed gay rights.

98 Other prominent Christian right organizations established in the late 1970s and early 1980s included the American Family Association (under the leadership of Donald Wildmon), Focus on the Family and

the Family Research Council (led by the anti-permissiveness psychologist James Dobson), the Council for National Policy (Tim LaHaye), Concerned Women for America (Beverly LaHaye), and the Traditional Values Coalition (Louis Sheldon).

99   FitzGerald, *Cities on a Hill*, pp. 178–80; Erling Jorstad, *The Politics of Moralism: The New Christian Right in American Life* (Minneapolis: Augsberg, 1981), p. 71.

100   Falwell, *Listen, America!*, p. 13.

101   Ibid., p. 74.

102   Seymour Martin Lipset, "Sources of the 'Radical Right,' " in Bell, ed., *The Radical Right*, pp. 307–71.

103   Brinkley, *Voices of Protest*, pp. 143–68, 265–83.

104   Hofstadter, "The Pseudo-Conservative Revolt – 1954," in *The Paranoid Style in American Politics, and Other Essays*, pp. 41–65.

105   Donald F. Crosby, *God, Church, and Flag: Senator Joseph R. McCarthy and the Catholic Church, 1950–1957* (Chapel Hill: University of North Carolina Press, 1978).

106   "Presidential Vote of Catholics," Center for Applied Research in the Apostolate, Georgetown University, at *http://cara.georgetown.edu/Presidential%20Vote%20Only.pdf* as of October 2012.

107   Rosalind Pollock Petchesky, *Abortion and Woman's Choice: The State, Sexuality, and Reproductive Freedom*, revised edition (Boston: Northeastern University Press, 1990), p. 254.

108   Leonard, "Independent Baptists," pp. 504–17.

109   Robert C. Liebman, "Mobilizing the Moral Majority," in Liebman and Wuthnow, eds., *The New Christian Right*, pp. 49–73.

110   Peele, *Revival and Reaction*, pp. 55–65.

111   Richard Viguerie and David Franke, *America's Right Turn: How Conservatives Used New and Alternative Media to Take Power* (Chicago: Bonus Books, 2004).

112   Falwell claimed in 1983 that the *Old-Time Gospel Hour* was carried on approximately 400 television stations each week and aired on nearly 500 radio stations daily, with the ministry employing more than 2,000 people. Jerry Falwell, *Nuclear War and the Second Coming of Jesus Christ* (Lynchburg, VA: Old-Time Gospel Hour, 1983), p. 45. According to Frances FitzGerald, revenues from the *Old-Time Gospel Hour* rose from $7 million in 1973 to $22 million in 1977, and raised about $115 million between 1977 through 1980 from the two and a half million people on its mailing lists. These revenues enabled Falwell to subsidize the Thomas Road Baptist Church's other ventures, including the Liberty Baptist College campus, and to bail out the church from its financial difficulties in 1980. FitzGerald, *Cities on the Hill*, pp. 152–5.

113   Armstrong, *The Electric Church*; Hadden and Shupe, *Televangelism*.

114 Research Articles – The Council for National Policy, at *http://www.seekgod.ca/topiccnp.htm* as of October 2012; Blumenthal, *Republican Gomorrah*, pp. 32–46.
115 American Legislative Exchange Council, at *http://www.alec.org/* as of October 2012.
116 Cited in Hadden and Shupe, *Televangelism*, p. 28.
117 Cited in Donald Heinz, "The Struggle to Define America," in Liebman and Wuthnow, eds., *The New Christian Right*, p. 136.
118 LaHaye, *The Battle for the Mind*, pp. 217–18.
119 Harding, *The Book of Jerry Falwell*, p. 241.
120 Bennett M. Berger, *The Survival of a Counterculture: Ideological Work and Everyday Life among Rural Communards* (New Brunswick, NJ: Transaction Publishers, 2004).
121 Harding, *The Book of Jerry Falwell*, pp. 143, 165, 244.
122 See Smidt, "Born Again Politics."
123 John McCain, speech in Virginia Beach, VA (February 28, 2000), at *http://www.nytimes.com/2000/02/29/us/the-2000-campaign-excerpt-from-mccain-s-speech-on-religious-conservatives.html?pagewanted=all&src=pm* as of October 2012.
124 Kevin Phillips, *American Theocracy: The Peril and Politics of Radical Religion, Oil, and Borrowed Money in the 21st Century* (New York: Viking, 2006); Gilgoff, *The Jesus Machine*.
125 Rousas John Rushdoony, *The Institutes of Biblical Law: A Chalcedon Study, with Three Appendices by Gary North* (Nutley, NJ: Craig Press, 1973); Rushdoony, *Christianity and the State* (Vallecito, CA: Ross House Books, 1986); Michelle Goldberg, *Kingdom Coming: The Rise of Christian Nationalism* (New York: Norton, 2006).
126 Gary North, *An Introduction to Christian Economics* (Nutley, NJ: Craig Press, 1973).
127 Gary North and Gary DeMar, *Christian Reconstruction: What It is, What It isn't* (Tyler, TX: Institute for Christian Economics, 1991).
128 Schaeffer, *A Christian Manifesto*, pp. 19, 20.
129 Leszek Kolakowski, *My Correct Views on Everything*, Zbigniew Jankowski, ed. (South Bend, IN: St. Augustine's Press, 2005), p. 137.
130 Steve Bruce, *The Rise and Fall of the New Christian Right: Conservative Protestant Politics in America, 1978–1988* (New York: Oxford University Press, 1988), pp. 79–80.
131 Richard Hofstadter, *Anti-intellectualism in American Life* (New York: Vintage, 1962); Hofstadter, *The Paranoid Style in American Politics, and Other Essays*; Seymour Martin Lipset, *Political Man: The Social Bases of Politics* (Garden City, NY: Doubleday, 1960); Lipset with Earl Rabb, *The Politics of Unreason: Right-Wing Extremism in America, 1790–1977* (Chicago: University of Chicago Press, 1978); Bell, ed., *The Radical Right*.

132 Sara Diamond, "The Thread of the Christian Right," *Z Magazine* (July/August 1995).

133 George Weigel, *Tranquillitas Ordinis: The Present Failure and Future Promise of American Catholic Thought on War and Peace* (New York: Oxford University Press, 1987); Damon Linker, *The Theocons: Secular America under Siege* (New York: Doubleday, 2006), pp. 117–46.

134 Diamond, *Roads to Dominion*, pp. 214–25, 236–41.

135 Falwell, *Nuclear War and the Second Coming of Jesus Christ*.

136 Cited in Paul Boyer, "When U.S. Foreign Policy Meets Biblical Prophecy," *AlterNet* (February 20, 2003), at *http://alternet.org/story/15221/* as of October 2012.

137 Clark, *Allies for Armageddon*.

138 Cited in Mark Wingfield, "Evangelical Theology Drives American Attitudes toward Israel and the Middle East," *Baptist Standard* (April 15, 2002), at *http://www.baptiststandard.com/2002/4_15/pages/mideast_evangelical.html* as of October 2012.

139 Aparna Kumar, "Christian Coalition Calls for Solidarity with Israel," *Religion News Service* (November 11, 2002), at *http://www.baptiststandard.com/2002/11_11/print/israel.html* as of October 2012; Chip Berlet and Nikhil Aziz, "Culture, Religion, Apocalypse, and Middle East Foreign Policy" (December 5, 2003), at *http://rightweb.irc-online.org/pdf/0312apocalypse.pdf* as of October 2012.

140 Walter Russell Mead, "God's Country?" *Foreign Affairs*, Vol. 85, No. 5 (September/October 2006), pp. 24–44.

141 Dr. Richard D. Land, Letter to President George W. Bush (October 3, 2002), at *http://en.wikisource.org/wiki/Land_letter* as of October 2012.

142 Joseph Chambers, *A Palace for the Antichrist* (Green Forest, AR: New Leaf Press, 1996); Tim LaHaye and Jerry B. Jenkins, *Are We Living in the End Times?* (Wheaton, IL: Tyndale House, 1999).

143 Jerry Falwell, "God is Pro-war," *WorldNetDaily* (January 31, 2004), at *http://www.wnd.com/2004/01/23022/* as of October 2012.

144 Charles Stanley, "A Nation at War" (February 2003), at *http://biblestudyplanet.com/s138.htm* as of August 2012; Charles Marsh, "Wayward Christian Soldiers," *New York Times* (January 20, 2006).

145 Harding, *The Book of Jerry Falwell*, p. 25.

146 Ibid., pp. 149–50.

147 Nancy Tatom Ammerman, *Baptist Battles: Social Change and Religious Conflict in the Southern Baptist Convention* (New Brunswick, NJ: Rutgers University Press, 1990). In the era of the founding and early republic, Baptists had always been perhaps the strongest supporters of the separation of church and state. Steven Waldman, *Founding Faith: Providence, Politics, and the Birth of Religious*

Freedom in America (New York: Random House, 2008). In keeping with the denomination's historical stance against the oppression of state religion, the Southern Baptist Convention (SBC) eight times over a period of two decades affirmed support for the Supreme Court ruling that school prayer was unconstitutional. The SBC passed a near-unanimous resolution in 1971 upholding the right of abortion if a mother was in any physical or emotional peril. By 1982, as Moral Majority members became powerful within the SBC, both of those positions were reversed. And at its 1984 convention, the SBC passed a resolution against the ordination of women as ministers because "God requires" their "submission." Sidney Blumenthal, "The Religious Right and Republicans," in Richard Neuhaus and Michael Cromartie, eds., *Piety and Politics: Evangelicals and Fundamentalists Confront the World* (Washington, D.C.: Ethics and Public Policy Center, 1987), pp. 271–86. By 2000, the SBC effectively renounced its traditional democratic principles in favor of the dominance of male pastors. Stephen M. Tipton's historical analysis of the conservative challenge to the United Methodist Church's Social Gospel provides yet another piece of evidence of the conscious strategy of the right to undermine mainline liberal Protestantism. Tipton, *Public Pulpits: Methodists and Mainline Churches in the Moral Argument of Public Life* (Chicago: University of Chicago Press, 2007).

148   Falwell, *Nuclear War and the Second Coming of Jesus Christ.*

149   Jerry Falwell, Christian Broadcast Network's *The 700 Club* (September 13, 2001), at *http://www.truthorfiction.com/rumors/f/falwell-robertson-wtc.htm* as of October 2012.

150   Tim LaHaye and Jerry B. Jenkins, *Left Behind: A Novel of Earth's Last Days* [book one] (Wheaton, IL: Tyndale House Publishers, 1995). The series now extends to sixteen books and several movie spinoffs.

151   John Hagee, *Final Dawn over Jerusalem* (Nashville: Thomas Nelson, 1998).

152   The political scientist Gary Jacobson conducted one piece of a survey for Polimetrix, Inc. following the 2006 midterm congressional election. After responding to an initial question about belief in divine intervention in general, respondents were asked, "Do you believe that George W. Bush was chosen by God to lead the United States in a global war on terrorism?" Twenty-nine percent of Republicans (N = 219) responded "yes"; 28 percent responded "don't know"; 43 percent responded "no." Jacobson interprets the "don't know" responses as indicating that they believe Bush *might* be God's chosen instrument. Gary Jacobson, Cooperative Congressional Election Study – UCSD Module (Palo Alto, CA: Polimetrix, Inc., 2006).

153   Tim LaHaye and Ed Hindson, *Global Warning: Are We on the Brink of World War III?* (Eugene, OR: Harvest House, 2007).

236

Chapter 4   Two Generations of Neoconservatism: From the Law of Unintended Consequences to the Cleansing Fire of Violence

1   The quote is from the famous 1845 *New York Morning News* column of the influential journalist and Democratic Party activist John L. O'Sullivan. Cited in Anders Stephanson, *Manifest Destiny: American Expansionism and the Empire of Right* (New York: Hill and Wang, 1995), p. 42.

2   Technically, one should refer to them as "nascent" neoconservatives, because the neoconservative label appeared only in 1973, when the democratic socialist Michael Harrington attached the name to the intellectual movement in a critical article in the journal *Dissent*. Harrington, "The Welfare State and Its Neoconservative Critics," *Dissent*, Vol. 20, No. 4 (September 1973), pp. 435–54. The name stuck, although some associated with the intellectual movement, such as Daniel Bell, always rejected the label.

3   Others associated with the first generation of neoconservatives included Daniel Bell, Seymour Martin Lipset, and Jeane Kirkpatrick. Robert Tucker, Walter Laqueur, and Peter Berger were often considered associates. It is difficult to declare who was a bona fide neoconservative and who was a fellow traveler. Neoconservatism wasn't a movement per se; there was no statement of principles to sign on to. As Irving Kristol was fond of saying, neoconservatism was, rather, a "persuasion."

4   Irving Kristol, " 'Civil Liberties,' 1952 – A Study in Confusion: Do We Defend Our Rights by Protecting Communists?" *Commentary* (March 1952), pp. 228–36.

5   Kristol, "On Negative Liberalism," *Encounter* (January 1954), p. 2.

6   Reinhold Niebuhr, *The Children of Light and the Children of Darkness: A Vindication of Democracy and a Critique of Its Traditional Defense* (New York: Charles Scribner's Sons, 1944).

7   Cited in Elsie O'Shaughnessy, "The Moynihan Mystique," *Vanity Fair* (May 1994), p. 58.

8   Irving Kristol, "What's Bugging the Students?" *Atlantic Monthly* (November 1965), p. 108.

9   Daniel Patrick Moynihan, "Politics as the Art of the Impossible," *The American Scholar* (Fall 1969), pp. 573–83.

10   Nathan Glazer, "The Campus Crucible: Student Politics and the University," *Atlantic Monthly* (July 1969), pp. 43–53; Allan Bloom, *The Closing of the American Mind* (New York: Simon & Schuster, 1987).

11   Jeane Kirkpatrick, "Neoconservatism as a Response to the Counterculture," in Irwin Stelzer, ed., *The Neoconservative Reader* (New York: Grove Press, 2004), p. 239.

12 Students for a Democratic Society, "Port Huron Statement" (1962), at *http://www.h-net.org/~hst306/documents/huron.html* as of October 2012; Stokley Carmichael and Charles V. Hamilton, *Black Power: The Politics of Liberation in America* (New York: Vintage Books, 1967).

13 Midge Decter, "A Letter to the Young (and to Their Parents)," *Atlantic Monthly* (February 1975), at *http://www.theatlantic.com/magazine/ archive/1975/02/a-letter-to-the-young-and-to-their-parents/4096/* as of October 2012. The notion and phrase "adversary culture" came from Lionel Trilling, the important mid-century literary critic who was something of a mentor to a few of the first generation of neoconservatives.

14 Daniel Bell, *The Cultural Contradictions of Capitalism* (New York: Basic Books, 1976); Bell, *The Winding Passage: Essays and Sociological Journeys, 1960–1980* (Cambridge, MA: Abt Books, 1980).

15 Mark Gerson, *The Neoconservative Vision: From the Cold War to the Culture Wars* (Lanham, MD: Madison Books, 1996), pp. 9–10.

16 Leo Strauss, *Natural Right and History* (Chicago: University of Chicago Press, 1953).

17 Seymour M. Hersh, "Selective Intelligence: Donald Rumsfeld Has His Own Special Sources. Are They Reliable?" *New Yorker* (May 12, 2003), quoting Stephen Holmes, a Strauss critic at New York University School of Law.

18 Owen Edwards, "The New York Wasp is Not an Endangered Species," *New York* (August 12, 1974). Jacob Heilbrunn, among others, makes a strong case that first-generation neoconservatives resented the American WASP establishment. WASPs, in their view, ignored the Holocaust and excluded Jews from the establishment. Even among second-generation neoconservatives, such as Douglas Feith, some resentment continues, especially of the State Department, which, supposedly, is historically run by WASPs. Jacob Heilbrunn, *They Knew They Were Right: The Rise of the Neocons* (New York: Doubleday, 2008), pp. 11–12, 58, 73, 83.

19 Melanie Phillips, "The Politics of Progress," *Jewish Chronicle* (January 1, 2004), at *http://www.melaniephillips.com/the-politics-of-progress-with-link-to-limmud-talk* as of October 2012.

20 Daniel Patrick Moynihan, "The Negro Family: The Case for National Action," Office of Policy Planning and Research, U.S. Department of Labor (March 1965).

21 Lee Rainwater and William L. Yancy, *The Moynihan Report and the Politics of Controversy: A Trans-action Social Science and Public Policy Report* (Cambridge, MA: MIT Press, 1967).

22 Nathan Glazer, *Affirmative Discrimination: Ethnic Inequality and Public Policy* (New York: Basic Books, 1975); Thomas Sowell, "Colleges Are Skipping Over Competent Blacks to Admit 'Authentic' Ghetto Types," *New York Times Magazine* (December 13, 1970);

Sowell, "'Affirmative Action': A Worldwide Disaster," *Commentary* (December 1989), pp. 21–41.

23   Nathan Glazer and Daniel Patrick Moynihan, *Beyond the Melting Pot: The Negroes, Puerto Ricans, Jews, Italians, and Irish of New York City* (Cambridge, MA: MIT Press, 1970).

24   James Q. Wilson, "What Makes a Better Policeman," *Atlantic Monthly* (March 1969), pp. 129–35.

25   James Q. Wilson and George L. Kelling, "Broken Windows: The Police and Neighborhood Safety," *Atlantic Monthly* (March 1982), pp. 29–38.

26   James Q. Wilson, "The Rediscovery of Character: Private Virtue and Public Policy," *The Public Interest* (Fall 1985), p. 16.

27   Irving Kristol, "Human Nature and Social Reform," *Wall Street Journal* (September 18, 1978); William Kristol, "The Politics of Liberty, the Sociology of Virtue," in Mark Gerson, ed., *The Essential Neoconservative Reader* (Reading, MA: Addison-Wesley, 1996), pp. 434–43; William J. Bennett, ed., *The Book of Virtues: A Treasury of Great Moral Stories* (New York: Simon & Schuster, 1993).

28   Daniel Patrick Moynihan, *Miles to Go: A Personal History of Social Policy* (Cambridge, MA: Harvard University Press, 1996), p. 63.

29   Irving Kristol, *Two Cheers for Capitalism* (New York: Basic Books, 1978), pp. 3–70. Notwithstanding Kristol's American version, the most famous of the New Class critiques was that of Milovan Djilas, *The New Class: An Analysis of the Communist System* (New York: Praeger, 1957). And still another intellectual forebear of Kristol's New Class was James Burnham, the Marxist-turned-*National Review* conservative who, himself channeling a version of Robert Michels's "iron law of oligarchy" perspective on bureaucracy, argued that managerial capitalism created a new class that had little commitment either to traditional social and political institutions or to the very existence of the nation-state. James Burnham, *The Managerial Revolution: What is Happening in the World* (New York: John Day, 1941); Robert Michels, *Political Parties: A Sociological Study of the Oligarchical Tendencies of Modern Democracy*, Eden and Cedar Paul, trans. (Glencoe, IL: Free Press, 1915). Moreover, virtually every social theorist worth his or her salt had been trying to make sense of the rise of the educated workforce, highly skilled in scientific, technical, and communicative or symbolic enterprises in the post-World War II period. Some theorists believed this development was a good one, others not. The neoconservatives clearly thought not. See Michael Harrington, "The New Class and the Left," in B. Bruce-Briggs, ed., *The New Class?* (New Brunswick, NJ: Transaction Books, 1979), pp. 123–39.

30 Michael E. Kazin, *The Populist Persuasion: An American History* (New York: Basic Books, 1995).

31 Michael Schudson, *Why Democracies Need an Unlovable Press* (Cambridge: Polity, 2008), pp. 108–25.

32 Jeane J. Kirkpatrick, "The Revolt of the Masses," *Commentary* (February 1973), pp. 58–72.

33 John B. Judis, *The Paradox of American Democracy: Elites, Special Interests, and the Betrayal of Public Trust* (New York: Pantheon, 2000).

34 Kristol, *Two Cheers for Capitalism*, p. 15.

35 Robert L. Bartley, "Business and the New Class," in Bruce-Briggs, ed., *The New Class?*, p. 59.

36 Chris Mooney, *The Republican War on Science* (New York: Basic Books, 2005); Naomi Oreskes and Erik M. Conway, *Merchants of Doubt: How a Handful of Scientists Obscured the Truth on Issues from Tobacco Smoke to Global Warming* (New York: Bloomsbury Press, 2010).

37 Sam Peltzman, *The Regulation of Automobile Safety* (Washington, DC: American Enterprise Institute, 1975); A.L. Nichols and Richard Zeckhauser, "Government Comes to the Workplace: An Assessment of OSHA," *The Public Interest* (Fall 1977), pp. 39–69; Murray Weidenbaum and Robert DeFina, *The Cost of Federal Regulation of Economic Activity* (Washington, DC: American Enterprise Institute, 1978).

38 Kristol, *Two Cheers for Capitalism*; Michael Novak, *The Spirit of Democratic Capitalism* (New York: Simon & Schuster, 1982). Kristol, who retained a sense of capitalism's destructive side, gave the free enterprise system two cheers; Novak's ever-sunny identification of capitalism and democracy gave it all three huzzahs.

39 Robert B. Horwitz, *The Irony of Regulatory Reform: The Deregulation of American Telecommunications* (New York: Oxford University Press, 1989), pp. 196–212; David Vogel, *Lobbying the Corporation: Citizen Challenges to Business Authority* (New York: Basic Books, 1978).

40 Steven M. Teles, *The Rise of the Conservative Legal Movement: The Battle for Control of the Law* (Princeton: Princeton University Press, 2009).

41 Irving Kristol, "Pornography, Obscenity, and the Case for Censorship," *New York Times Magazine* (March 28, 1971).

42 Irving Kristol, "The New Populism: Not to Worry" [1985], in Kristol, *Neoconservatism: The Autobiography of an Idea* (New York: Free Press, 1995), pp. 359–63.

43 Irving Kristol, "Room for Darwin and the Bible," *New York Times* (September 30, 1986).

44 Irving Kristol, "The Future of American Jewry," *Commentary* (August 1991), pp. 21–6; Kristol, "The Coming 'Conservative Century'"

[1993], in Kristol, *Neoconservatism: The Autobiography of an Idea*, pp. 364–8.

45 Irving Kristol, "America's 'Exceptional' Conservatism," in *Neoconservatism: The Autobiography of an Idea*, p. 380.

46 Irving Kristol, "The Political Dilemma of American Jews," *Commentary* (July 1984), pp. 23–9.

47 Nathan Abrams, *Norman Podhoretz and Commentary Magazine: The Rise and Fall of the Neocons* (New York: Continuum, 2010), pp. 205–7, 244, 264–8; Norman Podhoretz, "Should Jews Fear the Christian Right?" *New York Times* (July 23, 1994); Podhoretz, "In the Matter of Pat Robertson," *Commentary* (August 1995), pp. 27–32; Midge Decter, "The ADL vs. the Religious Right," *Commentary* (September 1994), pp. 45–7.

48 Steven M. Tipton, *Public Pulpits: Methodists and Mainline Churches in the Moral Argument of Public Life* (Chicago: University of Chicago Press, 2007), pp. 146–228; William Inboden, *Religion and American Foreign Policy, 1945–1960: The Soul of Containment* (Cambridge: Cambridge University Press, 2008).

49 Peter Steinfels, "Christianity and Democracy: Baptizing Reaganism," *Christianity and Crisis* (March 29, 1983), pp. 80–5.

50 *http://bridgeproject.com/?transparency?* as of October 2012.

51 See note 48 for Tipton.

52 Damon Linker, *The Theocons: Secular America under Siege* (New York: Doubleday, 2006).

53 See note 38 for Novak.

54 Richard John Neuhaus, *The Naked Public Square: Religion and Democracy in America* (Grand Rapids, MI: Eerdmans, 1984).

55 Linker, *The Theocons*, pp. 53–86.

56 *http://bridgeproject.com/?transparency?* as of October 2012.

57 Norman Podhoretz, *The Present Danger: "Do We Have the Will to Reverse the Decline of American Power?* (New York: Simon & Schuster, 1980), p. 91.

58 Norman Podhoretz, "Making the World Safe for Communism," *Commentary* (April 1976), pp. 31–42; Podhoretz, "The Abandonment of Israel," *Commentary* (July 1976), pp. 23–31; Podhoretz, "The Culture of Appeasement," *Harper's* (October 1977), pp. 25–32.

59 Norman Podhoretz, *Why We Were in Vietnam* (New York: Simon & Schuster, 1982).

60 Podhoretz, *The Present Danger*, p. 49.

61 Ibid., pp. 57, 12.

62 In defending the U.S. invasion of Cambodia in 1970, Nixon said, "If, when the chips are down, the world's most powerful nation, the United States of America, acts like a pitiful, helpless giant, the forces of totalitarianism and anarchy will threaten free nations and free institutions throughout the world." President Richard M. Nixon, "Address to the

Nation on the Situation in Southeast Asia" (April 30, 1970), at *http:// www.mekong.net/cambodia/nixon430.htm* as of October 2012.

63 Irving Kristol, "Does NATO Exist?" [1979], in *Reflections of a Neoconservative: Looking Back, Looking Ahead* (New York: Basic Books, 1983), pp. 241, 242.

64 Kristol, "Our Incoherent Foreign Policy" [1980], in *Reflections of a Neoconservative*, p. 235.

65 Key figures associated with the Coalition for a Democratic Majority were Senators Henry Jackson and Daniel Patrick Moynihan, along with Midge Decter, Norman Podhoretz, Jeane Kirkpatrick, Penn Kemble (executive director of the group), Max Kampelman (a former chief of staff for Senator Hubert Humphrey), and Ben Wattenberg (a former aide to President Lyndon Johnson). According to Benjamin Balint, the coalition's manifesto was drafted by Podhoretz and Decter. Benjamin Balint, *Running Commentary: The Contentious Magazine That Transformed the Jewish Left into the Neoconservative Right* (New York: PublicAffairs, 2010), p. 119.

66 Charles Tyroler, II, ed., *Alerting America: The Papers of the Committee on the Present Danger* (Washington: Pergamon-Brassey's, 1984); Gary Dorrien, *Imperial Designs: Neoconservatism and the New Pax Americana* (New York: Routledge, 2004), pp. 48–50.

67 Albert Wohlstetter, "Is There a Strategic Arms Race?" *Foreign Policy*, Vol. 15 (Summer 1974), pp. 3–20. The bomber and missile gaps of the late 1950s were based on extraordinarily spotty data, wild presumptions of Soviet weapons factory production, miscounting, and gross conjecture about Soviet military policy, at the root of which were the parochial turf interests of the Air Force and its allies in the Pentagon. Similarly, the military sometimes assumed, on scant evidence, very high damage expectations in the wake of a Soviet attack in order to justify massive new weapons systems. All military plans and numbers were part of the inter-service rivalries during the post-war era and the strategic exploitation of these rivalries by select politicians. A key element of John F. Kennedy's bid for the presidency in 1960, for instance, was the missile gap, which he pinned on the Eisenhower administration. But there was no missile gap. Indeed, Soviet nuclear capabilities at that time were far retarded in comparison with those of the United States. Fred Kaplan, *The Wizards of Armageddon* (New York: Simon & Schuster, 1983).

68 Team B, "Soviet Strategic Objections, An Alternative View: Intelligence Community Experiment in Competitive Analysis," CIA Classified Document (December 1976); unclassified, National Archives and Records Administration (1992).

69 Dorrien, *Imperial Designs*, pp. 51–2.

70 The pattern of overestimates of Soviet military strength and American weakness, along with fanciful conjecture about Soviet military policy,

characterizes each of the three key reports – the NSC-68 report of 1950, the 1957 Gaither Report, and the Team B report – which established the hawk position and largely determined U.S. military strategy since 1950. NSC-68, classified for more than two decades, contemplated rollback, militarizing the containment of the Soviet Union through the threat of nuclear reprisal. At *http://www.fas.org/irp/ offdocs/nsc-hst/nsc-68.htm* as of October 2012. This key early document has been described as more like a sermon in parts than a policy blueprint, a "synthesis of righteousness, pride in *patria*, and sense of the evil in other polities, as well as the belief in the spiritual potency of American ideas." Bruce Kuklick, "Commentary," in Ernest R. May, ed., *American Cold War Strategy: Interpreting NSC 68* (Boston: Bedford Books, 1993), p. 158. The reports created an environment of political fear difficult to resist and resulted in large military expenditures. The influential defense hawk Paul Nitze was central to all three reports. Fred Kaplan, "Paul Nitze: The Man Who Brought Us the Cold War," *Slate* (October 21, 2004), at *http://www.slate.com/ articles/news_and_politics/obit/2004/10/paul_nitze.html* as of October 2012.

71   Julian E. Zelizer, "Conservatives, Carter, and the Politics of National Security," in Bruce J. Schulman and Julian E. Zelizer, eds., *Rightward Bound: Making America Conservative in the 1970s* (Cambridge, MA: Harvard University Press, 2008), pp. 265–87; James Mann, *Rise of the Vulcans: The History of Bush's War Cabinet* (New York: Viking Penguin, 2004).

72   Jeane Kirkpatrick, "Dictatorships and Double Standards" [1979], in Gerson, ed. *The Essential Neoconservative Reader*, pp. 163–89.

73   Ibid., p. 186.

74   Irving Kristol, "The 'Human Rights' Muddle," *Wall Street Journal* (March 20, 1978).

75   Odd Arne Westad, *The Global Cold War: Third World Interventions and the Making of Our Times* (Cambridge: Cambridge University Press, 2005), pp. 331–4.

76   Elliott Abrams, Kenneth Adelman, William Bennett, Linda Chavez, Chester Finn, Fred Ikle, Robert Kagan, Max Kampelman, Jeane Kirkpatrick, William Kristol, Richard Perle, Richard Pipes, and Paul Wolfowitz worked in the Reagan administration. Dorrien, *Imperial Designs*, p. 10; Jerry W. Sanders, *Peddlers of Crisis: The Committee on the Present Danger and the Politics of Containment* (Boston: South End Press, 1983), p. 8.

77   Ronald Reagan, at *http://www.reagan.utexas.edu/archives/speeches/ 1983/30883b.htm* as of October 2012.

78   John Patrick Diggins, *Ronald Reagan: Fate, Freedom, and the Making of History* (New York: W.W. Norton & Co., 2007); Stefan Halper and

Jonathan Clarke, *America Alone: The Neoconservatives and the Global Order* (Cambridge: Cambridge University Press, 2004).

79　Norman Podhoretz, "The Neo-Conservative Anguish over Reagan's Foreign Policy," *New York Times Magazine* (May 2, 1982); Podhoretz, "The First Term: The Reagan Road to Détente," *Foreign Affairs*, Vol. 63, No. 3 (1984), pp. 447–64. With respect to Israel, neoconservatives had already begun to back the Israeli right-wing Likud Party, which advocated West Bank settlements as necessary for Israel's security, and fingered Arab intransigence as the central obstacle to any possible peace agreement. And because Israel represented a bulwark against Soviet expansion in the Middle East, any weakening of Israel was considered a blow to U.S. policy with regard to the USSR and thus a threat to American national security. Douglas Feith, "The Settlements and Peace: Playing the Links with Begin, Carter and Sadat," *Policy Review*, Vol. 8 (Spring 1979), pp. 25–40.

80　Norman Podhoretz, "How Reagan Succeeds as a Carter Clone," *New York Post* (October 7, 1986); Podhoretz, "The Fantasy of Communist Collapse," *Washington Post* (December 31, 1986).

81　For example, Robert Kagan and William Kristol, "Toward a Neo-Reaganite Foreign Policy," *Foreign Affairs*, Vol. 75, No. 4 (July/August 1996), pp. 18–32.

82　Jeane Kirkpatrick, "A Normal Country in a Normal Time," *National Interest* (Fall 1990), pp. 40–3. After 9/11, Kirkpatrick modified this stance.

83　Nathan Glazer, "A Time for Modesty," in Owen Harries, ed., *America's Purpose: New Visions of U.S. Foreign Policy* (San Francisco: Institute for Contemporary Studies, 1991), pp. 133–41.

84　Irving Kristol, "Defining Our National Interest," *National Interest* (Fall 1990), pp. 16–25.

85　Michael Mandelbaum, "Foreign Policy as Social Work," *Foreign Affairs*, Vol. 75, No. 1 (January/February 1996), pp. 16–32.

86　Francis Fukuyama, "The End of History?" *The National Interest* (Summer 1989), pp. 3–18.

87　Ben Wattenberg, "Neo-Manifest Destinarianism," *National Interest* (Fall 1990), pp. 51–4; Charles Krauthammer, "The Unipolar Moment," *Foreign Affairs* (Winter 1990/1), pp. 23–33; Joshua Muravchik, *Exporting Democracy: Fulfilling America's Destiny* (Washington, DC: American Enterprise Institute, 1991).

88　Project for a New American Century, "Statement of Principles" (1997), at *http://www.newamericancentury.org/statementofprinciples.htm* as of October 2012. PNAC was co-founded by William Kristol and Robert Kagan. The signatories to the "Statement of Principles" were a combination of neoconservatives and hawkish unilateralist Republicans out of power: Elliott Abrams, Gary Bauer, William J. Bennett, Jeb Bush, Dick Cheney, Eliot A. Cohen, Midge Decter, Paula

Dobriansky, Steve Forbes, Aaron Friedberg, Francis Fukuyama, Frank Gaffney, Fred C. Ikle, Donald Kagan, Zalmay Khalilzad, I. Lewis Libby, Norman Podhoretz, Dan Quayle, Peter W. Rodman, Stephen P. Rosen, Henry S. Rowen, Donald Rumsfeld, Vin Weber, George Weigel, and Paul Wolfowitz.

89 Robert Kagan and William Kristol, "Introduction: National Interest and Global Responsibility," in Kagan and Kristol, eds., *Present Dangers: Crisis and Opportunity in American Foreign and Defense Policy* (San Francisco: Encounter Books, 2000), p. 12.

90 Patrick E. Tyler, "U.S. Strategy Plan Calls for Insuring No Rivals Develop," *New York Times* (March 8, 1992); PBS, "Frontline: The War Behind Closed Doors: Excerpts from 1992 Draft 'Defense Planning Guidance,'" at *http://www.pbs.org/wgbh/pages/frontline/shows/iraq/etc/wolf.html* as of October 2012.

91 Richard Perle, "Iraq: Saddam Unbound," in Kagan and Kristol, eds., *Present Dangers*, pp. 107–8. Also David Wurmser, *Tyranny's Ally: America's Failure to Defeat Saddam Hussein* (Washington, DC: American Enterprise Institute Press, 1999); Donald Kagan and Frederick W. Kagan, *While America Sleeps: Self-delusion, Military Weakness, and the Threat to Peace Today* (New York: St. Martin's Press, 2000).

92 Robert Kagan and William Kristol, "Introduction: National Interest and Global Responsibility," in Kagan and Kristol, eds., *Present Dangers*, pp. 5–6; David Frum and Richard Perle, *An End to Evil: How to Win the War on Terror* (New York: Random House, 2003).

93 "U.S. Policy on Iraq Draws Fire in Ohio," *CNN Interactive* (February 18, 1998), at *http://www.cnn.com/WORLD/9802/18/town.meeting.folo/* as of October 2012.

94 Paul Wolfowitz, "Clinton's First Year," *Foreign Affairs*, Vol. 73, No. 1 (January/February 1994), pp. 28–43.

95 Halper and Clarke, *America Alone*, pp. 84–95.

96 Francis Fukuyama, *America at the Crossroads: Democracy, Power, and the Neoconservative Legacy* (New Haven: Yale University Press, 2006), pp. 31–6; Heilbrunn, *They Knew They Were Right*, p. 106.

97 Robert Kagan, *Of Paradise and Power: America and Europe in the New World Order* (New York: Knopf, 2003). It was with this analysis in the background that, in the face of European opposition to the Iraq War, Defense Secretary Donald Rumsfeld contemptuously denounced "old Europe" as barely worth dealing with.

98 Lawrence F. Kaplan and William Kristol, *The War over Iraq: Saddam's Tyranny and America's Mission* (San Francisco: Encounter Books, 2003), p. 56.

99 Harvey C. Mansfield, the Straussian political philosopher with whom some second-generation neoconservatives studied at Harvard,

rearticulated the view in his study *Manliness* (New Haven: Yale University Press, 2006).

100 John Gray, *Black Mass: Apocalyptic Religion and the Death of Utopia* (London: Allen Lane, 2007).

101 Hugo Grotius, *The Law of War and Peace (De Jure Belli Ac Pacis, Libri Tres.)*, Francis W. Kelsey, with Arthur E.R. Boak, trans. (Indianapolis: Bobbs-Merrill, 1925); Michael Walzer, *Arguing about War* (New Haven: Yale University Press, 2004).

102 Kaplan and Kristol, *The War over Iraq*, p. 64.

103 Ibid., p. 119.

104 Max Boot, "The Case for American Empire," *Weekly Standard*, Vol. 7, No. 5 (October 15, 2001); Niall Ferguson, *Colossus: The Price of America's Empire* (New York: Penguin Press, 2004).

105 George W. Bush, "A Distinctly American Internationalism," Ronald Reagan Presidential Library, Simi Valley, California (November 19, 1999), at *http://www.mtholyoke.edu/acad/intrel/bush/wspeech.htm* as of October 2012.

106 Project for the New American Century, Letter to President George W. Bush on the War on Terrorism (September 20, 2001), at *http://www.newamericancentury.org/Bushletter.htm* as of October 2012.

107 Richard Clarke, *Against All Enemies: Inside America's War on Terror* (New York: Free Press, 2004), p. 32.

108 The White House, The National Security Strategy of the United States of America (September 17, 2002), at *http://georgewbush-whitehouse.archives.gov/nsc/nss/2002/* as of October 2012.

109 Neta C. Crawford, "The Justice of Pre-emption and Preventive War Doctrines," in Mark Evans, ed., *Just War Theory: A Reappraisal* (Edinburgh: Edinburgh University Press, 2005), pp. 25–49.

110 George W. Bush, Second Inaugural Address (January 20, 2005), at *http://www.bartleby.com/124/pres67.html* as of October 2012.

111 Identifiable neoconservatives and fellow travelers in the Bush administration included Paul Wolfowitz, Elliott Abrams, Kenneth Adelman, John Bolton, Stephen Cambone, Paula Dobriansky, Stephen Hadley, Douglas Feith, Zalmay Khalilzad, I. Lewis Libby, William Luti, Richard Perle, Peter Rodman, and David Wurmser. Dorrien, *Imperial Designs*, p. 2. (Wolfowitz and Perle always rejected the neoconservative designation.) Note the large overlap with those who signed the Project for a New American Century's "Statement of Principles." But while Vice-President Cheney and Secretary of Defense Rumsfeld shared the inclination of interventionist unipolarism, they were more of a realist bent, albeit characterized by assertive nationalism: that is, willing to use military power to defeat threats to the United States but reluctant as a general rule to use American primacy to remake the world in its image. On this point see Ivo H. Daalder and James M. Lindsay, *America Unbound: The Bush Revolution in Foreign Policy*

(Washington, DC: Brookings Institution Press, 2003), p. 16. National Security Adviser Condoleezza Rice was identified with her realist mentor, Brent Scowcroft; Secretary of State Colin Powell flitted between realism and liberal internationalism, guided by the lessons of Vietnam, not Munich.

112 Kagan and Kristol, "Toward a Neo-Reaganite Foreign Policy," pp. 22–3.

113 Leon Kass, Chairman's opening remarks at the first meeting of the president's Council on Bioethics (January 17, 2002), at *http://bioethics.georgetown.edu/pcbe/transcripts/jan02/opening01.html* as of October 2012. Similar sentiments were articulated by many neo-conservatives, among them William J. Bennett, *Why We Fight: Moral Clarity and the War on Terrorism* (New York: Doubleday, 2002).

114 Richard John Neuhaus, "September 11 – Before and After," *First Things* (November 2001), p. 65.

115 The portentous phrase "clash of civilizations" came from Samuel P. Huntington's influential book of the same name, in which he argued that in the post-Cold War world the basis of conflict would come from culture and religious identities. Huntington, *The Clash of Civilizations and the Remaking of World Order* (New York: Simon & Schuster, 1996). The term, and a source of Huntington's ideas on Islam, derived from the work of the Princeton historian of the Islamic world and neoconservative fellow traveler Bernard Lewis. Lewis, "The Roots of Muslim Rage," *Atlantic Monthly* (September 1990). The centrality of the concept of the clash of civilizations is key to Richard Bonney's fine treatment of the war on terror, *False Prophets: The "Clash of Civilizations" and the Global War on Terror* (Oxford: Peter Lang, 2008). As for the term "evil," its use invariably transforms moral and political questions into religious ones. See Richard J. Bernstein, *The Abuse of Evil: The Corruption of Politics and Religion since 9/11* (Malden, MA: Polity Press, 2005).

116 Reinhold Niebuhr, *The Irony of American History* (New York: Scribner, 1952); Louis Hartz, *The Liberal Tradition in America: An Interpretation of American Political Thought since the Revolution* (New York: Harcourt, Brace, 1955); Seymour Martin Lipset, *American Exceptionalism: A Double-Edged Sword* (New York: Norton, 1996).

117 Walter A. McDougall, *Promised Land, Crusader State* (Boston: Houghton-Mifflin, 1997); Lloyd E. Ambrosius, *Wilsonianism: Woodrow Wilson and His Legacy in American Foreign Relations* (New York: Palgrave Macmillan, 2002); Hugh Heclo, *Christianity and American Democracy* (Cambridge, MA: Harvard University Press, 2007); Ted Widmer, *Ark of the Liberties: America and the World* (New York: Hill and Wang, 2008); Inboden, *Religion and American Foreign Policy, 1945–1960*; William Pfaff, *The Irony of Manifest*

Destiny: The Tragedy of America's Foreign Policy (New York: Walker, 2010).

118 Robert P. Jones and Daniel Cox, "Old Alignments, Emerging Fault Lines: Religion in the 2010 Election and Beyond" (Washington, DC: Public Religion Research Institute, November 2010).

119 Maureen Dowd, *Bushworld: Enter at Your Own Risk* (New York: GP Putnam's Sons, 2004); Jacob Weisberg, *The Bush Tragedy* (New York: Random House, 2008).

120 John J. Mearsheimer and Stephen M. Walt, *The Israel Lobby and U.S. Foreign Policy* (London: Allen Lane, 2007); Bonney, *False Prophets*.

121 Michael T. Klare, "The Coming War with Iraq: Deciphering the Bush Administration's Motives," *Foreign Policy in Focus* (January 16, 2003), at *http://www.fpif.org/articles/the_coming_war_with_iraq_deciphering_the_bush_administrations_motives* as of October 2012.

122 Daniel Yergin, "A Crude View of the Crisis in Iraq," *Washington Post* (December 8, 2002).

123 This subsection draws heavily on Michael MacDonald, *We Are the World: Regime Change in Iraq* (Cambridge, MA: Harvard University Press, forthcoming).

124 Donald Rumsfeld, *Known and Unknown: A Memoir* (New York: Sentinel, 2011).

125 "The Secret Downing Street Memo," *Sunday Times* (May 1, 2005), at *http://www.informationclearinghouse.info/article8709.htm* as of August 2012.

126 Sarah Lyall, "Ex-official Says Afghan and Iraq Wars Increased Threats to Britain," *New York Times* (July 21, 2010).

127 Cited in Bob Woodward, *Plan of Attack* (New York: Simon & Schuster, 2004), p. 281.

128 Bob Drogin, *Curveball: Spies, Lies, and the Con Man Who Caused a War* (New York: Random House, 2007).

129 Therein lies the importance of the "liberal hawks," the liberal internationalists and even some leftists who were convinced by the WMD claims and who supported the invasion of Iraq because of their commitment to international humanitarianism. After 9/11, they found in "Islamic totalitarianism" or "Islamofascism" an existential threat to the United States and western liberalism, seeing in militant Islam's animosity toward the West a "clash of civilizations" and September 11, 2001 as comparable to the Nazi assault of 1939. These included former U.S. Senator Bob Kerrey, former National Security Council staffer Kenneth Pollack, and the writers Philip Bobbitt, Will Marshall, Paul Berman, George Packer, Thomas Friedman, Christopher Hitchens, and many at the staff of the *New Republic* who supported Bush administration Iraq policy, and whom the incisive, biting political historian Tony Judt called "useful idiots." Judt, "Bush's Useful Idiots," *London Review of Books* (September 21, 2006), pp. 3–5.

130 One more look at the money. Between 1995 and 2001, the American Enterprise Institute took in $14.5 million from the Bradley Foundation alone, and topped $17 million by 2008. William Kristol's Project for a New American Century, so connected to the AEI that it rented office space from it, also benefited from the Bradley Foundation's largesse, to the tune of $1.8 million. Dorrien, *Imperial Designs*, p. 130. Other large conservative foundation grants to the AEI included the Smith-Richardson Foundation ($8 million), the Olin Foundation ($7.6 million), and the Sarah Scaife Foundation ($6.4 million). The Heritage Foundation received $21.2 million from Scaife, $14.2 from Bradley, $8 million from Olin, and $13 million from the Samuel Roberts Noble Foundation. The Hoover Institution received almost $10 million from Scaife, $5 million from Olin, and $4 million from the Walton Family Foundation. And the Cato Institute, to round out this financial look at the most important conservative think tanks, received $9.3 million from the Claude R. Lambe Charitable Foundation, $4 million from the David H. Koch Charitable Foundation, and almost $2 million from Scaife. These numbers reflect total cumulative donations, as of 2008. At *http://bridgeproject.com/?transparency?* as of October 2012.

131 Dorrien, *Imperial Designs*, p. 17.

132 Mann, *Rise of the Vulcans*. Of course, Cheney and especially Rumsfeld were far less interested in democracy promotion than in the unilateral assertion of American power. It's not clear whether it is accurate to label Cheney and Rumsfeld foreign policy realists. It seems more that they were so keen to restore power and war-making prerogative to the executive branch that they were simply interventionists. Since the time of Watergate, Cheney had endeavored to restore authority to the executive branch, especially via the president's commander-in-chief powers. The Iraq War was an excellent means of doing so, and Cheney's office was a hive of activity for neoconservatives and those keen to expand and exercise executive power. Jane Mayer, *Dark Side: The Inside Story of How the War on Terror Turned Into a War on American Ideals* (New York: Doubleday, 2008). Rumsfeld had so little interest in Iraq apart from its conquest that, in his emblematical combat over turf, he sabotaged the State Department's post-Iraq planning and had no Defense Department plan for the war's aftermath at all. PBS Frontline, "Bush's War" (2008), at *http://www.pbs.org/wgbh/ pages/frontline/bushswar/* as of October 2012. This was likely a function of the naïve expectation on the part of Rumsfeld and other high-ranking administration officials that the "decapitation" of Saddam as Iraq's leader would be accompanied by Iraqis dancing in the streets, welcoming American soldiers as liberators.

133 Cited in Heilbrunn, *They Knew They Were Right*, p. 236.

134 Cited in Abrams, *Norman Podhoretz and Commentary Magazine*, p. 242.

135 Gray, *Black Mass*.
136 George W. Bush, State of the Union address (January 29, 2002), at *http://www.washingtonpost.com/wp-srv/onpolitics/transcripts/sou012902.htm* as of October 2012.
137 Frum and Perle, *An End to Evil*, p. 114; Norman Podhoretz, "In Praise of the Bush Doctrine," *Commentary* (September 2002), pp. 19–28.
138 Ken Jowitt, "Rage, Hubris and Regime Change: The Urge to Speed History Along," *Policy Review*, Vol. 118 (April/May 2003), pp. 33–42.
139 Fukuyama, *America at the Crossroads*, p. 116.
140 "Think Tank with Ben Wattenberg: Interview with Richard Perle," Public Broadcasting System (November 14, 2002), at *http://www.pbs.org/thinktank/transcript1017.html* as of October 2012. And notice the language. The reverberation between Bush's foreign policy speeches and neoconservative public comments is palpable.
141 Lewis, "The Roots of Muslim Rage"; Lewis, "The Revolt of Islam: When Did the Conflict With the West Begin, and How Could It End?" *New Yorker* (November 19, 2001); Lewis, *What Went Wrong? Western Impact and Middle Eastern Response* (New York: Oxford University Press, 2002); Michael Hirsh, "Bernard Lewis Revisited," *Washington Monthly* (November 2004), at *http://www.washingtonmonthly.com/features/2004/0411.hirsh.html* as of October 2012.
142 Samir al-Khalil, *Republic of Fear: The Politics of Modern Iraq* (Berkeley: University of California Press, 1989), pp. 131, 109.
143 Guillermo O'Donnell, Philippe C. Schmitter, and Laurence Whitehead, eds., *Transitions From Authoritarian Rule: Prospects for Democracy* (Baltimore: Johns Hopkins University Press, 1986); Juan J. Linz and Alfred Stepan, *Problems of Democratic Transition and Consolidation: Southern Europe, South America, and Post-Communist Europe* (Baltimore: Johns Hopkins University Press, 1996).
144 Chalabi, it should be noted, had been, along with Wolfowitz, Perle, and Khalilzad, a protégé of sorts of Albert Wohlstetter and a favorite of Bernard Lewis. His connections to Rumsfeld and the high-ups in the Defense Department and to the closed circle of analysts convinced of Saddam Hussein's weapons of mass destruction are described in Hersh, "Selective Intelligence."
145 Jeane Kirkpatrick, "Dictatorships and Double Standards," p. 169.

Chapter 5   Richard Hofstadter's "Paranoid Style" Revisited: The Tea Party, Past as Prologue

1 NAE, "An Evangelical Declaration against Torture: Protecting Human Rights in an Age of Terror" (March 2007), at *http://www.nae.net/*

government-relations/endorsed-documents/409-an-evangelical-declaration-against-torture-protecting-human-rights-in-an-age-of-terror* as of October 2012.

2   Sam Rosenfeld and Matthew Iglesias, "The Incompetence Dodge," *The American Prospect* (November 10, 2005); Larry Diamond, *Squandered Victory: The American Occupation and the Bungled Effort to Bring Democracy to Iraq* (New York: Times Books, 2005); Thomas E. Ricks, *Fiasco: The American Military Adventure in Iraq* (New York: Penguin, 2006); David Rose, "Neo Culpa," *Vanity Fair* (November 3, 2006).

3   Devised chiefly by Frederick Kagan of the American Enterprise Institute, the surge was acclaimed by the administration and Kagan's fellow neoconservative enthusiasts of the war as prima facie evidence that with proper military doctrine and practice, the Iraq War could be, and was being, won. Frederick W. Kagan, "Choosing Victory: A Plan for Success in Iraq, Phase I Report" (Washington, DC: American Enterprise Institute, January 5, 2007), at *http://www.c-sspan.org/pdf/20061219_ChoosingVictory.pdf* as of October 2012.

4   Kate Zernicke, *Boiling Mad: Inside Tea Party America* (New York: Times Books, 2010).

5   Video of the Santelli rant at *http://www.youtube.com/watch?v=bEZB4taSEoA* as of October 2012.

6   No one seems to know the origin of the image, which is sometimes accompanied by the word "socialism." One clear link that was raised in the various newspaper and online discussions on the issue was to "The Joker" of the Batman comics and films, connoting a figure who is out of control, dangerous, and demonic. Given Obama's race, it's also hard not to associate the image with a kind of reverse minstrelsy (it looks like blackface around the eyes and mouth, but in reverse colors), in which, by becoming president, Obama pretends he is white. In the Tea Party context, it connotes that Obama is not one of us; he is demonic and must be feared. The image conveys a kind of racial panic. Of course, meanings such as this can rarely be fixed.

7   Elizabeth Price Foley, *The Tea Party: Three Principles* (Cambridge: Cambridge University Press, 2012).

8   David S. Brown, *Richard Hofstadter: An Intellectual Biography* (Chicago: University of Chicago Press, 2006).

9   Richard Hofstadter, *The American Political Tradition and the Men Who Made It* (New York: Knopf, 1948); Hoftstadter, *The Age of Reform: From Bryan to FDR* (New York: Knopf, 1955).

10 Richard Hofstadter, *Anti-intellectualism in American Life* (New York: Vintage, 1962).

11 T.W. Adorno, Else Frenkel-Brunswik, Daniel J. Levinson, and R. Nevitt Sanford, *The Authoritarian Personality* (New York: Harper, 1950).

12 Daniel Bell, ed., *The New American Right* (New York: Criterion Books, 1955); Bell, ed., *The Radical Right: The New American Right Expanded and Updated* (Garden City, NY: Anchor Books, 1963).

13 Richard Hofstadter, "The Pseudo-Conservative Revolt – 1954," in *The Paranoid Style in American Politics, and Other Essays* (New York: Knopf, 1965), pp. 43, 45.

14 Richard Hoftstadter, "Pseudo-Conservatism Revisited – 1965," in *The Paranoid Style in American Politics, and Other Essays*, pp. 83–4.

15 Hofstadter, "The Pseudo-Conservative Revolt – 1954," p. 60.

16 Ibid., p. 58.

17 Hofstadter, "Pseudo-Conservatism Revisited – 1965," pp. 71–3; Hofstadter, "Goldwater and Pseudo-Conservative Politics," in *The Paranoid Style in American Politics, and Other Essays*, pp. 100, 117.

18 Hofstadter, "The Paranoid Style in American Politics," in *The Paranoid Style in American Politics, and Other Essays*, pp. 30–1.

19 Ibid., p. 23.

20 Ibid., p. 24.

21 William Appleman Williams, "The Age of Reforming History," *The Nation* (June 30, 1956); C. Vann Woodward, "The Populist Heritage and the Intellectual," in *The Burden of Southern History* (New York: Vintage Books, 1960), pp. 141–66; David Potter, "The Politics of Status," *New Leader* (June 24, 1963), cited in Brown, *Richard Hofstadter: An Intellectual Biography*, p. 117; David Hackett Fischer, *Historians' Fallacies: Toward a Logic of Historical Thought* (New York: Harper & Row, 1970), p. 195.

22 Michael Paul Rogin, *The Intellectuals and McCarthy: The Radical Specter* (Cambridge, MA: MIT Press, 1967).

23 Todd Gitlin, "The Renaissance of Anti-Intellectualism," *The Chronicle of Higher Education* (December 8, 2000).

24 Jon Wiener, "America, Through a Glass Darkly," *The Nation* (October 23, 2006).

25 While it is true that the crazy and conspiratorial features of the Tea Party can be much embroidered and inflated by the movement's political opponents, nonetheless see the remarkable number of racist, outrageous, factually false, and verbally violent speeches, postings, and rallies detailed in Devin Burghart and Leonard Zeskind, *Tea Party Nationalism: A Critical Examination of the Tea Party Movement and the Size, Scope, and Focus of Its National Factions* (Kansas City: Institute for Research & Education on Human Rights, Fall 2010), at *http://justanothercoverup.com/wp-content/uploads/2010/11/TeaPartyNationalism.pdf* as of October 2012, and Will Bunch, *The Backlash: Right-Wing Radicals, Hi-def Hucksters, and Paranoid Politics in the Age of Obama* (New York: HarperCollins, 2010).

26 Jill Lepore, *The Whites of Their Eyes: The Tea Party's Revolution and the Battle over American History* (Princeton: Princeton University

Press, 2010); Jeffrey Rosen, "Radical Constitutionalism: The Tea Party's Exotic Ideas about the Country's Defining Document," *New York Times Magazine* (November 28, 2010).

27 David Brooks, "The Tea Party Teens," *New York Times* (January 4, 2010).

28 On literal and inerrant readings, and how the Bible and the Constitution work as parallel documents of ultimate authority for fundamentalists and originalists, see Vincent Crapanzano, *Serving the Word: Literalism in America from the Pulpit to the Bench* (New York: The New Press, 2000).

29 Amy Gardner, "Gauging the Scope of the Tea Party Movement in America," *Washington Post* (October 24, 2010), at *http://www.washingtonpost.com/wp-dyn/content/article/2010/10/23/AR2010102304000.html?hpid=topnews* as of October 2012. Theda Skocpol and Vanessa Williamson found considerably more Tea Party groups (about 1,000) and participation than did Gardner. Skocpol and Williamson, *The Tea Party and the Remaking of Republican Conservatism* (New York: Oxford University Press, 2012).

30 The Tenth Amendment reads: "The powers not delegated to the United States by the Constitution, nor prohibited by it to the States, are reserved to the States respectively, or to the people."

31 Bradford Plumer, "The Revisionaries," *The New Republic* (September 23, 2010); Jonathan Weisman, "GOP Hopefuls Fine-Tune Legislative Focus," *Wall Street Journal* (October 18, 2010). Recall GOP 2012 presidential hopeful Rick Santorum's public denigration of climate change as "junk science . . . an excuse for more government control of your life." The Rush Limbaugh Show (June 8, 2011), at *http://www.rushlimbaugh.com/daily/2011/06/08/the_rick_santorum_interview* as of October 2012.

32 Hofstadter, "The Paranoid Style in American Politics," p. 37.

33 The lifestyle issue and the surprisingly intense resentments attached to class-related markers of consumption point to the close interpenetration of politics and taste and the continuing salience of the work of the sociologist Pierre Bourdieu. For Bourdieu, consumption choices and judgments about taste are expressive of social position or class. Bourdieu, *Distinction: A Social Critique of the Judgment of Taste*, Richard Nice, trans. (Cambridge, MA: Harvard University Press, 1984).

34 CBS News, "Tea Party Supporters: Who They Are and What They Believe" (April 14, 2010), at *http://www.cbsnews.com/8301-503544_162-20002529-503544.html?tag=mncol;lst;1* as of October 2012; Skocpol and Williamson, *The Tea Party and the Remaking of Republican Conservatism*, pp. 19–44.

35 Lisa McGirr, *Suburban Warriors: The Origins of the New American Right* (Princeton: Princeton University Press, 2001); Zernicke, *Boiling*

Mad. A fascinating perspective on the prominence of women in the social conservatism of the 1980s and 90s, and thus relevant to the understanding of the Tea Party, is explored in Linda Kintz, *Between Jesus and the Market: The Emotions That Matter in Right-Wing America* (Durham, NC: Duke University Press, 1997). Kintz argues that the right was able to tap deeply into the emotional politics of traditional women's sense of the social – and theological – worth of their work as wives and mothers.

36 The direct roots of FreedomWorks and Americans for Prosperity were Citizens for a Sound Economy, an advocacy vehicle of the Koch brothers created in 1984. Ronald P. Formisano, *The Tea Party: A Brief History* (Baltimore: Johns Hopkins University Press, 2012), pp. 63–81.

37 Ibid., p. 87.

38 Michael E. Kazin, *The Populist Persuasion: An America History* (New York: Basic Books, 1995).

39 Robert P. Jones and Daniel Cox, "Old Alignments, Emerging Fault Lines: Religion in the 2010 Election and Beyond" (Washington, DC: Public Religion Research Institute, November 2010).

40 John M. O'Hara, *A New American Tea Party: The Counterrevolution against Bailouts, Handouts, Reckless Spending, and More Taxes* (Hoboken, NJ: Wiley, 2010), p. 4.

41 CBS News, "Tea Party Supporters: Who They Are and What They Believe."

42 The differences are rather striking between Tea Party and all respondents to the question:
"Who do you think is mostly to blame for the current state of the nation's economy?"

	Percentage all respondents	Percentage Tea Party supporters
Bush administration	32	5
Obama administration	4	10
Wall Street and financial institutions	22	15
Congress	10	28

CBS News/*New York Times*, "The Tea Party Movement: What They Think," (April 14, 2010), at *http://www.cbsnews.com/htdocs/pdf/poll_tea_party_041410.pdf?tag=contentMain;contentBody* as of October 2012.

43 "Original Content" (Steven Malanga), "Obama and the Reawakening of Corporatism," *RealClearMarkets* (April 8, 2009), at *http://www.realclearmarkets.com/articles/2009/04/obama_and_the_reawakening_of_c.html* as of October 2012.

44 Peter J. Wallinson, "The True Origins of This Financial Crisis," *The American Spectator* (February 2009), at *http://www.spectator.org/archives/2009/02/06/the-true-origins-of-this-finan* as of October 2012.

45 Glenn Beck Show, Glenn Beck discussions with Jonah Goldberg, Fox News Channel (June 1, 2009) at *http://www.foxnews.com/story/0,2933,524519,00.html*. Beck drew parallels between Obama and Hitler on several of his Fox News shows: April 1, 2009, at *http://mediamatters.org/video/2009/04/01/after-stating-i-am-not-saying-that-barack-obama/148835*; August 27, 2009, at *http://mediamatters.org/video/2009/08/27/beck-claims-obamas-civilian-national-security-f/153983*; and on his Premiere Radio Networks show: August 6, 2009 and August 12, 2009, at *http://www.mediamatters.org/tags/glenn-beck-program?p=165&s=15*, all as of October 2012.

46 Dinesh D'Souza, "How Obama Thinks," *Forbes* (September 27, 2010), at *http://www.forbes.com/forbes/2010/0927/politics-socialism-capitalism-private-enterprises-obama-business-problem.html* as of October 2012; Robert Costa, "Gingrich: Obama's 'Kenyan, Anti-colonial' Worldview," *National Review Online* (September 11, 2010), at *http://www.nationalreview.com/corner/246302/gingrich-obama-s-kenyan-anti-colonial-worldview-robert-costa* as of October 2012.

47 Frederic Bastiat, *The Law* [1850], Dean Russell, trans. (Irvington-on-Hudson, NY: Foundation for Economic Education, 1968).

48 Isaac W. Martin, *The Permanent Tax Revolt: How the Property Tax Transformed American Politics* (Stanford: Stanford University Press, 2008).

49 Jonah Goldberg, *Liberal Fascism: The Secret History of the American Left, from Mussolini to the Politics of Meaning* (New York: Doubleday, 2007); Amity Shlaes, *The Forgotten Man: A New History of the Great Depression* (New York: HarperCollins, 2007); Ron Paul, *The Revolution: A Manifesto* (New York: Grand Central Publishers, 2008); Albert Jay Nock, *Our Enemy, the State* [1935] (New York: Arno Press 1972); James Burnham, *The Managerial Revolution: What is Happening in the World* (New York: John Day, 1941); Frank Chodorov, *The Income Tax: Root of All Evil* (New York: Devin-Adair, 1954).

50 Leo Strauss, *Natural Right and History* (Chicago: University of Chicago Press, 1953).

51 W. Cleon Skousen, *The 5000 Year Leap: The 28 Great Ideas That Changed the World* (Washington, DC: National Center for Constitutional Studies, 2007).

52 W. Cleon Skousen, *The Naked Communist* (Salt Lake City: Ensign Publishing, 1958); Skousen, *The Naked Capitalist* (Salt Lake City: W. Cleon Skousen, 1971).

53 Mark Leibovich, "Being Glenn Beck," *New York Times Magazine* (October 3, 2010).

54 Alexander Zaitchik, *Common Nonsense: Glenn Beck and the Triumph of Ignorance* (Hoboken, NJ: Wiley, 2010); Sean Wilentz, "Confounding Fathers: The Tea Party's Cold War Roots," *The New Yorker* (October 18, 2010).

55 David Barton, *Original Intent: The Courts, the Constitution, and Religion* (Aledo, TX: WallBuilder Press, 1996); Barton, *Separation of Church & State: What the Founders Meant* (Aledo, TX: WallBuilder Press, 2007). Mark A. Beliles and Stephen K. McDowell, *America's Providential History* (Charlottesville, VA: Providence Foundation, 1989) is the standard textbook on American history used in many Christian schools and by the home school movement.

56 Beliles and McDowell, *America's Providential History*, p. 20.

57 Cited in Jon Ralston, "Angle: 'What's Happening (in America) . . . is a Violation of the 1st Commandment,' Entitlements 'Make Government Our God,'" *Las Vegas Sun* (August 4, 2010), at *http://www.lasvegassun.com/blogs/ralstons-flash/2010/aug/04/angle-whats-happening-america-violation-1st-comman/* as of October 2012.

58 "Marco Rubio on American Exceptionalism," at *http://www.Moonbattery.com/archives/2010/08/marco-rubio-on.html* as of October 2012.

59 Peter Montgomery, "Fractures, Alliances and Mobilizations in the Age of Obama: Emerging Analyses of the Tea Party Movement" Conference, Center for the Comparative Study of Right-Wing Movements (University of California, Berkeley, October 22, 2010).

60 Ben Smith, "Tea Parties Stir Evangelicals' Fears," *Politico* (March 12, 2010), at *http://www.politico.com/news/stories/0310/34291.html* as of October 2012.

61 Skocpol and Williamson, *The Tea Party and the Remaking of Republican Conservatism*.

62 Values Voter Summit (2012), at *http://www.valuesvotersummit.org/* as of October 2012.

63 Glenn Beck Transcripts, "American's Third Great Awakening," Fox News (September 3, 2010), at *http://www.foxnews.com/story/0,2933,600802,00.html* as of October 2012.

64 Jennifer Steinhauer, "Under Banner of Fiscal Restraint, Republicans Plan New Abortion Bills," *New York Times* (February 8, 2011). The restriction of abortion rights to instances of rape, incest, and endangerment to the life of the mother only was further pared back by suggesting that rapes where the woman does not put up a fight are not rapes, or are a different, lesser kind of rape, and that a subsequent pregnancy should not be eligible for abortion. In the 2012 Missouri Senate race, as we noted in chapter 1, the Republican candidate, Todd Akin, further muddied this bizarre issue by suggesting that a woman cannot become pregnant from forcible rape because under such circumstances her body naturally rejects the sperm. Further, in the race for the U.S.

Senate seat from Indiana, Richard Mourdock, the Tea Party Republican candidate, said in a debate that he did not support allowing abortions in the case of rape. Pregnancies conceived by rape should not be aborted because the conception was divinely willed. "I've struggled with it myself for a long time, but I came to realize that life is that gift from God. And even when life begins in that horrible situation of rape, that it is something God intended to happen." Jonathan Weisman, "Remark on Rape Jolts Senate Race in Indiana, and the Presidential Race, Too," *New York Times* (October 25, 2012).

65 Arthur Delaney and Michael McAuliff, "Paul Ryan Wants 'Welfare Reform Round 2,'" *Huffington Post* (March 20, 2012), at *http://www.huffingtonpost.com/2012/03/20/paul-ryan-welfare-reform_n_1368277.html* as of October 2012.

66 "Glenn's Soulmate?" Glenn Beck program (April 12, 2010), at *http://www.glennbeck.com/content/articles/article/196/39068/* as of October 2012.

67 Jennifer Steinhauer, "Tea Party Trains Its Influence on Reshaping Senate GOP," *New York Times* (August 2, 2012).

68 "Full Transcript of the Mitt Romney Secret Video," *Mother Jones* (September 19, 2012) *http://www.motherjones.com/politics/2012/09/full-transcript-mitt-romney-secret-video* as of November 2012.

69 Ashley Parker, "Romney Attributes Obama Win to 'Gifts'," *New York Times* (November 15, 2012).

70 James William Gibson, *Warrior Dreams: Violence and Manhood in Post-Vietnam America* (New York: Hill and Wang, 1994).

71 Alexander Zaitchik, "'Patriot' Paranoia," *Southern Poverty Law Center Intelligence Report* (Fall 2010), pp. 27–34; Barton Gellman, "America's Extreme Patriots," *Time* (October 11, 2010), pp. 26–33.

72 Friends for Liberty, at *http://www.friendsforliberty.com/* as of August 2012 (link no longer accessible).

73 David Barstow, "Lighting a Fuse for Rebellion on the Right," *New York Times* (February 16, 2010).

74 The anti-abortion movement, for example, which does have its violent fringe, plays on that territory. Francis Schaeffer occasionally alluded to violence in his speeches and writings, as did Richard John Neuhaus. Indeed, the section of Neuhaus's journal *First Things* on judicial activism included several essays that came close to advocating armed revolution. "The End of Democracy? Judicial Usurpation of Politics," *First Things*, Vol. 67 (November 1996), pp. 18–42.

75 David Gergen, "Like Perot Voters," *New York Times* online discussion, "What Tea Party Backers Want" (April 15, 2010), at *http://roomfordebate.blogs.nytimes.com/2010/04/15/what-tea-party-backers-want/?hp#david* as of October 2012.

76 University of California, San Diego Department of Communication Ph.D. students Muni Citrin and Reece Peck report on Tea Party convention in Las Vegas, July 2010 (personal communication).

77 In this regard, two books have been of key importance to Tea Party activists and intellectuals: Saul Alinsky, *Organizing for Radicals: A Practical Primer for Realistic Radicals* (New York: Random House, 1971) and Ori Brafman and Rod A. Beckstrom, *The Starfish and the Spider: The Unstoppable Power of Leaderless Organizations* (New York: Portfolio, 2006). Alinsky's book, written originally for leftist community organizers, provides an appropriable set of tools for any grassroots organizing drive. Brafman and Beckstrom's book is a popular business management text that extols the power of decentralized, leaderless organizations. The title's metaphor is a commentary on centralization and decentralization. A spider and starfish are both multi-legged creatures. A spider can be killed by cutting off its head. A starfish has no head per se; its "head," so to speak, is distributed throughout its "body." If the starfish is cut, it makes more starfish.

78 Skocpol and Williamson, *The Tea Party and the Remaking of Republican Conservatism.*

79 Brooks, "The Tea Party Teens."

80 "Ron Paul on Foreign Policy," at *http://www.ontheissues.org/2008/Ron_Paul_Foreign_Policy.htm* as of October 2012; Ron Paul, "A Tea Party Foreign Policy," *Foreign Policy* (August 27, 2010), at *http://www.foreignpolicy.com/articles/2010/08/27/a_tea_party_foreign_policy* as of October 2012; Glenn Beck with Joseph Perry, *Glenn Beck's Common Sense: The Case against an Out-of-Control Government, Inspired by Thomas Paine* (New York: Mercury Radio Arts/Threshold Editions, 2009).

81 Sarah Palin, speech to military families May 3, 2011, cited in Tony Lee, "The Emergence of a Sarah Palin Foreign Policy Doctrine?" *Human Events* (May 4, 2011), at *http://www.humanevents.com/article.php?id=43314* as of October 2012.

82 Ben Armbruster, "UPDATED: A Comprehensive Timeline of Mitt Romney's Foreign Policy Positions During the Campaign," *Thinkprogress* (October 22, 2012): *http://thinkprogress.org/security/2012/10/22/1054581/a-comprehensive-timeline-of-mitt-romneys-foreign-policy-positions-during-the-campaign/?mobile=nc* as of November 2012.

83 Peter Baker, "Strange Brew: Does the Tea Party Have a Foreign Policy?" *Foreign Policy* (September/October 2010), at *http://www.foreignpolicy.com/articles/2010/08/16/strange_brew* as of October 2012; Walter Russell Mead, "The Tea Party and American Foreign Policy – What Populism Means for Globalism," *Foreign Affairs* (March/April 2011), at *http://www.foreignaffairs.com/articles/67455/*

walter-russell-mead/the-tea-party-and-american-foreign-policy as of October 2012.

84 Pew Research Center for the People & the Press, "In Shift from Bush Era, More Conservatives Say 'Come Home, America'" (June 16, 2011), at *http://people-press.org/2011/06/16/in-shift-from-bush-era-more-conservatives-say-come-home-america/* as of October 2012.

85 Joseph E. Stiglitz and Linda J. Bilmes, "The True Cost of the Iraq War: $3 Trillion and Beyond," *Washington Post* (September 5, 2010), at *http://www.washingtonpost.com/wp-dyn/content/article/2010/09/03/AR2010090302200.html* as of November 2012.

86 Tax Policy Center, "The Bush Tax Cuts: What is Their Impact on Government Borrowing and Interest Payments?" at *http://www.taxpolicycenter.org/briefing-book/background/bush-tax-cuts/borrowing.cfm* as of October 2012.

87 The social theorist Stuart Hall engaged in the analysis of Thatcherism in this manner. Hall, *The Hard Road to Renewal: Thatcherism and the Crisis of the Left* (London: Verso, 1988); Hall, "The Toad in the Garden: Thatcherism among the Theorists," in Cary Nelson and Lawrence Grossberg, eds., *Marxism and the Interpretation of Culture* (Urbana: University of Illinois Press, 1988), pp. 35–74.

88 Jeff Zeleny, "In Iowa, Tea Party Trouble over Obama Poster," *New York Times* (July 14, 2010), at *http://thecaucus.blogs.nytimes.com/2010/07/14/tea-party-trouble-in-river-city/* as of October 2012.

89 Financial Services Modernization Act of 1999, Public Law 106–102, 113 Stat. 1338 (enacted November 12, 1999); Commodity Futures Modernization Act of 2000, Public Law 106–554, 114 Stat. 2763 (enacted December 21, 2000).

90 *The Financial Crisis Inquiry Report: Final Report of the National Commission on the Causes of the Financial and Economic Crisis in the United States* (New York: Public Affairs Books, 2011).

91 Gretchen Morgenson and Joshua Rosner, *Reckless Endangerment: How Outsized Ambition, Greed, and Corruption Led to Economic Armageddon* (New York: Times Books/Henry Holt, 2011).

92 James O'Connor, *The Fiscal Crisis of the State* (New York: St. Martin's Press, 1973); Claus Offe, "Structural Problems of the Capitalist State," in Klaus von Beyme, ed., *German Political Studies* (Beverly Hills: Sage, 1974), pp. 31–57; Jürgen Habermas, *Legitimation Crisis*, Thomas McCarthy, trans. (Boston: Beacon Press, 1975); Charles E. Lindblom, *Politics and Markets: The World's Political-Economic Systems* (New York: Basic Books, 1977); Peter B. Evans, Dietrich Rueschemeyer, and Theda Skocpol, eds., *Bringing the State Back In* (New York: Cambridge University Press, 1985).

93 On the Pecora investigation, see Michael E. Parrish, *Securities Regulation and the New Deal* (New Haven: Yale University Press, 1970).

94   Ron Suskind, *Confidence Men: Wall Street, Washington, and the Education of a President* (New York: Harper, 2011).

95   Louis Hartz, *The Liberal Tradition in America: An Interpretation of American Political Thought since the Revolution* (New York: Harcourt, Brace, 1955).

96   Mark Lilla, "The Tea Party Jacobins," *New York Review of Books* (May 27, 2010); Lilla, "The Beck of Revelation," *New York Review of Books* (December 9, 2010).

97   J.M. Bernstein, "The Very Angry Tea Party," *New York Times Opinionator* (June 13, 2010), at *http://opinionator.blogs.nytimes.com/2010/06/13/the-very-angry-tea-party/?src=me&ref=homepage* as of October 2012.

98   As a responder to the CBS News site on the Tea Party wrote, "There are basically two kinds of people in this country: those who want the government to take care of them and tell them what to do, and those who don't want the government to tell them what to do and only want the chance to take care of themselves." At CBS News, "Tea Party Supporters: Who They Are and What They Believe."

99   Lisabeth Cohen, *Making a New Deal: Industrial Workers in Chicago, 1929–1939* (New York: Cambridge University Press, 1990).

100 Richard Rorty, *Achieving Our Country: Leftist Thought in Twentieth-Century America* (Cambridge, MA: Harvard University Press, 1998); Todd Gitlin, *The Twilight of Common Dreams: Why America is Wracked by Culture Wars* (New York: Metropolitan Books, 1995).

101 Eric Alterman, "Cultural Liberalism is Not Enough," *New York Times* (April 8, 2012).

102 O'Hara, *A New American Tea Party*, p. 142.

103 Richard A. Viguerie, "From an Old School Conservative, Advice for the Tea Party," *Washington Post* (May 2, 2010), at *http://www.washingtonpost.com/wp-dyn/content/article/2010/04/30/AR2010043001109.html* as of October 2012; Viguerie, "Good Riddance to Establishment GOP," *Politico.com* (July 16, 2010), at *http://www.politico.com/news/stories/0710/39835.html* as of October 2012.

104 Mike McIntire, "Hidden under Tax-Exempt Cloak, Political Dollars Flow," *New York Times* (September 23, 2010); Jim Rutenberg, Don Van Natta, Jr., and Mike McIntire, "Offering Donors Secrecy, and Going on Attack," *New York Times* (October 12, 2010).

105 Jim Rutenberg, "With Another $1 Million Donation, Murdoch Expands His Political Sphere," *New York Times* (October 1, 2010). Paul Blumenthal, "Forbes 400 Contribute Record Amounts to Presidential Campaigns, Super PACs," *Huffington Post* (November 5, 2012), at *http://www.huffingtonpost.com/2012/11/05/forbes-400-campaign-contributions_n_2047750.html* as of November 2012.

106 *Citizens United v. Federal Election Commission*, 558 U.S. 50 (2010).

107 Climate change is but one case in point. The fossil fuel industries for decades have poured money into research institutions that produce studies questioning the science of global warming and challenging the economics of regulation or a carbon cap-and-trade system. Notwithstanding the fact that for all intents and purposes there is a consensus among scientists with expertise in climate issues, the skeptical industry claims are in turn treated as gospel by Rush Limbaugh and on other right-wing media outlets, and are accorded respectful treatment on mainstream media concerned with "balance." Naomi Oreskes and Erik M. Conway, *Merchants of Doubt: How a Handful of Scientists Obscured the Truth on Issues from Tobacco Smoke to Global Warming* (New York: Bloomsbury Press, 2010). The industry studies permeate the informational universe of those religious Christians who believe that God gave the earth to humans to use without interference and speak to people already inclined to distrust scientific experts. Just 14 percent of Tea Party supporters believe that global warming is an environmental problem that is having an effect now. John M. Broder, "Skepticism on Climate Change is Article of Faith for Tea Party," *New York Times* (October 21, 2010).

108 Doyle McManus, "The Death of the Moderate Republican," *Los Angeles Times* (November 18, 2012): *http://www.latimes.com/news/opinion/commentary/la-oe-mcmanus-column-moderates-in-congress-20121118,0,3364873.column* as of November 2012.

109 Ronald Brownstein, "Pulling Apart," *National Journal* (February 24, 2011), at *http://www.nationaljournal.com/magazine/congress-hits-new-peak-in-polarization-20110224* as of October 2012.

110 To speak of Fox News as a single thing is misleading, of course. Fox News is an amalgam of programs with particular norms, rhetoric, and modes of address. The daytime news shows approximate professional journalistic norms of objectivity and balance. The early morning, evening, and nighttime commentator shows are where Fox engages in direct ideological politics.

111 Skocpol and Williamson, *The Tea Party and the Remaking of Republican Conservatism*, pp. 121–55.

112 David Schoetz, "David Frum on GOP News: Now We Work for Fox," ABC News (March 23, 2010), at *http://blogs.abcnews.com/nightlinedailyline/2010/03/david-frum-on-gop-now-we-work-for-fox.html* as of October 2012.

113 David L. Bazelon, "FCC Regulation of the Telecommunications Press," *Duke Law Journal*, Vol. 1975, No. 2 (May 1975), pp. 213–51.

114 Fred Friendly, *The Good Guys, the Bad Guys, and the First Amendment: Free Speech vs. Fairness in Broadcasting* (New York: Random House, 1976); Heather Hendershot, *What's Fair on the Air? Cold War Right-Wing Broadcasting and the Public Interest* (Chicago: University of Chicago Press, 2011).

115 The complex history of the deregulation of American broadcasting and telecommunications is the subject of my book *The Irony of Regulatory Reform: The Deregulation of American Telecommunications* (New York: Oxford University Press, 1989).

116 Federal Communications Commission, Applications for Voluntary Assignments or Transfer of Control, 52 Radio Regulations 2d 1081 (1982).

117 James T. Hamilton, *All the News That's Fit to Sell: How the Market Transforms Information into News* (Princeton: Princeton University Press, 2004); Robert B. Horwitz, "On Media Concentration and the Diversity Question," *The Information Society*, Vol. 21, No. 3 (Summer 2005), pp. 181–204; William R. Bobbitt, *Us against Them: The Political Culture of Talk Radio* (Lanham, MD: Lexington Books, 2010).

118 Patricia Aufderheide, *Communication Policy and the Public Interest: The Telecommunications Act of 1996* (New York: Guilford, 1999).

119 Paul Farhi, "Limbaugh's Audience Size? It's Largely Up in the Air," *Washington Post* (March 7, 2009); Kathleen Hall Jamieson and Joseph N. Cappella, *Echo Chamber: Rush Limbaugh and the Conservative Media Establishment* (New York: Oxford University Press, 2010).

120 Harvey's show, with a weekly reach of 25 million, dispensed suspicion of intellectuals and foreigners, and resentment toward government bureaucrats through anecdotes, stories, and even the advertisements he delivered in his quirky manner. A typical Harvey program could be broadcast from a Tea Party stage today. In a broadcast aired in 1952, Harvey intoned, "No one came to this country originally or since to found a government. We came here to get away from government! They were not cowards . . . men of failure and frustration . . . academic theorists. They were successful men of business and agriculture, but they were scared. . . . They wanted little government . . . big people. And with freedom in their hearts and old buckskin shirts on their backs they headed off over the mountains. There was no TVA [Tennessee Valley Authority] out there . . . no price supports . . . no price control. No job for sure . . . no guaranteed rocking chair. . . . It's 1776 again. Right now!" Cited in Patricia Aufderheide, "Paul Harvey and the Culture of Resentment," in *The Daily Planet: A Critic on the Capitalist Culture Beat* (Minneapolis: University of Minnesota Press, 2000), p. 37. The TVA was a federally owned electricity provider created by the Roosevelt administration to supply electricity in the South.

121 A perennial complaint, given new relevance by, among others, Robert W. McChesney, *Corporate Media and the Threat to Democracy* (New York: Seven Stories Press, 1997).

122 Todd Gitlin, *The Whole World is Watching: Mass Media in the Making and Unmaking of the New Left* (Berkeley: University of California Press, 1980); Daniel C. Hallin, "The Passing of the 'High Modernism'

of American Journalism," *Journal of Communication*, Vol. 42, No. 3 (September 1992), pp. 14–25.

123 Cass R. Sunstein, *Republic.com* (Princeton: Princeton University Press, 2001); Sunstein, *Going to Extremes: How Like Minds Unite and Divide* (New York: Oxford University Press, 2009).

124 Justin Elliott, "How the 'Ground Zero Mosque' Fear Mongering Began," *Salon.com* (August 16, 2010), at *http://www.salon.com/news/politics/war_room/2010/08/16/ground_zero_mosque_origins* as of October 2012.

125 Cited in Maureen Dowd, "Going Mad in Herds," *New York Times* (August 22, 2010).

126 Sheldon S. Wolin, *Democracy Incorporated: Managed Democracy and the Specter of Inverted Totalitarianism* (Princeton: Princeton University Press, 2008), p. 9.

127 The Pew Forum on Religion and Public Life, "Growing Number of Americans Say Obama is a Muslim" (August 18, 2010), at *http://pewforum.org/Politics-and-Elections/Growing-Number-of-Americans-Say-Obama-is-a-Muslim.aspx* as of October 2012.

128 "$860 Billion Tax Cut Deal: Cost Breakdown," *CNNMoney.com* (December 10, 2010), at *http://money.cnn.com/2010/12/07/news/economy/tax_cut_deal_obama/index.htm* as of October 2012.

129 Wade Goodwyn, "GOP Governors Say Party Lost on Strategy, Not on Issues," *NPR News* (November 18, 2012): *http://www.npr.org/2012/11/18/165379129/gop-governors-say-party-lost-on-strategy-not-issues* as of November 2012.

130 I place the word "canalize" in quotes to recall its use by one of the earliest and still most compelling general essays on the limited yet powerful influence of mass media. Paul Lazarsfeld and Robert K. Merton, "Mass Communication, Popular Taste, and Organized Social Action," in Lyman Bryson, ed., *The Communication of Ideas* (New York: Harper, 1948), pp. 18–30.

131 Fareed Zakaria, "The Rise of Illiberal Democracy," *Foreign Affairs* (November/December 1997), at *http://www.fringer.org/wp-content/writings/fareed.pdf* as of October 2012.

132 Fareed Zakaria, *The Future of Freedom: Illiberal Democracy at Home and Abroad* (New York: Norton, 2003).

Chapter 6 Dogmatism, Utopianism, and Politics

1 Sam Tanenhaus, *The Death of Conservatism* (New York: Random House, 2009); Michael Lind, "The Three Fundamentalisms of the American Right," *Salon.com* (July 5, 2011), at *http://www.salon.com/2011/07/05/lind_three_fundamentalisms/* as of October 2012; Thomas E. Mann and Norman Ornstein, *It's Even Worse Than It*

Looks: How the American Constitutional System Collided with the New Politics of Extremism (New York: Basic Books, 2012).

2 Karl Popper, *The Open Society and Its Enemies* (London: Routledge, 1945); Jacob Talmon, *The Origins of Totalitarian Democracy* (London: Secker and Warburg, 1952); Isaiah Berlin, *Four Essays on Liberty* (Oxford: Oxford University Press, 1969); Hannah Arendt, *The Origins of Totalitarianism* (New York: Meridian Books, 1958).

3 Karl Mannheim, *Ideology and Utopia: An Introduction to the Sociology of Knowledge*, Louis Wirth and Edward Shils, trans. (New York: Harvest Books, 1936), p. 218.

4 Gary Greenwald, "David Brooks' Field Trip to the White House," *Salon.com* (July 17, 2007), at *http://www.salon.com/2007/07/17/brooks_24/* as of October 2012.

5 Peter Baker, "Bush Tells Group He Sees a 'Third Awakening,' " *Washington Post* (September 13, 2006).

6 Deborah Caldwell, "George W. Bush: Presidential Preacher," *Baptist Standard* (February 17, 2003), at *http://www.baptiststandard.com/2003/2_17/pages/bush_preacher.html* as of October 2012; Jim Wallis, "Dangerous Religion: George W. Bush's Theology of Empire," *Sojourners Magazine* (September/October 2003). George W. Bush, President's Address at the National Prayer Breakfast, *CNN.com* (February 6, 2003), at *http://transcripts.cnn.com/TRANSCRIPTS/0302/06/se.01.html* as of October 2012.

7 Kurt Eichenwald, *500 Days: Secrets and Lies in the Terror Wars* (New York: Touchstone/Simon & Schuster, 2012), p. 459.

8 David L. Chappell, for example, makes a compelling case that the civil rights movement was rooted in the extraordinary courage of southern blacks inspired by prophetic Christianity. Chappell, *A Stone of Hope: Prophetic Religion and the Death of Jim Crow* (Chapel Hill, NC: University of North Carolina Press, 2004).

9 Richard John Neuhaus, *The Naked Public Square: Religion and Democracy in America* (Grand Rapids, MI: Eerdmans, 1984). The book was premised, however, on the claim that not only has religion been banished from public discourse, but without religion the public square will be "naked" and democracy suffers.

10 D. Michael Lindsay, *Faith in the Halls of Power: How Evangelicals Joined the American Elite* (New York: Oxford University Press, 2007), pp. 26–7, 57.

11 David Iglesias, *In Justice: Inside the Scandal That Rocked the Bush Administration* (Hoboken, NJ: Wiley, 2008).

12 Rajiv Chandrasekaran, *Imperial Life in the Emerald City: Inside Iraq's Green Zone* (New York: Vintage, 2006), pp. 103–10.

13 The White House, "Fact Sheet: The Faith-Based and Community Initiative: A Quiet Revolution in the Way Government Addresses Human Need" (January 2008), at *http://georgewbush-whitehouse.*

archives.gov/news/releases/2008/01/20080129-8.html as of October 2012; Chris Hedges, *American Fascists: The Christian Right and the War on America* (New York: Free Press, 2006), pp. 13, 23–4.

14 John Rawls, "The Idea of Public Reason Revisited," *The University of Chicago Law Review*, Vol. 64, No. 3 (Summer 1997), pp. 765–807; Jürgen Habermas, "Religion in the Public Sphere," *European Journal of Philosophy*, Vol. 14, No. 1 (2006), pp. 1–25; Robert Audi and Nicholas Wolterstorff, *Religion in the Public Square: The Place of Religious Convictions in Political Debate* (Lanham, VA: Rowman & Littlefield, 1997).

15 Max Weber, "Politics as a Vocation" [1918], in H.H. Gerth and C. Wright Mills, eds., *From Max Weber: Essays in Sociology* (New York: Oxford University Press, 1946), pp. 77–128.

16 Reinhold Niebuhr, *Moral Man and Immoral Society: A Study in Ethics and Politics* [1932] (Louisville, KY: Westminster John Knox Press, 2001), pp. 80–1.

17 In realistic recognition of human frailty, Immanuel Kant wrote, "Out of the crooked timber of humanity, no straight thing was ever made." Reputed to be Isaiah Berlin's favorite quotation, he used part of it as the title of one of his collections of essays. Isaiah Berlin, *The Crooked Timber of Humanity: Chapters in the History of Ideas*, Henry Hardy, ed. (Princeton: Princeton University Press, 1990).

18 Labeling American exceptionalism as utopian is hardly a new insight. Early in the Cold War the vociferously anti-communist Niebuhr expressed the view that America's virtue – its innocence, the presumed nobility of its intentions – could easily become its vice. The central claim of *The Irony of American History* is that American exceptionalism is a perilous variety of utopianism. Niebuhr, *The Irony of American History* (New York: Charles Scribner's Sons, 1952).

19 Anne Norton, *Leo Strauss and the Politics of American Empire* (New Haven: Yale University Press, 2004), p. 179.

20 Norman Podhoretz, "The Case for Bombing Iran," *Commentary* (June 2007), at *http://www.commentarymagazine.com/article/the-case-for-bombing-iran/* as of October 2012.

21 Leszek Kolakowski, "Why an Ideology is Always Right," in *Modernity on Endless Trial* (Chicago: University of Chicago Press, 1990), pp. 232–3.

22 Richard J. Bernstein, *The Abuse of Evil: The Corruption of Politics and Religion since 9/11* (Malden, MA: Polity Press, 2005).

23 Reinhold Niebuhr, *The Children of Light and the Children of Darkness: A Vindication of Democracy and a Critique of its Traditional Defence* (New York: Charles Scribner's Sons, 1944), p. 183.

INDEX

abortion, 1–2, 14, 18, 87, 88, 89, 93, 95, 98, 106, 112, 126, 178
Abrams, Elliott, 130, 246n111
Acheson, Dean, 165
Adams, John Quincy, 24, 183
Adelman, Kenneth, 246n111
Adelson, Sheldon, 192–3
Adorno, Theodor, 161–2, 163
Afghanistan, 19, 106, 143, 182
African Americans, *see* civil rights; racism
Ahmadinejad, Mahmoud, 209–10
Ahmanson, Howard, 100
AIDS, 125, 157
AIG, 172, 187
Air Force, 30–1
al-Qaeda, 3, 110, 140, 145, 166, 167
Albright, Madeleine, 19, 138
Allen, Richard V., 52, 130
Alterman, Eric, 191, 260n101
America First Committee, 33, 177
American Civil Liberties Union (ACLU), 1–2, 46
American Conservative Union, 51, 94
American Council of Christian Churches (ACCC), 75, 76, 77
American Crossroads, 192
American Enterprise Institute, 41–2, 51, 52–3, 55, 150, 152

American exceptionalism, 15, 18, 25, 66, 89, 113, 138, 146–7, 152, 156, 177, 205
American Family Association, 99
American for Constitutional Action (ACA), 51
American Legislative Exchange Council, 94, 100
American Liberty League, 27–8
American Recovery and Reinvestment Act (2009), 158, 172
American Values, 178
Americans for Prosperity, 168, 170, 174, 179, 188
Amin, Idi, 129
Angle, Sharon, 177
Angola, 26, 106
anti-communism, 8, 12, 32–5, 39–43, 75–7, 97, 114–16, 126–35, 164, 202, 204
anti-intellectualism, 11, 58, 115, 120, 122, 161–2, 164, 166
anti-Semitism, 82, 115, 118, 124, 160, 161, 180
Anway Corporation, 98
Arendt, Hannah, 204
Arlington Group, 207
Armey, Dick, 108, 170, 192
Arminianism, 67, 71
associations, 51–5, 116–17

Atatürk, Kemal, 154, 155
atomic bomb, *see* nuclear weapons

Bachman, Michele, 181
Bakker, Jim, 83, 91
Baldwin, James, 127
Balkans, 136, 138–9, 142
banking, 50, 186, 187, 189
Baptists, 68, 70, 72, 78, 80, 98,
    108, 109
Baroody, William, 52, 53, 62
Bartley, Robert L., 122
Barton, David, 176
Bastiat, Frederic, 174, 176
Bauer, Gary, 178
Beck, Glenn, 173, 175–6, 178, 182,
    199
Beliles, Mark A., 176–7
Bell, Daniel, 44, 118, 162
Bellah, Robert, 67, 86
Berger, Bennett, 102
Berkowitz, Peter, 38
Berlin, Isaiah, 204
Berman, Paul, 248n129
Bible Institutes, 75, 80
Bilmes, Linda, 184
bin Laden, Osama, 142
black power, 115, 116
Blair, Tony, 149
Bloom, Allan, 115
Blumenthal, Sydney, 52
Bob Jones University, 103, 110
Bobbitt, Philip, 248n129
Bolton, John, 100, 246n111
Book of the Month Club, 42
Born Again Christians, 70, 72, 76,
    79, 90, 102
Bosnia, 136
Bourdieu, Pierre, 253n33
Bozell, L. Brent, 48
Bradley Foundation, 53, 125, 150
Bremer, Paul, 157
Bricker Amendment, 32–3, 40
broadcasting, 79–83, 99, 194–8
Brookings Institution, 51
Brooks, David, 167, 182

Bruce, Steve, 105
Brzezinski, Zbigniew, 133
Buchanan, Patrick, 52, 182
Buckley, William F., 8, 11, 30, 33,
    37, 38, 40, 48, 49, 51, 94, 180
Bundy, Edgar C., 76
Burke, Edmnund, 8, 10, 11, 28, 36,
    38, 41, 118, 119
Burnham, James, 38
Bush, George H., 131, 136–7
Bush, George W.
    anti-establishment conservatives
      and, 2, 3, 18–19
    appointments, 138, 145, 207,
      246n111
    axis of evil, 153
    budget deficit, 20
    Christian right and, 79, 108–9,
      111, 207–8
    dogmatism, 12
    failed presidency, 157
    foreign policy, 108–9, 182, 183,
      205
    infrastructure and, 187
    neoconservatives and, 141–50
    popular appeal, 166
    TARP, 172, 187
    theology, 205
    war on terror, 141–7
    see also Iraq War
Business Roundtable, 123

Cabot Lodge, Henry, 50
Calvinism, 66–7, 205
Cambodia, 241n62
Cambone, Stephen, 246n111
Campus Crusade for Christ, 108
Capra, Frank, 193
Carter, Jimmy, 84–5, 90–1, 106,
    128, 132, 133–4, 135, 150
Carthage Foundation, 125
Casanova, José, 67
Casey, William, 130
Catholicism., *see* Roman
    Catholicism
Cato Institute, 55

Center for Security Policy, 150
Center for Strategic and
    International Studies, 55, 151
Center for the Study of Public
    Choice, 55
Central Intelligence Agency (CIA),
    30–1, 131, 149
Chalabi, Ahmad, 149, 155
Chamber of Commerce, 53, 54, 55,
    123
Cheney, Dick, 137, 138, 151,
    246n111
Chiang Kai-shek, 77
Chicago School, 35
China, 31, 33, 34, 77, 136, 136–7
Chirac, Jacques, 205
Chodorov, Frank, 30
Christian Anti-Communism
    Crusade, 43, 76, 77
Christian Broadcasting Network,
    99, 103
Christian Coalition Road to
    Victory, 107–8
Christian Crusade, 76
Christian Freedom Foundation, 95,
    99
Christian Legal Defense and
    Education Fund, 85
Christian Patriots, 74
Christian Reconstructionism, 99,
    103–4
Christian right
    1970s rise, 63, 75, 78–111, 202–3
    American exceptionalism, 146–7,
        156, 205
    broadcasting, 79–83, 99
    Bush, George W. presidency and,
        157, 207
    Catholicism and, 97–8
    constituency, 7
    evangelicalism, 71
    evolution, 13–16
    foreign policy, 18–19, 105–11,
        125, 146–7
    Fourteenth Amendment and, 79,
        84–9

fundamentalism, 71–8
    Iraq War and, 105, 107,
        108–9
    mobilization of resources,
        98–100
    modernism and, 68–71
    neoconservative alliance with,
        123–6, 145
    networks, 98–100
    New Evangelicalism, 71–2
    political entrepreneurs, 91–7
    political values, 13–15
    Protestantism, 65–111
    Reagan and, 17, 64, 95, 100,
        101, 125
    religious ideology and politics,
        100–5, 206
    secularization thesis, 64–7
    slogans, 1–2
    Social Gospel and, 16
    Tea Party and, 177
    televangelism, 79–83
    terminology, 71–2
    theocracy, 104–5
    utopianism, 204–5
Christian School Action, 85, 91
Christian Voice, 95, 99
Chrysler, 172
Church League of America, 74
Churchill, Winston, 117
Citigroup, 186, 187
civil religion, 14, 86, 203, 204
civil rights, 14, 48, 55–60, 57, 63,
    76, 78, 79, 84–9, 93, 95, 115,
    201, 203
Civil War, 68, 193
Claremont Institute, 100
Clarke, Richard, 142
clash of civilizations, 146
climate change, 2, 12, 122, 142,
    159, 166, 169
Clinton, Bill, 2, 135–6, 138–40,
    142, 167
Club for Growth, 188
Coalition for a Democratic
    Majority (CDM), 130

Cold War, 26, 34, 77, 126–35, 173, 182, 204
Collins, Charles Wallace, 56, 57
colonialism, 26, 141, 158
Colson, Charles, 126
Committee of One Hundred, 47
Committee on the Present Danger (CPD), 130, 131–2
Concerned Women for America, 99, 207
conservation, 193
Conservative Caucus, 96
Constitution
    First Amendment, 65, 177
    Tenth Amendment, 168
    Fourteenth Amendment, 14, 17, 57, 59, 62, 79, 84–9
    Seventeenth Amendment, 168
    Bricker Amendment, 32–3, 40
    Equal Rights Amendment, 91, 93, 95
    textual guide, 8
contraception, 14
Coors, Joseph, 54, 98, 100
corporatism, 173, 184, 199
Coughlin, Charles, 29, 82, 97
Council for National Policy (CNP), 99, 100
counterculture, 14, 60, 100, 114–16, 121, 123, 203, 209
Cowie, Jefferson, 59
creationism, 3, 73–4, 99–100
    see also Scopes trial (1925)
Cruz, Ted, 179
culture wars, 17, 125, 157, 177, 178

Darby, John Nelson, 69
Darwinism, 3, 68, 70–1, 124
    see also social Darwinism
Davis, John W., 27–8
Dearlove, Richard, 149
Decter, Midge, 114, 116, 124
Defenders of the Christian Faith, 74
Defense Intelligence Agency, 149

defense spending, 20, 44–6
    see also military-industrial complex
Democrats
    Catholicism, 98
    civil rights and, 55–9, 190, 203
    decline, 189–91
    Dixiecrats, 29, 56–9, 190, 193
    health care reforms, 159
    ideology, 194
    Jacksonian Democrats, 47
    New Deal, see New Deal
deregulation
    eonomy, 17, 52–3
    financial, 186, 189
    mass media, 195–7
DeVos, Richard, 98
Dewey, Thomas, 6
Diamond, Sara, 106
Diggins, John Patrick, 134–5
Dillon, C. Douglas, 50
Disciples of Christ Church, 76
Discovery Institute, 99–100
Disraeli, Benjamin, 11, 41
Dixiecrats, see Democrats
Dobriansky, Paula, 246n111
Dobson, James, 87, 91, 100, 103
Dolan, John Terry, 52
Dominionism, 103–4
Dorrien, Gary, 150
du Pont family, 28
due process, 14, 57, 84
Dulles, John Forster, 165

Eagle Forum, 207
Earhart Foundation, 52
Echo Park Evangelistic Association, 80
Edwards, Lee, 52
Egypt, 153
Eichenwald, Kurt, 205
Eisenhower, Dwight, 6, 32, 43, 46, 50, 127, 165
El Salvador, 106
Enlightenment, 39, 65, 69, 175

Equal Employment Opportunities Commission (EEOC), 85
equal protection, 14, 57, 84, 95
Equal Rights Amendment, 1, 93, 95
equality, 5, 190
Establishment conservatism, 6–7, 9
Ethics and Public Policy Center, 55
euthanasia, 126
Evangelicalism, meaning, 71
Evans, M. Stanton, 52
evolution, *see* Darwinism
exceptionalism, *see* American exceptionalism

facts, denial and invention, 9–10
Falwell, Jerry
  anti-Semitism, 124
  broadcasting, 83, 99
  Christian right stalwart, 126
  Christian School Action, 91
  communist conspiracy, 77
  defending segregation, 78
  foreign policy, 108, 109
  Liberty University, 103
  on moral decay, 87–8
  Moral Majority, 78, 94, 95–7
  on nuclear war, 107
  power, 100
  premillennialism, 101–2, 110
  private academy, 84
  slogans, 2
  theology, 102
Family Research Council, 99, 103, 178, 207
Fannie Mae, 186
FBI, 43
Federal Communications Commission (FCC), 82–4, 195–6
Federal Council of Christian Churches, 75, 81
Federal Emergency Management Agency (FEMA), 167
Federal Radio Commission, 80–1
Federal Reserve, 43, 176, 180, 186

Feith, Douglas, 136, 149, 150, 246n111
feminism, 2, 87, 89, 93, 125, 179–80
feudalism, 38
Feulner, Edwin, 54, 91, 100
financial crisis, 186–8, 189, 199, 201
Fitzgerald, Frances, 78
Focus on the Family, 87, 99, 100, 103, 207
Ford, Gerald, 90, 95, 131
foreign policy
  1940s, 24–32
  1950s, 33–5, 40
  anti-communism, 126–35
  Bush, George W. administration, 141–56
  Christian right and, 18–19, 105–11, 125, 146–7
  first-generation neoconservatives, 126–35
  Goldwater, 33–4, 49
  influence, 3
  neoconservatives, 18, 24–5, 126–41
  old right and, 31
  post-Cold War, 136–41
  presidential power, 31, 32, 39, 40
  Realism, 24, 25, 136, 140
  Tea Party, 182–4
  Truman Doctrine, 25, 26, 32, 33–4
  values, 7–8
  war on terror, 141–7
Formisano, Ronald, 171
Foundation for Economic Education, 28, 41–2, 43, 55
Fox News, 150, 151–2, 158, 173, 175–6, 192, 194–9
Frankfurter, Felix, 165
Franks, Tommy, 149
Freddie Mac, 186
Freedom Works, 168, 170, 174, 179, 188, 192

French Revolution, 5, 36, 38, 140, 153
Friedman, Milton, 35, 96
Friedman, Thomas, 248n129
Friends for Liberty, 180
Frum, David, 150, 194
Fukuyama, Francis, 136
Fuller seminary, 72
fundamentalism, 71–8, 102–3
fusionism, 8, 38–40, 45, 48, 96, 178–9, 182

Galbraith, John Kenneth, 129
General Motors, 52, 172
Germany, 31, 126, 130
Gingrich, Newt, 192–3, 198
Gitlin, Tod, 166
Glass, Carter, 29
Glazer, Nathan, 114, 115, 118, 119, 135
global warming, *see* climate change
Goldberg, Jonah, 175
Goldman Sachs, 186
Goldwater, Barry
 1964 campaign, 39, 42
 Christian right and, 76, 77, 94–5
 civil rights and, 55–6
 Conscience of a Conservative, 48–50
 defeat, 8, 51, 202
 explaining, 11
 foreign policy, 33–4, 49
 Hofstadter and, 199
 John Birch Society and, 43
 legacy, 2, 201–2
 movement operatives, 91
 on presidential power, 40
 rise, 46–51
 Southern constituency, 56
 supporters, 52, 77, 93, 94, 163, 164, 181
 Tea Party and, 170
 white vote, 57
 Why Not Victory?, 33–4
Goodman, Paul, 127
GOP, *see* Republican Party

Gorbachev, Mikhail, 18, 134–5
Gore, Al, 166
Graham, Billy, 72, 77, 83, 101–2
Graham, Daniel O., 100, 131
Graham, Franklin, 198
grassroots, 41–51, 168–9
Gray, John, 153
Great Depression, 5–6, 73, 189
Great Society, 14, 57, 60, 63, 98, 113, 118, 119, 120
Greece, 32
Ground Zero, 197–8
Guatemala, 106
Gulf War (1991), 19, 136, 138, 147
guns, 95, 180

Habermas, Jürgen, 207
Hadley, Stephen, 246n111
Haiti, 142
Harding, Susan, 101, 102, 110
Hargis, Billy James, 43, 76–7, 83, 195
Harrington, Michael, 127
Hartz, Louis, 38, 188
Harvey, Paul, 196
Hayek, Friedrich, 28, 35, 37, 42, 48, 49, 53, 118, 174
healthcare, 4, 12, 158, 159, 168, 169, 172, 179
Heclo, Hugh, 65, 73
Hegel, Georg Wilhelm Friedrich, 136
Helms, Jessie, 108
Henry, Carl, 77, 110
Heritage Foundation, 52, 54–5, 91, 94, 150
Hezbollah, 142, 153
Hiss, Alger, 165
Hitchens, Christopher, 248n129
Hitler, Adolf, 4, 29, 74, 82, 126, 173, 181, 185–6, 209–10
Hobbes, Thomas, 172
Hofstadter, Richard
 on fundamentalism, 75
 on mass media, 194

Hofstadter, Richard (cont.)
  new paranoid style, 166–74,
    184–5
  old liberalism, 188–9
  paranoid style, 11–13, 160–5,
    210
  on post-war prosperity, 30
  social psychology, 199–201
  status anxiety, 12. 13, 105, 163,
    165, 166, 170, 184–5,
    199–200
homosexuality, 2, 89. 87, 93, 95,
  112, 125, 178
Hook, Sidney, 114
Hoover, Herbert, 41
Hoover, J. Edgar, 42
Hoover Institution, 51, 106, 150
House Un-American Activities
    Committee (HUAC), 42, 46,
    75
Hudson Institute, 55
human rights, 24, 108, 132–3,
    135–6. 138, 140, 141, 178
Hunt, Nelson Bunker, 98, 100
Huntington, Samuel P., 247n115
Hurricane Katrina, 167

immigration, 24, 161, 163, 171
individualism, 5, 30, 37, 39, 46,
    48, 59, 185, 188–9, 189
Institute for Contemporary Studies,
    55
Institute for Educational Affairs
    (IEA), 53
Institute for Religion and
    Democracy (IRD), 100, 125
Institute on Religion and Public
    Life, 126
intellectuals, see anti-intellectualism
Intercollegiate Society of
    Individualists (ISI), 30, 47,
    51–2
International Council of Chriistian
    Churches, 75
International Monetary Fund, 25
Internet, 192, 197

Iran, 20, 132, 133–4, 153, 157,
    209–10
Iraq War
  Christian right and, 105, 107,
    108–9
  critique, 18, 19–20, 153–6, 157,
    183–4, 207–8
  irrationality, 105
  justification, 147–9, 154–6, 166,
    207–8
  neoconservative project, 2, 3,
    19–20, 113, 138, 140, 142,
    147–53, 205
  opposition, 182
  planning, 139, 142–3
  utopianism, 209
  WMD, 3, 20, 138, 148–9, 166
Iraqi National Congress (INC),
    149
Islam, 197–8
isolationism, 6–7, 24, 30, 32–3, 75,
    128, 140, 142, 145, 182–3
Israel
  Christian right and, 19, 69, 89,
    101–2, 107–11
  neoconservatives and, 115, 124,
    129, 134, 147–8, 156, 183

Jackson, Andrew, 24, 47, 188–9
Jackson, Henry M. "Scoop," 130
Jacobson, Gary, 236n152
Jefferson, Thomas, 182, 188–9
Jewish Institute for National
    Security Affairs, 150
Jim Crow, 119
John Birch Society, 43–4, 45, 46,
    47, 76, 163, 175, 176, 179,
    180–1
Johnson, Lyndon, 14, 51, 57, 58,
    60, 118, 193, 203
Jowitt, Kenneth, 153
Judt, Tony, 248n129
just war, 19, 106, 108, 140, 152

Kagan, Robert, 136, 139, 146
Kampelman, Max, 130

Kant, Immanuel, 265n17
Kaplan, Lawrence, 136, 141
Kass, Leon, 146
Kazin, Michael, 47
Kelling, George L., 120
Kennan, George, 114
Kennedy, John F., 127, 242n67
Kerrey, Bob, 248n129
Kerry, John, 192
Keyes, Alan, 108
Keynesianism, 11, 16, 20, 21, 23, 29, 46, 54, 55, 63, 158, 159, 190, 203
Khalilzad, Zalmay, 138
Khrushchev, Nikita, 43
Kirk, Russell, 38, 39, 41
Kirkland, Lane, 130
Kirkpatrick, Jeane, 115, 116, 117, 121, 132–3, 135, 155
Kissinger, Henry, 127
Koch, Charles and David, 55, 170, 192, 193
Kolakowski, Leszek, 105, 210
Korean War, 25–6, 34, 40, 127
Krauthammer, Charles, 150
Kresge Foundation, 52
Kristol, Irving, 16, 53–4, 62, 114, 115, 117, 118, 120–4, 127, 129–30, 133, 135, 151, 209
Kristol, William, 136, 141, 146, 150
Ku Klux Klan, 76
Kyoto Protocol, 142

LaFollette, Robert, 193
LaHaye, Tim, 88, 100, 101–2, 126
Land, Richard D., 108–9
Landon, Alf, 28
Lassiter, Matthew, 59
Lebanon, 142, 153
Lenin, Vladimir Ilyich, 4, 186
Leninism, 10, 153
Lewis, Bernard, 154
Libby, I. Lewis, 138, 246n111
liberal consensus, 6–7, 8, 24–33, 116, 121, 202–3

liberal internationalism, 24–5, 129–30, 132–3, 135, 137–8, 140, 142–3, 145, 147
libertarianism, values, 35–6, 39
Liberty University, 103
Libya, 153
Lilla, Mark, 188
Lilly Endowment, 52
Limbaugh, Rush, 196, 198, 261n107
Lincoln, Abraham, 193
Lind, Michael, 152
Lindsey, Hal, 101–2
Linker, Damon, 125
Lipser, Seymour Martin, 105
Locke, John, 7, 38, 188
Lugar, Richard, 179
Lukas, J. Anthony, 59
Lutherans, 68, 70, 108, 110
Luti, William, 246n111
Lynchburg Christian Academy, 96

MacArthur, Douglas, 27, 34
McAteer, Ed, 95, 100, 107
McCain, John, 79, 103
McCarthy, Joseph, 11, 31, 34–5, 42, 48, 75, 76, 173–4
McCarthyism, 97–8, 114, 160–5, 199
McConnell, Scott, 151–2
McDowell, Stephen K., 177
Macfarland, Charles S., 81
McGirr, Lisa, 45–6, 59, 170
McGovern, George, 121, 129
Machen, J. Gresham, 75, 88
McIntire, Carl, 43, 75–6, 77, 83, 88, 102, 177, 195
McKinley, William, 146
McPherson, Aimee Semple, 80
McVeigh, Timothy, 180
Makiya, Kanan, 154
Malanga, Steven, 173
Mandelbaum, Michael, 135
Manhattan Institute, 55, 150, 173
Manicheanism, 9, 146, 164
Manifest Destiny, 113, 146

Manion, Clarence, 47–8
Mannheim, Karl, 27, 41, 204
Manningham-Buller, Eliza, 149
Mansbridge, Jane, 93
Marsden, George, 73
Marshall, George, 31, 165
Marshall, Will, 248n129
Marshall Plan, 25, 50
Marx, Karl, 37
Marxism, 4, 104, 113, 116
mass media, 151, 194–9, 200
  see also broadcasting
materialism, 26, 37, 97, 136,
  210
Mead, Walter Russell, 108, 109
Medicare, 4, 115, 168, 169, 170,
  175
Methodists, 68, 70
Meyer, Frank, 38
military expenditure, 20, 44–6
military-industrial complex, 8, 45,
  50, 115–16, 202
Mills, C. Wright, 50
Mises, Ludwig von, 28, 35, 49
Mobil Oil, 52
modernism, 68–70
Mont Pelerin Society, 28, 35, 41
Moore, Roy, 108
Moral Majority, 78, 94, 95–7,
  98–9, 103, 105, 124, 157
Morgenthau, Hans, 114
Morley, Felix, 30
Mowry, George, 29
Moynihan, Daniel Patrick, 9, 114,
  115, 118–20
Mozambique, 106
Muravchik, Joshua, 136
Murdoch, Rupert, 150, 192, 193
Mussolini, Benito, 82

National Affairs Briefing, 100, 101
National Association of
  Evangelicals (NAE), 71–2, 77,
  134, 157
National Association of
  Manufacturers (NAM), 28, 43

National Baptist Convention, 108
National Christian Action Coalition
  (NCAC), 85, 95, 99
National Conference of Catholic
  Bishops (NCCB), 98
National Conservative Political
  Action Committee, 96
National Council of Churches, 76
National Labor Relations Board
  (NLRB), 85–6
National Layman's Council, 74
National Prayer Breakfast, 205
National Recovery Administration,
  23
National Right to Life, 98, 207–8
National Security Council, 30–1
National Student Association
  (NSA), 51
nativism, 24, 160
NATO, 25, 43, 127, 138–9
NBC, 81
neoconservatives
  Bush, George W. presidency,
    141–56
  Christian right alliance with,
    123–6, 145
  civil rights and, 14
  critique of counterculture,
    114–16, 121, 123
  first generation, 112–35, 154,
    155
  foreign policy, 18, 24–5, 126–41
  Iraq War and, 2, 3, 19–20, 113,
    138, 140, 142, 147–53, 205
  Israel and, 115, 124, 125, 129,
    134, 147–8, 156, 183
  media and, 151
  New Class and, 14–15, 120–3,
    203, 209
  second generation, 18, 19, 117,
    120, 130, 135–41, 150, 154,
    209
  utopianism, 18–19, 209–10
  worldview, 13–15
neoliberalism, 17–18
Netanyahu, Benjamin, 108

networks, 98–100, 191–9
Neuhaus, Richard John, 124, 126, 146, 206, 257n74
New Class, 14–15, 16, 58, 62, 120–4, 172, 203, 209
New Deal
    1970s strain on, 63–4
    breakdown of coalition, 16, 21–2
    business opposition, 9, 28, 62
    Catholics and, 97, 98
    coalition, 6, 24, 55–7, 59, 61
    conservative loathing of, 8, 14, 47
    first-generation neoconservatives and, 16, 34–5, 37, 39, 117
    foundations, 23–4
    fundamentalist opposition, 74
    globalization and, 21
    Goldwater and, 46
    history, 5–7
    Hofstadter and, 160–2
    old right and, 6, 27–33, 193
    status quo, 190
    Tea Party and, 159–60, 174–5
New Evangelicalism, 71–2, 77
new left, 114–16, 126, 129
New South, 59, 78
Nicaragua, 106, 132
Niebuhr, Reinhold, 114, 208, 210
9/11, see terrorism
Nitze, Paul, 131
Nixon, Richard, 49, 53, 58, 60–2, 61, 89–90, 127, 151
Norquist, Grover, 100
Norris, J. Frank, 73
North, Gary, 101, 104
North, Oliver, 108
North Korea, 153
Novak, Michael, 124, 126
nuclear disarmament, 18, 43, 106
nuclear weapons, 26–7, 31, 137–8, 139, 140

Obama, Barack
    anti-establishment conservatives and, 2–3, 12
    budget deficit, 20

citizenship status, 159, 166–7, 174, 180
    economic stimulus, 172, 187
    reelection, 3, 4, 62, 179, 201
    religion, 198
    Tea Party and, 3–4, 158, 166–7, 171–5, 178, 180–1, 183, 184, 185–6, 192, 198, 200
Occupy Wall Street, 191
Odom, William, 19
O'Hara, John, 191
Okenga, Harold, 77
Olin Foundation, 51, 53, 125, 150
Olmert, Ehud, 108
OPEC, 63
Operation Rescue, 88
Orwell, George, 128

Packer, George, 248n129
paleo-conservatives, 24, 25, 30, 145, 182
Palestinian Authority, 142, 153
Palin, Sarah, 169, 182–3
paranoid style, see Hofstadter, Richard
Patriot and Militia, 179–82
Paul, Ron, 104, 173, 175, 182
Paul, St, 68
Pax Americana, 137, 141
Pearl Harbor, 30
Pelley, William Dudley, 74
Pentecostals, 72, 80, 81–2, 99, 110
Perkins, Tony, 178
Perle, Richard, 130, 136, 138, 150, 153–4, 246n111
Perlstein, Rick, 42
Perry, Robert, 100, 192, 193
Petchetsky, Rosalind, 98
Pew, J. Howard, 77
Phillips, Howard, 52, 91, 95, 96, 100
Pipes, Daniel, 136
Pipes, Richard, 130, 131
Planned Parenthood, 178

Podhoretz, Norman, 114, 117, 124–5, 126–9, 130, 134, 148, 209–10
Poland, 134
political culture, 188–9
Pollack, Kenneth, 248n129
Popper, Karl, 204, 210
populism, 3, 8, 15, 17, 47, 58–9, 61, 97, 116, 120–1, 123, 160–1, 163, 166, 171–3, 179–80, 184, 186, 188–9
Postdam Conference, 31
postmillennialism, 66, 68–9, 100
Powell, Lewis F., 53, 62, 151
premillennialism, 18, 100–2, 107, 108, 110, 153
Presbyterians, 68, 70, 75, 110
presidential power, 26, 31, 32, 33, 39–40
preventive war, 27, 117, 143, 145, 149, 152, 209
producerism, 15, 171, 173, 179
Prohibition, 70, 74, 161, 206
Project for the New American Century (PNAC), 137–8, 150
Promise Keepers, 108
property values, 4–5, 35–6
Protestantism, 39–40, 46, 65–111, 116, 203
see also specific denominations

racism, 55–60, 63, 68, 74, 116, 119, 123, 171–2, 180
Rand, Ayn, 35–6, 45, 174, 178
RAND Corporation, 131, 132
rape, 4, 178
Reagan, Ronald
appointments, 132
Catholic support, 98
Christian right and, 17, 64, 95, 100, 101, 125
constituency, 14
deregulation of broadcasting, 195–6
foreign policy, 106, 125, 134–5
institutional change, 62
landmark, 2, 17–18, 112, 174, 203
rollback agenda, 112
Southern constituency, 57
Realists, 24, 25, 136, 140
Reed, Ralph, 103
relativism, 10, 146
religion, see Christian right; specific religions
Religious Roundtable, 95, 99, 100
Republic Steel, 52
Republicans
1938 elections, 29
2010 elections, 158, 159, 194
2012 elections, 3, 178–9, 194, 200
Christian right activism, 103
counter-establishment, 51–5
establishment, 50, 51
foreign policy opinions, 183
funding, 193
Hofstadter on, 163–4
political shift, 193–4, 203–4
Protestantism, 98
religious beliefs, 111
Republican in Name Only (RINO), 9
South, 57, 61, 203
takevover by anti-establishment conservatives, 1, 3–4
Tea Party and, 158, 181, 192, 194–5, 210
revivalism, 67–72, 77, 79, 83, 99
Ribuffo, Leo, 74
Rice, John R., 74
Rieder, Jonathan, 59, 60
Riesebrodt, Martin, 87
rights revolution, see civil rights
Ríos Montt, Efraín, 106
Roberts, Oral, 83
Robertson, Pat, 83, 89, 91, 99, 100, 102–3, 106, 108, 110, 207
Robison, James, 83, 95
Rockefeller, Nelson, 47, 50
Rodman, Peter, 246n111

Roman Catholicism, 37, 40, 63, 68, 70, 73, 74, 97–8, 124, 126, 163
Romney, Mitt, 79, 178, 179, 183, 193
Roosevelt, Franklin, 5–6, 23–4, 27, 28, 29, 30, 56, 74, 165, 175, 190
  see also New Deal
Roosevelt, Theodore, 193
Rossiter, Clinton, 41
Rostow, Eugene, 130
Rove, Karl, 10, 11, 192
Rubio, Marco, 182, 183
Rumsfeld, Donald, 130, 139, 148–9, 151, 157, 246n111
Rushdoony, Rousas, 99–100, 100, 103–4
Rusher, William, 48, 51, 52
Rutherford, Joseph, 80–1
Ryan, Paul, 178–9
Rycroft, Matthew, 149

Saddam Hussein, 3, 19, 20, 107, 109, 111, 136, 138, 140, 142, 147–9, 153–4
Santelli, Rick, 158, 171
Santorum, Rick, 2, 3, 178
Saudi Arabia, 153
Scaife, Richard Mellon, 54, 100, 193
Scaife, Sarah, 125
Scaife Foundation, 52, 125, 150
Schachtman, Max, 120
Schaeffer, Francis A., 88, 104–5, 110
Schlafly, Phyllis, 49–51, 91, 93, 94, 180
Schlesinger, Arthur, 41, 114, 129
school prayer, 14, 79
Schumpeter, Joseph, 147
Schwarz, Frederick, 43, 76, 77
Scopes trial (1925), 70–1, 73–4, 75, 79
Second Great Awakening, 71

secularism, 16, 62, 64–7, 87–8, 91, 113, 124, 126
Serbia, 138–9
sexual revolution, 87
Shlaes, Amity, 175
Shuler, Robert, 81
Silver Legion, 74
Simon, William E., 53, 62, 151
Singlaub, John K., 100
Skocpol, Theda, 177–8
Skousen, W. Cleon, 175–6
slavery, 68, 69, 108, 119, 171
Smith, Al, 27–8
Smith, Bailey, 100, 124
Smith, Rogers, 75
Smith Richardson Foundation, 150
social Darwinism, 5, 35, 70
Social Gospel, 16, 66, 70, 122
social science, 7, 16–17, 21, 118, 121–2, 161
Social Security, 41, 115, 168, 170, 175
Somalia, 136, 142
Somoza, Anastasio, 132
Southern Baptist Convention, 72, 100, 108, 109, 110
Soviet Union
  anti-communism of first-generation neoconservatives, 126–35, 148, 202
  Christian right and, 101, 106, 107
  disintegration, 135, 137
  Goldwater and, 11, 49
  nuclear attack of, 7
  old right and, 26, 27, 32, 33–4
  Reagan and, 18, 134–5
  self-righteousness, 210
Sowell, Thomas, 119
Spain, 146
Spencer, Herbert, 35
Stalin, Joseph, 31, 43
Stalinism, 114, 120
Standard Oil, 52
Stanley, Charles, 109

status anxiety, 44, 105, 161, 163, 165, 166, 170, 184–5
Stiglitz, Joseph, 184
Strategic Defense Initative, 137–8
Strauss, Leo, 117, 175
Sumner, William Graham, 35
Sun Oil Company, 77
Suskind, Ron, 10, 187
Swaggart, Jimmy, 83
Swift Boat Veterans for Truth, 192
Syria, 142, 153

Taft, Robert A., 28, 31–2, 33, 40, 74, 183
Taft–Hartley Act (1947), 16, 31, 56
Talmon, Jacob, 204
TARP (Troubled Asset Relief Program), 172, 187
taxation
    discriminatory schools, 84–5, 91
    illegitimacy, 9–10
    John Birch Society and, 43
    Reagan policy, 17
    reform, 85–6
    Republican policies, 3
    Tea Party and, 174–5, 176
Taxpayer Protection Pledge, 2, 9
Taylor, Charles, 19
Tea Party
    2010 elections, 158, 159, 194
    2012 elections, 194
    American political culture and, 188–9
    anti-elitism, 21, 167, 169, 173, 176, 180, 182
    anti-federal government, 170–1
    billboards, 1, 4
    decline of left alternative, 189–91
    demographics, 169–70, 172, 199
    emergence, 9, 20, 158–60, 210
    foreign policy, 182–4
    funds, 191–3
    grassroots localism, 168–9
    Hofstadter thesis and, 160, 165, 166–74
    ideology, 158–9, 174–82

    illiberal democracy, 199–201
    institutional structures and, 184–99
    media and, 194–9, 200
    networks, 191–9, 200
    Obama and, 3–4, 158, 166, 167, 171–5, 178, 180–1, 183, 184, 185–6, 192, 198, 200
    organizations, 168, 179
    producerist populism, 171
    racism, 171–2, 180
    rage, 3, 11, 210
    slogans, 12, 167, 173, 185–6
    structural analysis, 185–8
    takeover of Republicans, 158
Tea Party Express, 168, 179
Tea Party Nation, 168
Tea Party Patriots, 168
Team B, 130, 131–2
Teheran Conference (1943), 31
televangelism, 79–83
terrorism
    9/11, 1–2, 18, 110, 142–7
    9/11 myths, 167
    neoconservative policy making, 113
    war on terror, 40, 113, 141–7
Terry, Randall, 88
theocracy, 104–5
Third Great Awakening, 19, 178, 205
Third World, 26, 106, 107, 129–30, 134, 157
Thurmond. Strom, 56, 57
Tipton, Steven, 125
Tocqueville, Alexis de, 11, 28, 65, 66, 116–17, 118, 201
torture, 3, 40, 157
Traditional Values Coalition, 99, 207
traditionalism, tenets, 36–8
Trotskyism, 113, 120–1
Truman, Harry, 27, 29–32, 34, 40, 56, 127, 146, 165
Truman doctrine, 25, 26, 32, 33–4
Turkey, 32, 154

UNICEF, 76
United Kingdom, 149
United Nations, 24, 25, 27, 46, 76, 77, 110, 138–9, 140, 143, 167
UNPROFOR, 139
U.S. Steel, 52
utopianism, 18–19, 104–5, 130, 133, 148, 153, 156, 204–5, 209–10

Values Action Team, 207
Values Voter Summit, 178
Vietnam War, 16, 26, 60, 63, 76, 114–15, 121, 127–9, 179, 203
Viguerie, Richard, 52, 91, 93, 94, 95, 96, 99, 192

Walker, Edwin, 76
Wallace, George, 56–9
Wallace, Henry, 27
Wanniski, Jude, 54
war on terror, *see* terrorism
Warren, Earl, 43, 79, 165
Warren, Rick, 157
WASPs, 117, 163
Watergate, 89–90, 92, 126
weapons of mass destruction, 3, 20, 137, 138, 140, 143, 148–9, 166
Weaver, Richard, 38, 39
Weber, Max, 204, 208
Weigel, George, 106
Welch, Robert, 43
welfarism, 48–9

Westad, Arne, 26
Weyrich, Paul, 54, 91–3, 94, 95, 100, 207
White, F. Clifton, 47
Wiener, Jon, 166
Will, George F., 19
Willentz, Sean, 176
William Volker Fund, 28
Williamson, Vanessa, 177–8
Wills, Garry, 61
Wilson, James Q., 119–20
Wilson, Woodrow, 40, 146, 176
Winrod, Gerald B., 74
Winthrop, John, 146
Wohlstetter, Albert, 131, 139
Wolfowitz, Paul, 130, 131, 136, 137–8, 150, 155, 246n111
World Bank, 25
World Council of Churches, 74, 76
World War I, 6, 70
World War II, 30
Wurmser, David, 246n111
Wuthnow, Robert, 78, 89, 90, 92

Yalta Conference (1945), 31, 33
Young Americans for Freedom (YAF), 47, 48, 51–2, 93
Youth for Christ movement, 71–2
Yugoslavia, 136, 138–9, 142

Zaitchick, Alexander, 176
Zakaria, Fareed, 201
Zionism, 108, 129, 183